HOW TO USE THE HEAVENLY BANQUET DEVOTIONAL

WHAT YOU NEED TO HAVE:

You need to have a quiet place—free from any disturbance

You need to have a good Bible, preferably with chain references

You need to have a pen and paper to jot down lessons learned.

WHAT STEPS YOU NEED TO FOLLOW:

Step 1: Start with prayer and praises. Thank God for a new day and ask Him for His blessings as you banquet with Him.

Step 2: Read the Bible text (s) carefully

Step 3: Read the Devotional carefully. *Note the comments and where applicable answer the questions.*

Step 4: Meditate on what you have read in the Bible and the Devotional.

Step 5: Ask God to speak to you. There may be some **Commands** He wants you to obey, **Warnings** He wants you to pay attention to, **Issues** He wants you to address, **Examples** He wants you to follow, **Fruits** He wants you to bear and **Promises** He wants you to claim.

Step 6: Write down whatever the Holy Spirit has laid in your heart. Things written are not easily forgotten.

Step 7: Pray concerning your need and intercede for others.

Thank God for the opportunity to banquet with Him.

CONTENTS

JANUARY

FEBRUARY

MARCH

1. Clean Hands & Pure Heart
2. Sin—Energy Sapper
3. Responsible Citizenry
4. The Godly vs. The Ungodly
5. The Incomparability Of God
6. Discern The Time!
7. Our Place Of Origin
8. Being Lazy!
9. Trust In The Lord
10. Interpersonal Relationship
11. An Earthly Vision
12. A Geographical Calling
13. Being Inquisitive
14. Overwhelming Evidence
15. Lost, But Restored
16. Closed-Door Mentality
17. Preach The Word!
18. Faith, Hope And Love
19. A Taker Turned Giver
20. In Him!
21. Prophecies About Christ
22. Always Be Thankful To God
23. An Ideal House Or Home?
24. Known In Heaven
25. Prayer A Spiritual Discipline
26. Work, Rest And Sleep
27. The Power Of Faith
28. Test The Spirits
29. An Eye-Covenant
30. The Rich And The Poor
31. A Promise Of Restoration

APRIL

1. Hated Without A Cause
2. Caution! Eat Worthily
3. What's Written Is Written
4. Victory Celebration
5. He is risen!
6. Contend For The Faith
7. What A Forgiving Father!
8. Hallmarks of an Ideal Leader
9. Christ's Rescue Mission (CRM)
10. It's Heart, Not Eye Service
11. Water The Seed You Sow
12. The Foolishness of Greed
13. Touching The Untouchable
14. Follow Me!
15. "So, I Prayed"
16. A Three-Fold Ministry
17. An Abiding Relationship
18. Trial & Persecution
19. Business-As-Usual Attitude
20. Stony-Heart Hearers
21. Joshua's Rededication Sermon
22. Are You Living A Disguised Life?
23. Let God Prepare You
24. Personalize The Lyrics
25. Anxiety Syndrome
26. A Continuum Of God's Blessing
27. A Worthy Epistle
28. Life's Priority
29. Avenge Not!
30. Known By Their Fruits

MAY	JUNE
1. Not forgotten!	1. He's Greater Than All
2. Sanctification	2. Beauty For Ashes
3. Mystery Of Death Revealed	3. The Prince of Life & Peace
4. Divine Intervention	4. The Spirit Of Unbelief
5. A Measured Life Span	5. Be Different!
6. Sought, Found & Followed	6. God Confounds The Wise
7. He's From Above	7. The 'Moderation' Cliché
8. An Unearned Inheritance	8. Soul-winning Opportunity
9. Don't Get Hooked Up!	9. Lost, Found & Restored
10. A Mother's Greatest Gift	10. The Bette Covenant
11. Weep Before Him In Prayer	11. Divinely Commissioned
12. Faith Contenders	12. Temple Not Made with Hands
13. Gifted For Service	13. Sin—A Dysfunctional Gene
14. Demonstrating God's Power	14. Beware!
15. The Virtue Of Patience	15. Commandments & Doctrines
16. My Times Are In God's Hand	16. Tine Is Running Out!
17. Stay On the Right Lane	17. Salvation—A Revealed Mystery
18. God's 'Alert' Mechanism	18. Witnessing/Soul Winning
19. Adam The Dust	19. Talk Less; Pray More
20. Light And Salt	20. Praise & Dance Before Him
21. Despised And Rejected	21. Godly Fatherhood
22. Faith	22. Sow In Tears; Reap In Joy
23. Crowned With Glory & Honor	23. Spiritual Parentage
24. Sinless, Empathetic High Priest	24. A Slavery Switch
25. Thank Him In Advance	25. The Power of Influence
26. The Lord—My Strength	26. Return To Your God
27. Shun Disorderly Behavior	27. An Aborted Ministry
28. The Blood Of Jesus Christ	28. Slow Down!
29. External Appearance	29. Brighten Up!
30. My Rock And My Salvation	30. Christianity, Not Religiosity
31. God's Unsearchable Ways	

JULY

1. I Called & He Answered
2. Holy Spirit Baptism
3. Exceedingly Abundant Grace
4. The Priced Of Freedom!
5. Keeping The World At Bay
6. Bribery & Corruption
7. Losing A God Night's Sleep?
8. Lord: Show, Lead And Teach Me
9. The Mystery of Life
10. Divinely Ambushed
11. Transformation & Renewal
12. Mighty And Strong
13. God's Mercy & Compassion
14. A Life Journey
15. God's Glorious Landscape
16. God's Mysterious Way
17. God—My Help And Hope
18. An Altar To the Lord
19. The "Why" Question
20. No Swearing!
21. A Final Warning
22. Christ Is Our Peace
23. What A Horrible Ending!
24. Living A Disguised Life?
25. Safety In The Lord's Presence
26. Christ—Our Advocate
27. What A Lowly Title!
28. The Rock Higher Than I
29. The Legacy Of Woes
30. Going Ahead Of God?
31. The Church—Outside & Within

AUGUST

1. Rivers of Living Water
2. What A Happy Man!
3. Christ's Majestic Glory
4. The Lord Was With Joseph
5. When Heaven Communicates
6. True & Effective Discipleship
7. Christ In You is Greater
8. Dutiful Martha
9. The Weapon Of Praise
10. The God Of Provision
11. Stir Up One Another
12. Christ—The Bread of Life
13. Trying Times!
14. The Inward Beauty
15. The Invincible God
16. Becoming Brand-New In Christ
17. Asleep, Not Dead
18. Covenant Breakers
19. Sin—A Spiritual Barrier
20. How To Know A Fool
21. God's Judgment Upon The Land
22. Love In Action
23. Lose To Gain
24. Stubborn & Rebellious Spirit
25. What A Great Salvation!
26. A Spiritually Healthy Heart
27. Not By Works!
28. Tough Love!
29. "Even The winds...Obey Him"
30. Down The Memory lane
31. Don't Standby And Gaze

NOVEMBER

1. Peace In Tribulation
2. Have The Mind Of Christ
3. Gain By Losing
4. The Power Of Prayer
5. Dual Rebuke!
6. Know God, Know Wisdom
7. A Credible List Of Witnesses
8. Excellency Of The Lord
9. The Need For Confession
10. The Unveiled Gospel
11. Have An Eternal Perspective
12. Divinely Resisted
13. Quench Your Spiritual Thirst
14. A Camouflage Christianity?
15. 'And His Cup Was Full'
16. The Trees Of God For Adam
17. "Message Of The Cross"
18. An Abundant Life Invitation
19. Beloved Of The Lord
20. Be Steadfast In the Lord
21. Away With 'Zig-Zag' Loyalty
22. Delivered and Preserved
23. Strength Through Weakness
24. Mouth & Heart Confession
25. Alone With The Lord
26. The 'Unbelieving Believers'
27. Give And Gain
28. The God Of Breakthroughs
29. Reject God, Reject Life
30. Good And Bad Fasting

DECEMBER

1. In Search Of Wisdom?
2. The Big And Little Foxes
3. Break Not The Divine Hedge!
4. Respect God's House
5. The Futility Of Idolatry
6. Lord, Draw Me Nearer
7. Seven Things God Hates
8. Multitude-Driven Christianity
9. Seed, Soil And Stone
10. Skeptics Of God's Power
11. Freedom Without Probation
12. Godly & Ungodly Submission
13. Spiritual Pep-Talk
14. Quintessential Relevance
15. Spare The Rod, Spoil The Child
16. Order Out Of Chaos!
17. A Positive Influence
18. A Futile Reliance
19. God's Inseparable Love!
20. Patience And Perseverance
21. A Time To Ponder
22. 911 Call To Heaven
23. The Godly
24. Having Christ's DNA
25. The Joy Of Christmas
26. Sacrificial Servant-hood
27. A Blurred Spiritual Vision
28. Divinely Relocated
29. Stay True To The End
30. False Prophets
31. Be Spiritually Prepared

JANUARY

DEVOTIONALS

THE YEAR OF ABUNDANT BLESSING

While the earth remains, seedtime and harvest, cold and heat, winter and summer, and day and night shall not cease (Genesis 8:22).

READ: GALATIANS 6:6-10

Genesis 8: 22 informs us that as long as the earth remains, sowing and harvesting shall not cease. This year is the year of abundant blessing—a year that a lot of people will harvest God's blessings. God wants us to harvest His blessings, just as a farmer harvests his farm crops. But, in order for harvest to take place, there must be some sowing. Sowing is like an investment. The kind of seed you sow, the quality of the seed you sow and where it is sown determine the degree of harvest.

Harvesting is contingent upon sowing and what people sow is what they harvest. Verse 8 of our text reads, *"For he who sows to his flesh will of the flesh reap corruption, but he who sows to the Spirit will of the Spirit reap everlasting life. "*If you sow spiritually, you harvest spirituality; but if you sow carnally you harvest carnality. If you sow financially, you harvest financial gains. If you sow love, you harvest love; but if you sow bitterness, you harvest bitterness. If you sow abundantly, you reap abundant harvest. But if on the other hand, you sow stingingly or sparingly, you will reap sparingly (2 Corinthians 9:6). In V9 of our text, we are enjoined, *"Let us not grow weary while doing good, for in due season we shall reap if we do not lose heart."* Sowing is not always an easy thing to do for the following reasons: **1.** Sowing demands **wisdom**. A diligent farmer does not sow his seeds on the wayside, but in the soil (Read Mark 4:3-4). **2.** Sowing demands **faith.** It takes faith for a famer to sow and wait for the day of harvesting. **3.** Sowing demands **sacrifice.** If a farmer is not willing to sacrifice his seedlings, time and energy during the sowing season, he cannot reap during the harvest season. **4.** Sowing demands **patience**. A farmer sows and patiently waits for the seed to germinate, grow and bear fruits. The above principles should be applied, if you want to experience abundant blessing this year. Learn to sow good quality seed, be diligent in sowing, have faith in God as you sow and be patient after sowing.

Reflection: Check the kind and quality of seed you sow in God's vineyard as well as in people's lives. Are they spiritual or carnal?

Word for today: *Sowing bountifully, reap bountifully.*

KEEP THE VISION ALIVE

Where there is no revelation, the people cast off restraint; but happy is he who keeps the law (Proverbs 29:18)

READ: HABAKKUK 2:1-4

The Bible makes it clear that where there is no vision (revelation), the people are not restrained. May I add that, where the people fail to respond to a vision or revelation, they remain stagnant. Verse 1 of our text reveals how Habakkuk waited on God to receive His revelation. God gave him a vision and asked him to write it down (Habakkuk 2:1-2). Whenever and whatever vision God has given you, endeavor to write it down. Something that is written is not easily forgotten. The vision of any ministry or Church defines its operation. Whenever God gives a vision, He also provides the wherewithal to fulfill it. A vision often has a visionary and sometimes a mission component to it, as was the case with Ezekiel. God showed Ezekiel the vision of dry bones, which reflected the spiritual condition of the children of Israel. Thereafter, God commissioned him to prophesy and say to the people, *"O my people, I will open your graves and cause you to come up from your graves, and bring you into the land of Israel."* (Ezekiel 37:12). God sent Ezekiel to the people with a message of restoration

There are three important things to note about a God-given vision:
1. The vision should be celebrated.
Nehemiah celebrated the accomplishment of the vision which the LORD had sown in his heart—to rebuild the broken walls of Jerusalem. He gathered the priests, the singers and the people as they rejoiced at the dedication of the rebuilt wall (Read Nehemiah 12:27-43). It is good to celebrate a God-given vision, rather than a man-made vision.
2. The vision should be sustained. Nehemiah sustained his God-given vision through prayer and watchfulness. He prayerfully completed the rebuilding of the wall in spite of the conspiracy of Sanballat and Tobiah (Read Nehemiah 4:4-9, 15-18; 6:1-9).
3. The vision should be cautiously shared. Nehemiah shared his vision cautiously with his fellow Jews (Read Nehemiah 2:16-18).

Reflection: Do you have a God-given vision this year? Prayerfully fulfill it.

Word for today: *A vision not well handled goes unfulfilled.*

2

ENTER WITH THANKSGIVING

Make a joyful shout to the LORD, all you lands! Serve the LORD with gladness; Come before His presence with singing (Psalm 100:1-2).

READ: PSALM 100:4-5

That you entered into the New Year, healthy and hearty, is a blessing that calls for joyous celebration and thanksgiving to God. Remember, many who had wished to make it into the New Year could not do so. That you were able to cross over into the New Year is nothing short of God's favor. Since you have entered into the New year alive and well, it is important that you also enter into God's gate with thanksgiving. Verse 4 of our text reads, *"Enter into His gates with thanksgiving, and into His courts with praise. Be thankful to Him, and bless His name."* In the ancient times, Gate *represented* the realm of the king's power, while Court *represented* his seat of authority. The Psalmist writes, *"Enter into His gates with thanksgiving"* and *"His courts with praise."* What he is basically saying is that you should approach the awesome presence of God with thanksgiving and praise. May this be your attitude as you enter into the New Year, in Jesus name.

Verse 5 of our text reveals why you should enter into the LORD's gate with thanksgiving. 1. *"For He is good."* *(v5a)*. We should enter into the LORD's gate with thanksgiving because He is good. If you recount His mercies upon your life in 2014, you will have cause to thank Him. Remembering His hand of protection and provision will make you fall before Him in adoration and thanksgiving. 2. *"His mercy is everlasting."* *(v5b)*. God's mercy is from everlasting to everlasting—meaning that it lasts till eternity. In other words, God's mercy towards you has no end.

3. *"His truth endures to all generations."* *(v5c)*.

Indeed, God's truth (His Word) endures to all generations, otherwise, you and I wouldn't have been beneficiaries of God's Word today. The truth in the Bible has endured thousands of years, and still remains the same—powerful and effective. A grateful heart is a graceful heart. He that is grateful to God is a beneficiary of His grace.

Reflection: Did you usher the New Year with thanksgiving to God or to self?

Word for today: *Make your New Year thanksgiving a continuous habit.*

A CONSISTENT WALK WITH GOD

After he begot Methuselah, Enoch walked with God three hundred years, and had sons and daughters (Genesis 5:21-22).

READ: JEREMIAH 35:1-10

God demands our consistent walk with Him. He is disappointed whenever we are not consistent in our walk with Him. We may do all the singing, dancing, giving and even praying, but if we are not consistent in our walk with Him, God is not pleased. God hates "flip-flopping" Christians. He wants us to be steadfast and consistent in our walk with Him. Our Lord Jesus Christ re-emphasized the need for consistency in His letter to the Laodicean Church (Read Revelation 3:14-19). Genesis 5: 21-27 gives us an account of two individuals who lived opposite lives. At the age of 65, Enoch began to walk with God and lived for 300 years doing so, bringing the total numbers of years that he lived to 365. On the other hand, Enoch's son, Methuselah, lived 969 years, and there is no record that he walked with God, meaning that he lived for self without God. After living for 969 years, Methuselah died. The difference between Enoch who walked with God and Methuselah who did not walk with God became evident at the end of their lives. Enoch was raptured, while Methuselah died. Methuselah *represents* an unbeliever who refuses to align himself with God, while Enoch *represents* a believer who walks with God. Methuselah lived much longer than Enoch, but because he failed to walk with God, there was nothing spectacular about him. It is not how long we live that matters; it is what we do with our lives that counts. Longevity is good, but longevity without Christ is a disaster and a waste.

Our text is a classic example of a consistent walk with God. Due to the inconsistency of the children of Israel, God decided to use the Rechabites to teach them some lessons on the importance of being consistent in walking with Him. God asked Jeremiah to offer the Rechabites free wine, which they refused, because their father had instructed them against drinking any wine. The Rechabites were so consistent in their walk with God that decades after their father had gone, they refused to compromise their faith and spiritual standard. They were commended by God (Read Jeremiah 35:18-19).

Reflection: Can you truly say that you have been a consistent Christian?

Word for today: *A consistent walk with God has an eternal reward.*

BE ANGRY AND SIN NOT!

Cease from anger, and forsake wrath; do not fret--it only causes harm (Psalm 37:8).

READ: EPHESIANS 4:26-27

Verse 26 of our text reads, *"Be angry, and do not sin": do not let the sun go down on your wrath."* How can one be angry and not sin? Is it possible? The answer to this question is in v27 of our text, which reads, *"Nor give place to the devil."* The NIV translation puts it more clearly, *"Do not give the devil a foothold."* The easiest way to open the door for the devil into your life is through anger and bitterness. Remember, the devil comes to steal, kill and destroy (John 10:10). Once he is let in to our human heart, he does exactly that. The Bible does not say we should not be angry, for anger is a part of our human emotions. Our Lord Jesus Christ expressed His angry emotions towards all those who desecrated the temple by converting it into a commercial house. Matthew 21: 12-13 read, *"Then Jesus went into the temple of God and drove out all those who bought and sold in the temple, and overturned the tables of the money changers and the seats of those who sold doves. And He said to them, "It is written, 'My house shall be called a house of prayer,' but you have made it a 'den of thieves.'"* Our Lord Jesus Christ did not go to sleep with His emotional anger. To have done so would have given the devil a stronghold. Similarly, you and I should not allow the sun to go down on our anger. In other words, we should not go to bed with anger and bitterness in our hearts. Anyone who goes to bed with anger and bitterness in his or her heart is opening the door for the devil into his or her life. The devil knows the Scriptures very well.

In Genesis 4:1-8, we learn of how Cain, due to anger, killed his brother Abel. God honored Abel's sacrifice, but dishonored that of Cain. This made Cain to become angry. The Bible does not tell us for how long Cain harbored his anger against Abel. However, the phrase, *"And it came to pass",* suggests that there was time frame between when Cain became angry and the time he killed Abel. Cain went to bed with anger and bitterness several days. As a result, the devil came in and sowed the seed of murder in his heart and encouraged him to carry it out. He does the same thing today.

Reflection: Do you have a hang-over of anger and bitterness against anyone?

Word for today: *Uncontrolled anger is a spiritual cancer; it kills.*

NOTHING IS HIDDEN FROM GOD

For there is nothing hidden which will not be revealed, nor has anything been kept secret but that it should come to light (Mark 4:22).

READ: MATTHEW 10:24-26

As human beings, we have the tendency to hide things from others. Trying to hide things from people is the consequential effect of sin. The Bible records that after Adam and Eve sinned, they tried to hide from God without success (Read Genesis 3:9-10). Ever since, human beings have always tried to hide their deeds and actions from God. Since Adam and Eve did not succeed in hiding from God, what makes people think that their evil ways can be hidden from God? Just as there is no hiding place for the wicked, so is there no hiding place for their evil works.

There are four things about human beings that cannot be hidden. **1. The intents of the human heart**. Through God's Word the intents of the human heart are made bare. The Bible declares, *"For the word of God is living and powerful, and sharper than any two-edged sword, piercing even to the division of soul and spirit, and of joints and marrow, and is a discerner of the thoughts and intents of the heart. And there is no creature hidden from His sight, but all things are naked and open to the eyes of Him to whom we must give account.* "You may try to hide from a fellow human being, the intents of your heart, but not so with God. God knows everything. **2. The sinfulness of human beings**. David committed murder in order to hide his sin of adultery with Uriah's wife (Read 2 Samuel chapter 11). God made it clear to David that nothing was hidden from Him. How shocked David must have been when he was confronted by Nathan with these words, *"For you did it secretly, but I will do this thing before all Israel, before the sun."* (12:12). **3. The unspoken words in the human heart.** When three angelic visitors broke the good news to Abraham and Sarah about their becoming parents at the ages of hundred and ninety years respectively, they both laughed and said something in their hearts (Read Genesis 17:17; 18:12-15). What they said was not hidden from God. **4. The human existence.** King David knew this very well. Read his take on this universal truth in Psalm 139:7-12.

Reflection: Have you been doing things in secret or hiding things from God?

Word for today: *God fills the heaven and earth—nothing is hidden from Him.*

6

MERCY & GRACE

*Mercy and truth have met together; Righteousness and peace have kissed
(Psalm 85:10).*

READ: TITUS 3:1-8

Two words that form the bedrock of our salvation are **Mercy** and **Grace**. According to Vine's expository dictionary, the word Mercy "is the outward manifestation of pity; it assumes need on the part of him who receives it, and resources adequate to meet the need on the part of him who shows it." In other words, mercy is something someone in dire need receives, because it is always available. God is the only one who is capable of providing mercy to everyone who needs it. God is rich in mercy, hence He has made salvation available to mankind (Ephesians 2:4; Titus 3:5). He is so merciful that while the human race was lost in sin, He sought it by sending His Son, Jesus Christ to redeem it. Our Lord Jesus Christ during His earthly ministry reiterated this message when He told the Jews, *"The Son of Man has come to seek and to save that which was lost"* (Luke 19:10). Grace is basically an unmerited divine favor. Verse 5 of our text reads, *"Not by works of righteousness which we have done, but according to His mercy He saved us, through the washing of regeneration and renewing of the Holy Spirit."* So, we see that God's **mercy** forgives our sins and saves us. At the same time, His **grace** justifies us. We read, *"having been justified by his grace we should become heirs according to the hope of eternal life."* (v7). Mercy and grace are like twin brothers—inseparable.

John records an account of how our Lord Jesus Christ demonstrated mercy and grace on a woman who was about to be stoned by a mob, because she was caught in adultery. The woman's accusers brought her to Jesus to seek permission for her to be put to death in keeping with the Mosaic law (See Leviticus 20:10). But, both the woman and her accusers were shocked at how Jesus applied His divine attributes of mercy and grace in dealing with the issue. Jesus told the accusers, *"He who is without sin among you, let him throw the first stone at her."* (John 8:7). No one dared throw the first stone, because they were equally guilty sinners, as the woman. **Mercy** forgave this woman and saved her life, while **Grace** justified her for eternal life.

Reflection: Do you accuse others of the same thing that you are guilty of?

Word for today: *Avail yourself of God's mercy and grace today.*

7

THE NEW BIRTH

Jesus answered and said to him, "Most assuredly, I say to you, unless one is born again, he cannot see the kingdom of God" (John 3:3).

READ: JOHN 3:1-8

Birth is a natural phenomenon which every living creature must experience, in order to exist. Human beings are born into this world with old sinful nature, inherited from Adam. In order to experience a righteous relationship with God, man needs a re-birth through faith in the finished work of Christ. The issue of new birth as a pre-requisite for eternal life was made crystal clear by Christ. Our text gives us an account of what took place during an interesting conversation between Nicodemus and Jesus Christ. Nicodemus approached Jesus by night with these commendable words, *"Rabbi, we know that you are a teacher come from God; for no one can do these signs that you do unless God is with him."* In reply, Jesus shifted the focus from Himself to the Kingdom of God. He told Nicodemus, *"Most assuredly, I say to you, unless one is born again, he cannot see the kingdom of God."* (John 3:3). Nicodemus asked, *"How can a man be born when he is old? Can he enter a second time into his mother's womb and be born?"* (v4). From his question, Nicodemus showed a lack of understanding in spiritual matters. Many people today still ask the same kind of question that Nicodemus asked: "How can this be?", "How can a man who is old be born again?" Our Lord Jesus answered Nicodemus' question in verses 5-6 of our text: *"Most assuredly, I say to you, unless one is born of water and the Spirit, he cannot enter the kingdom of God. That which is born of the flesh is flesh, and that which is born of the Spirit is spirit."* Jesus, by His answer to Nicodemus, revealed a three-fold truth. **First,** the new birth has nothing to do with the physical body. **Second,** the new birth is a spiritual experience, not a physical manifestation. **Third,** the Spirit of God and water are tools for the new birth. Water refers to the Word of God (Read Ephesians 5:26; John 15:3; 17:17 and 1 Peter 1:22-23). Only the Word of God can cleanse sin; physical water cannot.

A sinner is spiritually dirty before God! Just as the physical water washes physical dirt, so does the Word of God (Spiritual water) cleanses spiritual dirt, called sin. A sinner who hears and believes the Word of God is cleansed by it.

Reflection: Have you been cleansed by the Word of God? Are you born again?

Word for today: *Embrace the New Year with the new birth in Christ.*

GET THE WORD OUT!

*The fruit of the righteous is a tree of life, and he who wins souls is wise
(Proverbs 11:30).*

READ: ROMANS 10:14-17

Someone has rightly compared the sharing of the gospel to a kind-hearted effort of a sighted man in preventing the blind from falling into a ditch. Indeed, someone without Christ is spiritually blind and, if left alone, will certainly fall into eternal ditch, called hell. Just like the physically blind needs a guide, so does the spiritually blind. There is an urgent need for every born—again Christian to get the Word of God out to dying sinners. The unfolding events today show how much the world is engulfed in spiritual darkness. The unbelieving souls are spiritually blind and therefore, need an urgent spiritual rescue mission.

Verses 14-15 of our text pose four heart-searching questions: The first question is *"How then shall they call on Him in whom they have not believed?"* The implication of this question is that one has to believe in Christ before calling on Him. Paul told the Philippian jailer, *"Believe on the Lord Jesus Christ, and you will be saved, you and your household."* (Acts 16:31). Belief must precede salvation. The second question is, *"And how shall they believe in Him of whom they have not heard?"* Again, this question implies that without the communication of the gospel, it is difficult, if not impossible, for salvation to take place. Any wonder why our Lord Jesus Christ commanded every believer, *"Go into the world and preach the gospel to every creature."* (Mark 16:15). People need to hear the gospel in order for them to believe in Christ. No matter how foolish the gospel may sound in the ears of a sinner, it is the only way to link a sinner up with his Savior. 1 Corinthians 1:18 reads, *"For the message [preaching] of the cross is foolishness to those who are perishing, but to us who are being saved it is the power of God."* The third question is, *"And how shall they hear without a preacher?"* Indeed, someone has to communicate the gospel for conversion to take place in the human soul. The fourth question is, *"And how shall they preach unless they are sent?"* The great commission is for every believer in Christ. Share the gospel with others today.

Reflection: Has the preaching of the gospel saved you? Help to save others.

Word for today: *He who wins souls is wise. Are you?*

9

PHONY & INEFFECTIVE CURSES

[The Ammonites and Moabites]...had not met the children of Israel with bread and water, but hired Balaam to curse them. However, God turned the curse into a blessing. (Nehemiah 13:2).

READ: 1 SAMUEL 14:24-27

People dread curses, because a curse is "an appeal or prayer for evil or misfortune to befall someone or something." In certain parts of the world, curses are pronounced on individuals by witch doctors or voodoo priests. Some curses are effective, while others are not. If you are a child of God, living a life of righteousness, no curse pronounced on you shall prosper, because, He that is in you is greater than the source of the curse (Read 2 Kings 6:16; 1 John 4:4).

In our text, we read of how king Saul took an indiscreet oath and pronounced a curse on his fighting men at the battle field. He said, *"Cursed is the man who eats any food until evening, before I have taken vengeance on my enemies. So none of the people tasted food."* By placing a curse on them, king Saul was denying his starving army the opportunity to eat something. Saul's pronounced curse was phony and ineffective. It was phony, because no one in his right mind would prevent hungry, fighting soldiers from eating something when food is available. Starving soldiers don't fight very well. Saul placed the curse upon his fighting men for self-glorification, rather than as a fighting strategy against the enemy. Saul's curse was ineffective because Jonathan, his son, defied it. Verse 27 of our text reads, *"But Jonathan had not heard his father charge the people with the oath; therefore he stretched out the end of the rod that was in his hand and dipped it in a honeycomb, and put his hand to his mouth; and his countenance brightened."* Jonathan who was not present when his father pronounced the curse tasted some honey and in so doing, was refreshed. In spite of the fact that Jonathan was not present when the curse was pronounced, King Saul wanted Jonathan dead. Look at what he said, *"God do so and more also; for you shall surely die, Jonathan."* (v44). But, the people refused to give in to King Saul's demand (v45). Not only was Saul's curse ineffective, his order to kill Jonathan was defied.

Reflection: As a leader, mind the kind of pronouncements you make.

Word for today: *No one can curse whom the LORD has blessed.*

DIVINE FAVOR

*"And the LORD gave the people favor in the sight of the Egyp-
tians...'." (Exodus 11:3).*

READ: GENESIS 39:19-23

Another word for favor is **goodwill.** God's favor is not based on who
we are, but who He is. It is an unmerited gift! For example, Abraham had no righteous credentials to qualify him for God's call upon his life,
yet, he enjoyed God's favor. He was called out of his idolatrous family to become the father of a great nation, due to God's favor (Genesis 12:1-3). Mary
became the mother of Jesus Christ, based on God's favor. In Luke 1:30-31 we
read, *"Then the angel said to her, 'Do not be afraid, Mary, for you have found
favor with God. And behold, you will conceive in your womb and bring forth a
Son, and shall call His name JESUS."* The angelic message to Mary about becoming the mother of Jesus, showed how favored she was before God. There
were other virgins in Nazareth, but Mary was the favored one.

Joseph was a favored child among his siblings. God favored him by revealing to him in a dream how he would become great (Genesis 37:7,9). Sometimes, God's favor in your life can cause people to hate and envy you. This was
what happened to Joseph. Joseph's brothers hated and envied him due to God's
favor upon his life (v8,11). When Joseph was thrown into the pit by his brothers, God's favor brought him out of the pit (v24, 28); when he was sold into
slavery, God's favor followed him down to Egypt; when he found himself in
Potiphar's house, God's favor followed him there (39:1-4); when he was
thrown into the prison, God's favor also followed him into the prison cell.
There is nothing anyone can do to remove God's favor over your life; only you
can destroy it! This can happen through sinful lifestyle and disobedience to
God's Word. God's favor is sustained through obedience to His Word. The
children of Israel could not sustain God's favor due to their rebellious attitude
towards God (Read Numbers 14:26-28). In our text, we notice how God's favor
played out so well in Joseph's life, while in prison. God gave him favor before
the prison keeper, who promoted him from being an ordinary prisoner to becoming a supervisory prisoner. As a believer in Christ, do you know that you
are a favored child of God? Read Zechariah 2:8; 1 Peter 2:9-10)

Reflection: Do you toy with or appreciate God's favor in your life?

Word for today: *No one can destroy God's favor in your life, except you.*

11

GOD'S ABIDING PRESENCE

And He said, "My Presence will go with you, and I will give you rest." (Exodus 33:14)

READ: ACTS 27:21-26

God's abiding presence makes a lot of difference in the life of every child of God. It made a difference in the lives of the children of Israel, as they journeyed from Egypt to the Promised Land. For forty years, they did not cultivate any crop, yet they never lacked food to eat; God fed them with heavenly food. They had no where to buy clothes, yet they had enough clothes to wear for the duration of forty years. There were no incidents of people being killed by wild animals, nor was there any report of epidemic disease among the people, because God's presence was with them. When God's presence is with you, you are safe, secure and shielded. God's abiding presence was with Paul and Silas in the prison cells. The Bible makes it clear that at midnight, while they were praying and singing hymns to God, His presence came down. We read, *"Suddenly, there was a great earthquake, so that the foundations of the prison were shaken; and immediately all the prison doors were opened and everyone's chains were loosed."* (Acts 16:25-26).

God's abiding presence was also with Paul on the high seas. On his way to Rome as a prisoner, to appear before Caesar, Paul and those travelling with him experienced a shipwreck. In the midst of chaos, fear and uncertainty, Paul the prisoner became Paul the encourager, because God's presence was with him. Paul spoke with authority, *"And now I urge you to take heart, for there will be no loss of life among you, but only of the ship. For there stood by me this night an angel of the God to whom I belong and whom I serve, saying, 'Do not be afraid, Paul; you must be brought before Caesar; and indeed God has granted you all those who sail with you. Therefore take heart, men, for I believe God that it will be just as it was told me."* (Acts 27:22-25). God's abiding presence dispels fear in the midst of danger, provides courage in time of despair and protects life in the face of death. Moses knew the importance of God's abiding presence when he told God, *"If your presence does not go with us, do not bring us from here."* (Exodus 33:15). May God's presence abide with you this year.

Reflection: How genuine is your relationship with God to attract His presence?

Word for today: *God's presence abides with those who fear Him.*

BE COMMITTED & ESTABLISHED

Trust in the LORD with all your heart...in all your ways acknowledge Him, and He shall direct your paths (Proverbs 3:5-6).

READ: PROVERBS 16:1-3

Psalm 37:5 reads, *"Commit your way to the LORD, trust also in Him, and He shall bring it to pass."* Every born-again believer in Christ is a child of God—God has become his or her Father. God, our heavenly Father, wants every child of His to have a personal relationship with Him, just as a son would have with his earthly father. God is interested in what goes on in our lives as His dear children. Not only does He want us to succeed in this present life, He also wants us to be with Him in heaven forever (Read John 17:20,24; 3 John 2). A recalcitrant child does not do very well with his father. The same thing applies to us in our relationship with God. God warns, *"If you are willing and obedient, you shall eat the good of the land."* (Isaiah 1:19). The surest way to succeed in life is to trust in the LORD and commit your ways to Him. This means accepting the gift of eternal life through Christ Jesus and depending on Him and His Word.

There is a common parlance which says, *"Man proposes, but God disposes."* What this means is that as humans, we can do all the planning we want. But, except God grants His permission, such plans will not see the light of the day. Verse 1 of our text underscores this fact. We read, *"The preparations of the heart belong to man, but the answer of the tongue is from the LORD.* Indeed, any plan outside of God will not have a fruitful ending. Our Lord Jesus Christ gave a parable of a rich guy who was foolish in planning his future. God had blessed his farm so much that he ran out of storage space for his produce (Read Luke 12:13-21). In his plan for the future, this guy used the words, **"I will"** four times regarding what he would do going forward. There was no mention of **"If God wills."** This guy's plan was flawed, because, he kept God out of it. Verse 3a of our text tells us what our attitude should be regarding whatever plan we might make. We should commit it to the LORD. When we do this, then God will enable such a plan to succeed (v3b).

Reflection: Do you have plans for this year? Learn to bring God into them and it shall be well with you.

Word for today: *Without commitment to God, plans go haywire.*

THE FORGIVENESS YARDSTICK

And if he sins against you seven times in a day, and seven times in a day returns to you, saying, 'I repent,' you shall forgive him (Luke 17:4).

READ: MATTHEW 18:21-22

The issue of how often one should forgive those who have offended one is open to debate among people, including Christians. Christ Himself addressed the issue of forgiveness during one of His teaching sessions. From our text we notice that Peter had asked a question in this regard, *"Lord, how often shall my brother sin against me, and I forgive him? Up to seven times?"* (Matthew 18:21). Peter based his yardstick of forgiveness on seven offences, probably, because seven is God's number of completeness. Our Lord Jesus answered Peter's question in this manner, *"I do not say to you , up to seven times, but up to seventy times seven."* (v22). Christ's answer must have taken Peter aback. To forgive someone who has sinned against you 490 times, of the same offence is next to incredulity. In other words, it is unlikely to happen, that someone will sin against you 490 times of the same offence in one day. In order for this to happen, the committal of such a sin would take place nearly every 3 minutes in a day. Since, it is nearly impossible for someone to sin against you every 3 minutes of the day, of the same sin, Jesus' answer can be interpreted to mean that the yardstick for forgiving any sin committed against you is **endless forgiveness.**

Some people have often ask this relevant question regarding forgiveness, "What if your offending brother refuses to say sorry?" They cite Jesus' statement in Luke 17:4, which reads as follows, *"And if he sins against you seven times in a day, and <u>seven times in a day returns to you, saying, 'I repent,'</u> you shall forgive him."* To such people, the element of sorry should be in place before forgiveness can even take place. But, the Bible makes it clear that our Lord Jesus Christ never demanded, "Sorry" as a prerequisite for forgiving those who were crucifying Him. Instead, He prayed, *"Father forgive them, for they do not know what they do."* (Luke 23:34). Stephen, while being stoned to death based on a false accusation, did not demand **"Sorry"** from his accusers before pleading with God to forgive them for their murderous act (Acts 7:60)

Reflection: We know much we've sinned and how often God has forgiven us!

Word for today: *Forgiveness is the by-product of a genuine love.*

THE KISS & THE HIDDEN SWORD!

And one of those who stood by drew his sword and struck the servant of the high priest, and cut off his ear (Mark 14:47).

READ: LUKE 22:49-53

Two interesting incidents took place in the Garden of Gethsemane, during the arrest of our Lord Jesus Christ by the Jewish religious authority. The first was Judas' kiss of Jesus. The Bible tells us that *"Judas, one of the twelve went before them and drew near to Jesus to kiss Him."* (Luke 22:47). In the Eastern world, a kiss on the neck was, and still is, the traditional way of greeting a loved one. In their letters to the early Church, Paul and Peter urged them to kiss one another with a holy kiss (Read Romans 16:16; 1 Corinthians 16:20; 2 Corinthians 13:12; 1 Thessalonians 5:26) He was very careful to use the word "holy" to differentiate it from a worldly kiss, which bothers on sensuality and immorality. Judas' kiss was different from the normal kiss; it was not a kiss of love, but a kiss of identification. Prior to Judas' kiss, the Jewish religious leaders had problem identifying the person of Christ. So, in order to ensure that they did not make a mistake, Judas agreed to identify Christ with a kiss. Mark 14:44-46 read, *"Now His betrayer had given them a signal, saying, 'Whomever I kiss, He is the One; seize Him and lead Him away safely'. As soon as He had come, immediately he went up to Him and said to Him, 'Rabbi, Rabbi!' and kissed Him. Then they laid their hands on Him and took Him."* Judas's kiss was an unholy kiss of betrayal.

The second incident that took place during Christ's arrest was the cutting of Malchus' ear. Unknown to anyone, Peter had a sword on him. Probably, due to Jesus' statement to them regarding His imminent arrest, Peter prepared for the worst by hiding a sword under his garment (Matthew 26:31-32). It was not surprising, therefore, that he used it in cutting off the high priest's servant's ear. Peter missed the guy's head and got his ear anyway. But for Jesus' gracious touch and healing, Malchus would have bled to death. Peter's sword was hidden and deadly. There is another kind of sword that is hidden, sharp and deadly. It is called the **human tongue.** The human tongue, though hidden in the mouth, is a deadly sword. It can kill and set a nation ablaze (Read James 3:1-10).

Reflection: Peter's hidden sword revealed his unpreparedness to die.

Word for today: *Unholy kiss and hidden sword are from the devil, avoid them.*

15

THE REAL PEACE

Peace I leave with you, my peace I give to you; not as the world gives do I give to you. Let not your heart be troubled, neither let it be afraid (John 14:27).

READ: JOHN 14:27-28

The opposite of peace is war and anxiety. Christ's post-resurrection greetings to His disciples included these words, "Peace be with you." and "Peace to you." Understandably, Christ's disciples were devastated by His death. They were so afraid of the Jews that they remained behind closed doors (John 20:19); they were so worried and uncertain about the future that they went about feeling disappointed (Luke 24:13-27); they were so discouraged regarding their calling that they called it quits (John 20:2-4). Jesus pronounced peace upon His disciples because their hearts were very much troubled. Jesus is the Prince of peace (Isaiah 9:6 and only He can provide real peace.

There are four kinds of peace. First is the **Peace of God** (Philippians 4:7; Colossians 3:15). This kind of peace sustains the believer in Christ in time of difficulties. Second is the **Peace from God** (Galatians 1:3). This is the kind of peace that God bestows upon believers, based on the atoning death of Christ. Third is **Peace with God** (Romans 5:1). This is the kind of peace that a believer in Christ experiences, sequel to salvation. The fourth is **World peace** (John 14:27). We read, *"Peace I leave with you, my peace I give to you; not as the world gives do I give to you."* In His statement, our Lord Jesus differentiates His peace from that of the world. Indeed, Christ's peace is bestowed on His followers, while World peace is negotiated by warring individuals; Christ's peace is guaranteed in heaven, while world peace is written on paper, and can fall apart any time; Christ's peace is eternal, while world peace is temporal. The world operates in crisis and will not know any peace, because it crucified the Prince of peace. Verse 28 of our text reads, *"You have heard me say to you, 'I am going away and coming back to you,' If you loved me, you would rejoice because I said, 'I am going to the Father,' for my Father is greater than I."* Christ's promise to return for all who believe and love Him, should give us cause to rejoice. The storms may rage, the wind may blow, you should not be afraid .

Reflection: Have you experienced the real peace that is in Christ Jesus?

Word for today: *The pursuit of peace outside of Christ is counter-productive.*

DELIVERANCE IN ZION

"The eyes of the Lord GOD are on the sinful kingdom, and I will destroy it from the face of the earth, yet I will not destroy the house of Jacob...." (Amos 9:8).

READ: OBADIAH 1:15-18

The rivalry between Esau and Jacob, which started from their mother's womb (Genesis 25:22-26), played itself out during their life time (v29 -34) and continued even after they had gone. The descendants of Esau are the Edomites, while the descendants of Jacob are the Israelites. The rivalry between Esau and Jacob grew into animosity with successive generations. Twice, the Edomites exhibited their animosity towards the children of Israel. The first was their refusal to grant the children of Israel passage through their cities on their way to the Promised land (Read Numbers 20:14-21).The second was the Edomites' indifference to the plight of the children of Israel during the invasion by King Nebuchadnezzar's soldiers. Not only did the Edomites rejoice over the invasion of Jerusalem, they also helped the invading army to achieve their purpose.

God remembered the injustice and ill-treatment meted out by the Edomites to the children of Israel in their time of affliction (Read Obadiah 1:12-14). V15-16 of our text contain the pronouncement of God's judgment upon the Edomites for their lack of love towards the children of Israel. God said that the way they had treated the children of Israel would be the same way they would be treated by their enemies. Treat others the way you would like to be treated, because, "What goes around, comes around!" Edom would be invaded, but, Mount Zion shall experience deliverance from the LORD (v17,19). Following its divine deliverance, Mount Zion shall operate in holiness for the house of Jacob to possess their possessions (v17). In the Old Testament, Mount Zion refers to the city of God's people—the Israelites. In the New testament, Mount Zion takes a spiritual meaning. It speaks of God's spiritual Kingdom—the heavenly Jerusalem (Hebrews 12:22-23; Revelation 14:1). Anyone who identifies with Christ is ushered into God's Kingdom, where he or she enjoys the power of deliverance and victory in Christ. Edom *represents* the world, Mount Zion *represents* God's Kingdom.

Reflection: Have you been delivered from the powers of darkness?

Word for today: *When God delivers, He also blesses.*

HE CARES FOR YOU

You will seek me and find me, when you search for me with all your heart (Jeremiah 29:13).

READ: JEREMIAH 29:11-14

The lyrics of a popular hymn by Civilla D. Martins, (1869-1948), entitled *"God will take care of you"* speaks volumes of God's omnipotence in providing and caring. Indeed, God cares for all those who put their trust in Him. During their Babylonian captivity, God still cared for the children of Israel. Look at what He told them through prophet Jeremiah, *"I know the thoughts that I think toward you, says the LORD, thoughts of peace and not of evil, to give you a future and a hope." (Jeremiah 29:11).* God's promise of caring is relevant to all believers in Christ today. As a child of God, be rest assured that God cares for you. If He could care for the birds of the air and the animals in the forest, what makes you think that He wouldn't care for you, who are created in His image. There are numerous examples in the Bible of how God miraculously cared for people. He cared for Elijah in a time of severe famine. God hooked Elijah up with unlikely sources—the ravens and a widow, because He cared for him. These two characters have one thing in common— poverty and uncertainty, yet God used them to feed Elijah. As was the case with Elijah, God can provide for you through unlikely sources. God also cared for Joseph by making him a successful man, while he was in the house of Potiphar (Read Genesis 39:1-4). Christ cared for His disciples on the high seas. The wind blew and the storm raged, yet their boat did not sink, because He cared for them. Do you know that God's presence in your life can cause the wind of adversity, sickness and poverty to cease in your life?

There are four inhibitors to knowing that God cares for you: **1. Satan's deceit**. Satan can speak lies into your minds in time of difficulties, to make you feel that God doesn't care. Learn to listen to God rather than Satan (Read Genesis 2:16-17) **2. Lack of understanding of how God operates.** God operates differently from the way we do. Otherwise, how can shouting bring down the walls of Jericho (Joshua 6:16). **3. Lack of faith** (Read Romans 1:17; Hebrews 11:6). **4. Misplaced priorities in life** (Read Matthew 6:33).

Reflection: Do you feel abandoned and uncared for by God? Don't feel so.

Word for today: *That you are alive means that God still cares for you.*

THE LORD'S WILL BE DONE

So when he would not be persuaded, we ceased, saying, "The will of the Lord be done." (Acts 21:14).

READ: LUKE 11:1-4

One of the disciples of our Lord Jesus Christ approached Him with an important request, *"Lord, teach us to pray, as John also taught his disciples."* (Luke 11:1). In response, Jesus taught them, *"When you pray, say, 'Our Father in heaven, Hallowed be your name. Your Kingdom come, your will be done on earth as it is heaven.'"* The element of God's will in prayer is very important. God wants His will to be done on earth as it is done in heaven. God owns both heaven and earth. In heaven, God's will prevails; He wants the same thing done here on earth. **What is God's will?** Simply put, "God's will" is God's divine purpose, plan, discretion and determination, which cannot be overridden or changed by anyone. Having taught His disciples to include the element of God's will in their prayers, our Lord Jesus demonstrated what He taught them, while agonizing in prayer in the Garden of Gethsemane. Twice in His prayers, Christ invoked the will of God to be done. In Matthew 26: 39 we read, *"He went a little farther and fell on His face, and prayed, saying, 'O My Father, if it is possible, let this cup pass from me; nevertheless, not as I will, but as You will.'"* Our Lord Jesus prayed to His Father about the possibility of removing death on the cross from His salvation plan for mankind. But suddenly, He realized that God's will could not be changed or overridden, so He added to His prayer, *"Nevertheless, not as I will, but as you will".* Verse 42 reads, *"Again, a second time, He went away and prayed, saying, 'O My Father, if this cup cannot pass away from me unless I drink it, your will be done.'"* God's will supersedes our human will.

Knowing the fate that was awaiting Paul in Jerusalem, based on divine revelation, the Christians persuaded him not to go because they did not want to lose him (Read Acts 21:8-12). But, Paul was determined to go, even if it meant his dying. Therefore, the disciples concluded with these words *"The will of the Lord be done."* (v13-14). Sometimes, carrying out God's will can cost us our friends or even our own lives. That notwithstanding, learn to do God's will.

Reflection: How ready and willing are you to do God's will?

Word for today: *Anything done according to God's will, honors Him.*

HE CAN'T BE BOUGHT!

And when Simon saw that through the laying on of the apostles' hands the Holy Spirit was given, he offered them money (Acts 8:18).

READ: ACTS 8:14-19

Money plays a vital role in our social and economic lives. If used correctly, money is good, but if used wrongly, it becomes a problem. In the ancient time, as it is today, many people have used money to buy their way and suppress the truth. For instance, the Jews used money to suppress the truth regarding Christ's triumphant resurrection. Matthew 28: 12-15 read, *"When they had assembled with the elders and consulted together, they gave a large sum of money to the soldiers, saying, 'Tell them, His disciples came at night and stole Him away while we slept.' And if this comes to the governor's ears, we will appease him and make you secure. So they took the money and did as they were instructed; and this saying is commonly reported among the Jews until this day.'"* As at the time Matthew wrote the gospel, it was a common saying among the Jews, that the body of Jesus Christ was stolen away by His disciples, while the soldiers stationed at the tomb to prevent that from happening slept. This kind of lie was only possible due to the power of bribe money. It is not unlikely that Paul prior to his conversion was among those who peddled this kind of lie. But, after his encounter with Jesus on the Damascus road, such a lie was put to rest in his mind.

Our text reveals how deceitful money can be. The Bible makes it clear that Simon was a sorcerer, who *"astonished the people of Samaria"* through the power of sorcery. As a result, everyone gave heed to him and even acknowledged him as someone who possessed the great power of God. Due to the conversion galore that took place in the city of Samaria, Simon believed in Christ and was consequently baptized along with others. When the apostles laid their hands on the new converts, they all received the Holy Spirit. Simon was fascinated by what he saw. Rather than ask to be prayed for to receive the Holy Spirit, Simon offered the apostles money in exchange for the Holy Spirit. Peter cursed him and his money. Holy Spirit and His gifts cannot be bought or faked. Those who merchandize spiritual giftedness will give account to God.

Reflection: Do you seek power? Seek Christ for in Him dwells all power.

Word for today: *Bribe money is a cursed money; avoid it.*

A BALANCED-LIFE APPROACH

"And you shall remember the LORD your God, for it is He who gives you power to get wealth..." (Deuteronomy 8:18).

READ: PROVERBS 30:7-9

Verse 8-9 of our text reads, *"Remove falsehood and lies far from me; Give me neither poverty nor riches-- Feed me with the food allotted to me; lest I be full and deny You, and say, 'Who is the LORD?' Or lest I be poor and steal, and profane the name of my God.."* Agur, the writer of Proverbs chapter 30 took a balanced approach to the issues of life. In fact, he asked God for a balanced life—a life that will enable him experience neither wealth nor poverty. In other words, he wanted to be free from the pride of being wealthy and the suffering of being poor. What a balanced approach to life issues! If everyone were to think like Agur, this planet would be a nice and peaceful place to live. Unfortunately, this is not the case! There is an inordinate ambition for riches by the powerful and a pathetic struggle for survival by the poor. Agur chose the middle ground—to be neither rich nor poor. Wealth can open the door to pride and utter disregard for God. On the other hand, poverty can lead to suffering and stealing. Agur concludes by asking the LORD to feed him with the food allotted to him—meaning that God will provide him with daily bread.

Three C's to sustaining a balanced-life approach to issues of life.
1. Contentment
God wants us to be content with what we have. May we never behave like the proverbial dog that lost the bone he had by diving into the water for the mirage of the bone he saw (Read 1 Timothy 6:6-8 and Hebrews 13:5).
2. Commitment.
The Bible commands, *"Commit your way to the LORD, trust also in Him, and He shall bring it to pass."* (Psalm 37:5). When you commit your way to the LORD, He will enable you to have a balanced -life approach to issues of life (Read Proverbs 16:3).
3. Commencement. Commence each day with the Lord and you will have the strength to live a balanced life in Him daily (Read Psalm 63:1).

Reflection: How balanced is your life in Christ Jesus? Write it down.

Word for today: *Know God; know the way to live a balanced life.*

BE HEAVENLY MINDED

But he, being full of the Holy Spirit, gazed into heaven and saw the glory of God, and Jesus standing at the right hand of God (Acts 7:55).

READ: COLOSSIANS 3:1-4

To be heavenly minded *speaks* of being conscious of God's glory, Christ's imminent return and the heavenly bliss that awaits the believer in Christ. The early Christians lived the lives of heaven mindedness. As they were beaten, hounded, bound and thrown to hungry lions, they never wavered in their faith because they were heavenly minded. Take, for instance, someone like Stephen. The Bible records that he was *"full of the Holy Spirit, gazed into heaven and saw the glory of God, and Jesus standing at the right hand of God."* (Acts 7:55). He told his accusers what he saw, *"Look! I see the heaven opened and the Son of Man standing at the right hand of God!"* (v56). Stephen was full of the Holy Spirit and heavenly minded. Any wonder why he was able to look into heaven? If you are Spirit filled, you will be able to connect with heaven in your spirit, while you are praying, or singing or meditating on the Word of God. Don't forget, carnality cannot connect with heaven.

Our Lord Jesus Himself warns us to be heavenly minded, in His teaching about the cares of life. He said, *"Seek you first the Kingdom of God and His righteousness, and all these things shall be added to you."* (Matthew 6:33). Seeking the things of heaven amounts to being heavenly minded. In our text, we are reminded to do the same thing. Verses 1 and 2 of our text read, *"If then you were raised with Christ, seek those things which are above, where Christ is, sitting at the right hand of God. Set your mind on things above, not on things on the earth."* From our text we notice that seeking after heavenly things is contingent upon being risen with Christ. If one has not risen with Christ, he or she cannot seek the things which are above. Being risen with Christ *speaks* of accepting Christ as your Lord and Savior, dying to sin and living a life of holiness in Him (Read Romans 6:4; Galatians 2:20). Verse 3 of our text reiterates the need to be dead to sin in order to be heavenly minded, while v4 tells us of the benefit of being heavenly minded—appearing in glory with Christ when He returns.

Reflection: Are you heavenly minded? What are your priorities in life?

Word for today: *The heavenly minded are spiritually molded.*

INTERCESSORY PRAYER

*Then the people cried out to Moses, and when Moses prayed to the LORD, the
fire was quenched (Numbers 11:2).*

READ: COLOSSIANS 1:9-12

An Intercessory Prayer is usually very effective, except when God's sovereign Will overrules. When God was about to destroy the cities of Sodom and Gomorrah, Abraham interceded on their behalf. We read, *"And the LORD said, "Because the outcry against Sodom and Gomorrah is great, and because their sin is very grave, I will go down now and see whether they have done altogether according to the outcry against it that has come to me; and if not, I will know."* (Genesis 18:20-21). After telling Abraham of God's intention to destroy the cities of Sodom and Gomorrah, the angelic messengers departed, *"but Abraham stood still before the LORD."* (v22). Abraham interceded for people of Sodom and Gomorrah six times before the LORD (Read Genesis 18:23-33). Again, when the children of Israel angered God through their complaint, God sent "fire which burned among them, and consumed some in the outskirts of the camp." But, when *"the people cried out to Moses, and when Moses prayed to the LORD, the fire was quenched."* (Numbers 11:1-2). God visited Miriam with leprosy for opening her mouth too wide to insult Moses (12:1-10). But Moses ended up interceding for her. We read, *"So Moses cried out to the LORD, saying, 'Please, heal her O God, I pray.'"* (v13). In another occasion, God wanted to get rid of the children of Israel for their rebellious attitude and to raise a new set of people through Moses. But Moses interceded for them by talking God out of it. Through Moses' intercessory prayer, God pardoned the people (Read Numbers 14:1-25).

Prior to His death on the cross, our Lord Jesus Christ offered an intercessory prayer to His Father for His disciples and all those who will believe in Him through their ministry (Read John 17:9, 15, 20). In our text, we read of Paul's intercessory prayer for the Church in Colossae. He asked the Lord to grant them knowledge, spiritual understanding and to strengthen them in the power of God's might and to enable them walk worthy of the Lord. Ask God to give you an interceding heart.

Reflection: Do you intercede for your enemies? (Read Matthew 5:44).

Word for today: *Intercessory prayer is a plea to God for those in need.*

23

AN AMAZING TRANSFORMATION!

Now, therefore, you are no longer strangers and foreigners, but fellow citizens with the saints and members of the household of God (Ephesians 2:19).

READ: EPHESIANS 2:11-13

The transformation that takes place when someone experiences a spiritual re-rebirth is phenomenal. When someone becomes born again, he or she graduates from a sinner to a saint; from a candidate of hell to a candidate of heaven; from being God's enemy to being God's son; ; from a hater of God's Word to a doer of God's Word; from being worldly minded to being heavenly minded.

Our text reads, *"Therefore remember that you, once Gentiles in the flesh--who are called Uncircumcision by what is called the Circumcision made in the flesh by hands—that at that time you were without Christ, being aliens from the commonwealth of Israel and strangers from the covenants of promise, having no hope and without God in the world. But now in Christ Jesus you who once were far off have been brought near by the blood of Christ."* From our text, we notice that Paul wrote to remind the Gentile Christians about the transformation that has taken place in their lives as a result of their faith in Christ Jesus. The same holds true for every believer in Christ today. Our text reveals a five-fold condition of a Gentile sinner prior to his or her spiritual transformation.

1. He was *uncircumcised* (Ephesians 2:11). In Biblical parlance, Gentiles were referred to as "Uncircumcised", alias, second-hand citizens (Read 1 Samuel 14:6; Jeremiah 9:25, 26). For instance, David referred to Goliath as an "Uncircumcised Philistine." (1 Samuel 17:26,36).

2. He was *"without Christ"* (Ephesians 2:12). This means that he had no claim to salvation in God (Read John 4:19-22).

3. He was *"an alien from the Commonwealth of Israel"* (Ephesians 2:12)

4. He was *"a stranger from the covenant of promise"* (v12).

5. He was *"without God and hope in this world"* (v12).

But, all the above inhibitions were removed as a result of Christ's death, burial and triumphant resurrection. Praise God!

Reflection: Has Christ transformed you yet? Are there any visible evidence?

Word for today: *An amazing transformation takes place through Christ.*

YOU'RE IMPORTANT TO GOD

See, I have inscribed you on the palms of my hands; your walls are continually before me. (Isaiah 49:16).

READ: ISAIAH 49:15-18

In our text, God asked the children of Israel a very important question, *"Can a woman forget her nursing child, and not have compassion on the son of her womb?"* God Himself answered the question, *"Surely they may forget."* (Isaiah 49:15). Indeed, it is possible that a woman will forget her nursing child. We learn in the Bible of a woman who boiled her infant child for food, due to a severe famine in the land of Samaria (Read 2 Kings 6:24-29). The world in which we live is witnessing an unprecedented level of wickedness. It is not uncommon today to hear stories of mothers, who have abandoned their sucking babies. Some mothers have even dumped their new born babies into dumpsters, while others have gotten rid of their babies by throwing them into the river. The issue of a mother forgetting her sucking child is of spiritual relevance to believers in Christ. Although, a mother may forget her nursing child, God has promised not to forget you because you are His child. Everyone who accepts Christ as Lord and Savior becomes a child of God. God goes further by saying that whoever touches His people touches the apple of His eyes (Zechariah 2:8). Although this statement was directed to the children of Israel at the time of their Babylonian captivity, it is very relevant to every believer in Christ. As a believer in Christ, the blessings of Abraham are upon you (Read Genesis 12:3; Galatians 3:26-29). Whoever touches an innocent child of God is looking for trouble! You are important to God.

Verse 16 of our text reads, *"See, I have inscribed you on the palms of my hands; your walls are continually before me."* God says that He has inscribed you on the palms of His hands, meaning that you are secure in Him. The Holy Spirit also confirmed this promise through apostle Paul (Read Romans 8:35). In verse 17 of our text, God said, *"Your sons shall make haste; your destroyers and those who laid you waste shall go away from you."* If you align yourself with God, your spiritual relevance in Christ will attract God's blessings upon you, before your enemies. They will be stunned by what God does in your life.

Reflection: How spiritually relevant are you in serving God?

Word for today: *To become important to God, identify with Christ.*

AN OPEN-HANDED GIVER

He who gives to the poor will not lack, but he who hides his eyes will have many curses (Proverbs 28:27).

READ: ACTS 20:33-35

Giving starts from the mind. One has to be open-minded in order to be open-handed in giving. Giving is like sowing a seed. The more open-handed you are in sowing, the bigger your harvest. Our Lord Jesus commands, *"Give, and it will be given to you: good measure, pressed down, shaken together, and running over will be put into your bosom. For with the same measure that you use, it will be measured back to you."* In this statement, our Lord Jesus introduces the principle of giving. If you give open-handedly, you will receive an open-handed reward—a fully-loaded reward. But, if on the other hand you give tight-fistedly, you will in return receive a tight-fisted reward. Those who are tight-fisted in giving will find it hard to receive God's blessings, because there is no room in their palms for such a reward. God drops his blessings on open hands, not on tight-fisted hands. Therefore, open your hands in giving, in order to attract God's blessings. Paul commended the Thessalonian Christians for their open-handedness in giving. We read, *"For I bear witness that according to their ability, yes, and beyond their ability, they were freely willing, imploring us with much urgency that we would receive the gift and the fellowship of the ministering to the saints. And not only as we had hoped, but they first gave themselves to the Lord, and then to us by the will of God."* (2 Corinthians 8:3-5). The Thessalonian Christians *"first gave themselves to the Lord"* As a result, they were able to be open minded in their giving to the Lord's work. Unfortunately, some people refuse to give their money to the Church, because they think that by doing so, they are enriching the pastor of the Church. They forget that they are giving to God and not the pastor.

In our text, Paul reminded the Church in Ephesus that he never *"coveted anyone's silver or gold or apparel."* Paul was by profession a tent maker (Acts 18:1-3). So, he applied his skill of tent-making in fending for himself and those with him. He reminds us, *"It is more blessed to give than to receive."* (Acts 20:35). Learn to be open-handed in your giving to God's work this year.

Reflection: Remember, God owns everything you have, and even you.

Word for today: *Don't be tight-fisted; be open-handed in your giving to God.*

UNITED IN CHRIST

"There is one body and one Spirit, just as you were called in one hope...one Lord, one faith, one baptism; one God and Father of all..." (Ephesians 4:4-6).

READ: GENESIS 11:1-9

The Church is diverse in culture, but united in Christ. That means cultural differences should not disrupt the Church; rather, they should help the Church to move forward in Christ. Culture is as old as mankind; it is linked to a spoken language. Language plays an important role in sustaining a culture. Hence, those who speak the same language, invariably, share similar cultural identity. The diverse cultures we have today is the result of a confused language. In other words, a confused language gave birth to our cultural differences. Verse 1 of our text reads, *"Now the whole earth had one language and one speech."* But, all that changed when mankind decided to flout God's injunction to *"fill the whole earth and subdue it."* (Genesis 1:28). After the flood, mankind didn't want to spread out. Rather, they decided to take a vertical, rather than a horizontal approach in filling the earth. Verse 4 of our text reads, *"And they said, "Come, let us build ourselves a city, and a tower whose top is in the heavens; let us make a name for ourselves, lest we be scattered abroad over the face of the whole earth."* In response, the *"LORD said, 'Indeed the people are one and they all have one language, and this is what they begin to do; now nothing that they propose to do will be withheld from them. Come, let us go down and there confuse their language, that they may not understand one another's speech.'"* (v6-7). Mankind were united in their effort to build a tower to make a name for themselves. In response, the trinity was united in making sure that it did not happen by confusing their language.

In the midst of all the chaos of cultural and lingual differences, believers in Christ are united in Christ Jesus. Christ's death on the cross has removed the cultural and lingual barriers that have haunted mankind. Today, people from every culture can worship God irrespective of their cultural and lingual differences. We are united in Christ (Colossians 3:11). Interestingly, the original language of mankind that was lost at the tower of Babel will be restored during Christ's millennial reign (Read Zephaniah 3:9).

Reflection: Are you united in Christ or haunted by cultural barriers?

Word for today: *Culture will fade away, but Christ will remain.*

NO TESTING, NO TESTIMONY

"...let those who suffer according to the will of God commit their souls to Him in doing good, as to a faithful Creator ." (1 Peter 4:19).

READ: 1 PETER 4:12-16

Another word for testing is trial. Testing begets testimony; for he who lacks testing lacks testimony. Without the testing of our faith, there will be no testimony of what God can do. A steadfast faith in God often produces testimony, and testimony honors God. Peter's letter to the early Church as it went through a period of severe trial and testing holds true for us today. Verses 12-13 of our text read, *"Beloved, do not think it strange concerning the fiery trial which is to try you, as though some strange thing happened to you; but rejoice to the extent that you partake of Christ's sufferings, that when His glory is revealed, you may also be glad with exceeding joy."* As a believer in Christ, there must be a time of testing and trial of your faith. When this happens, don't chicken out. Testing of your faith can come in various forms, such as, but not limited to, persecution, suffering, affliction, denial of your rights, threats, beatings and even imprisonment for the sake of the gospel. May the testing of our faith bring glory to God, rather than shame, for the judgment of God must start from the Church of God (1 Peter 4:17).

Let's take a look at two tested Biblical characters who had testimonies:
1. Joseph. Joseph went through a period of severe testing. He was thrown into a pit and later sold into slavery by his siblings (Genesis chapter 37). Under false accusation, Joseph was thrown into prison. God allowed Joseph to be tested in order to bless and promote him. After his testing, Joseph was promoted to become the Prime Minister of Egypt. God also blessed him with two sons. The names of Joseph's sons reveal his testimony: *"God has made me forget all my toil and all my father's house."* (Genesis 41:51). *"God has caused me to be fruitful in the land of my affliction."* (v52). What is your testimony?
2. Daniel. Daniel's enemies conspired against him and consequently he was thrown into the lions' den. After passing the test of faith, Daniel had a testimony. Read Daniel 6:21-22.

Reflection: Can you remember when last you gave a testimony?

Word for today: *Testing and trial strengthen our Christian faith.*

28

THE WOMAN IN A BASKET

And because lawlessness will abound, the love of many will grow cold. But he who endures to the end shall be saved (Matthew 24:12-13).

READ: ZECHARIAH 5:5-11

Zechariah was shown a vision of a woman in a basket. The vision was aimed at correcting the *"spirit of secularism and greed"* that held the children of Israel captive in his days. Nonetheless, the vision gives us some insight into an end-time world government system. Zechariah's vision has two symbolisms: a **woman** and a **basket** (*Hebrew ephah*). In Hebrew, an *ephah* is a unit of measurement, especially for meal flour. In the Scriptures, it is not uncommon to find where a woman symbolizes the spiritual lethargy of the people. For instance, in His parable of the leaven, our Lord Jesus Christ used the symbolism of a woman to indict the Jewish religious leaders for their indifference to the Kingdom of heaven (Matthew 13:33). In Revelation 2:20, Christ used the woman, Jezebel to symbolize sexual immorality and idolatry among the heathen nations. Again, John in his vision at the Island of Patmos saw a vision of a woman sitting on a scarlet beast, which symbolizes "political power" and world-wide apostasy (Revelation 17:1-6).

In Zechariah's vision, the **woman** represents, *"the religious aspect of satanic world system."*, while the **basket** (*Hebrew ephah*) represents *"the godless economic and commercial aspects of satanic world system."* Human beings don't live in baskets. Verse 8a of our text tells us the character of the woman in the basket. We read, *"Then he said, 'This is Wickedness.'"* That this woman is named, *"Wickedness"* reveals the degree of wickedness associated with ungodly world governments. Verse 8b tells us about the fate of the woman. She was *"thrust down into the basket"* which had a lead cover over it. Verses 10-11 reveal the destination of the basket. We read, *"So I said to the angel who talked with me, 'Where are they carrying the basket?' And he said to me, 'To build a house for it in the land of Shinar; when it is ready, the basket will be set there on its base.'"* Humans don't live in baskets. The fact that the woman in Zechariah's vision was conveyed in a basket points to a world-wide religious decline and apostasy that will mark the end time.

Reflection: Are you prepared to meet the Lord?

Word for today: *Get reconciled to God before it is too late.*

29

QUESTIONING GALORE!

Then one of them, a lawyer, asked Him a question, testing Him, and saying, "Teacher, which is the great commandment in the law?" (Matthew 22:35-36).

READ: MATTHEW 22:15-22

Matthew chapter 22 can aptly be called, 'Question & Answer' chapter. It contains four questions—three from the Jewish rulers and one from Christ. Our Lord Jesus Christ answered the three questions asked by the Jewish rulers, but they could not answer the only question He posed to them.

Question #1 by the Herodians: *"Teacher, we know that you are true, and teach the way of God in truth; nor do you care about anyone, for you do not regard the person of men. 'Tell us, therefore, what do you think? Is it lawful to pay taxes to Caesar, or not?'"* (Matthew 22:16-17). **Christ's answer:** *"Render therefore to Caesar the things that are Caesar's, and to God the things that are God's."* (v21).

Question #2 by the Sadducees: *"Teacher, Moses said that if a man dies, having no children, his brother shall marry his wife and raise up offspring for his brother. Now there were with us seven brothers. The first died after he had married, and having no offspring, left his wife to his brother. Likewise the second also, and the third, even to the seventh. Last of all the woman died also. Therefore, in the resurrection, whose wife of the seven will she be? For they all had her."* (v24-28). **Christ's answer:** *"In the resurrection they neither marry nor are given in marriage, but are like angels of God in heaven."* (v30).

Question #3 by a lawyer: *"Teacher, which is the great commandment in the law?"* (v36). **Christ's answer:** *"You shall love the LORD your God with all your heart, with all your soul, and with all your mind. You shall love your neighbor as yourself"* (v37,39). **Question #4 by Christ:** *"What do you think about Christ? Whose Son is He?"* They answered, 'The Son of David.' (v42) Christ's follow-up question, *'How then does David call Him, Lord?'* (v43) *'If David calls Him, Lord, how is He his Son.'"* (v45). The questions asked by the Jewish rulers were malicious—aimed at entrapping Christ, while Christ's question to them was aimed at revealing their ignorance about His deity.

Reflection: Are you fond of asking motive-driven questions?

Word for today: *Motive-driven questions are better not answered.*

ASSURANCE OF SALVATION

"These things I have written to you who believe in the name of the Son of God, that you may know that you have eternal life…" (1 John 5:13).

READ: 1 JOHN 5:10-13

Salvation is an act of faith. God in His Word, has promised salvation to as many as believe in His Son, Jesus Christ (John 3:16). You need not expect any changes in your physical body, when you accept Christ into your life. The changes that are expected in you are spiritual, which will begin to manifest externally in your daily life. When Jesus comes into your life, you become a child of God (John 1:12). The question is: How can I know that I have been saved? This is the question some Christians ask, especially those who are new in the faith or who have recently given their lives to Christ.

The only way to know if you have been saved, is to believe what the Bible says about your salvation. The Bible says that if you believe in Jesus Christ, you will be saved. It is not a thing that takes place in future; rather, it is something that takes place the moment you accept Jesus Christ (Read John 3:18, 36 and 1 John 5:13). Take for instance, the criminal on the cross with Jesus Christ; he experienced salvation the moment he believed in Christ. In Luke 23:42-43 we read, *"Then he [the criminal] said to Jesus, 'Lord, remember me when you come into your kingdom.'"* In response, Jesus said to him, *"Assuredly, I say to you, today you will be with me in Paradise."* In most cases, the devil plays in the minds of people to make them doubt their salvation in Christ. He reminds them of their sinful past and makes them think that their sins can never be forgiven, due to their magnitude. If you are one of such people, read 1 John 1:9. As a born-again Christian, you become a member of God's chosen generation, a royal priesthood, and a special individual (1 Peter 2:9). You do not work for salvation; it is a free gift of God (Ephesians 2:8-9). However, you need to do something to grow in it (Read Philippians 2:12). **Work out your salvation** *speaks* of engaging in a spiritual discipline that will make you grow and mature in faith, which includes daily reading of God's Word, prayer, soul-wining and fellowshipping with other believers in Christ. Rebuke the devil if he tries to make you doubt your salvation in Christ (James 4:7).

Reflection: Are you saved? Or do you doubt your salvation?

Word for today: *Salvation is instant; sanctification is progressive.*

31

FEBRUARY

DEVOTIONALS

34

LOOSE HIM & LET HIM GO

Therefore if the Son makes you free, you shall be free indeed (John 8:36).

READ: JOHN 11:38-44

*L**oose him and let him go.** These were the words of our Lord Jesus Christ to a weeping crowd that was gathered at the grave of Lazarus. Lazarus had been dead and buried for four days before the arrival of Christ. We learn that Jesus became emotional on approaching the grave of Lazarus, His friend. In verse 38 of our text we read, *"Then Jesus, again groaning in Himself, came to the tomb. It was a cave, and a stone lay against it."* Do you know that God has emotions? The things we do and the things that happen around us do touch His heart. Verse 39 reads, *"Jesus said, 'Take away the stone.' Martha, the sister of him who was dead, said to Him, 'Lord, by this time there is a stench, for he has been dead four days.'"* Martha, the sister of Lazarus objected to Jesus' demand for the stone at the gate of Lazarus' tomb to be taken away. According to her, doing so will produce some stench, because the body had been there for four days. Sister Martha didn't know why Jesus asked that the stone should be removed. In order for a miracle to take place, the stone had to be removed. Unless the spiritual stone of doubt is removed, it is difficult to experience God's miracle in your life. After the stone was removed, Jesus "cried with a loud voice, 'Lazarus, come forth." (v43). In response, Lazarus came forth—with his hands and feet bound with grave clothes and the face wrapped with a cloth. Then "Jesus said to them, *'Loose Him and let him go."* (v44).

Yes, Lazarus was alive, yet he was bound. Some Christians are like Lazarus; they are physically alive, yet spiritually bound. As a result, they cannot function properly. Hence we have three classes of people in the Church today: **First**, those who are born again, with their spiritual grave clothes removed. Such people crave for the things of God, live holy lives and grow spiritually in serving God. **Second,** those who are born again, but with spiritual grave-clothes on. Such Christians are spiritually suppressed by demons, due to their connection with demonic powers prior to their repentance. **Third,** those who are spiritually dead, with grave clothes wrapped around them.

Reflection: Are you constantly having spiritual attacks? You need help.

Word for today: *Spiritual bondage is the worst kind of bondage.*

A TWO-FOLD TRANSITION

*We know that we have passed from death to life, because we love the brethren.
He who does not love his brother abides in death (1 John 3:14).*

READ: JOHN 5:24-30

Verse 24 of our text reads, *"Most assuredly, I say to you, he who hears my word and believes in Him who sent me has everlasting life, and shall not come into judgment, but has passed from death into life."* Opposite of life is death. There are two kinds of transition in life that are open to everyone. **First** is the transition from physical life to physical death. Every human being experiences this kind of transition when life departs the physical body. When Adam sinned, God pronounced the curse of transition from physical life to physical death upon him. Ever since, humankind has been experiencing this kind of transition—being the descendants of Adam (Read Genesis 3:1-19). In Theological parlance, this condition is called **Adamic nature.** Our Adamic nature guarantees our transition from physical life to physical death. **Second** is the transition from spiritual death to spiritual life. One who is spiritually **dead in sin** becomes spiritually **dead to sin** and alive in Christ. Anyone who is without Christ is spiritually dead. That is the message our Lord Jesus is conveying in verse 25 of our text. We read, *"Most assuredly, I say to you, the hour is coming, and now is, when the dead will hear the voice of the Son of God; and those who hear will live."* That Christ begins His message with the phrase, "Most assuredly" underscores the importance and seriousness He attaches to what He says. Transition from spiritual death to spiritual life takes place the moment you come to God through faith in Christ Jesus.

A two-fold transition results in a two-fold resurrection. Verses 28-29 of our text read, *"Do not marvel at this; for the hour is coming in which all who are in the graves will hear His voice and come forth—those who have done good, to the resurrection of life, and those who have done evil, to the resurrection of condemnation."* When Christ returns, all those who have experienced the transition from spiritual death to spiritual life, even though they are physically dead, will experience the resurrection of life, while those who reject Christ will experience the resurrection of condemnation. May that never be your portion!

Reflection: Do you live by Adamic or Christ-like nature?

Word for today: *Spiritual transformation guarantees a resurrection of life.*

FROM GRACE TO GRASS?

"If, after they have escaped the pollutions of the world...they are again entangled in them and overcome, the latter end is worse...than the beginning" (2 Peter 2:20).

READ: HEBREWS 10:26-31

Believers in Christ operate on a spiritual frequency called **grace.** Unfortunately, some have chosen to operate under grass, rather than grace. In the end, such people see themselves fall from grace to grass. In this context, **Grace** speaks of *an elevated and enviable position in Christ Jesus*, while **Grass** speaks of *a fallen and despicable condition in the world*. In our elevated position in Christ, we enjoy the following benefits: **1. In Salvation— *We have been transferred from the power of darkness into the Kingdom of Christ*.** In Colossians 1:13 we read, *"He has delivered us from the power of darkness and conveyed us into the kingdom of the Son of His love."* Indeed, as many as have accepted Christ as Lord and Savior have received the gift of eternal life (John 1:12; 3:16). **2. In Position—*We are seated in heavenly places in Christ Jesus*.** *"He [God] raised us up together and made us sit together in heavenly places in Christ Jesus (Ephesians 2:6).* **3. In Power—*We have been empowered to trample upon satanic forces*.** *"Behold, I give you the authority to trample on serpents and scorpions, and over all the power of the enemy, and nothing shall by any means hurt you." (*Luke 10:19). **4. In Blessing—*We have been blessed with spiritual blessings in heavenly places in Christ*.** *"Blessed be the God and Father of our Lord Jesus Christ, who has blessed us with every spiritual blessing in the heavenly places in Christ" (Ephesians 1:3).*

In v29 of our text, there are three things to be avoided in order not to fall from grace to grass. **First,** avoid trampling the Son of God underfoot, by bringing shame to His name. **Second,** avoid trivializing the blood of Christ that saved you. **Third,** avoid insulting the Holy Spirit by grieving Him. King Saul was elevated by God (1 Samuel 10:1-13), but he fell from grace to grass by consulting a witch doctor (Read 1 Samuel 31:1-10). Ananias and his wife fell from grace to grass by lying to God in their giving (Acts 5:1-11). May you never fall from grace to grass in your relationship with God.

Reflection: Do you operate under Grace or under Grass?

Word for today: *It is unfruitful to operate under grass, instead of grace.*

37

LUGGAGE OR BAGGAGE?

"Alas, sinful nation, a people laden with iniquity, a brood of evildoers, children who are corrupters...they have gone backward." (Isaiah 1:4).

READ: MATTHEW 11:28-29

Whenever you check-in your belonging at the Airline counter, it is labeled, **luggage.** But, on arrival to its destination, the same luggage becomes **baggage.** In fact, the Airline tells you where to claim your baggage. Why does your checked-in luggage become a baggage? The reason is simple. It is because you are home-bound with it. As long as your luggage stays with the Airline, it remains a luggage, but when you claim it, it becomes a baggage. There is a spiritual truth in this analogy. The opposite is the case when you come to Jesus with your baggage. You check in your baggage and go home with a luggage of blessing. **Baggage** *speaks* of diverse spiritual and material problems you bring to Jesus, while **Luggage** *speaks* of spiritual and material blessings you go home with, after being with Jesus.

Our text reads, *"Come to me, all you who labor and are heavy laden, and I will give you rest."* If I were to paraphrase Jesus' statement, it would look something like this: ***Come to me all you who are burdened with all sorts of baggage in exchange for a luggage of blessing from me***. In Jesus, a baggage becomes a luggage. When you come to Jesus with your baggage of sin, sorrow, bitterness, anxiety, hatred and anger, you go home with a luggage of His blessings. For instance, Zacchaeus came to Jesus with a baggage of cheating and corruption in his life. After Jesus became a Guest at his house, Zacchaeus never remained the same. He left his baggage at the feet of Jesus, in exchange for His blessings. Since Zacchaeus' life changed for the better, he was able to say, *"Look, Lord, I give half of my goods to the poor; and if I have taken anything from anyone by false accusation, I restore fourfold."* (Luke 19:8). In response, Jesus told Zacchaeus, *"Today salvation has come to this house, because he also is a son of Abraham; for the Son of Man has come to seek and to save that which was lost."* (v9-10). Have you been carrying some baggage in your life? Why not take a cue from Zacchaeus? Pray for forgiveness and ask Jesus to come into your life. Your baggage will become a luggage in Christ.

Reflection: Are you heavy laden with the baggage of life? Come to Jesus now.

Word for today: *Only Jesus can turn a baggage into a luggage of blessings.*

POWER IN GOD'S WORD

He sends out His command to the earth; His word runs very swiftly (Psalm 147:15).

READ: PSALM 19:7-11

There is tremendous power in God's Word. God created the world with His Word. In Genesis 1:3 we read, *"Then God said, 'Let there be light'; and there was light.'"* For additional evidence of God's Word in creation, read Genesis 1: 6, 9,11,14,20,24 and 26. God brought the world into being through His spoken Word and will judge the world by His Word (John 12:48). The Word of God is so powerful that it rattles and destroys satanic kingdom. One day as our Lord Jesus Christ was preaching in the Synagogue, a man with demons became so uncomfortable on hearing the Word of God that he blurted out, *"Let us alone! What have we to do with You, Jesus of Nazareth? Did You come to destroy us? I know who You are--the Holy One of God."* (Mark 1:24). In Hebrews 4:12, we are reminded of how powerful God's Word is. We read, *"For the word of God is living and powerful, and sharper than any two-edged sword, piercing even to the division of soul and spirit, and of joints and marrow, and is a discerner of the thoughts and intents of the heart.."* No instrument is powerful enough to discern what goes on in the human mind. People are subjected to lie detector in order to determine the truthfulness of what they say. Sometimes, a smart guy can beat a lie detector, because it is incapable of *"dividing the soul and spirit, and of joints and marrow,* and discerning *"the thoughts and intents of the heart"* Man-made instrument is incapable of doing what the Word of God does, because of the power associated with the Word of God.

In our text we notice the various names given to the Word of God:
1. It is the **Law of the LORD**, which converts the soul (v7a)
2. It is the **Testimony of the LORD**, which makes the simple wise (v7b)
3. It is the **Statute of the LORD**, which rejoices the heart (v8a).
4. It is the **Commandment of the LORD**, which enlightens the eyes (v8b).
5. It is the **Fear of the LORD,** which cleanses forever (v9a).
6. It is the **Judgment of the LORD,** which ensures righteousness (v9b).

Reflection: Does the power of God's Word manifest in your life?

Word for today: *He who takes in God's Word taps into God's power.*

39

COME TO THE MOUNTAIN TOP!

Then Moses went up into the mountain, and a cloud covered the mountain (Exodus 24:15).

READ: EXODUS 24:12-18

God told Moses, *"Come up to me on the mountain and be there; and I will give you tablets of stone, and the law and commandments which I have written, that you may teach them."* Could God not have given Moses the Ten commandments somewhere else, rather than the mountain top? The purpose God asked Moses to meet Him at the mountain top was two-fold: **First**, to give Moses the Ten commandments, and **second,** to have fellowship with Moses. God likes to fellowship with His people. God's command to Moses to come to the mountain top has some spiritual lessons for us. A Mountain top *speaks* of the height or state of spiritual condition in which divine manifestation takes place. As a Christian, do you know that God wants to meet you at the mountain top of prayer, the mountain top of praise and worship, the mountain top of holiness, the mountain top of service?

God wants us to operate from a spiritual mountain top, because: **1.** Mountain is a place of preparation. God met Moses at Mount Horeb, where he was prepared and assigned the task of delivering the children of Israel from their Egyptian bondage (Read Exodus chapter 3). **2.** Mountain is a place of victory. While Joshua and his men were fighting the Amelekites on the plain, Moses went to the Mountain with his rod in his hand. Aaron and Hur kept Moses' hand up until victory was achieved (Exodus 17:8-13). **3.** Mountain is a place of transformation. After Moses had been with the LORD for forty days and forty nights, he was so transformed that his face shone like light—so bright that the children of Israel could not behold his face (Exodus 34:27-30). **4.** Mountain is a place of inspiration. Jesus delivered His inspired teaching to His disciples at the mountain top (Matthew 5:1-16). **5.** Mountain is a place of revelation. Christ took Peter, James and John to the mountain, where He was transfigured. God revealed Christ's glory and identity to them (Read Matthew 17:1-9). **6.** Mountain is a place of security. Lot was asked to run to the mountain for safety (Read Genesis 19:17). **7.** Mountain is a place of reassured hope (Acts 1:10-11).

Reflection: How often do you meet with God at the mountain of prayer?

Word for today: *A mountain-top experience is unique. Seek it!*

FULFILL YOUR MINISTRY

But you be watchful in all things, endure afflictions, do the work of an evangelist, fulfill your ministry (2 Timothy 4:5).

READ: 1 TIMOTHY 4:12-16

A calling is a divine appointment; a ministry is the responsibility associated with such an appointment. When God calls you, He assigns a ministry to you. This means that there is no calling of God that is void of a ministry. Paul had this truth in mind, when he wrote young Timothy regarding his calling. First of all, he reminded Timothy about the spiritual gift that God has deposited in his life (2 Timothy 1:6). As a freshman in the ministry, Timothy was warned against anyone who might try to undermine his youthfulness as he fulfilled his ministry. God is not hindered by age; He can use both the old and the young alike. After all, He used infant Samuel to warn Eli—an old man, about an end to his ministry and an impending doom upon him and his family (Read 1 Samuel chapter 3).

In our text, Paul gave Timothy ten tips for ministerial fulfilment.
1. *Let no one despise your youth* (v12a). Do you have a ministry? Don't be deterred by age in fulfilling it. **2**. *Be example to other believers (v12b).*As you serve in fulfilling your ministry, be a good example to others. **3**. *Give attention to the reading of God's Word (v13).* Reading of God's Word goes together with studying it (Read 2 Timothy 2:15). **4**. *Give attention to exhortation (v13).* **Exhortation** speaks of the preaching of God's Word for the edification of the saints. **5**. *Give attention to doctrine (v13).* This speaks of the teaching of God's Word. **6**. *Do not neglect the gift in you (v14).* If you are gifted in the Body of Christ, make use of such gifts. **7**. *Meditate on these things (v15).* Meditation on God's Word and His Will enhances your spirituality. **8**. *Take heed to yourself (v16a).* This means being careful not to bring shame to Christ. **9**. *Take heed to the doctrine (v16b).* This means to guard against false doctrines. **10**. Continue in them (v16c). This means to be consistent in what you have learned. It is sad to see how some so-called men of God have allowed their calling and ministry to be eclipsed by greed, worldly cares and pleasures. God demands accountability from everyone He has called (Read 2 Corinthians 5:10).

Reflection: Are you called? Do you have a ministry? Have you fulfilled it?

Word for today: *No ministry, no calling and no calling, no ministry.*

STAND FIRM!

Now I praise you, brethren, that you remember me in all things and keep the traditions just as I delivered them to you (1 Corinthians 11:2).

READ: 2 THESSALONIANS 2:13-17

In 1 Corinthians 16:13 we read, *"Watch, stand fast in the faith, be brave, be strong."* These were Apostle Paul's words of exhortation to the Church in Corinth. Paul's exhortation which contains four action words, holds true today for all believers in Christ. Let's take a look at these action words: **"Watch"** means "to be on guard." As a Christian believer, you ought to be on guard all the time, *"because your adversary the devil walks about like a roaring lion, seeking whom he may devour."* (1 Peter 5:8). Be watchful for the temptation of sinful desire, pride of life and worldliness. **"Stand fast"** means to hold on tenaciously to what you believe—sound Biblical doctrines. You should hold fast to sound doctrines, because a time will come when people will *"depart from the faith, giving heed to seducing spirits and doctrines of demons."* (1 Timothy 4:1). **"Be brave"** means to be bold and courageous in the face of threats and danger, due to your faith in Christ Jesus (Read 2 Timothy 1:7). **"Be strong"** means to be spiritually strengthened by the power of the Holy Spirit. It is the Holy Spirit that empowers you in Christ; human strength will fail you (Read Ephesians 3;16; 6:10).

Verse 15 of our text reads, *"Therefore, brethren, stand fast and hold the traditions which you were taught, whether by word or our epistle."* The problem some Christians have is the inability to stand firm in faith; they are easily swayed aside and swept away by sweet-talking preachers, who come in sheep's clothing, but are inwardly wolves. There are four things you should do to remain firm in the Lord. **First,** resolve to feed on God's Word daily (Colossians 3:16). **Second,** resolve to pray daily, at least for 30 minutes. Spending 1hour out of the 24 hours that make up the day, in God's presence, is the wisest investment of time you can ever make daily. **Third,** resolve to act on the word of God. Hearing, reading, meditating and even, preaching the Word of God without acting on it is unprofitable (Read James 1:22-25). **Fourth,** resolve to share the gospel with others regularly (Read Proverbs 11:30; Matthew 28:19-20).

Reflection: Is your faith in Christ shaky or wobbly due to life challenges?

Word for today: *To stand firm in life is to be anchored in Christ.*

A LIFE TURNED AROUND

He answered and said, "Whether He is a sinner or not I do not know. One thing I know: that though I was blind, now I see." (John 9:25).

READ: ACTS 9:20-22

One of the reasons why Christ came is to turn people's lives around. When Christ turns your life around, you will never remain the same; things will change for the better in your life. For example, when Christ turned the life of Nicodemus around, Nicodemus never remained the same. He came to Jesus at night, probably, to avoid being spotted by someone as identifying with Christ, being a Pharisee and a ruler of the Jews (John 3:1). After Christ had turned his life around, Nicodemus' behavior towards Christ changed. When the Jewish religious authority tried to judge Christ in absentia, Nicodemus defended Christ by saying, *"Does our law judge a man before it hears him and knows what he is doing?"* (John 7:51). Again, at Christ's burial, it was Nicodemus who brought a mixture of myrrh and aloes, weighing about one hundred pounds, to prepare Christ's body for burial (19:39). When Christ turned the life of a man born blind around by restoring his sight, the man publicly declared, *"Whether He [Christ] is a sinner or not I do not know. One thing I know: that though I was blind, now I see."* (John 9:25). When Christ turns your life around, you cannot but testify about Him (Read 1 John 1:3 and Acts 4:20). Christ turned the lives of Peter, Andrew, James and John around, when He called and promoted them from being "fisher men" to "fishers of men." (Read Mark 1:16-20).

Our Lord Jesus still turns people's lives around today. When Christ turns your life around, He turns your circumstances around as well. Some years ago, a young man whose wife attended our Church ran into a big problem. Unknown to him, some junior staff who didn't like him, conspired and stole an official car assigned to him. This meant that he had to replace the car or lose his job. This incident drove him to Christ, after which both his life and circumstances were turned around. Rather than being fired, he was promoted and transferred to a better and more congenial working environment.

Reflection: Can you testify of how and when Christ turned your life around?

Word for today: *A turned-around life lives for Christ daily.*

TWO IMPORTANT STEPS IN LIFE

*"For I have no pleasure in the death of one who dies, says the Lord GOD.
'Therefore turn and live!'" (Ezekiel 18:32).*

READ: EZEKIEL 18:21-28

The step one takes in life defines one's future. If one takes the right step, one is likely to succeed in life. But, if on the other hand, one takes the wrong step, one is more likely to experience failure in life. There are two important steps one can take in life: One is a **forward step**, the other is a **backward step.** Each of these steps has consequences. A **forward step** *speaks* of walking in the path of righteousness, while a **backward step** *speaks* of meddling with sin. From our text, we notice how these two steps can play out in people's lives. Verses 21-22 which deal with a forward step read as follows, *"But if a wicked man turns from all his sins which he has committed, keeps all my statutes, and does what is lawful and right, he shall surely live; he shall not die. None of the transgressions which he has committed shall be remembered against him; because of the righteousness which he has done, he shall live."* The LORD says that when a sinner takes a step forward in repentance and righteous living, he or she shall not die, but live. A step forwards is the right step in establishing a relationship with God. Normally, whenever a person moves forward, he or she leaves certain things behind. Similarly, when someone takes a step forward in Christ, he or she must leave the old life and lifestyle behind. A forward step in Christ is good; it leads to eternal life. God does not take pleasure in the death of a sinner (Read Ezekiel 18:32).

Verse 24, 26 of our text deal with a backward step. A backward step occurs when a Christian backslides and reverts to his or her sinful old lifestyle. God hates backsliding. When one backslides, all of one's works of righteousness are forgotten. A backward step leads to destruction, while a forward step leads to salvation (Read 2 Peter 2:20-22). King Solomon took a backward step in his life by following after Baal to appease his idolatrous wives (1 Kings 11:1-8). See v9 for the consequences of his action. Nineveh took a forward step by repenting of her sins and God spared it (Jonah 3:5-10).

Reflection: What kind of step do you take in life—forward or backward?

Word for today: *A step forward in Christ leads to eternal life.*

"PUT OFF & PUT ON"

If then you were raised with Christ, seek those things which are above, where Christ is, sitting at the right hand of God (Colossians 3:1).

READ: COLOSSIANS 3:1-10

Sometimes we wonder why we don't see the kind of miracles that the early Church experienced. As a result, we feel that God is too far away from us. God is not far away from us; our sins have hidden His face from us (Read Isaiah 59:1-3). There is no way one can experience God's miraculous power while still meddling with sin. In order for the **natural** to experience the **supernatural,** there must be some emptying. Our Lord Jesus gave a good analogy of this in one of His teachings (Read Matthew 9:16-17). You cannot put a *new wine* into an *old wine bottle.* A new wine *represents* a new life in Christ, while an old bottle *represents* the sinful nature of humankind. Verses 9-10 read, *"Do not lie to one another, since you have <u>put off</u> the old man with his deeds, and have <u>put on</u> the new man who is renewed in knowledge according to the image of Him who created him."* We are to **put off** the old man and **put on** the new man. The old man *speaks* of one's sinful nature—the Adamic legacy in man that likes to sin. The new man *speaks* of one's regenerated nature in Christ that seeks to please God. The old man has ten deadly characteristics which must be put off, and the new man has five characteristics which must be put on.

Characteristics of the old man are as follows (Colossians 3:5, 8). **Sexual immorality**—*"any form of illicit sexual relationship"* . **Impurity**— *"moral uncleanness, impure thoughts"* ; **Evil desire**—*"wanting something that is sinister and vile in order to satisfy one's desire."*; **Greed**—*"Unquenchable appetite to acquire more for self."* ; **Anger**—*"A continuous attitude of hatred that remains bottled up within."* ; **Rage**—*"Outbursts of anger or quick temper for selfish reasons."* ; **Malice**—*"Desire to harm others or see others suffer.";* **Slander**— *"Destroying another person's good reputation by lies, gossip, spreading rumors, etc."* Characteristics of the new man include the following: **Compassion, Kindness, Humility, Gentleness and Patience** (Colossians 3:12). You must put off the **old man** and put on the **new man.**

Reflection: Can you write down the things you have put off in your life?

Word for today: *Old and new pieces of cloth don't blend very well.*

CHRIST IS COMING SOON!

*For yet a little while, And He who is coming will come and will not tarry
(Hebrews 10:37).*

READ: REVELATION 22:6-11

The coming of our Lord Jesus Christ seems to have taken a back seat in the hearts of many Christians. People are so preoccupied with earthly things that the issue of the Lord's return has become a fable to many. The devil is responsible for this. Before going to the cross, our Lord Jesus Christ said to His disciples, *"Let not your heart be troubled; you believe in God, believe also in me. In My Father's house are many mansions; if it were not so, I would have told you. I go to prepare a place for you. And if I go and prepare a place for you, I will come again and receive you to Myself; that where I am, there you may be also."* (John 14:1-3). It is about two thousand years since Christ made the above statement. Due to the long intervening period between the time Christ made the statement and now, His return seems delayed, prompting a lot of people, including some Christians, to doubt Christ's return. As humans, we often forget that Heavenly Calendar is different from Earthly Calendar. Apostle Peter gave us some insight into a Heavenly Calendar in relation to Christ's return. He wrote, *"But, beloved, do not forget this one thing, that with the Lord one day is as a thousand years, and a thousand years as one day."* (2 Peter 3:8). Based on the Heavenly Calendar, two thousand years since Christ's ascension are just two days in the eyes of the Lord. Therefore, Christ was right to have told John nearly two thousand years ago of His imminent return.

Signs of Christ's return are all over the place. Let's consider some of them. Matthew 24:4-14 contains about twelve of them: **1.** Universal deception (v4); **2.** False Christs (v5); **3.** Wars and rumors of wars (v6-7a); **4.** Universal famine (v7b); **5.** Universal pestilence—diseases (v7c); **6.** Universal earthquakes (v7d); **7.** Universal betrayals (v10a); **8.** Universal hatred (v10b); **9.** False prophets (v11); **10.** Unprecedented iniquity—crime and lawlessness (v12a); **11.** Lack of love (v12b); **12.** Universal reach with the gospel (v14). The above signs are with us today!

Reflection: Are you ready for the Lord's return? Don't be caught unawares!

Word for today: *Unpreparedness for Christ's coming will send some to hell.*

THE POWER OF GOD'S LOVE

"...Neither death nor life, nor angels nor principalities nor powers...shall be able to separate us from the love of God which is in Christ Jesus our Lord (Romans 8:38-39).

READ: EPHESIANS 3:14-19

John 3:16 is a very popular verse in the Bible. It reads, *"For God so loved the world that He gave His only begotten Son, that whoever believes in Him should not perish but have everlasting life."* In this verse, we see God's gift of love to mankind in His Son—Christ Jesus. Love for mankind motivated God to give His Son as a sacrificial lamb. When God asked Abraham to sacrifice his only son—Isaac, He was conveying an important message to Abraham regarding His love for mankind. Just as Abraham's son Isaac was offered as a sacrifice, so would God offer His own Son—Jesus as a sacrifice for the sins of the world. Abraham's sacrifice of Isaac foreshadowed God's sacrificial offering of Christ to the world. What an act of love! We are the object of God's love, because God is love (1 John 4:16). Since we are God's children, His love should flow from us to others. The power of God's love in us will impact those around us.

Verses 18-19 of our text read, *"[That you] may be able to comprehend with all the saints what is the width and length and depth and height—to know the love of Christ which passes knowledge; that you may be filled with all the fullness of God."* Paul describes the power of God's love as being four-dimensional. **The width**—*so wide that it stretches from eternity to eternity*; **the length**—*so long that it has no beginning and no end*; **the depth**—*so deep that it is anchored on Christ*; **the height**—*so high that it emanates from heaven.* Indeed, the power of God's love is unsearchable, hence it defies human understanding. Romans 5:5 reads, *"Now hope does not disappoint, because the love of God has been poured out in our hearts by the Holy Spirit who was given to us."* There is power in God's love. When God's love is poured out in our hearts, we will be able to face persecution, suffering and trials with hope (v3-4). Let's learn to love God because He first loved us (1 John 4:19).

Reflection: How much do you reciprocate God's love in your life?

Word for today: *God's love is powerful—embrace it today.*

THE NEED FOR SPIRITUAL COMPASS

Your word I have hidden in my heart, that I might not sin against you! (Psalm 119:11).

READ: PROVERBS 3:1-6

Can you imagine a sailor or a pilot setting out on a journey without a navigational system? Any sailor or pilot who ventures to sail or fly without a compass is headed for a disaster. The same thing applies to our journey in life. We are on a spiritual journey in this world and how dearly we need spiritual compass to ensure a successful journey! The compass for a successful spiritual journey is the **Word of God**. No wonder the Psalmist declared, *"Your word is a lamp to my feet, and a light to my path."* (Psalm 119:105). If you make the Word of God the navigational tool in your life, you will never go astray.

Our text contains some tips on how to journey through life successfully. There are things you need to do and benefits for doing them. **First,** do not forget the Word of God: *"My son, do not forget my law, but let your heart keep my commands"* (v1). Verse 2 spells out the benefit, *"For length of days and long life and peace they will add to you."* Obedience to the Word of God ensures longevity and peace as you journey through life. All who flouted the Word of God did not end well in life. **Second,** do not forsake mercy and truth: *"Let not mercy and truth forsake you; bind them around your neck, write them on the tablet of your heart (v3).* Verse 4 tells of the benefit for doing so, *"And so find favor and high esteem in the sight of God and man."* (v4). Those who are God-fearing and honest in making wealth, are more likely to be merciful to people. But, those who are wicked and dishonest in their ways are merciless in their dealings with others. Such a wicked behavior saps one's energy and shortens one's life. **Third,** do not depend totally on your human wisdom: *"Trust in the LORD with all your heart, and lean not on your own understanding. In all your ways acknowledge Him."* (v5-6a). The benefit: *"He shall direct your paths."* (6b). Life's journey entails a lot of the unknown. Allow God who is Omnipotent and Omniscient to provide, protect and direct you aright in life.

Reflection: Have you been navigating through life blind-folded spiritually?

Word for today: *A life's journey without spiritual compass is disastrous.*

48

AWFUL PRAYER PARTNERS!

Then He came to the disciples and found them asleep, and said to Peter, "What? Could you not watch with me one hour?" (Matthew 26:40).

READ: MATTHEW 26:36-46

The Bible asks, *"Can two walk together, unless they are agreed?"* (Amos 3:3). Indeed, if there is no agreement, two people cannot walk together, let alone work together. Corporate agreement is very important in achieving a corporate goal. It is not uncommon to hear people talk about having prayer partners. There is nothing bad in having a prayer partner. After all, the Bible encourages us to do so. Our Lord Jesus told His disciples, *"Again I say to you that if two of you agree on earth concerning anything that they ask, it will be done for them by my Father in heaven. For where two or three are gathered together in my name, I am there in the midst of them."* (Matthew 18:19-20). Based on the above statement by Jesus, the principle governing answer to corporate prayer is four-fold. **First,** there must be a gathering of believers. **Second,** there must be unity of purpose. **Third,** there must be a request made. **Fourth,** such a request must be made in the name of Jesus Christ.

Our Lord Jesus demonstrated what He taught His disciples about corporate prayers, when He took them along to the Garden of Gethsemane. On getting there, Jesus made the disciples His prayer partners. Our text reads, *"Then Jesus came with them to a place called Gethsemane, and said to the disciples, Sit here while I go and pray over there. And He took with Him Peter and the two sons of Zebedee, and He began to be sorrowful and deeply distressed."* (v36-37). Jesus told His prayer partners, *"Stay here and watch with me."* (v38). Unfortunately, rather than pray, His prayer partners were sleeping. Twice Christ scolded them for sleeping, instead of praying along with Him (See v40,43). Our Lord Jesus warned them, *"Watch and pray, lest you enter into temptation. The spirit indeed is willing, but the flesh is weak."* (v41). He who fails to pray becomes an easy target for the devil. Christ's disciples were awful prayer partners. Any wonder that they all fled when the chips started falling? (v56).

Reflection: How sincere and committed a prayer partner are you?

Word for today: *Those who pray together get along spiritually.*

GOD OF COMFORT

Nevertheless God, who comforts the downcast, comforted us by the coming of Titus (2 Corinthians 7:6)

READ: 2 CORINTHIANS 1:3-7

Words of comfort are to the afflicted, what a cup of cold water is to a thirsty man. When people go through sufferings, trials and persecutions, they need doses of comforting words. As believers in Christ, we ought to comfort other fellow believers in times of crisis. More importantly, we need comforting words from our heavenly Father. God knows how to comfort His people. He comforted Christ during His earthly ministry. Preparatory to going to the cross, Jesus Christ, the Son was comforted by God the Father. Faced with the overwhelming burden of bearing the sins of the world, Jesus prayed, *"Now my soul is troubled, and what shall I say? Father, save me from this hour? But for this purpose I came to this hour. Father, glorify your name."* (John 12:27-28a). In response, *"a voice came from heaven, saying, 'I have both glorified it and will glorify it again.'* (v28b). The voice was so loud that it sounded like a thunder to those around (v29). Christ was comforted by His Father with assuring words of triumph. Stephen was comforted by God as he was about to be put to death by Jewish religious leaders. The Bible records, *"But he, being full of the Holy Spirit, gazed into heaven and saw the glory of God, and Jesus standing at the right hand of God, and said, 'Look! I see the heavens opened and the Son of Man standing at the right hand of God!'"* (Acts 7:55-56). God comforted Stephen by allowing him to see the glory of the place into which he was about to be ushered.

Verses 3-4 of our text read, *"Blessed be the God and Father of our Lord Jesus Christ, the Father of mercies and God of all comfort, who comforts us in all our tribulation, that we may be able to comfort those who are in any trouble, with the comfort with which we ourselves are comforted by God."* Paul spoke of how believers in Christ are comforted by God in times of trials and persecutions, citing himself as an example. May God of comfort, comfort you in all that you go through in Jesus name.

Reflection: Are you afflicted and downcast? Call on God of comfort for help.

Word for today: *God's comforting words go deeper than human pep-talk.*

GOD—THE SOURCE OF WISDOM

For the LORD gives wisdom; from His mouth come knowledge and under-standing (Proverbs 2:6)

READ: PROVERBS 2:1-7

God is the Source of wisdom. By His infinite wisdom, heaven and earth were created. Since God is the Source of wisdom, doesn't it make sense to seek wisdom from Him? Solomon sought wisdom from God and was blessed with unprecedented measure of wisdom ever known to mankind (Read 1 Kings 3:4-12). Do you know that God is willing and prepared to bless you with wisdom, if you ask? In James 1:5 we read, *"If any of you lacks wisdom, let him ask of God, who gives to all liberally and without reproach, and it will be given to him."*

Our text tells us that *"God gives wisdom"* and *"stores up sound wisdom for the upright."* (v6,7). God does not grant His wisdom to those who lack His fear in their lives. The Bible declares, *"The fear of the LORD is the beginning of wisdom; a good understanding have all those who do His commandments."* What this verse is saying is that wisdom stems from having the fear of God. In other words, any wisdom that is void of the fear of God, is not genuine. It is earthly, not heavenly; sensual, not spiritual; demonic, not Christ-like (James 3:15). Without the fear of God, you cannot experience God's wisdom. Joseph had the fear of God in him; he rejected the sexual advances of Potiphar's wife (Genesis 39:7). The fear of God in Joseph prompted him to answer Potiphar's wife with these words, *"Look, my master does not know what is with me in the house, and he has committed all that he has to my hand. There is no one greater in this house than I, nor has he kept back anything from me but you, because you are his wife. How then can I do this great wickedness, and sin against God?"* God was listening when Joseph made this statement. Since the fear of God is the beginning of wisdom, God decided to endow Joseph with the wisdom of interpreting dreams—the wisdom that took him from the prison to the palace (Read Genesis chapters 40-41). Daniel's fear of God earned him God's wisdom of interpreting dreams (Read Daniel 1:8-9; 2:14-23).

Reflection: Do you have the fear of God in your life? Do you have wisdom?

Word for today: *He that lacks God, lacks wisdom.*

CREATION VS. INVENTION

"Shall the clay say to him who forms it, 'What are you making?' Or shall your handiwork say, 'He has no hands'?" (Isaiah 45:9b).

READ: JOB 38:1-7

The story of Job in the Bible is very pathetic; he suffered family, social, financial, economic losses in one day. As if that wasn't enough, the devil afflicted him with terrible boils. Job's problem and suffering was so huge that his wife advised him to curse God and die. To her Job was better dead than alive (Read Job 1:6-22 and 2:1-9). In the course of Job's suffering, a lot of things must have gone through his mind—silent complaints and unanswered questions to which God responded. Our text reads, *"Then the LORD answered Job out of the whirlwind, and said: Who is this who darkens counsel by words without knowledge? Now prepare yourself like a man; I will question you, and you shall answer me."* (v1-3). God asked Job some heart-searching and mind-boggling questions about creation, First, *"Where were you when I laid the foundations of the earth..."* (v4). Neither Job nor any other human being has been able to answer this question regarding the earth's foundation. Human beings have, through scientific knowledge, been able to determine that the earth is flat, not round, but are yet to find the earth's foundation. Something huge and flat as the earth is, must have a foundation on which it rests. No one knows the foundation and boundary of the earth except God, its Creator. Due to our limited knowledge, we have used the word, "Space" to delineate the earth's boundary.

God is the Creator, human beings are the inventors. In creation, God, the Creator, created something out of nothing. In other words, He brought into being something that had not existed before. But, in invention, through God-given knowledge, human beings are able to put together materials created by God for the benefit of humankind. In invention, products are usually patented to establish ownership and avoid piracy. In creation, the opposite is the case. After creation, God didn't need any patency for His creative work, because no one can duplicate God's creation. God created light, but Edison invented electricity. If God hadn't created light, there wouldn't have been any thought of electricity.

Reflection: Heaven rejoiced over the earth's creation (Job 38:7). Do you?

Word for today: *Remember, God is the Creator, not the inventor.*

52

THE TALE OF TWO GARDENS

"Jesus...went out with His disciples over the Brook Kidron, where there was a garden, which He and His disciples entered (John 18:1).

READ: GENESIS 2:15-17

The Bible has the records of two incidents that took place in two different locations and two different era. One incident took place in a place called Garden of Eden, and is recorded in the Old Testament, while the other incident took place in a place called, Garden of Gethsemane, and is recorded in the New Testament. Both incidents held the keys to the future of humankind. The incident that took place in the Garden of Eden involved Adam's disobedience to God's command. After creating Adam, God *"put him in the garden of Eden to tend and keep it."* (Genesis 2:15). Verses 16 and 17 read, *"And the LORD God commanded the man, saying, 'Of every tree of the garden you may freely eat; but of the tree of the knowledge of good and evil you shall not eat, for in the day that you eat of it you shall surely die."* God's command to Adam was very clear, yet Adam chose to disobey God, resulting in suffering and death to humankind (Read Genesis 3:1-19).

In the Garden of Gethsemane, Christ triumphed by choosing to die in obedience to His Father's will. He prayed, *"O my Father, if it is possible, let this cup pass from me; nevertheless, not as I will, but as you will."* (Matthew 26:39). Christ obeyed the Father and prepared Himself to die in order to reverse the curse from Adam's disobedience. The first Adam failed in the garden of Eden, while the last Adam—Christ triumphed in the garden of Gethsemane. Adam was **put in** the garden of Eden, but after he sinned, He was **put out** of the garden. In Genesis 3:23-24 we read, *"Therefore the LORD God sent him out of the garden of Eden to till the ground from which he was taken. So He drove out the man; and He placed cherubim at the east of the garden of Eden, and a flaming sword which turned every way, to guard the way to the tree of life."* Interestingly, Adam's garden of habitation became a place of ejection due to his sin, while the garden of Gethsemane—a place of Christ's rejection became our place of acceptance due to His obedience.

Reflection: Which of the two incidents would you like to identify with?

Word for today: *Christ took care of our sins in the garden of Gethsemane.*

THE TRUTH HURTS

And you shall know the truth, and the truth shall make you free (John 8:32).

READ: ACTS 7:51-54

Some people cannot stand the truth, because their ways are evil; they even try to eliminate the truth in order to protect their ego. Not only does the truth hurt; it liberates. Our Lord Jesus told His Jewish audience, *"And you shall know the truth, and the truth shall make you free."* (John 8:32). By the truth, Jesus was referring to the undiluted Word of God. The Jewish religious leaders had head knowledge of the Law, but lacked heart knowledge of God's Word, hence they could not understand what Jesus was saying. Their reply to Jesus, *"We are Abraham's descendants, and have never been in bondage to anyone. How can you say, 'You will be made free?'"* (v33) underscores their lack of spiritual understanding. Head knowledge of the Scriptures puffs up and enslaves, but heart knowledge liberates. For instance, prior to his conversion, Paul was puffed up with head knowledge of the Law (Philippians 3:4-6). But, after his conversion, he received a heart knowledge about Christ and then declared, *"I have been crucified with Christ; it is no longer I who live, but Christ lives in me; and the life which I now live in the flesh I live by faith in the Son of God, who loved me and gave Himself for me. I do not set aside the grace of God; for if righteousness comes through the law, then Christ died in vain."* (Galatians 2:20-21). Have you experienced a heart knowledge about Christ? Have you known the truth?

Just as being told the truth hurts, rejecting it kills. Jesus told the unbelieving Jews, *"You will die in your sins; for if you do not believe that I am He, you will die in your sins."* Today, those who refuse to believe the truth—God's Word, die in their sins; they die without salvation and spend eternity in hell. In our text, we notice how hurt the Jewish religious leaders were when they were told the truth regarding their rebellious attitude toward God's Word by Stephen (v51-53). Rather than become sorrowful and repentant, they *"were cut to the heart and gnashed at Stephen with their teeth."* (v54). Although they stoned Stephen to death, they could not kill the truth that was told them by Stephen.

Reflection: Do you get hurt when told the truth? If so, examine yourself.

Word for today: *To be spiritually liberated, take in spiritual truth.*

WATCHERS OF THE POOR

He who has pity on the poor lends to the LORD, and He will pay back what he has given (Proverbs 19:17).

READ: PSALM 41:1-3

Our text reads, *"Blessed is he who considers the poor; The LORD will deliver him in time of trouble. The LORD will preserve him and keep him alive, and he will be blessed on the earth; you will not deliver him to the will of his enemies. The LORD will strengthen him on his bed of illness; you will sustain him on his sickbed."* The poor refers not only to those who have no money, but also to those "who suffer illness and misfortune through no fault of their own." God is the "Defender, Deliverer and Sustainer" of the poor (Read Psalm 10:2,9; 35:10; 69:33; 109:16; 140:12).

In our text, we notice a seven-fold package of blessings for whoever shows compassion to the poor. **First,** he is blessed of the LORD (v1a). When one is blessed of the LORD, one enjoys God's package of goodness, which includes, good health, promotion, provision, protection, prosperity, longevity and peace. **Second,** "the LORD will delivered him in time of trouble" (v1b). Each day, as we ask the LORD to deliver us from trouble, let us remember that lack of compassion towards the poor could hinder an answer to such prayer. **Third,** "the LORD will preserve and keep him alive" (v2a). In time of danger, God has promised to deliver those who show compassion to the poor. **Fourth,** the LORD will bless him on the earth" (v2b). **Fifth,** "the LORD will not deliver him to his enemies" (v2c). In other words, if you are compassionate to the poor, the LORD will not allow your enemies to overtake you. **Sixth,** "the LORD will strengthen him on his sickbed" (v3a). **Seventh,** "the LORD will restore (heal) him on his sickbed" (v3b). These seven-fold divine blessings are meant for those who show compassion to the poor, because the poor will never cease in the land (Deuteronomy 15:11). Dorcas was so compassionate to the poor, that all the widows converged on her death-bed weeping and displaying *"the tunics and gowns which Dorcas had made while she was with them."* Any wonder why God brought her back to life? (Acts 9:39-41).

Reflection: How compassionate are you to the poor around you?

Word for today: *Those who care for the poor are blessed by God.*

THE WITHERED FIG TREE

"He came to it and found nothing on it but leaves, and said to it, 'Let no fruit grow on you ever again.' Immediately the fig tree withered away" (Matthew 21:19).

READ: MARK 11:20-24

In ancient Israel, two important seed crops were of immense economic value to the people. One was the vine—from which wine was made; the other was the fig tree, which produced edible fruits. Both of these crops are used metaphorically in the Bible, to illustrate the spiritual condition of the children of Israel. In the Old Testament, the LORD compares the nation of Israel to an unfruitful vineyard, which produced nothing, except wild grapes, in spite of all the cares—the spiritual investments He made in it (Read Isaiah 5:1-7). In the New Testament, we notice that the incident of the withered fig tree was an indictment of the spiritual barrenness of the Israelites. Mark 11:12-14 reads, *"Now the next day, when they had come out from Bethany, He was hungry. And seeing from afar a fig tree having leaves, He went to see if perhaps He would find something on it. When He came to it, He found nothing but leaves, for it was not the season for figs. In response Jesus said to it, 'Let no one eat fruit from you ever again.' And His disciples heard it."* The fig tree was cursed for two reasons: **First,** it failed to bear fruits; **second**, it presented a false appearance of fruitfulness. It had green leaves suggesting fruitfulness, but in reality, lacked fruits. Just like the fig tree, some Christians present false appearance of spirituality. Externally, they look religious, but internally they are bereft of spiritual fruit. They claim to have faith, but are barren in their work of faith.

There are three important spiritual lessons to take away from the withered fig tree story: **1. God hates spiritual barrenness.** Christ even said it, *"I am the true vine, and my Father is the vinedresser. Every branch in me that does not bear fruit He takes away; and every branch that bears fruit He prunes, that it may bear more fruit"* (John 15:1-2). **2. God hates false appearance of Christianity**. If you claim to be a Christian, then bear the spiritual fruit. **3. A divine curse is very devastating.** No creature is immune to a divine curse.

Reflection: In spiritual things, are you fruitful or barren?

Word for today: *A withered fig tree is only good for the fire.*

WHAT DO YOU WANT?

Therefore I say to you, whatever things you ask when you pray, believe that you receive them, and you will have them (Mark 11:24).

READ: LUKE 18:35-43

*W*hat *do you want me to do for you? (*Luke 18:41a). This was the question our Lord Jesus Christ asked a blind man, who cried out to Him, *"Jesus, Son of David, have mercy on me!"* (v38). Jesus' question got an immediate response from the blind guy, *"Lord, that I may receive my sight."* (v41b). The blind guy knew what his need was and made it known to the Lord. If Jesus were to ask you the same question today, what would be your response? Would your response be based on priority of needs or wants? It is important to be specific in our requests to God. This will enable us to be appreciative of God's faithfulness, when answers to our requests come through. Specificity in prayer promotes specificity in testimonies regarding answered prayers. Let's avoid flurries of ambiguity in our prayers. God already knows what we need, just as He knew what the blind man needed. Christ's question to the man was not aimed at knowing the man's need, but at soliciting the man's attention and faith in receiving God's miracle. By his request, the blind man demonstrated absolute faith in Christ Jesus. Do you know that God does not impose His blessing upon anyone who is not interested in seeking after Him? If you align yourself with God, you will experience His manifold blessings.

Verses 42-43 of our text read, *"Then Jesus said to him, 'Receive your sight; your faith has made you well. And immediately he received his sight, and followed Him, glorifying God. And all the people, when they saw it, gave praise to God.'"* Christ's miracle of healing did four things in the life of the blind man. **First,** it demonstrated the man's faith in Christ. Jesus told him, *"Your faith has made you well."* (v42). **Second,** it demonstrated Christ's power over circumstances. Remember, Christ's power is bigger than your problems. **Third,** it enabled the guy to follow Jesus (v43a). Had he not received his sight, he would not have followed Jesus. **Fourth,** it brought glory to God. *"All the people when they saw it [what happened], gave glory to God."* (v43b).

Reflection: Do you have a prayer list?

Word for today: *Have faith in God and be specific in your payers.*

THE PREEMINENT CHRIST

"He is before all things, and in Him all things consist" (Colossians 1:17).

READ: COLOSSIANS 1:13-18

Our Lord Jesus Christ asked His disciples, *"Who do men say that I, the Son of Man, am?" So they said, 'Some say John the Baptist, some Elijah, and others Jeremiah or one of the prophets.'"* (Matthew 16:13-14). Having hear their various answers, Christ then asked a follow-up question, *"But who do you say that I am?"* (v15). Only Peter ventured an answer, *"You are the Christ, the Son of the living God."* (v16) The perception of the Jewish religious leaders of Christ was flawed. He was not a reincarnated prophet in the person of John the Baptist, or Jeremiah or Elijah. Christ is the Son of God. Peter got it right! Look at what Jesus told Peter, *"Blessed are you, Simon Bar-Jonah, for flesh and blood has not revealed this to you, but my Father who is in heaven."* (v17). Indeed, no one can truly identify Christ as the Son of God without the help of the Spirit of God. Hence, so many people still struggle with the idea of Christ being the Son of God and yet dying on the cross. God can not die, they argue. But, they forget that Christ did not die as God, He died as human, hence He was called the Son of Man. During His earthly ministry, Christ had a dual identity: He was the Son of Man and the Son of God. As the Son of Man, He was human; but as the Son of God, He is God.

As the Son of God, Christ is preeminent—meaning He is above all things both in heaven and on earth. Our text reveals the seven characteristics of Christ's preeminence. **1.** Through His blood we are redeemed. (v14). The blood of goats could only cover sin, but lacked the power to redeem the human soul from sin. **2.** He is the image of the invisible God. (v15a). God expressed Himself in human form through His Son—Jesus Christ. **3.** He is the first born (first in rank) over all creation (v15b); He is not the first of God's creation. **4.** By Him all things were created—visible and invisible, whether thrones or dominions, or principalities or powers (v16). **5.** He is the Head of the Church (v18a). **6.** He is the firstborn from the dead—the first to resurrect without having to die again (v18b) **7.** He is preeminent in all things (v18c).

Reflection: What is your perception of Christ? Who is He to you?

Word for today: *The signature of Christ's preeminence is all over creation.*

58

SMALL, BUT POWERFUL

"The tongue is a little member and boasts great things. See how great a forest a little fire kindles!" (James 3:5).

READ: JAMES 3:1-8

The average length of the human tongue—from the oropharynx to the lip—is 4 inches (10cm). Indeed, the tongue is a relatively small organ in the body, yet it causes a lot of havoc. The human tongue is created to fulfill three functions: **First,** to enable speech take place. **Second,** to determine the taste of food and water. **Third,** to facilitate food digestion. The human tongue is good if used properly, but bad if used improperly.

Our text lists nine negative characteristics of the human tongue.
1. The tongue boasts of great things (v5). The human tongue is capable of boasting of great things—greater than the human body it occupies. Hitler boasted of how he would have tea in London the next morning, in his quest to conquer the world, during the Second World War. Like every boasting of humans, he never lived to fulfill his dream. The Bible makes it clear that, *"death and life is in the power of the tongue, and those who love it will eat its fruit."* (Proverbs 18:21). What you say with your tongue can destroy your whole body.
2. The tongue is a fire (v6a). The word "fire" is used metaphorically to describe the chaos and havoc associated with wrongful use of the tongue.
3. The human tongue is a world of iniquity (v6b).
4. The tongue defiles the whole body (v6c).
5. The tongue sets on fire the course of human nature (v6d).
6. The tongue is set on fire by hell (v6e).
7. The tongue cannot be tamed (v8a).
8. The tongue is an unruly evil (v8b).
9. The tongue is full of deadly poison (v8c).
The human tongue is a small, but very powerful organ in the body. The way it is used determines the rise or fall of its host. The Bible declares *"The tongue of the wise promotes health."* and *"Whoever guides his mouth and tongue keeps his soul from troubles."* (Proverbs 12:18b; 21:23).

Reflection: How honorably do you use your tongue?

Word for today: *The tongue of a fool utters foolish talks.*

FOUNDATION MATTERS

If the foundations are destroyed, what can the righteous do? (Psalm 11:3).

READ: LUKE 6:46-49

Lately, there have been incidents of collapsed buildings, especially in developing countries, due to shaky foundations. Unfortunately, such incidents have claimed the lives of innocent people. Victims of collapsed buildings don't have a way of knowing about the foundation of the buildings they occupy. The look of a building from the outside may convey an impression of a solid building, while the foundation is shaky. Some buildings lack good foundation, even though they look nice externally. Unfortunately, when people look at a building from the outside and conclude that all is well, they get a rude awakening, when such a building collapses on them. Hence, foundation matters!

In our text, we notice that our Lord Jesus Christ gave an illustration of the importance of a solid foundation in building a house. Jesus compared two houses built on different foundations—one on a rock, the other on a sand. The house built on a rocky foundation withstood the wind and storm, while the house built on a sandy foundation collapsed (v48-49). The same principle applies to our spiritual lives. The spiritual foundation of our lives matters a lot. Some Christians have shallow spiritual foundation and as a result, they are not able to fight spiritual battles against the devil, even though they know the spiritual tools to use against the devil. The kind of spiritual foundation you have as a Christian determines your scope of spiritual victory over the forces of darkness. If you have a solid spiritual foundation, you are more likely to withstand the forces of spiritual attacks, deceptions of the devil, including false teachings from the pit of hell. Those who have shaky spiritual foundation fall prey to the devil and his cohorts. There are three important truths about a good spiritual foundation. **First**, a good spiritual foundation takes time to be laid. It took Christ three years of intensive teaching to lay a good spiritual foundation for His disciples. **Second**, a good spiritual foundation has to be properly laid—done the right way. **Third,** a good spiritual foundation needs to be laid with the right materials. Is your spiritual foundation solid?

Reflection: Is your spiritual foundation built of Christ and the Word of God?

Word for today: *Don't allow anything to destroy your spiritual foundation.*

BIBLE—THE WORD OF GOD

Every word of God is pure; He is a shield to those who put their trust in Him (Proverbs 30:5).

READ: ISAIAH 40:6-8

The Word of God, otherwise, known as the Scripture or the Bible is God's letter or message to humankind. It is meant to direct human beings to live in peace, prosperity and comfort on earth. Neglecting it means neglecting divine instruction for a victorious life. God created the world by His Word; He rules the world through His Word and will judge the world by His Word. God is in His Word and has magnified His Word above His name (Psalm 138:2b). As believers in Christ, we ought to uphold the whole counsel of God, so that it will be well with us. The Acronym for the Bible—Word of God is as follows:

B————Blessed

I————Information

B————-Bringing

L————-Life

E————--Eternal

Blessed information bringing life eternal

There are few questions regarding the Word of God. **First, how do we know that the Bible is the authentic Word of God?** The Bible is the authentic Word of God, because of what God says (Read 2 Peter 1:20-21). The Bible is the Word of God, written by holy men of God, under the inspiration of the Holy Spirit. **Second, why has God made the Bible available to us?** It is to correct, reproof, instruct and direct us in the way of righteousness (2 Timothy 3:16-17). **Third, what are the consequences of adulterating the Word of God?** (Read Revelation 22:18-19). **Fourth, what role does the Word of God play in our lives?** It guides us (Psalm 119:11, 105); sanctifies us (John 17:17) and heals us (Psalm 107:20; Matthew 8:8).

Reflection: How seriously do you take the Bible—the Word of God?

Word for today: *Make the Bible your daily spiritual companion.*

WHY JESUS?

Neither is there salvation in any other: for there is no other name under heaven given among men by which we must be saved (Acts 4:12).

READ: JOHN 1:11-13

There are those who believe that they can go to heaven without having to go through Jesus Christ. In fact, I have heard some people, including some Christians, make statements like this: "Just as there are several roads to get to one's destination, so are there several roads to get to heaven." Or, "The way you get to heaven is not as important as getting there. The important thing is that you get there." Such statements are borne out of people's ignorance and false belief systems, which tend to belie the Word of God and make Christ seem like a liar. But, Christ is not a liar; He is the truth. Christ, in His own word tells us how to get to heaven. In John 14:6 we read, *"Jesus said to him, 'I am the way, the truth, and the life. No one comes to the Father except through me.'"* It is better to believe what Christ says, than to believe what a human being says. Christ is the only way to God.

The question is, **Why Christ? Why is He the only Way to God?** To arrive at the answer, one has to look back at the origin of man's sin and God's immediate plan for his redemption. Genesis 3:15 reads, *"And I will put enmity between you and the woman, and between your seed and her Seed; He shall bruise your head, and you shall bruise His heel."* Right from the day man sinned, God put in place a master plan to redeem mankind from sin through His Son, Christ Jesus. In Genesis 3:15, God was talking to Satan, who impersonated the serpent to deceive Eve. The seed of Satan is none other than the unbelieving Jews (See John 8:44), while the Seed of the woman is Christ. The bruising of Satan's head and the bruising of the Seed's heel took place on the cross. As the Jews bruised the heel of Christ with those cruel nails, the head of Satan was also bruised. Right now, Satan no longer has the power to hold any human being captive. Whoever is under Satan's bondage is there by choice, because there is total deliverance in Christ Jesus. Christ came to destroy the works of Satan—sin and death (1 John 3:8b). Only Jesus Christ has the power of crushing Satan's head for good. Praise the Lord!

Reflection: Have you been trying to reach God without Christ?

Word for today: *Jesus is the only Way to God, embrace Him today.*

MARCH

DEVOTIONALS

CLEAN HANDS & PURE HEART

"The righteous will hold to his way, and he who has clean hands will be stronger and stronger (Job 17:9).

READ: PSALM 24:1-6

Verse 3-4 of our text reads, *"Who may ascend into the hill of the LORD? Or who may stand in His holy place? He who has clean hands and a pure heart, who has not lifted up his soul to an idol, nor sworn deceitfully."* **"Clean hands** and **"pure heart"** are metaphors for the godly spiritual condition; it conveys the thought of righteous living. The writer of this text understands the closeness of the heart to the hand. Thoughts emanate from the heart and the hands execute them. If there were no hands, the thoughts of the heart will remain dormant and unexecuted. On the other hand, if there were no heart, the hands won't have anything to execute. The evil thoughts of the heart and the execution of such thoughts end up defiling the whole body.

We cannot approach the throne of God with unclean hands and impure heart, hence the need to evaluate ourselves whenever we come into the presence of God. Unconfessed sin mars our relationship with God. Apostle John writes, *"If we say that we have no sin, we deceive ourselves, and the truth is not in us. If we confess our sins, He is faithful and just to forgive us our sins and to cleanse us from all unrighteousness. If we say that we have not sinned, we make Him a liar, and His word is not in us."* (1John 1:8-10). John's message is principally aimed at the believers, although it can apply to the unbelievers as well. The above text refutes the doctrine of **sinless perfection.** We are sinners saved by grace. If you sin, confess it to God and ask Him for forgiveness. But, don't keep committing and confessing the same sin over and over. Doing so, makes mockery of God's grace. In Romans 6:1-2, apostle Paul asks a very important question, *"Shall we continue in sin that grace may abound? Certainly not! How shall we who died to sin live any longer in it?"* Proverbs 28:13 reads, *"He who covers his sins will not prosper, but whoever confesses and forsakes them will have mercy."* If we approach God with "clean hands and pure heart" we shall be blessed (Psalm 24:5).

Reflection: What you see, think and do affect your spirituality, so be careful.

Word for today: *Be you holy for God is holy.*

SIN—ENERGY SAPPER

For sin shall not have dominion over you, for you are not under law but under grace (Romans 6:14).

READ: JOSHUA 7:10-12

Sin saps one's physical and spiritual energy as was the case with Samson. The Bible records that the "Spirit of the LORD began to move in Samson" which enabled him to do exploits. One day, as the Spirit of the LORD came upon Samson, he single-handedly killed a lion and tore it into pieces with bare hands (Judges 14:6). When Samson sought a revenge for not being allowed to have his Philistine wife, he again single-handedly "caught three hundred foxes, tied the foxes tail to tail, put torches between them, set fire on the torches and sent the foxes into the standing grains of the Philistines and got them completely burnt down. The next day, the Philistines noticed that their stock of grains had been gutted by fire and upon investigation, they discovered that the culprit was Samson (Read Judges 15:1-7). Not only did Samson burn their grains, he attacked and slaughtered the Philistines (v8). Samson was able to do all these exploits due to his God-given energy. But, when he started lying on the laps of a harlot, things changed. Due to Delilah's persistent persuasion, Samson gave away the secret of his God-given energy. After his head was shaven, Samson's energy left him. He was bound with ropes, his eyes plucked out and made a laughing stock by his enemies. Eventually, Samson took his own life along with thoseof his enemies (Read chapter 16). Samson didn't have to die that way. Sin sapped Samson's energy and caused his early demise!

Our text contains a classic example of how sin can sap people's energy. The children of Israel had overrun the city of Jericho through the power of God. To conquer a walled city without any weapon was a miracle, because God fought the battle. But, the sin of Achan sapped their energy as they tried to conquer a smaller, nearby city called Ai. The Bible records that the children of Israel "fled before the men of Ai", who killed and chased them out of their city (Joshua 7:4-5). It was a humiliating defeat. They had sinned through Achan and could not "stand before their enemies." (v11). Sin saps energy.

Reflection: Have you been toying with sin, thinking it doesn't hurt?

Word for today: *Sin saps both physical and spiritual energy. Watch it!*

RESPONSIBLE CITIZENRY

"I exhort.. that supplications, prayers....be made for all men...that we may lead a quiet and peaceable life in all godliness and reverence" (1 Timothy 2:1-2).

READ: 1 PETER 2:13-17

As believers in Christ, we have dual responsibilities in the society: One is civil; the other is spiritual. Our civil responsibilities are tied to our spiritual responsibilities. In other words, the way we discharge our civil responsibility by and large affects the way we carryout our spiritual responsibility. Sloppiness in the discharge of our civil responsibility can mar our testimony for Christ. For instance, someone who claims to be a Christian and ends up stealing public money has dented his testimony for Christ. He or she will find it very hard to condemn corruption in the society. Our civil responsibilities as believers include submission to civil authority. Our spiritual responsibility to the society is to pray for our leaders. 1 Timothy 2:1-2 reads, *"Therefore I exhort first of all that supplications, prayers, intercessions, and giving of thanks be made for all men, for kings and all who are in authority, that we may lead a quiet and peaceable life in all godliness and reverence"* Christians are part of the society. Since a good government flows from a good society, while a corrupt government flows from a corrupt society, it is important that we pray for the government and the society.

Our text reads, *"Therefore submit yourselves to every ordinance of man for the Lord's sake, whether to the king as supreme, or to governors, as to those who are sent by him for the punishment of evildoers and for the praise of those who do good."* (1 Peter 2:13-14). Our Lord Jesus was submissive to the civil authority during His earthly ministry. Once He was approached with the question of the legitimacy of paying taxes to Caesar. By His answer, the people were convinced that payment of taxes was the right thing to do (Read Luke 20:20-26). On another occasion, when the people demanded that Christ should pay the temple tax, Christ obliged (Read Matthew 17:24-27). Submission does not mean subjugation. Any ordinance of men that defies or contradicts the Word of God should be refused (Read Daniel 3:13-18; Acts 4:18-20).

Reflection: Do you discharge your civil responsibilities honorably?

Word for today: *We are accountable to God for our stewardship.*

THE GODLY VS. THE UNGODLY

Since we are receiving a kingdom which cannot be shaken, let us have grace,
by which we may serve God acceptably with reverence and godly fear
(Hebrews 12:28).

READ: PSALM 1:1-6

I am yet to see someone who shuns God's blessings. No matter how wicked and ungodly one is, one still yearns for life. God's blessing is as generous as it is universal. Any where you go, you can see it. It is there in your family, on your job, in your career, etc. In fact, the life you have is an evidence of God's blessing. However, in order to ensure and sustain the blessedness associated with the life God has given you, you need to align yourself with Him. Many people turn their lives—God's blessing—into a curse due to their rebellious attitude towards God. A son who rebels against his father does not receive his father's blessing; he receives a curse, instead. The same principle applies to our relationship with God. God is the Creator and therefore a heavenly Father to as many as come to Him through His Son, Jesus Christ (John 1:12). If anyone continues to live a sinful life, how do you expect such a person to be blessed by God. God does not reward iniquity; He punishes iniquity!

Our text draws a contrast between two categories of people—the godly and the ungodly. Verses 1-3 contain the characteristics of the godly, while v4-6 tell us about the characteristics of the ungodly. Who are the godly and who are the ungodly? *The godly are those who fear and love God, who have accepted God's salvation in Christ and live in righteousness.* On the other hand, *the ungodly are those who hate righteousness, live in sin and refuse the salvation that is in Christ Jesus.* Church membership does not necessarily make one godly; Christ relationship does. Without Christ in one's life, a godly life is difficult to attain. God sees godliness in us through the prism of His dear Son, Christ Jesus. The blessings of the godly include productivity, longevity and prosperity (v3), while the condemnation of the ungodly includes instability, failure and untimely death (v4-6). As you go about your daily life, you are either godly or ungodly, there is no middle ground. Think about it!

Reflection: Which of the two do you belong to: the godly or the ungodly?

Word for today: *Godliness promotes holiness.*

THE INCOMPARABILITY OF GOD

He gives power to the weak, and to those who have no might He increases strength (Isaiah 40:29).

READ: ISAIAH 40:25-26

Verse 25 of our text reads, *"To whom then will you liken me, or to whom shall I be equal? says the Holy One."* This question comes direct from God to idol worshippers and all those who liken Him to graven images, made with human hands. A similar question is reflected in v18, where Isaiah the prophet asks idolaters, *"To whom then will you liken God? Or what likeness will you compare to Him?"* Indeed, our God cannot be comopared to man-made gods; He is "holy and distinct from all others."

God's creation reveals the greatness of His power. Verse 26 of our text tells us what to do to appreciate God's greatness in creation. It reads, *"Lift up your eyes on high, and see who has created these things, who brings out their host by number; He calls them all by name, by the greatness of His might and the strength of His power; not one is missing."* "Lift up your eyes" means, "take a look at the skies." By asking human beings to "lift their eyes on high", God is making human beings responsible for discerning His greatness as the Creator, and failure to do so, amounts to guilt (Read Romans 1:18-20). Indeed, any right-thinking individual who takes a look at the skies will appreciate God's creative power. For instance, on a bright sunny day, all you see is an expanse of sky stretching far to the horizon. At night, you can see the sky dotted with innumerable twinkling stars. The sun and moon are created to give light in the day and at night respectively. These elements are held in position through God's power (Psalm 89:11-13). God "calls all creatures by name" and holds them together by the greatness of His power." (v26). No one is equal to the Almighty God. According to Matthew Henrys, "proud people make themselves equal with God; covetous people make their money equal with God." In fact, "whatever is esteemed, loved, feared or hoped in, more than God, is considered equal with God." Is there anything hindering you from acknowledging God as the Creator and you as His creature? Read Psalm 14:1.

Reflection: Take time to reflect on God's greatness in creating you.

Word for today: *God cannot be compared with man-made gods.*

69

DISCERN THE TIME!

See then that you walk circumspectly, not as fools but as wise, redeeming the time, because the days are evil (Ephesians 5:15-16).

READ: LUKE 12:54-56

Discernment is the "process of exhibiting keen insight and good judgment." It is the ability to have an insight into current trend of events in relation to what the Scriptures say about the end time. God wants us, as believers in Christ to be discerning of the end time, based on current events. Our Lord Jesus Christ gave an analogy of weather conditions in discerning the end time. Our text reads, *"Then He also said to the multitudes, 'Whenever you see a cloud rising out of the west, immediately you say, 'a shower is coming'; and so it is. And when you see the south wind blow, you say, 'There will be hot weather'; and there is."* (v54-55). At the time of Jesus, people did not have the kind of scientific instruments to measure the weather, as we have today. They relied on windy and cloudy conditions to discern weather—if it was going to be a rainy or hot day. For example, sighting a "rising cloud from the west indicated that there was going to be rain, while a southerly wind indicated a hot day. Our Lord Jesus indicted His audience for their lack of discernment of the times in which they lived. He told them, *"Hypocrites! You can discern the face of the sky and of the earth, but how is it you do not discern this time?* Christ's presence ushered in the Kingdom of God, yet the people failed to discern it; they chose to reject Him, instead (Read Matthew 12:22-28). In addition, the people lacked the ability to discern the impending doom awaiting the temple and inhabitants of Jerusalem—an event that led Jewish dispersal to date.

Lack of discernment is dangerous! There are several reasons whey some people lack discernment regarding the end time. They include **unbelief, worldly care** and **pride of life.** Those who lack the discipline of discerning the time do not believe that the world will ever end, but that it will continue for ever. They forget that anything that has a beginning must have an end. Their skeptical attitude is described by apostle Peter (Read 2 Peter 3:1-13). Those who fail to discern the time, are more likely to be caught unawares when Christ returns in glory.

Reflection: Do you discern the time? Are you conscious of Christ's return?

Word for today: *Lack of discernment often leads to disaster.*

70

OUR PLACE OF ORIGIN

The LORD God formed man of the dust of the ground, and breathed into his nostrils the breath of life; and man became a living being (Genesis 2:7).

READ: GENESIS 2:4-7

One's place of origin is very important in that, it reveals one's personal, ethnic and cultural identity. Every human being has a place of origin—it is called **dust,** otherwise known as sand. The Bible tells us about the origin of human beings. In Genesis 2:7 we read, *"And the LORD God formed man of the dust of the ground, and breathed into his nostrils the breath of life; and man became a living being."* God formed Adam from the dust of the ground, after which He breathed in him the breath of life and Adam became a living soul. We can see that Adam's place of origin was the dust and since everyone is the offspring of Adam, our place of origin is actually the same as Adam's—the dust. After Adam and Eve sinned against God by obeying the devil rather than obeying God, they both died spiritually and physically, though the physical death came much later (Read Genesis 3:6-11; 5:5). God's pronouncement on Adam marked Adam's burial—the return to his place of origin. We read, *"In the sweat of your face you shall eat bread till you return to the ground, for out of it you were taken; for dust you are, and to dust you shall return."* (Genesis 3:19). After his death, Adam returned to his place of origin— the dust. Ever since, everyone who dies has to return to his place of origin, called dust. Just as the remains of an Ambassador is returned to his country of origin for burial, so does the remains of every human being returns to his place of origin—the mother earth, after death.

Through a naturalization process, you can change your nationality, but not your place of origin. The same thing applies to spiritual identity. Just as people change their physical nationality, so do those who accept Christ change their spiritual nationality from sinners to saints, from children of disobedience to children of God (John 1:12). At death, the physical bodies of believers in Christ go to the dust, by virtue of their place of origin. However, by virtue of their nationality in Christ, their souls go to the Lord. Therefore, the grave is not the final place for believers in Christ.

Reflection: Has your nationality changed for good in Christ?

Word for today: *After a rebirth comes a change in spiritual nationality.*

BEING LAZY!

A lazy man buries his hand in the bowl, and will not so much as bring it to his mouth again (Proverbs 19:24).

READ: PROVERBS 26:13-16

Another word for **laziness** is **idleness**. Laziness is a vice; hard work is a virtue. God has not created human beings to be lazy. Indeed, there is no laziness in God's creation vocabulary. Otherwise, after his creation, God wouldn't have kept Adam in the Garden of Eve to tend—cultivate it. Genesis 2:8 and 15 read, *"The Lord planted a garden eastward in Eden, and there He put the man whom He had formed. Then the LORD God took the man and put him in the garden of Eden to tend and keep it."* Adam was quite industrious, not lazy. Our text addresses the problems associated with being lazy. A lazy man is full of excuses. Rather than go to the farm, a lazy man complains of lions prowling the streets (v13). A lazy man is compared to "a door that turns on its hinges" (v14). Rather than make use of his hands, a lazy man "buries his hands in his bosom." (v15).

Five reasons why people are lazy: 1. Procrastination. Procrastination is a brother to laziness. Postponing something that ought to be done today till another day, for no just reason, is an invitation to laziness. **2. Fear of failure.** The fear of being labelled a failure can lead to becoming lazy. It is better to try and fail, than to not try at all. **3. Lack of motivation.** When people are unmotivated, they tend to slide into lazy behavior. **4. Excuses.** People who are lazy are often full of excuses. An Apartment building worker posted a speed limit sign which read: **11 mph.** How come **11 mph?** Why not **10 mph?"** someone asked. He replied, "It is earsier to paint." What an excuse! **5. Reliance on others.** Being dependent on other people can lead to laziness. Paul condemns this kind of behavior in 2 Thessalonians 3:10-12. **Five problems with being lazy: 1. Poverty** (Proverbs 10:4; 13:4; 19:15). **2. Penury** (Proverbs 12:24). **3. Wastefulness** (18:9). **4. Covetousness** (21:25-26). When people are lazy, they tend to become jealous and covetous. **5. Restlessness** (26:14). Determine not to be lazy this year.

Reflection: Do you procrastinate? Are you afraid of failure?

Word for today: *Remember, laziness is a brother to poverty.*

TRUST IN THE LORD

Trust in the LORD with all your heart, and lean not on your own understanding (Proverbs 3:5).

READ: PSALM 73:25-28

The Psalmist must have been going through some unpleasant experiences when he penned down the words in our text.. After a deep reflection he asked, *"Whom have I in heaven but you? And there is none upon earth that I desire besides you. My flesh and my heart fail; but God is the strength of my heart and my portion forever."* The Psalmist understood God's sovereignty over all his problems and fears and concluded that "God is eternal; all that is temporal will fail." Like the Psalmist, we must do the following things as we face life's challenges. **1. We must chose God** (v25a). Choosing God means putting our faith in Him. **2. We must have a desire for Him** (v25b). **3. We must prefer Him above others** (v25b). **4. We must draw closer to Him** (v28a). **5. We must declare His works** (v28b). It is when we come closer to God that we can declare or testify of His works. We cannot testify of God's works unless we are aligned with Him. Our testimony of God's work should be permanent, not temporary; firsthand, not secondhand; real, not imaginary. Don't depend on other people's testimony about God; have one yourself. God is real, trust in Him and you will be amazed what he would do for you. In the midst of overwhelming challenges, your heart may fail. But remember, God is "the strength of your heart." It is He who strengthens the human heart. "God is not only better than all on earth, but more excellent than all in heaven." Hence, you should trust in Him. Human beings will fail you, but God will never fail you.

Based on our text, there are three important truths about the believer's strength in God. **First,** God is the <u>Author</u> of the believer's strength. Our Lord Jesus told His disciples, without me you can do nothing." (John 15:5; Hebrews 12:2). **Second,** God is the <u>Perfecter</u> of the believer's strength (Psalm 148:8). **Third,** God is the <u>Preserver</u> of the believer's strength (Psalm 41:1-2; 91:1; 121:7-8). No matter what you are going through today, don't give up on God, because he has not given up on you.

Reflection: How often do you bring your problems to the Lord?

Word for today: *Those who trust in the Lord are never disappointed.*

INTERPERSONAL RELATIONSHIP

"Be of the same mind toward one another. Do not set your mind on high things, but associate with the humble." (Romans 12:16).

READ: PHILIPPIANS 2:1-4

God the Father, Son and Holy Spirit enjoy inter-personal relationship. In sovereignty, the three are one. For instance, while in the Island of Patmos, the majestic glory of the Trinity and their interpersonal relationship were revealed to John. Read Revelation chapters 4 and 5. In Creation, the three are one. The Spirit of God *"was hovering—(incubating) the face of the waters."* (Genesis 1:1-2). After the incubation of the waters by the Holy Spirit, God spoke and creation took place. Christ is the spoken Word of God (v3). If God had not spoken, creation would not have taken place. The Word of God—Christ, brought about creation (Read John 1:1-3; Colossians 1:16). Genesis 1:26 reads, *"Then God said, 'Let Us make man in Our image, according to Our likeness; let them have dominion over the fish of the sea, over the birds of the air, and over the cattle, over all the earth and over every creeping thing that creeps on the earth."* The statement, **"Let us"** indicates plurality of persons—God the Father, the Son and the Holy Spirit in the creation of man. Also in Re-creation, the three are one. God the Father initiated the salvation plan for mankind (Genesis 3:25); God the Son executed it (Luke 1:31-33) and God the Holy Spirit consummated it (v34-35).

Since God the Father, Son and Holy Spirit enjoy interpersonal relationship, the children of God cannot do otherwise. Christ prayed the Father for interpersonal relationship among the believers: *"I do not pray for these alone, but also for those who will believe in Me through their word, that they all may be one, as you, Father, are in me, and I in you; that they also may be one in us, that the world may believe that you sent me."* (John 17:20-12). In our text, Paul echoes the same thing. *"Be of one mind."* (v2) *"Do nothing through selfish ambition, but esteem others better than self"*(v3), *"Look out for the interest of other believers in Christ"* (v4).

Reflection: What is your interpersonal relationship with others like?

Word for today: *Pray for good relationship among believers in Christ.*

AN EARTHLY VISION

"All that is in the world—the lust of the flesh, the lust of the eyes, and the pride of life--is not of the Father but is of the world" (1 John 2:16).

READ: MATTHEW 4:8-11

A vision is an "unusual capability in discernment or perception." There are at least five kinds of vision that people identify with:

1. Heavenly vision—*a supernatural revelation that comes with a divine message.* This is the kind of vision that God gives to His servants (Examples: Read Genesis 15:1-6; Ezekiel 37:1-14; Acts 10:9-16; 16:6-10).

2. Earthly vision—*a natural perception of the world with its pursuits, glamor and allurement.* This is the kind of vision that the devil showed Jesus during the temptation encounter (Read Luke 4:5-8; see also1 John 2:15-17).

3. Hallucinatory vision—*a perception of events or objects that are not real.* This is the kind of vision that is associated with mental illness.

4. Satanic vision—*a revelation of hidden things with the help of demonic powers.* This was the kind of vision that King Saul had, when he consulted a witch doctor (Read 1 Samuel 28:7-14).

5. Mental vision—*a mental image produced by the manipulation of the mind.* This was the kind of vision the false prophets of the children of Israel had. It was a vision of deception and falsehood (Read Jeremiah 23:16-17).

Our text reads, *"Again, the devil took Him up on an exceedingly high mountain, and showed Him all the kingdoms of the world and their glory. And he said to Him, 'All these things I will give you if you will fall down and worship me.' Then Jesus said to him, 'Away with you, Satan! For it is written, 'You shall worship the LORD your God, and Him only you shall serve.' Then the devil left Him, and behold, angels came and ministered to Him.'"* (v8-11). The devil took Jesus to *"an exceedingly high mountain and showed Him the world and their glory"* and demanded to be worshipped in exchange for worldly kingdoms. Jesus **rebuked** the devil for making such a demand. May that be our attitude to Satan whenever he tempts us through worldly visions of lust of the flesh, lust of the eyes and the pride of life." (1 John 2:16).

Reflection: What kinds of vision do you relate to?

Word for today: *Heavenly vision is life, Satanic vision is death.*

A GEOGRAPHICAL CALLING

"Depart, for I will send you far from here to the Gentiles." (Acts 22:21)

READ: ACTS 16:6-10

A geographical calling is a divine assignment which enables you to serve in a particular geographical area. When Ruth clung to Naomi—insisting that she would return with her to the land of the Jews, little did she know that she was embarking on a geographical calling. She was willing to leave her gods and people, and venture into a foreign land. Her statement to Naomi says it all: *"Entreat me not to leave you, or to turn back from following after you; for wherever you go, I will go; and wherever you lodge, I will lodge; your people shall be my people, and your God, my God. Where you die, I will die, and there will I be buried. The LORD do so to me, and more also, if anything but death parts you and me."* (Ruth 1:16-17). The LORD literally sent Ruth to serve in a Jewish land due to her faith in Jehovah God. Ruth served faithfully, and how faithfully she was rewarded by God! (Read Ruth 4:13-22; Matthew 1:5).

We see in our text, another example of a geographical calling. Verse 6 reads, *"Now when they had gone through Phrygia and the region of Galatia, they were forbidden by the Holy Spirit to preach the word in Asia."* Paul had some divine directives regarding his calling (Read Acts 9:15; 22:18, 21). Having completed their missionary journey in and around Galatia, Paul and his team *"were forbidden by the Holy Spirit to preach the word* (gospel) *in Asia"*—the Roman province of Asia. The Holy Spirit must have seen a more pressing need for the gospel in Macedonia than in Asia. So, *"a vision appeared to Paul in the night. A man of Macedonia stood and pleaded with him, saying, 'Come over to Macedonia and help us.'"* In response to that vision, Paul and his team changed course and took the gospel to Macedonia (v10). Sometimes, fulfilling a geographical calling can land you in hot waters. Notice that it was in Philippi, a city in the province of Macedonia that Paul cast out the demon of divination from a girl—an act that landed him and Silas in prison (Acts 16:23-24). But, God was with them (v25-34). God knows where He wants us to serve.

Reflection: In your unfamiliar geographical location, do you still serve God?

Word for today: *Divinely led ministry produces divinely led dividend.*

76

BEING INQUISITIVE

"When they had come together, they asked Him, saying, Lord, will You at this time restore the kingdom to Israel?" (Acts 1:6)

READ: JOHN 21:18-23

J ust before He ascended into heaven, a dialogue took place between our Lord Jesus Christ and His disciples. Acts 1:4-5 reads, *"And being assembled together with them, He commanded them not to depart from Jerusalem, but to wait for the Promise of the Father, 'which,' He said, 'you have heard from me; for John truly baptized with water, but you shall be baptized with the Holy Spirit not many days from now.'"* In response to Jesus' statement, the disciples asked, *"Lord, will you at this time restore the kingdom to Israel?"* (v6). Prior to His death and resurrection, during one of His teaching sessions, Christ had made it clear that His Kingdom was not of this world (John 18:36). Since Christ's Kingdom was not of this world, the disciples wanted to know when Israel would be free from their Roman oppressors and Davidic throne restored. In answer to their inquiry, Jesus said, *"It is not for you to know times or seasons which the Father has put in His own authority. But you shall receive power when the Holy Spirit has come upon you; and you shall be witnesses to me in Jerusalem, and in all Judea and Samaria, and to the end of the earth."* (v7). Jesus was, and is, more interested in the preparation of souls for the heavenly Kingdom, than the establishment of earthly kingdom.

Yes, God has created us with inquiring minds, but being too inquisitive is dangerous; it can make us confused human beings. The devil sometimes capitalizes on our inquisitiveness to sow lies in our minds as truth. After Peter's restoration (John 21:15-17), Jesus spoke to him about his destiny —how he would die, using some figurative language (v18-19). Then Peter became inquisitive on seeing John approaching. He asked Jesus two questions, *"Lord who is the one who betrays you?"* (v20). *"Lord, what about this man?"*— referring to John (v21). Jesus' answer was misunderstood (v22-23). Just like the disciples, how often we misunderstand God's Word. When Christ spoke of the **leaven of the Pharisees**, the disciples mistook it for bread (Read Matthew 16:5-12).

Reflection: Are you inquisitive about things that don't matter?

Word for today: *Irrelevant inquisitiveness is unproductive to your soul.*

OVERWHELMING EVIDENCE

And there are also many other things that Jesus did, which if they were written one by one, I suppose that even the world itself could not contain the books that would be written. Amen. (John 21:25).

READ: JOHN 20:30-31

An evidence is something you present to authenticate the truthfulness of a matter. In the court of law, any case that lacks evidence has lost its credibility and therefore is without merit. If we were to prove the deity of Christ from the stand-point of human evidence, the evidence is overwhelming. The deity of Christ is not in doubt, except in the minds of the skeptics. The devil is responsible for making people doubt or deny the deity of Christ for the following reasons: **First,** to rob people of the opportunity to be saved. If the devil succeeds in making people doubt or deny the deity of Christ, he has succeeded in making them candidates for hell (Read John 1:18; 6:46-47; 15:23-25). **Second,** to keep people in perpetual bondage of Satan. Anyone who denies the deity of Christ, remains the servant of Satan (Read John 12:31-32; Luke 10:17-18). **Third,** to keep people in bondage of sin (Read John 8:23-24).

Regarding the overwhelming evidence of Christ's deity, Apostle John writes, *"And truly Jesus did many other signs in the presence of His disciples, which are not written in this book; but these are written that you may believe that Jesus is the Christ, the Son of God, and that believing you may have life in His name."* (John 20:30-31). From the Scriptures, we can garner four kinds of evidence to prove the deity of Christ. **1. Scriptural evidence.** He is the "the Mighty God and the Everlasting Father" (Read Isaiah 9:6; John 1:1-2;Titus 2:13). **2. Oral evidence.** He is God incarnate (Read Matthew 1:23; 3:17; 17:5; Luke 1:35; Mark 15:37-39). **3. Visible evidence.** He healed the sick, cast out demons, raised the dead and fed thousands with five loaves of bread and two fish (Read Mark 3:10-12; 6:34-44). He resurrected after three days (Matthew 28:1-8). 4. **Transformational evidence** (John 8:36). That Christ transforms lives today is an evidence of His deity. No other deity can do what Christ has done, is doing and will do.

Reflection: Are you one of those who deny and or doubt Christ's deity?

Word for today: To deny Christ's deity is to deny God's deity.

LOST, BUT RESTORED

"So the man of God entreated the LORD, and the king's hand was restored to him, and became as before." (1 Kings 13:6b)

READ: 1 KINGS 13:1-6

King Jeroboam overstepped his boundary when "he stood by the altar to burn incense." (1 Kings 13:1). Verses 2-3 of our text read, *"Then he cried out against the altar by the word of the LORD, and said, 'O altar, altar! Thus says the LORD: 'Behold, a child, Josiah by name, shall be born to the house of David; and on you he shall sacrifice the priests of the high places who burn incense on you, and men's bones shall be burned on you.' And he gave a sign the same day, saying, 'This is the sign which the LORD has spoken: Surely the altar shall split apart, and the ashes on it shall be poured out.'"* Jeroboam's action prompted the man of God from Bethel to pronounce God's judgment upon the altar. But as Jeroboam tried to arrest the man of God, his hand was arrested by God, "he could not pull it back to himself" (v4). But, when he acknowledged his folly, he asked the man of God to plead with God for the restoration of his hand. So, the man of God pleaded with God and Jeroboam's hand was restored (v6). How gracious and merciful God is! God is willing to restore that which the devil has stolen, if He sees genuine repentance in us.

In the Garden of Eden two things were lost, but restored in Christ. The **first** was the River of life (Genesis 2:10). Adam and Eve enjoyed a river which flowed out of Eden. That river symbolized the river of life. It was lost due to sin but restored in Christ due to Christ's righteousness (Read John 4:13-14; Revelation 22:1). The **second** was the Tree of life (Genesis 3:23-24). Adam and Eve were driven out of the garden of Eden to stop them from eating the tree of life and live forever in their sinful condition. The tree of life in the garden of Eden is now in heaven (Read Revelation 22:2). Through His death and resurrection, Christ restored the tree of life to all believers in Him. Revelation 22:14 reads, *"Blessed are those who do His commandments, that they may have the right to the tree of life, and may enter through the gates into the city."*

Reflection: Have you lost your joy, peace and hope? Christ can restore them.

Word for today: *Salvation—What is lost in Adam is restored in Christ.*

79

CLOSED-DOOR MENTALITY

"At evening...when the doors were shut where the disciples were assembled, for fear of the Jews...Jesus came and stood in their midst." (John 20:19).

READ: JOHN 20:19-20

Our text reads, *"Then, the same day at evening, being the first day of the week, when the doors were shut where the disciples were assembled, for fear of the Jews, Jesus came and stood in the midst, and said to them, 'Peace be with you.' When He had said this, He showed them His hands and His side. Then the disciples were glad when they saw the Lord."* Fear drove Christ's disciples behind closed door. Christ had died and had been buried; they felt all hope was lost, that the Jewish religious leaders who killed their Master would come after them. Some believers behave the same way today. When things don't go the way they have planned, they feel disappointed and go behind **spiritual closed door**—weep, cry, complain, whine, have pity party and even stop going to Church. Closed door mentality feeds on fear and failure. While the disciples remained behind closed door, due to fear, Christ appeared in their midst and said to them, *"Peace be with you."* (v19). Christ knows how to meet people in their closed-door situation.

God doesn't want us to operate with a closed-door mentality. Since the disciples had developed a closed-door mentality, they lost heir focus—left their high calling of *"fishers of men"* and went after worldly trade of *fishermen.* The result was disappointing—they caught nothing (Read John 21:1-3). In Revelation 3:8, we read of an open door. John, one of the disciples who were behind closed door for fear of the Jews, was told of an open door by Christ. When Christ opens a door for you, no one can shut it, except you. Any door He shuts, no one can open it. **Three ways to sustain Christ's open door: First,** acknowledge your inadequacies. You "have a little strength." says the Lord (Revelation 3:8a) **Second,** obey God's Word (v8c) "[You] have kept my Word." Obedience to God's Word keeps the door open. **Third,** Don't deny Christ (v8d). Yes, persecutions and trials will come, but they should not make you to deny Christ.

Reflection: Do you operate with a closed-door mentality?

Word for today: *Away with closed door mentality, embrace Christ by faith.*

PREACH THE WORD!

"And as you go, preach, saying, 'The kingdom of heaven is at hand.'" (Matthew 10:7).

READ: 2 TIMOTHY 4:1-5

Paul charged Timothy, with God and Jesus Christ as witnesses, to preach the Word of God (2 Timothy 4:1). In v2, Paul gave Timothy five-fold commands to follow. The same command is applicable to us today.

Command #1: Preach the Word—to proclaim the gospel of Christ Jesus. Preaching God's Word demands courage, boldness, passion and persistence.

Command #2: Be ready in season and out of season. This means "to be persistent whether the time is favorable or unfavorable"

Command #3: Convince. The word, **convince,** is the same as **persuade**. Like Timothy, we are to persuade those who have erred from the truth—carefully and patiently explaining to them sound Biblical doctrine.

Command #4: Rebuke. Like Timothy, we are to rebuke those who live in sin and urge them to repent.

Command #5: Exhort. The word **exhort** is the same as **encourage.** Again, like Timothy, we are to encourage others to grow in faith and in the knowledge of our Lord Jesus Christ. Why must the Word of God be preached? The Word of God must be preached because, it is the only means of repentance from sin and salvation in Christ (Read Romans 1:16-17). Another reason why the Word of God must be preached is that, failure to do so will legitimize false doctrines. Even with the preaching of God's Word, people are still giving heed to false doctrines. Can you imagine what would happen, if the Word of God were not preached? Satan would have a field day.

It is a pity that some people don't like to pay heed to sound Biblical doctrines because: **1.** It will convict them of their sinful ways. **2.** It will make demands from them that they would not like to follow. **3.** They are fulfilling the Scriptures (Read Mark 4:12; 2 Timothy 4:3). Most people fulfill the Scriptures without knowing it. One can fulfil the Scriptures in a positive or negative way based on one's attitude toward the Word of God.

Reflection: How do you receive the Word? Do you share it with others?

Word for today: *To preach the Word is to have the Word in you.*

FAITH, HOPE AND LOVE

The work of righteousness will be peace, And the effect of righteousness, quietness and assurance forever (Isaiah 32:17).

READ: ROMANS 5:1-5

Faith, hope and love are tripartite Christian virtues associated with our salvation in Christ. The three work in close consort. Verses 1-2 of our text read, *"Therefore, having been justified by faith, we have peace with God through our Lord Jesus Christ, through whom also we have access by faith into this grace in which we stand, and rejoice in hope of the glory of God."* In this text, we notice the interconnectivity of **faith**, **hope** and **love**. You cannot have hope if you lack faith in Christ; nor can you have faith in Christ without experiencing the love of God. Love of God draws us closer to Christ; faith in Him justifies us before God, while hope of eternal life drives our passion for Him. Faith in Christ justifies every sinner. For example, the thief on the cross was justified due to his faith in Christ. He pleaded, *"Lord, remember me when you come into your kingdom. "*, and Jesus responded, *"Assuredly, I say to you, today you will be with me in Paradise. "* (Luke 23:42-43). This guy came to the cross a sinful, guilty, condemned criminal. But, faith in Christ changed his status from a sinner to a saint; from a criminal to a candidate of Paradise. The power of faith is so great that it can **transform** (Luke 19:8-9); **save** (23:42-43); **cleanse** (Matthew 8:1-3); **heal** (Mark 10:46-52) and **justify** (Romans 5:1).

Verse 3a of our text reads, *"And not only that, but we also glory in tribulations. "* Paul is not saying that he enjoyed tribulations, rather, he glorified God as he went through them. We should learn to glorify God rather than question Him whenever we go through trials and persecutions, because tribulations produce perseverance in us. In other words, tribulation toughens our faith in Christ. Perseverance produces character and character produces hope. Verse 5 reads, *"Now hope does not disappoint, because the love of God has been poured out in our hearts by the Holy Spirit who was given to us. "* Since hope is the product of faith, hope in God never disappoints. God is faithful in all His promises (Read Romans 4:21; Hebrews 10:23).

Reflection: Do you have the virtues of faith, hope and love?

Word for today: *Faith, hope and love are the catalysts of Christian character.*

A TAKER TURNED GIVER

"Remember the words of the Lord Jesus, that He said, 'It is more blessed to give than to receive.'" (Acts 20:35).

READ: LUKE 19:1-10

There are some people who like to take or receive from others, but find it hard to give back. Even when they have more than enough, they still find it difficult to part with what they have. In American slang, such people are called, "takers" Whenever a taker becomes a giver, something transformational has taken place. This was the case of Zacchaeus, the tax collector. Tax collectors at the time of Jesus were very corrupt and notorious in the way they discharged their duties. They were fond of surcharging tax payers for their personal profit. The extra fees they imposed on tax payers put undue financial burden on the people. As a result of their corrupt practices, tax collectors were despised and hated by the Jews, who regarded them as extorters of the Roman empire. So, it was not surprising that John the Baptist addressed the evil practice of the tax collectors in his "repentance" sermon to the people. Luke 3:12-13 reads, *"Then tax collectors also came to be baptized, and said to him, 'Teacher, what shall we do?' And he said to them, 'Collect no more than what is appointed for you.'"*

Our text tells a story of how Zacchaeus, the **taker** became Zacchaeus, the **giver.** After his transformational encounter with Jesus, Zacchaeus promised to restitute all that he had stolen from people as a tax collector. Verse 8 of our text reads, *"Then Zacchaeus stood and said to the Lord, 'Look, Lord, I give half of my goods to the poor; and if I have taken anything from anyone by false accusation, I restore fourfold.'"* Our Lord Jesus who sees in secret, saw Zacchaeus' genuine repentance and sincere heart of restitution and said to him, *"Today, salvation has come to this house, because he also is a son of Abraham, for the Son of Man has come to seek and to save that which was lost."* (v9-10). Zacchaeus' restitution gesture was based on the law of restitution (Read Exodus 22:1; Leviticus 6:4-5). When God touches your life, you will never remain the same; you will become a productive tool in the hands of God.

Reflection: How productive have you been in God's Kingdom work?

Word for today: *An encounter with the Lord turns a life around.*

IN HIM!

In Him we have redemption through His blood, the forgiveness of sins, according to the riches of His grace (Ephesians 1:7).

READ: EPHESIANS 1:3-14

There are three Persons in the God-head: God the Father, God the Son, and God the Holy Spirit. The three are co-equal, co-existent and co-eternal. In Theological parlance, this concept is known as Trinity. A rational mind cannot understand the concept of Trinity. Let's use the analogy of water to explain the concept of Trinity. **Water, water vapor** and **Ice** are one, and inseparable object. For instance, if you <u>boil</u> water, it becomes vapor; if you <u>freeze</u> water, it becomes ice; if you <u>melt</u> the ice, it becomes water. Just as water, water vapor and ice are inseparable, so is God the Father, God the Son and God the Holy Spirit inseparable. In His humanity, Christ was incarnate God, hence His name was called Emmanuel—God with us (Matthew 1:23). Since Christ is part of Trinity, God chose Him as the means of salvation for humankind. Christ's atoning death, burial and triumphant resurrection satisfied God's demand for the penalty of our sin and restoration of our relationship with Him.

Through His substitutionary death, every believer in Christ becomes complete in Him (Colossians 2:10). Our text contains about six, **"In Him"** phrases and can aptly be called, **'In Him'** text, because of who we are in Christ. Let's consider the seven **"In Him's"** about Christ:
1. In Him all things consist (Read John 1:1-3 and Colossians 1:17). In Christ all things hold together—your life, future, career, finances, family, etc.
2. In Him we are complete. Colossians 2:9-10 read, *"For in Him dwells all the fullness of the Godhead bodily; and you are complete in Him, who is the head of all principality and power."*
3. In Him we are blessed with spiritual blessings in heavenly places (Read Ephesians 1:3). **4. In Him we are chosen** (v4). **5. In Him we have redemption** (Ephesians 1:7; Acts 4:12). **6. In Him we have obtained an inheritance** (Ephesians 1:11). **7. In Him we have trusted and believed** (v13). If you put your confidence in Christ, you will not be disappointed (Read Romans 9:33; 10:11).

Reflection: Do you know that you are complete in Christ as a Christian?

Word for today: *Trust draws us to Him; Belief grants us salvation in Him.*

PROPHECIES ABOUT CHRIST

And they made His grave with the wicked—but with the rich at His death, because He had done no violence, nor was any deceit in His mouth (Isaiah 53:9).

READ: ISAIAH 53:1-12

Prophecy is the foretelling of an event. True prophecy comes from God, while false prophecy comes from the devil. Christ's advent is a monumental event in the history of humankind, and every aspect of it was prophetic. Prior to Christ's incarnation, over two thousand years ago, there were series of prophecies about His life. Today, every word of those prophecies has been fulfilled to the letter. Christ's life is both prophetic and documentary: Prophetic, because Old Testament prophets spoke about it; documentary because there is a written evidence of the fulfilment of such prophecies.

There are seven aspects of prophecies about Christ's life, which have been fully fulfilled., and which merit our consideration:
1. Prophecy about His incarnation (Isaiah 7:14; 9:6). *Fulfilment:* (Read Matthew 1:20-23; Luke 2:1-20). Christ's birth was prophesied in the Old Testament and fulfilled in the New Testament.
2. Prophecy about His ministry—to preach, heal, and set the captives free (Isaiah 61:1-3). *Fulfilment:* (Read Luke 4:18-19; Matthew 4:23-25; 9:35)
3. Prophecy about His suffering (Isaiah 53:4-7). *Fulfilment:* (Read Luke 18:31-34; Mathew 27:27-37, 39-44).
4. Prophecy about His death (Isaiah 53:8). *Fulfilment:* (Read Luke 23:44-49).
5. Prophecy about His burial (Isaiah 53:9). *Fulfilment:* (Read Matthew 27:57-61).
6. Prophecy about His resurrection (Psalm 16:10; 49:15). *Fulfilment:* (Read Matthew 28:1-8).
7. Prophecy about His ascension (John 6:62). *Fulfilment:* (Read Acts 1:9; 2:32-35). No Philosopher or a religious founder or a political leader, can boast of the above credentials in regard to his birth, life, ministry, death and resurrection. Since the prophecies about Christ and His ministry have been fulfilled, what is your thought about Him?

Reflection: Do you know that Christ came and died for you?

Word for today: *Your view about Christ today, defines your place in eternity.*

ALWAYS BE THANKFUL TO GOD

In everything give thanks; for this is the will of God in Christ Jesus for you (1 Thessalonians 5:18).

READ: LUKE 17:11-19

Ten lepers met Jesus Christ as He entered a village. Due to their leprous condition, these men could not approach Christ; hence they stood afar off. Just as the disease of leprosy prevented these lepers from approaching Christ, so does sin (spiritual leprosy) prevent a sinner from approaching Christ. Indeed, anyone who lives in sin finds it hard to approach Christ, unless he or she is drawn by the power of the Holy Spirit. These lepers did something: *"They lifted their voices and said, 'Jesus, Master, have mercy on us!'"* (Luke 17:13). In response, Jesus told them, *"Go, show yourselves to the priests."* As they went, *"they were cleansed."* (v14). How wonderful it would be for anyone living under the bondage of sin to lift his or her voice and call on the name of the Lord for help! (Read Romans 10:13). Verses 15-16 of our text read, *"And one of them, when he saw that he was healed, returned, and with a loud voice glorified God, and fell down on his face at His feet, giving Him thanks. And he was a Samaritan."*

Jesus commended one of the lepers who came back to give thanks, but chided the other nine for their ingratitude. We read, *"So Jesus answered and said, 'Were there not ten cleansed? But where are the nine? Were there not any found who returned to give glory to God except this foreigner?'"* Jesus got only 10% thanks in return for all He did. Could this be true of our attitude towards Him? **Why should we thank God?** We should thank God for many reasons, including the following: **1.** He has made us (Psalm 100:3a). **2.** We are His people (v3b). **3.** Our sins are forgiven (Psalm 103:3a). **4.** He heals our diseases (v3b). **5.** He redeems our lives from destruction (v4a). **6.** He has bestowed His mercies upon us (v4b). **7.** He has satisfied us with good things, including good health (v5). **How should we thank God? First,** with praise on our lips (Psalm 63:3; 119:171); **Second,** with our substance Psalm 116:17-18; **Third,** with our whole being (Romans 12:1).

Reflection: How often do you thank God for your salvation and protection?

Word for today: *Any thanks without a surrendered life to Christ is worthless.*

AN IDEAL HOUSE OR HOME?

"I have known him, in order that he may command his children and his house-hold after him, that they keep the way of the LORD, to do righteousness and justice." (Genesis 18:19).

READ: EPHESIANS 5:22-25; 6:1-4

A good number of people strive to own an ideal house—where they hope to live until retirement. In most cases, such people end up having ideal house, but not ideal homes. There is a difference between a house and a home. What makes a house a home is not its furnishing, cost or location, but people living in it. As long as a house is not occupied, it remains a house, not a home. In addition, what makes a house an ideal home is not the class of people living in it, but the presence of God in such a home. People make an empty house to become a home, while Christ makes an 'empty' home to become an ideal home. This means that any home without Christ is spiritually empty. Not long ago, a couple built a dream house in a very expensive and beautiful neighborhood. The house had all the trappings of an exquisite edifice, but after five years, their marriage hit the rock! The house was sold as they went through a divorce. This couple had built a dream house, but not a ideal home. Without Christ, the storm of life can blow a home apart.

In our text, we notice what it takes to have an ideal home:
1. Acceptance and presence of Christ in the home (Ephesians 5:22-23). Christ's presence at the wedding in Cana of Galilee made all the difference when they ran out of wine. His presence will supply every need of the home—including peace (Read John 2:1-12). **2. Wife's submission to her husband** (v22). Lack of submission creates chaos in the home. Remember, submission is not subjugation. **3. Husband's love for the wife** (v25,28). If a husband loves his wife, the wife will respond by submitting. **4. Children's obedience to their parents** (6:1-3). When children are disobedient to parents, they dig their graves early in life. **5. Respect for the children** (6:4). When parents dishonor their children by being cruel and abusive, they create bitterness and barrier in their relationship.

Reflection: What do you have—an ideal house or an ideal home?

Word for today: *An ideal home has the fear of God in it.*

KNOWN IN HEAVEN

"The Spirit Himself bears witness with our spirit that we are children of God, and if children, then heirs—heirs of God and joint heirs with Christ…" (Romans 8:16-17).

READ: 1 JOHN 3:1-3

Three things make a person to be known in a place: First, a person's **identity.** Information about yourself—name and status will make others know you in a place. Second, a person's **responsibility.** If for instance you are employed in a place, people will get to know you as a worker there. But, the day you cease to work there, your responsibility to such a place stops, and over time, you will no longer be known there. Third, a person's **relationship**. Those who have built some kind of relationship with people tend to be associated with them. For instance, if you frequent a place, people there see you often and overtime, you become known there. So we see that for one to be known in a place, one has to identify with such a place and what goes on there. The same principle applies to heavenly things. Identifying with heavenly things shows your connectivity with heaven (Read Colossians 3:1-3).

Our text reveals that those who belong to Christ are not known in the world; however, they are known in heaven. We read, *"Behold what manner of love the Father has bestowed on us, that we should be called children of God! Therefore the world does not know us, because it did not know Him. Beloved, now we are children of God; and it has not yet been revealed what we shall be, but we know that when He is revealed, we shall be like Him, for we shall see Him as He is, and everyone who has this hope in Him purifies himself, just as He is pure."* Based on our text, in order to be known in heaven, one has to fulfil the following spiritual conditions: **1. You must become a child of God** (1 John 3:1a; John 1:12). This means repenting of your sins and accepting Christ as your Lord and Savior. **2. You must not identify with the world, but with Christ** (v1b; Read 1 John 2:15-16). **3. You must live a life of purity** (1 John 3:3; Read Hebrews 12:14). On Christ's return, those who are known in heaven will be like Him. What a special honor and privilege to be known in heaven!

Reflection: Are you known in heaven or in the world?

Word for today: *It's better to be known in heaven, than in the world.*

88

PRAYER: A SPIRITUAL DISCIPLINE

Then He spoke a parable to them, that men always ought to pray and not lose heart (Luke 18:1).

READ: REVELATION 8:1-5

Prayer is an act of communicating with God; it is the means by which the children of God gain victory over Satan. A prayerful Christian is a powerful Christian. In our text, we notice how powerful the prayers of believers in Christ can be. John's description of the revelation he had gives us some insight into what happens when you pray as a believer in Christ. Verses 3-5 of our text read, *"Then another angel, having a golden censer, came and stood at the altar. He was given much incense, that he should offer it with the prayers of all the saints upon the golden altar which was before the throne. And the smoke of the incense, with the prayers of the saints, ascended before God from the angel's hand. Then the angel took the censer, filled it with fire from the altar, and threw it to the earth. And there were noises, thunderings, lightnings, and an earthquake."* From John's description, we notice four things: **1.** There is an angel, whose responsibility it is to offer incense daily to God. **2.** The angel mixes the prayers of the saints with the incense. **3.** The incense with the prayers of the saints ascends to God. **4.** God answers the prayer of the saints through natural phenomena of thunder, lightning, and earthquake. Prayers accepted in heaven can produce great changes on earth. Therefore, it is very important that as a believer in Christ, you give yourself to prayer. According to John Bunyan, "Prayer is a <u>shield</u> to the soul, a <u>sacrifice</u> to God, and a <u>scourge</u> to Satan."

In order to have a result-oriented prayer, you may want to adopt the following principles: **First, you should pray in faith,** "for without faith it is impossible to please God." (Hebrews 11:6. Read Mark 11:24; James 1:5-8). **Second, you should pray with perseverance** (Luke 18:1-8). **Third, you should pray in the name of Jesus** (John 14:13-14; 16:23-24). **Fourth, you should pray in accordance with God's will** (1 John 5:14-15). Prayer is a spiritual discipline and only those who are spiritually disciplined can pray (Read 2 Timothy 1:7). Peter failed to pray and ended up denying his Master three times.

Reflection: Do you have the spiritual discipline to pray? If not, why not?

Word for today: *He who fails to pray fails to win spiritual battles.*

WORK, REST AND SLEEP

When Jesus heard it, He departed from there by boat to a deserted place by Himself (Matthew 14:13).

READ: MARK 6:30-33

C an you imagine what life would look like, if we were to continue working without rest or sleep? People will drop dead! Our human body is not designed to work without rest and sleep. Work, rest and sleep enhance the wellbeing of our physical body: Work builds and strengthens the body, rest relaxes it, and sleep refreshes it. For instance, anyone who fails to engage in any physical activity, is likely to develop some physical ailments and anyone who works, but fails to rest or sleep will become sick. On the other hand, anyone who spends time resting and sleeping without working becomes lazy and impoverished. So, there must be a balancing act between work, rest and sleep.

In our text, we notice Christ's concern for His disciples regarding their lack of rest. After a busy day's work, *"the apostles gathered to Jesus and told Him all things, both what they had done and what they had taught."* (Mark 4:30). In response, Jesus told them, *"Come aside by yourselves to a deserted place and rest a while."* (v31). Another word for "deserted" is "quiet". Our Lord Jesus Christ encouraged His apostles to rest after a busy day's work. The apostles were so busy that they hardly had time to eat. In obedience to their Masters command, the apostles "departed to a deserted (quiet) place" for a rest. Just as Christ asked His apostles to have some rest, after a busy day's work, so does He all His followers. Work without rest and sleep has led to a lot of premature deaths, even among Christians. I have had some people, including pastors, quote the Bible out of context, to justify their workaholic behavior—working without rest. They quote verses like John 4:31-34 and 9:4. These verses relate to Christ's ministry of salvation for humankind. In application, there is no evidence to support working without resting in these verses. We are productive when our bodies are replenished through rest and sleep, but are unproductive when these two important elements of life are lacking.

Reflection: Are you a workaholic? Do you undermine the importance of rest?

Word for today: *All work and no rest makes one a spiritual dullard.*

THE POWER OF FAITH

And He said to her, "Daughter, your faith has made you well. Go in peace, and be healed of your affliction." (Mark 5:34).

READ: JOSHUA 2:8-14

God honors faith, because there is power in it. The power in the faith of Abraham evoked these words of blessing from God, *"By Myself I have sworn, says the LORD, because you have done this thing, and have not withheld your son, your only son—blessing I will bless you, and multiplying I will multiply your descendants as the stars of the heaven and as the sand which is on the seashore; and your descendants shall possess the gate of their enemies. In your seed all the nations of the earth shall be blessed, because you have obeyed My voice."* (Genesis 22:15-18). The power in Abraham's faith is still at work today in the lives of many (Read Galatians 3:29). The power in Abraham's faith made him a friend of God (2 Chronicles 20:7; Isaiah 41:8). In the New Testament, we notice how the power of faith healed the woman with severe hemorrhage. She said, *"If only I may touch His clothes, I shall be made well."* Immediately, she touched the clothes of Jesus, *"her blood was dried up, and she felt in her body that she was healed of the affliction."* (Mark 5:28-29). Not only did the power in this woman's faith heal her, it sucked some power out of Jesus (v30; 34).

Our text is a classic example of how powerful faith is. Rahab was a harlot who hid the spies that were sent by Joshua to spy the land of Jericho. Based on her faith in the God of the Hebrews, Rahab accommodated the spies and requested that she and her family members be spared (Joshua 2:11-13). In the story of Rahab, we learn four lessons about the dynamics of faith:
1. Faith without works is useless. Rahab put her faith to work by hiding the spies. Faith requires action (Read James 2:14-22).
2. Faith involves risk taking. Rahab took a huge risk by hiding the spies.
3. Faith qualifies the unqualified. Rahab was qualified to be named in the book of genealogy of the faithful (Read Matthew 1:5; Hebrews 11:31; James 2:25). **4. Faith saves.** Rahab was saved by her faith in Jehovah God.

Reflection: Can you testify to the power of faith in your life?

Word for today: *Don't underestimate the power of faith in God.*

91

TEST THE SPIRITS

"Every spirit that does not confess that Jesus Christ has come in the flesh is not of God..." (1 John 4:3).

READ: 1 JOHN 4:1-6

Verses 1-2 of our text read, *"Beloved, do not believe every spirit, but test the spirits, whether they are of God; because many false prophets have gone out into the world. By this you know the Spirit of God: Every spirit that confesses that Jesus Christ has come in the flesh is of God."* John's letter to the Church was aimed at countering some false teachings about the incarnation of Christ. John's letter was as relevant to the 1st century Church as it is relevant to the 21st century Church. John warns the Church to test every spirit, to see "whether they are of God." At the time John wrote his letter, many false prophets had infiltrated the body of Christ with false doctrines about Christ's incarnation. Prominent among them were the Docetists, who taught that "Christ did not have a physical body" and Cerinthus, a false teacher of John's day, who denied the incarnation by teaching that "the divine Christ descended on the human Jesus at His baptism and then departed before His crucifixion." Unfortunately, different kinds of spirit operate freely in the Church of Christ today undetected. They range from the spirit of pride, corruption, materialism, seduction, lying, false teaching, etc.

The slave girl who kept announcing the identity of Paul and Silas for three days would easily have passed for a young prophetess today, with a large following. But, when Paul cast out the demon in her, it became obvious that she was possessed. Although what she said was correct, the source of her message was demonic (Read Acts 16:16-18). We are enjoined to test the spirits, whether they are of God. There are three important reasons why we should test the spirits operating in the Church of the living God. **First,** because there are many false prophets out there (1John 4:1). **Second,** because Satan likes to transform himself into an angel of light (2 Corinthians 11:13-14). **Third,** because false doctrine can lead people to hell (1 Timothy 4:1; 2 Peter 2:1-3). So, be very careful of what you hear and swallow.

Reflection: Can you test the spirits operating in people around you?

Word for today: *The Bible and the Holy Spirit enable us to test the spirits.*

AN EYE-COVENANT

But I say to you that whoever looks at a woman to lust for her has already committed adultery with her in his heart (Matthew 5:28).

READ: JOB 31:1-4

A covenant is an agreement, written or unwritten, between two people or an entity. Some eye-covenants are good; others are bad. A good eye-covenant is the covenant you make with your eyes not to behold anything that will defile your spirit. It is an agreement entered into between your eyes and God to glorify Him always with your eyes. When someone decides to feed his or her eyes with X-rated movies and pornography, he or she has entered into a bad covenant with his or her eyes to fulfil lustful desires. But, if on the other hand, someone decides not to feed his or her eyes with visual trash, then such an individual has made a good covenant with his or her eyes. The writer of our text understood the power in what the human eyes see and declared, *"I have made a covenant with my eyes; why then should I look upon a young woman?"* (Job 31:1). The eye is the gate-way to your soul. Whatever goes through it lodges in your mind, and will from time to time, replay itself. By virtue of your faith in Christ, you have been sanctified for God's use, including your eyes. In other words, you have entered into an eye-covenant with God not to behold anything that defiles, because you are His child (Read Romans 6:11-14).

Remember, as a believer in Christ, any violation of your eye-covenant with God spells disaster. David was a king and a man after God's heart (See 1 Samuel 13:13-14; Acts 13:22). But, when he violated his eye-covenant with the LORD, he got into a big trouble! One evening, as David walked around the balcony of his palace, he violated his eye-covenant by looking lustfully at Uriah's wife taking a bath. What David saw played so intensely in his mind that he committed adultery with Uriah's wife (1 Kings 11:1-5). As he tried to cover up his sin, David committed murder by masterminding the death of Uriah (vv6-21). As a man of God, do you cast lustful eyes on a woman? As a woman of God, do you cast seductive eyes on a man? As a Spirit-filled Christian, how do you make use of your eyes.

Reflection: Is your eye-covenant a good or bad one? What do you behold?

Word for today: *A good eye-covenant filters trash out of your mind.*

THE RICH AND THE POOR

The poor will never cease from the land; therefore...you shall open your hand wide to your brother, to your poor and your needy, in your land (Deuteronomy 15:11).

READ: JAMES 1:9-11

The world in which we live does not operate on a level plain, hence we have opposites: like good or bad, tall or short, big or small, white or black, hot or cold, rich or poor, etc. One day, when Christ returns, the current life of opposites will give way to life of oneness and completeness to as many as believe in Him. The Bible declares, *"Beloved, now we are children of God; and it has not yet been revealed what we shall be, but we know that when He is revealed, we shall be like Him, for we shall see Him as He is. And everyone who has this hope in Him purifies himself, just as He is pure."* (1 John 3:2-3). The United Nations as well as other well-meaning philanthropic organizations have been doing their best to eradicate poverty. The harder they try, the more elusive success seems to be. Based on the Word of God, poverty cannot be eradicated; but, it can be minimized. Deuteronomy 15: 11 reads, *"For the poor will never cease from the land; therefore I command you, saying, 'You shall open your hand wide to your brother, to your poor and your needy, in your land.'* What we should be doing is to help the poor around us to make life much easier for them, but not to eradicate poverty. Poverty is not a disease that can be eradicated; it is the consequence of man's rebellion against God. God did not create Adam with poverty. But, after Adam sinned and was driven out of the Garden of Eden, poverty set in. As a punishment for his rebellion, God cursed the ground—a curse that remains to date, which opened the door to poverty, misery and suffering of humankind (Read Genesis 3:17-19).

James, the writer of our text admonishes us, *"Let the lowly brother glory in his exaltation."* (James 1:9). "A lowly brother" means a Christian brother who is poor. A Christian brother who is poor should glorify God that he has been exalted in Christ, while a Christian brother who is rich should glorify God that he can use his wealth in serving God. Neither poverty nor riches last forever.

Reflection: Do you glorify God in your rich or poor condition?

Word for today: *Riches and poverty are lives of opposites that glorify God.*

A PROMISE OF RESTORATION

"For I will restore health to you and heal you of your wounds, 'says the LORD.'" (Jeremiah 30:17).

READ: JOEL 2:25-27

When God makes a promise you can bank on Him—He will always follow through on it, even though it may tarry. For instance, God promised Abraham that in him "all the families of the world would be blessed." (Genesis 12:3). After two thousand years, God fulfilled that promise by sending His Son, Jesus Christ—descendant of Abraham, as a Savior of the world. By virtue of His incarnation, everyone who responds to the salvation that is in Christ, becomes the beneficiary of God's promise to Abraham. During His covenant with Abraham, God told him, *"Know certainly that your descendants will be strangers in a land that is not theirs, and will serve them, and they will afflict them four hundred years."* God promised Abraham, *"The nation whom they serve I will judge; afterward they shall come out with great possessions."* Indeed, after four hundred years, God delivered the children of Israel from Egyptian bondage with His mighty arm, through His servant Moses. God is a promise keeper!

When the children of Israel sinned against God, He punished them by sending a swarm of locust to devastate their farmlands. Being a merciful God, He also promised them restoration through prophet Joel. We read, *"I will restore to you the years that the swarming locust has eaten, the crawling locust, the consuming locust, my great army which I sent among you. You shall eat in plenty and be satisfied and praise the name of the LORD your God, who has dealt wondrously with you. And my people shall never be ashamed ."* (Joel 2:25-26). God's promise of restoration holds true to everyone who puts his or her confidence in Him. If you truly repent of your sins and come to God through faith in Christ Jesus, God will restore your wasted years. He will bless you, promote you, heal you, redeem your life from destruction, renew your strength and satisfy your mouth with good things (Psalm 103:3-5). No matter how sinful you may have been, once you repent and turn to Christ, God will restore you.

Reflection: Do you have wasted years of sinfulness?

Word for today: *Only God can restore what the locusts of sin have eaten.*

APRIL

DEVOTIONALS

HATED WITHOUT A CAUSE

If the world hates you, you know that it hated me before it hated you (John 15:18)

READ: JOHN 15:18-25

Hatred is an act of intense displeasure, animosity and hostility against someone, hence the Bible likens it to murder. In Matthew 5:21-22 we read, *"You have heard that it was said to those of old, 'You shall not murder, and whoever murders will be in danger of the judgment.' But I say to you that whoever is angry with his brother without a cause shall be in danger of the judgment. And whoever says to his brother, 'Raca!' shall be in danger of the council. But whoever says, 'You fool! shall be in danger of hell fire.'"* Those were strong words from Christ about hatred.

Our Lord Jesus was hated without a cause by the Jewish religious leaders. They accused Him falsely before Pilate, *"We found this fellow perverting the nation, and forbidding to pay taxes to Caesar, saying that he Himself is Christ, a King."* (Luke 23:2). After questioning Jesus, Pilate declared, *"I find no fault in this Man."* (v4). But, hatred for Jesus made them more resolved and fierce in their accusation (v5). Pilate sent Christ to Herod for trial, in whose jurisdiction Galilee was, since Christ was from Galilee. After examining Jesus, Pilate came out with the verdict: *"I have found no fault with the Man concerning those things of which you accuse Him. No, neither Herod, for I sent you back to him; and indeed nothing deserving death has been done by Him."* (v14-15). In spite of Herod's and Pilate's verdicts of 'not guilty', hatred still motivated the Jewish religious leaders to cry out for Christ's death (v18). The more Pilate wanted to release Jesus on the account of lack of evidence, the more the Jewish leaders "shouted, 'Crucify Him, crucify Him." (v21). Three times Pilate wanted to release Jesus, but each time, hatred drove the Jewish religious leaders to demand His crucifixion. The Mosaic law demanded a fair trial before someone could be put to death (Numbers 35:29-31). But in the case of Jesus, fairness was on trial, because he was hated without a cause (John 15:25).

Reflection: Do you hate or love Jesus Christ?

Word for today: *Those who hate Christ love death.*

CAUTION! EAT WORTHILY

Therefore whoever eats this bread or drinks this cup of the Lord in an unworthy manner will be guilty of the body and blood of the Lord (1 Corinthians 11:27).

READ: 1 CORINTHIANS 11:27-34

No restaurant will dare warn its hungry customers to be careful of what they are eating. Any restaurant that does so will be out of business. The driving force of every restaurant has always been profit, rather than the consequences of what you eat. But, when it comes to the Lord's supper, the opposite is the case. Since God's Kingdom is not about making financial profit, but about preparing souls for eternity, the Bible cautions on how not to eat the Lord's supper. The Lord's supper is a covenant meal between Christ and His followers, instituted prior to His going to the cross (Read Luke 22:14-20). The Lord's supper, otherwise known as the Holy communion, does not guarantee anyone a place in heaven; however, it does demonstrate one's faith and commitment to Christ Jesus. If the eating of Holy communion could guarantee someone a place in heaven, Judas would have been there, because he partook of it with the Lord Jesus. Read what Jesus said about Judas, *"But behold, the hand of my betrayer is with me on the table. And truly the Son of Man goes as it has been determined, but woe to that man by whom He is betrayed!"* (v21-22). Read also John 17:12.

In our text Paul warns, *"Whoever eats this bread or drinks this cup of the Lord in an unworthy manner will be guilty of the body and blood of the Lord." But let a man examine himself, and so let him eat of the bread and drink of the cup* (v27-28).What does it mean to eat in an **unworthy manner? 1.**It means to eat with an unconfessed sin (1 John 1:8-10). **2.** It means to eat with bitterness, anger and hatred within (1 John 3:15). **3.** It means to eat without having a personal relationship with Christ (Read John 1:12; 3:18, 36). Verses 29-30 spell out the consequences of eating the Lord's supper carelessly. Anyone who eats the Lord's supper while meddling with sin digs his of her early grave. Hence, it is important to examine yourself before you participate in the Lord's Supper. Many who neglected the warning of self-examination have died prematurely.

Reflection: How have you been eating? Carefully or carelessly?

Word for today: *Self-examination is crucial while dining with King Jesus.*

WHAT'S WRITTEN IS WRITTEN

"Behold, we are going up to Jerusalem, and all things that are written by the prophets concerning the Son of Man will be accomplished." (Luke 18:31).

READ: JOHN 19:17-24

JESUS OF NAZARETH, THE KING OF THE JEWS: That was the inscription written by Pilate and placed on the cross of Jesus (John 19:19). It was written in the three principal languages of the then world: Hebrew *representing* the Jews, Greek *representing* the Gentiles and Latin *representing* the Roman empire (v20). But, the chief priests took an exception to the inscription by Pilate. Allowing the inscription to stay as it is would lend legitimacy to Christ's claim as the King of the Jews, which He is. So, they approached Pilate with this request, "Do not write, 'The King of the Jews.' but 'He said, 'I am King of the Jews.'" (v21). Pilate's response was prompt and precise, *"What I have written, I have written."* (v22). What Pilate wrote about Christ has already been written in the Scriptures about Him; Pilate was only reiterating the fact. Herod, unknowingly echoed what the Scripture had already written about Christ. Let's consider some of them: **1.** It is written that Christ is the King of the Jews (Isaiah 9:6-7; Matthew 2:2;11). **2.** It is written that Christ is the sacrificial Lamb of God (Isaiah 53:4-6; John 1:29). **3.** It is written that Christ is the Savior of the world (Matthew 1:21). **4.** It is written that Christ's garment would be divided (Psalm 22:18; John 19:23-24). **5.** It is written that Christ's bones would not be broken (Psalm 34:20; John 19:31-33). **6.** It is written that Christ's side would be pierced (Zechariah 12:10; John 19:34). It is written that Christ would be raised from the dead (Psalm 16:10;Matthew 17:23-24).

As we celebrate Good Friday, let's not forget what makes the Friday a good one. The Friday in which Christ was crucified became a good Friday because His death brought salvation to humankind. All that was written about Him were fulfilled to the letter in order to make the Friday in which Christ died a good one. He was conceived of the Holy Spirit, born of a virgin, healed the sick, proclaimed the good news, died, buried and rose triumphantly.

Reflection: Do you know what is written about you in the Scriptures?

Word for today: *What is written in the Scriptures makes us God-dependent.*

VICTORY CELEBRATION

But thanks be to God, who gives us the victory through our Lord Jesus Christ
(1 Corinthians 15:57).

READ: EXODUS 15:1-5

Victory is sweet, but it is expensive! No victory ever comes without a price, either to the victor or the victim. Since victory is sweet, it evokes joyful emotions and calls for celebration. After the miraculous crossing of the Red Sea on foot, the children of Israel celebrated their victory over Pharaoh's army as they watched it sink to the bed of the sea.

The children of Israel celebrated their victory over Pharaoh's army in four ways, as seen in our text.
1. They celebrated with songs of praise to God. Verses 1-2 read, *"Then Moses and the children of Israel sang this song to the LORD, and spoke, saying: "I will sing to the LORD, for He has triumphed gloriously! The horse and its rider He has thrown into the sea! The LORD is my strength and song, and He has become my salvation; He is my God, and I will praise Him; my father's God, and I will exalt Him."* Any celebration that does not glorify God exalts self and Satan. We should sing and praise God in our victory celebration.
2. They celebrated by calling God by His name. Verse 3 reads, *"The LORD is a man of war; the LORD is His name."* If you call God by His name, it shows you are appreciative of who He is.
3. They celebrated by recounting what God had done. They sang, *"Pharaoh's chariots and his army He has cast into the sea; His chosen captains also are drowned in the Red Sea. The depths have covered them; they sank to the bottom like a stone."* (v4-5). It is good to recount what the LORD has done, each time we celebrate the victory He has given us over the forces of darkness. Learn to celebrate the Lord's victory over the powers of Satan in your life, family, marriage, career, education and destiny. The more you celebrate the LORD's victory, the more confident you become, as you look forward to what He would do next (v14-16).

Reflection: To whom do you ascribe your victory and success in life?

Word for today: *Christ paid the utmost price for our victory.*

HE IS RISEN!

"Do not be alarmed. You seek Jesus of Nazareth, who was crucified. He is risen! He is not here. See the place where they laid Him." (Mark 16:6).

READ: MATTHEW 28:1-8

After Christ was buried, as the Bible records the *"chief priests and the Pharisees gathered together to Pilate, saying, 'Sir, we remember while He was still alive, how that deceiver said, 'After three days I will rise.' Therefore, command that the tomb be made secure until the third day, lest His disciples come by night and steal Him away, and say to the people, 'He is risen from the dead.' so the last deception will be worse than the first."* In response to their request, Pilate told them, *"You have a guard; go your way, make it secure as you know how. So they went and made the tomb secure, sealing the stone and setting the guard."* (Matthew 27:62-66). Every effort was made by the Jewish religious leaders to prevent Christ's body from being stolen by His disciples from the tomb, to create the impression that He had risen from the dead. Christ's body was not stolen! If it were stolen, people would have found out where it was buried. In addition, He would not have appeared to numerous people after His resurrection, in His physical body, with all the nail prints on His hands.

On the third day, after His burial, Christ rose triumphantly from dead! Verse 2 of our text reads, *"And behold, there was a great earthquake; for an angel of the Lord descended from heaven, and came and rolled back the stone from the door, and sat on it."* The angel did not raise Christ from the dead; God the Father did. Nor did he roll away the stone from the grave to facilitate Christ's resurrection. The angel was at the tomb to announce Christ's resurrection to His disciples, while the earth quake ushered his arrival. The countenance of the angel "was like lightning, and his clothing as white as snow." (v3). The stone with which the tomb was securely sealed became a stool for the angel of the Lord. The angelic announcement was heart warming, "He is risen! Come and see where the Lord lay." They saw and were joyful.

Reflection: Has Christ risen in your life?

Word for today: *The joy of Easter is that Christ is risen from the dead.*

CONTEND FOR THE FAITH

*For to you it has been granted on behalf of Christ, not only to believe in Him,
but also to suffer for His sake (Philippians 1:29).*

READ: JUDE 1:3-4

There is an ongoing conflict between the Kingdom of God and the kingdom of Satan. The conflict which started from heaven led to Satan's being cast out of heaven. Satan used to be called Lucifer and was one of the archangels of God. He was so beautifully decorated with glory that he was called, "Son of the morning." But, when pride led him to attempt to overthrow God, he was cast out of heaven (Read Isaiah 14:1-15). Ever since Satan and host of demons loyal to him were cast out heaven, Satan has vowed to ruin God's creation, especially human beings created in God's image. The war Satan could not win in heaven, he tries to win by attacking human beings, created in the image of God. He succeeded in doing so through deceiving Adam and Eve to disobey God. In order to counteract Satan's defeat of Adam and Eve, God made an elaborate and lasting plan for the redemption of humankind, by sending His Son, Jesus Christ to bruise the head of Satan on the cross (Read Genesis 3:15). When Christ was born, Satan again made frantic effort to destroy Him through Herod. God was smarter than Herod and his murderous plan. By a divine intervention, infant Jesus was spared the sword of Herod (Read Matthew 2:7-16).

Satan targets the Church of the living God, hence our text enjoins us to contend earnestly for the faith (Jude 1:3). Satan has tried so hard to stop the spread of the gospel. He has also masterminded the killing of the saints for centuries to stamp out Christianity; the burning of the Scriptures to eradicate the Word of God. For centuries, Satan has raised false teachers to adulterate the truth in order to undermine the Word of God. But, in all these, Satan has not succeeded and will never succeed. He knows that he can not win the fight and his days are numbered, so he resorts to attacking the easy targets of God's creation—the human beings, especially the believers in Christ. Contend for the faith on your knees.

Reflection: Do you contend for the faith? Don't be a potato Christian.

Word for today: *Only the violent in spirit can contend for the faith.*

WHAT A FORGIVING FATHER!

Bless the LORD, O my soul, and forget not all His benefits: who forgives all your iniquities, who heals all your diseases (Psalm 103:2-4).

READ: 1 JOHN 1:8-10

Our text reads, *"If we say that we have no sin, we deceive ourselves, and the truth is not in us. If we confess our sins, He is faithful and just to forgive us our sins and to cleanse us from all unrighteousness. If we say that we have not sinned, we make Him a liar, and His word is not in us."* (1 John 1:8-10). There are three fundamental truths about our sinful nature in our text: First, we can not claim to be sinless. To do so will amount to self-deception, because, even on our best days, we are still vulnerable to temptation and sin. Second, God is faithful to forgive and cleanse us of our sins. Third, there is need to confess our sins to God. John addressed his letter to believers in Christ. His letter was aimed at debunking the false doctrine of sinless perfection of his time. Believers are not perfect, but sinners saved by grace. As believers in Christ, our perfection is in Christ Jesus. Faith in Christ does not eradicate our sinful nature; it transforms and liberates our souls from sin domination. By obeying the Word of God, we would not allow sin to dominate us. The more we obey the Word of God, the more we are able to overcome sin.

God is a forgiving Father! Every day, He demonstrates His Omnipotent forgiving power over our sins. The Bible records how the sins of a paralytic, who was conveyed through a roof-top by his friends, were forgiven. Jesus told him, *"Son, your sins are forgiven you."* (Mark 2:1-5). That Jesus first of all forgave the man's sins before healing him underscores the correlation of sin and sickness, although not all sicknesses are associated with sin. The story of the woman caught in adultery gives us some insight into the magnificence of God's forgiveness. From the hands of a mob, Jesus rescued the woman from death, forgave her sins and told her, *"Go and sin no more."* (John 8:11). God is willing to forgive our sins if we confess and resolve not to repeat them.

Reflection: Are there sins that you have been dealing with in your life? Are there bad habits that you cannot overcome?

Word for today: *No sin is ever bigger than God's forgiving power.*

HALMARKS OF AN IDEAL LEADER

And whoever of you desires to be first shall be slave of all (Mark 10:44).

READ: LUKE 22:24-30

The world's view of greatness is totally different from Christ's view of greatness. The world views greatness in terms of acquisition of power and exercise of authority over people, while Jesus views greatness in terms of humility and service to others. Based on the world-view standard, the greater your power, the wider your scope of influence over people. But with Christ, greatness assumes a different meaning. Christ's disciples were not aware of this fact, otherwise, they would not have engaged in an argument as to who was the greatest among them. Verse 24 of our text reads, *"Now there was also a dispute among them, as to which of them should be considered the greatest."* Ironically, while Jesus was faced with the reality of dying, His disciples were busy arguing among themselves who the team leader would be after He had gone. How disappointed they must have been when Christ explained to them what it takes to be a leader. Jesus told them, *"The kings of the Gentiles exercise lordship over them, and those who exercise authority over them are called 'benefactors.' But not so among you; on the contrary, he who is greatest among you, let him be as the younger, and he who governs as he who serves."*

From what Jesus told His disciples, we notice that an ideal leader must imbibe the following character traits:

1. He or she must show respect to others. In the world, those who are lords exercise authority over their subjects. We read, *"The kings of the Gentiles exercise lordship over them, and those who exercise authority over them are called benefactors."* (v25). In Christ, things are different.

2. He or she must labor for others. *"Whoever is "greatest among you, let him be as the younger, and he who governs as he who serves"* (v26).

3. He or she must serve in humility (v27). *"For who is greater, he who sits at the table or he who serves? Is it not he who sits at the table? Yet I am among you as the One who serves."* (v27). As a leader, learn to be humble.

4. He or she must be willing to suffer hardship (v28).

Reflection: What kind of a leader are you at home, at work and in the Church?

Word for today: *Like Christ, an ideal leader leads by example.*

CHRIST'S RESCUE MISSION(CRM)

"God demonstrates His own love toward us, in that while we were still sinners, Christ died for us." (Romans 5:8).

READ: LUKE 19:9-10

In the United States, during a time of disaster, two **"R"** efforts come into play in dealing with the situation. The first is **Rescue** effort. In a Rescue effort, attempt is made to rescue those who are alive, but trapped in a wreckage. At the conclusion of the Rescue effort, comes the recovery effort. In a **Recovery** effort, the bodies of the dead are recovered for family members of the victims. During a Rescue effort, instructions are given by the rescuers to enable the victims come to safety. Failure to heed such instructions makes the rescue effort difficult, dangerous and deadly. The same principle applies to Christ's **Rescue Mission**—to rescue human souls from the bondage of Satan, sin and death. Christ does not engage in a recovery mission; but in a rescue mission, because, according to the Word of God, *"It is appointed for men to die once, but after this the judgment."* (Hebrews 9:27). Christ made the case for the futility of recovery effort clear when He said, *"God is not the God of the dead, but of the living."* (Luke 20:38). Christ came into this world to rescue those who are still alive before they die and go to hell.

In order to be rescued from the bondage of Satan, sin and death, one has to follow the instructions from Christ, the Rescuer, as contained in God's instruction manual called the Bible.
Rescue Instruction #1. Totally surrender to Christ. *"Come unto me all you who labor and are heavy laden"* (Matthew 11:28a). That instruction is from Christ to all those who need to be rescued from Satan, sin and eternal death.
Rescue Instruction #2: Be willing to identify with Christ's suffering. *"Take my yoke upon you."* (v28b). A yoke is a symbol of burden bearing and suffering. Christ's yoke is easy and His burden is light , so identify with it.
Rescue Instruction #3: Be prepared to learn from Christ (v28c). *"Learn from me for I am gentle and lowly in heart..."*. It is by a total surrender to Christ's Lordship that one can be rescued from the bondage of Satan, sin and eternal death.

Reflection: Have you been spiritually rescued by Christ?

Word for today: *Only those rescued by Christ have eternal life.*

IT'S HEART, NOT EYE SERVICE

Bondservants, obey in all things your masters according to the flesh, not with eye service, as men-pleasers, but in sincerity of heart, fearing God (Colossians 3:22).

READ: EPHESIANS 6:5-9

Two parts of the human body play significant role in serving. One is the heart. Every effort you put in serving originates from the heart. If the heart is not willing to serve or receptive to service, it becomes very difficult to accomplish any task. Second is the eye. With the eye you are able to not only see, but evaluate the work you are doing. So, we see that the heart and the eye are very important in whatever service we render, be it secular or ecclesiastical.

Our text warns us against eye service, but encourages us to apply heart service in all that we do. **Eye service** is performing an activity in order to please on-lookers. Simply stated, it is an act of serving to attract attention to self. Many people like to do eye service at their work places, in their homes, and in the house of God. Eye service takes away the focus from Christ to self. Although the service you render in the house of God may not be visible to the human eyes, remember that God who sees in secret will reward you openly and adequately in due time (Matthew 6:3-4). **Heart service** is the service you render wholeheartedly; the duty you perform without seeking to be noticed. Heart service is aimed at pleasing God, while eye service is aimed at pleasing men. It is self-promoting and God-demoting. God is not pleased when we render eye service to Him or to others. Verses 5-7 of our text read, *"Bondservants, be obedient to those who are your masters according to the flesh, with fear and trembling, in sincerity of heart, as to Christ; not with eye service, as men-pleasers, but as bondservants of Christ, doing the will of God from the heart, with goodwill doing service, as to the Lord, and not to men."* As a public servant, do you render eye or heart service to your employers? As a servant of God, do you render heart or eye service in the Church? As an employer, do you offer honest wages to your employees, or do you exploit them for your personal gains?

Reflection: How do you serve the Lord and those around you?

Word for today: *Remember, our heavenly Master sees how we serve.*

WATER THE SEED YOU SOW

"Therefore I also after I heard of your faith in the Lord Jesus and your love for all the saints, do not cease to give thanks for you, making mention of you in my prayers." (Ephesians 1;15-16).

READ: EPHESIANS 1:15-23

T he ancient city of Ephesus was very notorious for its idol worship; chief among their idols was the Roman goddess of fertility, named Diana. Paul's ministry in Ephesus yielded much fruit, for the Holy Spirit swept across the city of Ephesus and there was a tremendous conversion of souls, so much so, that *"many who had practiced magic brought their books together and burned them in the sight of all. And they counted up the value of them and it totaled fifty thousand pieces of silver."* (Acts 19:19). Through Paul's ministry, many souls were emancipated from the worship of Dian and changed to the worship of Jehovah God.

Paul did not abandon the seeds of God's Word which he sowed in people's lives in the city of Ephesus; he continually watered them with prayers. Verses 15-16 of our text read, *"Therefore I also, after I heard of your faith in the Lord Jesus and your love for all the saints, do not cease to give thanks for you, making mention of you in my prayers."* A farmer normally irrigates the farm after seed planting and through proper irrigation, the seeds are able to germinate, grow and bear fruits. The same principle applies to sowing the seed of God's Word in people's heart. God's Word is like a seed; it needs to be watered with prayers after it has been sown. As you sow and water the seed with your payers, God will cause it to germinate and bear much fruits (Read1Corinthian 3:6-8). Paul was specific in his prayers to God for the Ephesian Christians. **First,** he thanked God for their conversion (Ephesians 1: 16). **Second,** he asked God to give them *"the spirit of wisdom and revelation in the knowledge of Him."* (v17). **Third,** he prayed that God would enlighten their spiritual eyes to understand what the hope of their calling was and the riches of God's inheritance in their lives. (v18). **Fourth,** Paul prayed for them to experience the exceeding greatness of God's power (v19).

Reflection: How often do you water the seed you sow with prayers?

Word for today: *A watered seed germinates and grows well.*

THE FOOLISHNESS OF GREED

Not that I speak in regard to need, for I have learned in whatever state I am, to be content (Philippians 4:11).

READ: 1 TIMOTHY 6:6-10

Greed is folly! Writing about the foolishness of greed, Frank Buchman, in his book: *Remaking the world* wrote, *"There is enough in the world for everyone's need, but not enough for everyone's greed."* Laurence J. Peter in his humor had this to say about the greedy, *"As a farmer said, 'I am not greedy, all I want is the next land to mine.'"* So, we see that greed is not the absence of goods, but the inability to control the appetite for more of it; it is lack of contentment for what one has. Our text reads, *"Now godliness with contentment is great gain. For we brought nothing into this world, and it is certain we can carry nothing out. And having food and clothing, with these we shall be content."* (v6-8). The Bible makes it clear that "godliness with contentment is great gain." This means that without godliness, contentment is hard to achieve. Greed is driven by the demon of acquisition. A greedy person can be compared to an insane person. Just like an insane person likes to acquire and surround himself or herself with a lot of things, so does a greedy person love to acquire material things, even when they don't make sense. An insane person loves acquiring things because he or she is mentally sick, while a greedy person loves acquiring things because he or she is spiritually sick.

In our text we notice three reasons why greed is foolishness:
1. Greed is foolishness because material wealth is vanity. No matter how much wealth one acquires, it all ends here. *"For we brought nothing into this world, and it is certain we can carry nothing out."* (v7). Isn't it a sign of foolishness for one to keep acquiring something that one cannot go with on one's journey to eternity? **2. Greed is foolishness because material wealth can ensnare (v9).** Those who are greedy of material wealth "fall (are ensnared) into foolish and harmful lusts." **3. Greed is foolishness because material wealth can lead to sorrow (v10).** Have money, but don't love it.

Reflection: Do you have an insatiable appetite for material wealth?

Word for today: *Only spiritual riches last into eternity.*

TOUCHING THE UNTOUCHABLE

"And the LORD spoke to Moses, saying: 'Command the children of Israel that they put out of the camp every leper…'" (Numbers 5:1-2).

READ: MATTHEW 8:1-4

In the Scriptures, the LORD gave the children of Israel some strict instructions on how to treat a leper. A leper was to be put away from the people. In Leviticus 13:45-46 we read, *"Now the leper on whom the sore is, his clothes shall be torn and his head bare; and he shall cover his mustache, and cry, 'Unclean! Unclean!' He shall be unclean. All the days he has the sore he shall be unclean. He is unclean, and he shall dwell alone; his dwelling shall be outside the camp."* From the above text, we notice that it was incumbent upon a leper to do the following three things: **First,** he was to tear his clothes, bare his head and cover his mustache—all signs of mourning. **Second,** he was to introduce himself to the passersby with a shout, "Unclean! unclean!" wherever he went. The idea was that by introducing himself as unclean, people would avoid coming near the leper. **Third,** he was to stay outside the camp. In other words, he was to live a secluded life. Based on the above restrictions regarding a leper, Naaman would not have qualified for the position of an Army General in Israel, living side by side with people (Read 2 Kings 5:1-4).

During Christ's earthly ministry, the above restrictions on lepers were in place. But, a leper took a bold step to defy such restrictions. Verse 2 of our text reads, *"And behold, a leper came and worshiped Him, saying, 'Lord, if you are willing, you can make me clean.'"* This leper defied every inhibition and came to Jesus for his healing. He was not supposed to do so, but need drove him to Jesus. In response, Jesus did what no one could ever do, *"He put out His hand and touched him, saying, 'I am willing, be cleansed; immediately, his leprosy was cleansed.'"* (v3). Jesus's compassionate touch cleansed and transformed this leper. Just as the leper defied the law of inhibition, came to Jesus by faith and received his physical healing, so must a sinner defy every inhibition of shame and unbelief, and come to Jesus for spiritual healing. Leprosy is like sin. Jesus is willing to touch a sinner, if the sinner is willing to come to Him.

Reflection: Do you have inhibitions in coming to Jesus for soul healing?

Word for today: *Jesus has the compassion to touch the untouchable sinner.*

FOLLOW ME!

Then another of His disciples said to Him, "Lord, let me first go and bury my father."But Jesus said to him, "Follow me, and let the dead bury their own dead." (Matthew 8:21-22).

READ: MATTHEW 4:18-22

Follow me! That was the statement of Jesus to Peter, Andrew, James and John, preceding their call to discipleship. All of these men responded positively by following Jesus. In doing so, they left four things in exchange for something better: **1.** They left their fishing occupation for a vocation. Christ told them, *"I will make you fishers of men"* (Matthew 4:19). Hitherto, the expression "fishers of men" was non-existent. This means that Peter, Andrew, James and John were unfamiliar with their new occupation. Nonetheless, they trusted Jesus and followed Him. **2.** They left their means of livelihood for a Source of livelihood in Christ. By following Christ, they made Him their Source of livelihood. Indeed, once you leave your means of livelihood for the cause of the gospel, Christ becomes your Source of livelihood; He will provide for you (Read Philippians 4:19). **3.** They left their earthly father for a heavenly Father (Matthew 4:21). Following Christ, changes your status—God becomes your Father and you become His child (John 1:12). **4.** They left their friends for the friendly Jesus (Read Luke 12:4; John 15:13-15). In another occasion, Jesus called a tax collector named Matthew with the same statement, "Follow me." (Luke 5:27). In response, Matthew *"left all, rose up and followed Him."* (v28). After Peter's restoration, the last statement from Christ to him was, "Follow me". Christ made this statement earlier to Peter when he was called (Matthew 4:19). After his denial of Christ, it was appropriate to repeat the same statement to Peter after his restoration (John 21:19).

Jesus has made a call to you, "Come to me" (Matthew 11:28). Have you responded to that call? If not, why not? It is only by responding to Christ's call that you will be able to follow Him. Unfortunately, many people claim to be followers of Christ, without first of all, responding to His call for repentance and salvation. Without coming to Jesus, it is impossible to follow Him.

Reflection: Can you place your finger on when you responded to Jesus' call?

Word for today: *Jesus calls no one without a purpose.*

"SO, I PRAYED"

Then the king said to me, "What do you request?" So I prayed to the God of heaven (Nehemiah 2:4).

READ: NEHEMIAH 2:4-8

Prayer should be a part of our daily routine. We should pray when things are tough; we should also pray when things are good. In whatever we do, we should not neglect prayers. We should pray before and after we have eaten. No matter how hungry you may be, don't forget to pray before you pounce on the food. Stories have been told of people who ended up in the hospital, after a meal. Pray before you leave your house; pray when you get to the office, before you start the day's work; pray and thank God whenever you come back from work. As a believer in Christ, learn to pray before you offer any counsel to someone. Some years ago, someone came to me for advice regarding how to handle the sudden death of his sister back in Africa. As I always do, I asked him to close his eyes for prayer before I would say anything. In the course of our prayer, the Holy Spirit ministered to me that he was making up the story of his sister's death in order to collect money from sympathizers. I confronted him about it and he owned up that he was lying. In fact, he had no biological sister alive. He said that he came up with that 'strategy' in order to raise money to meet some financial obligations.

Nehemiah commenced and ended his rebuilding effort with prayers. He poured out his heart in prayer for God to restore His people (Nehemiah 1:4-11). He prayed before giving the king an answer to his question (2:4). Nehemiah's purpose for praying before answering the king was two-fold: First, for God to grant him wisdom and boldness to relate his needs to the king. Second, for God to soften the king's heart in order to obtain favor from the king. How graciously God answered Nehemiah's prayer! The king granted him permission to go and rebuild the broken walls of Jerusalem and provided him the wherewithal to do so (v6-8). Nehemiah prayed against Sanballat's derision, conspiracy and attack against the rebuilding effort (4:7-9; 6:1-9). He prayed against Shemaiah's false prophesy to stall God's work (v10-14).

Reflection: Do you pray before venturing into something?

Word for today: *Taking a leap without praying makes for a terrible landing.*

113

A THREE-FOLD MINISTRY

Then Jesus went about all the cities and villages, teaching in their synagogues, preaching the gospel of the kingdom, and healing every sickness and every disease among the people (Matthew 9:35).

READ: MATTHEW 4:23-25

Luke 4:18 gives us a synopsis of Christ's earthly ministry. It reads, *"The Spirit of the LORD is upon me, because He has anointed me to preach the gospel to the poor; He has sent me to heal the brokenhearted, to proclaim liberty to the captives and recovery of sight to the blind, to set at liberty those who are oppressed; to proclaim the acceptable year of the LORD."* From this text, we notice a three-fold ministry of Christ, each of which was fulfilled before He went to the cross. Prior to the commencement of His earthly ministry, the Spirit of the LORD descended upon Christ at River Jordan, after His water baptism by John the Baptist. We read, *"When He had been baptized, Jesus came up immediately from the water; and behold, the heavens were opened to Him, and He saw the Spirit of God descending like a dove and alighting upon Him. And suddenly a voice came from heaven, saying, 'This is My beloved Son, in whom I am well pleased.'"* (Matthew 3:16-17). In His humanity, Christ was anointed by the Holy Spirit to carry out His three-fold ministry as foretold by prophet Isaiah (Read Isaiah 61:1-2).

Based on our text of Matthew 4:23, Christ's three-fold ministry were as follows: **1. Teaching:** Jesus *"went about teaching in their synagogue."* He taught the multitude about various issues of life, ranging from God's blessedness (Matthew 5:1-10), to persecution for righteousness sake (11-12); living exemplary life (v13-16); fulfilment of the law (v17-20); heart murder (v21-22); forgiveness (v23-26); adultery (v27-28); sacredness of marriage (v31-32); oath taking (v33-37); loving your enemies (v43-48); how to pray (Matthew 6:5-13).
2. Preaching: Jesus *"went about preaching the gospel of the Kingdom."* Preaching of the gospel is central to salvation (Read Matthew 24:14; 28:19-20).
3. Healing: Jesus *"went about healing all kinds of diseases among the people."* Verses 24-25 of our text speak of the scope of such healings.

Reflection: Can you identify your ministry in the Body of Christ?

Word for today: *Follow in the footsteps of Christ's Ministry (John 14:12).*

114

AN ABIDING RELATIONSHIP

If you abide in me, and my words abide in you, you will ask what you desire, and it shall be done for you (John 15:7).

READ: JOHN 15:1-8

The word "Abide" appears seven times in our text: "**Abide** in me"; "Unless it **abides** in the vine"; "Unless you **abide** in me." (v4); "He who **abides** in me" (v5); "If anyone **abides** in me" (v6); "If you **abide** in me and my words **abide** in you" (v7). As a believer in Christ, our Lord Jesus Christ emphasizes the need for you to abide in Him and He in you (John 15:4). **What does it mean to abide in Christ?** According to Nelson's New King James Version Study Bible, "To abide in Christ" means, "to dwell, to stay, to settle in, to sink deeper" in Christ Jesus. Abiding in Christ is tied to fruit-bearing. Verse 4 of our text reads, *"As the branch cannot bear fruit of itself unless it abides in the vine, neither can you, unless you abide in me."* Indeed, if the branch of a vine does not abide in the tree, it cannot bear fruit. The same abiding principle applies to our relationship with Christ. If there is no abiding, there will be no fruit bearing! Have you ever wondered why some people stay in Church for years without bearing any fruit? The reason is that such people have failed to abide in Christ; they abide in the Church, but not in Christ.

How can one abide in Christ? John 15:10 tells us how. *"If you keep my commandments, you will abide in my love, just as I have kept my Father's commandments and abide in His love."* So, we see that abiding in Christ has to do with obeying the Word of God. **What are the benefits of abiding in Christ?** You become fruitful and you receive answers to your prayers (John 15:4,7). **What are the consequences for not abiding in Christ?** Verse 6 of our text has the answer: *"If anyone does not abide in me, he is cast out as a branch and is withered; and they gather them and throw them into the fire, and they are burned."* Anyone who does not abide in Christ Jesus is cast away as was the case with Judas. How does the believer know that Christ abides in him or her? Through the presence of the Holy Spirit (2 Corinthians 1:22; Ephesians 1:13; 4:30).

Reflection: In whom do you abide? And who abides in you?

Word for today: *An* abiding *relationship with Christ enhances fruit-bearing.*

115

TRIAL & PERSECUTION

They will put you out of the synagogues; yes, the time is coming that whoever kills you will think that he offers God service (John 16:2).

READ: 2 TIMOTHY 3:10-13

The words, trial and persecution don't seem to resonate well with the New-age Christianity. Anything, but suffering for Christ's sake is acceptable. Sermons about holiness, purity, love, forgiveness, eternal life, trial and persecution are no longer popular. In their places, sermons geared towards prosperity and how to undo your enemies resonate—filling the pulpits on Sundays and hitting the air waves each day. And how eager people like to hear such sermons. Isn't this the fulfilment of the Scripture which says, *"For the time will come when they will not endure sound doctrine, but according to their own desires, because they have itching ears, they will heap up for themselves teachers; and they will turn their ears away from the truth, and be turned aside to fables."* (2 Timothy 4:3-4). In the early Church, going through trial and persecution was a way of life. As believers in Christ went through trials and persecutions, the Church experienced rapid growth. Trials and persecutions became the fuel that propelled the engine of spreading the gospel. It is said that where trial and persecution abound, soul harvesting also abounds. On the other hand, where trial and persecution are lacking, soul harvesting is also lacking. The Church today lacks passion for soul harvesting due to the absence of trial and persecution.

Trials and persecutions are part of our Christian faith. Our Lord Jesus said it: *"Blessed are you when they revile and persecute you, and say all kinds of evil against you falsely for my sake."* (Matthew 5:11). John 15:20 reads, *"Remember the word that I said to you, 'A servant is not greater than his master.' If they persecuted me, they will also persecute you. If they kept my word, they will keep yours also.'"* As a Christian believer, if you live a life void of trials and persecutions, you need to re-examine your commitment to Christ. You might be compromising with sin or the world. 2 Timothy 3:12 says it all, *"All who desire to live godly in Christ Jesus will suffer persecution."*

Reflection: Are you scared of trials and persecutions for Christ's sake?

Word for today: *Rejoice and be glad over your trials and persecutions.*

BUSINESS-AS-USUAL ATTITUDE

Therefore you shall observe all my statutes and all my judgments, and perform them: I am the LORD (Leviticus 19:37).

READ: LEVITICUS 19:35-37

Business as usual refers to "the normal conduct of business, regardless of current circumstances, especially difficult events, which pose a potential negative impact"; "having things go along as usual." In the Kingdom of God, there is no room for business as usual. This means that when missteps are made, one has to correct such mistakes to prevent any recurrence. It is not uncommon to find people, especially those in business ventures, indulge in bad business practices. Even when caught and punished, they quickly revert to business-as-usual attitude. We also find this kind of behavior among politicians in the developing countries. During electioneering campaigns, they pretend to be angels and promise the people to right the wrongs of their predecessors. But, no sooner they are elected into power, than they revert to business-as-usual attitude of looting the treasury and impoverishing the people. In every business endeavor as well as political activity, God demands honesty; anything less incurs His wrath. Whenever people engage in business-as-usual attitude in acquiring wealth through fraudulent means, they are, in effect, digging their own graves as well as that of their posterity. Dishonest practices of parents linger much longer after they are gone, so, watch how you make your wealth. Ill gotten wealth is a curse! Read what the Scripture says about it, *"Bread gained by deceit is sweet to a man, but afterward his mouth will be filled with gravel."* (Proverbs 20:17).

In our text, God gave the children of Israel specific instructions regarding how to make wealth. The same instructions hold true for everyone. We read, *"You shall do no injustice in judgment, in measurement of length, weight, or volume. You shall have honest scales, honest weights, an honest ephah, and an honest hin: I am the LORD your God, who brought you out of the land of Egypt."* The way we make wealth must be God-honoring.

Reflection: How do you conduct your business—through cheating or bribery?

Word for today: *Heaven is out of bounds to business-as-usual attitude.*

STONY-HEART HEARERS

But be doers of the word, and not hearers only, deceiving yourselves (James 1:22).

READ: MARK 4:5-6, 16-17

Jesus' parable of the sower in our text, speaks of seed that fell on stony ground, *"where it did not have much earth; and immediately it sprang up because it had no depth of earth, but when the sun was up, it was scorched, and because it had no root it withered away."* (Mark 4:5-6). Notice in this text that the seed "sprang up immediately, because it had no depth of earth." In other words, it lacked enough soil to sustain itself. If the seed had enough soil, it wouldn't have sprung up too fast. When a seed is planted on a good soil, it doesn't spring up immediately. Rather, it first of all produces roots which find their way into the soil before sprouting. Otherwise, it is left without any nutrition and is vulnerable to the heat of the sun. That was what happened to the seed that fell on the stony ground in Christ's parable. Since there was not enough soil around it, the seed quickly sprouted without any root in the soil to sustain it. This is typical of temporal believers, who confess Christ when things are good, but deny Him when persecution and hardship arise. Paul associated Dermas with this kind of temporal belief system. In his letter to the Church in Colosse, Paul wrote, *"Luke the beloved physician and Demas greet you."* (Colossians 4:14). But, in his letter to Timothy, Demas was not so commended. We read, *"Demas has forsaken me, having loved this present world, and has departed for Thessalonica."* (2 Timothy 4:10). Demas who was temporal in his belief system, like the seed that fell on the stony ground, couldn't handle trials, sufferings and persecutions for Christ's sake. So, he decided to go back into the world.

In His interpretation of the parable of the sower, Christ likened the seed that fell on the stony ground to someone who *"immediately receives the Word of God with gladness, endures only for a time"*, but stumble due to tribulations and persecutions (Mark 4:15-16). A temporal believer lacks deep spiritual root to withstand trials and persecutions associated with the Christian faith.

Reflection: What kind of a hearer have you been?

Word for today: *Temporal believers don't do well spiritually.*

JOSHUA'S REDEDICATION SERMON

So the people answered and said: "Far be it from us that we should forsake the LORD to serve other gods." (Joshua 24:16).

READ: JOSHUA 24:15-18

Rededication often comes with a recommitment! That was the message Joshua was trying to communicate to the children of Israel prior to his death. The people had not been consistent in their worship of God; they had forgotten how far the LORD had brought them. So, Joshua organized a rededication service in which he preached what sounded like a farewell sermon.

Our text tells us what transpired during the rededication service. Interestingly, the people responded positively to the three **C's** of Joshua's rededication sermon which are as follows:**1. CHOICE:** In his sermon, Joshua stressed the importance of choice. He told the people, *"And if it seems evil to you to serve the LORD, choose for yourselves this day whom you will serve, whether the gods which your fathers served that were on the other side of the river, or the gods of the Amorites, in whose land you dwell. But as for me and my house, we will serve the LORD."* (Joshua 24:15). Joshua made it clear to the people that choice was central to serving God. He told them to choose between serving Jehovah God and the gods of the Amorites, in whose land they dwelt. The people's response was positive, *"Far be it from us that we should forsake the LORD to serve other gods."* (v16). **2. COMMITMENT**: Joshua spoke about the need for commitment, when he told the people, *"You cannot serve the LORD, for He is a holy God. He is a jealous God; He will not forgive your transgressions nor your sins."* (v19) Again, the people's reply was positive: *"No, but we will serve the LORD!"* (v21)
3. CONSECRATION: Joshua told the people, *"Put away the foreign gods which are among you, and incline your heart o the LORD God of Israel."* (v23). In reply, the people said to Joshua, *"The LORD our God we will serve, and His voice we will obey!"* (v24). In order to please God, one has to live a life of consecration to Him (Read Hebrews 12:14; 1 Peter 1:15-16).

Reflection: Have you rededicated your life to Christ?

Word for today: *Recommitment is the product of a rededicated life.*

119

ARE YOU LIVING A DISGUISED LIFE?

And the king of Israel said to Jehoshaphat, "I will disguise myself and go into battle; but you put on your robes." So the king of Israel disguised himself, and they went into battle (2 Chronicles 18:29).

READ: 2 CHRONICLES 18:28-34

Whenever people disguise themselves, they want to hide their identity from others. Sometimes, when criminals want to commit heinous crimes, they mask their faces. In fact, it is not uncommon to see trobbers wear masks over their faces during bank robberies, to avoid detection. King Ahab hated prophet Micaiah, because according to him, he *"never prophesied good concerning him, but always evil."* (2 Chronicles 18:7). As if that wasn't enough, Zedekiah, Ahab's favorite prophet, confronted Micaiah with a dirty slap and said, *"Which way did the spirit from the LORD go from me to speak to you."* (v23). King Ahab commanded that Micaiah be put in prison and subjected to inhumane treatment until he returned from battle in peace. Micaiah, who could not be intimidated, told King Ahab clearly, *"If you ever returned in peace, the LORD has not spoken by me."* (v27).

If God's wrath is upon someone, no amount of disguise will save such an individual. That was what happened to King Ahab. Based on Micaiah's prophetic pronouncement against him, King Ahab decided to disguise himself as he went to the battle field with Jehoshaphat. Even though King Ahab hated Micaiah, he still recognized him as the man of God. In spite of his disguised appearance, God's wrath caught up with Ahab—he was struck and killed in the battle field in fulfilment of Micaiah's prophecy (v33-34). It is unfortunate that just like King Ahab, many disguise themselves in the Church today. They appear like shepherds of the flock, but inside of them are ravening wolves; they mask themselves with holy appearance, but inside of them is rottenness. They talk the talk, but don't walk the walk of a Christian. When people disguise themselves to do things contrary to God's will, they often end up in a disaster. In spite of his good deeds, King Josiah disguised himself in order to fight a war he had no business meddling with and consequently died (2 Chronicles 35:20-25). What a pity!

Reflection: Do you live a disguised life? Do you have a spiritual face mask?

Word for today: *A disguised life leads to disgrace, suffering and death.*

LET GOD PREPARE YOU

But the Lord said to him, "Go, for he is a chosen vessel of mine to bear my name before Gentiles, kings, and the children of Israel." (Acts 9:15)

READ: JEREMIAH 1:1-9

God does not use an unprepared vessel for His work. When He calls; He also prepares. For instance, when God called Abraham, He prepared him to become the father of a great nation by separating him from his heathen family. God told him, *"Get out of your country, from your family and from your father's house."* (Genesis 12:1). Without the separation from his idolatrous family, there was no way Abraham could have been used by God. Prior to making use of Moses, God called and prepared him. From a burning bush, God spoke to him about his calling—to deliver the children of Israel from their Egyptian bondage (Exodus 3:1-10). When God calls, He often prepares you for the task ahead. He may not give you all the details, but He will surely tell you what the calling is all about. When God calls and prepares you, it makes the work of the ministry much easier, fruitful and fulfilling. Unfortunately, some people jump into the bandwagon of ministers of God without being called of God. Most of the time, such people break away from their parent Churches to start their own, out of envy, pride or jealousy. There is nothing wrong in starting a Church; but, there is every thing wrong when it is done for selfish motives and more importantly, without God's calling and approval. Starting a Church or ministry without God's calling and preparation will ultimately meet with a colossal failure. Christ builds His Church, using those whom He has chosen and prepared (Matthew 16:18).

Our text is a good example of how God calls and prepares a vessel for His own use. When God called Jeremiah, He prepared him by touching his mouth to become His mouthpiece to the children of Israel. God also told him what his task would be and the challenges he would face, but promised to be with him (Jeremiah 1: 8,9, 17-19). God may not call you to be a pastor, an evangelist, or a bishop. It is important that you know God's calling in your life, and allow Him to prepare you to fulfill such a calling.

Reflection: Are you called by God? Have you allowed Him to prepare you?

Word for today: *An unprepared vessel is like a painful tooth in the mouth.*

PERSONALIZE THE LYRICS

I will lift up my eyes to the hills—From whence comes my help? My help comes from the LORD, Who made heaven and earth (Psalm 121:1-2).

READ: PSALM 121:1-8

When we read Psalms or sing choruses, it is sometimes good to personalize the lyrics of what we read or sing. In so doing, the lyrics of such a Psalm or chorus become more meaningful and relevant to our needs. For instance, where the lyric has pronouns like, "We", "They", "He" or "She", we replace them with first person singular pronoun "I". This will make the Psalm or chorus more meaningful and personal. Let's take a look at Psalm 91:9-16. In this Psalm, we notice that from v3-13, the writer used the third person pronoun in the nominative and possessive case, such as "you" and "yours" in his sentences. But, from v14-16, he changed the nominative case from, "you" to "he" and the objective case from "you" to "him". The replacement of personal pronouns like "We" You" and "Us" with "I" and "Me" makes a Psalm or a chorus more personal and relevant to one's need. You will no longer be reading or singing in a generalized, but personal manner.

Our text, Psalm 121 is a song of Ascent with very powerful lyrics—sung during the annual "going up" to the great feasts at Jerusalem by the children of Israel (Read Deuteronomy 16:16). The lyrics of Psalm 121 sounds like a prayer, full of personal pronouns like "You" and "Your". But, a personalized version of it will be something like this, which will be more relevant to your needs:
V3 "He will not allow *my* foot to be moved, He who keeps *me* will not slumber.
V5 The LORD is *my* keeper; the LORD is *my* shade at *my* right hand."
V6 The sun shall not strike *me* by day, nor the moon by night."
V7 The LORD shall preserve *me* from all evil; He shall preserve *my* soul.
V8 The LORD shall preserve *my* going out and *my* coming in, from this time forth and even forevermore." Whenever you hear a chorus, you should first of all understand what the lyrics say, then personalize the lyrics as you sing the song, so that they become relevant to your needs. It is unprofitable to sing a chorus or read a Psalm without having the understanding of the lyrics.

Reflection: How personal is your communication with God?

Word for today: *A personalized lyric is like a custom-made good.*

ANXIETY SYNDROME

Anxiety in the heart of man causes depression, but a good word makes it glad (Proverbs 12:25).

READ: PHILIPPIANS 4:4-7

Anxiety is a "state of uneasiness and apprehension." Most of the time, fear, worry, uncertainty, unmet needs, unfulfilled dreams contribute to people becoming anxious. Anxiety is as old as creation. But, God did not create human beings with anxiety; rather, anxiety came about as a result of rebellion against God. When Adam and Eve sinned, the Bible has it that they became afraid and tried to hide from God (Genesis 3:9-10). Ever since, human beings have lived with anxiety syndrome—a syndrome that has been exacerbated due to human quest for material wealth, political power and social recognition. In a fast-paced society in which we live, people are constantly under pressure. As the pressure increases, so does the level of people's anxiety over their lives, jobs and future increase. Over time, such a high level of anxiety leads to mental illness, known as anxiety disorder. In the United States alone, about 40 million adults—18 and older, suffer from anxiety disorder yearly, and it costs the country about 42 billion dollars in terms of treatment.

Knowing the devastation that anxiety could cause, Christ warns against worrying about the issues of life. In Matthew 6:34 we read, *"Therefore, do not worry about tomorrow, for tomorrow will worry about its own things. Sufficient for the day is its own trouble."* Worry does not solve any problem; it makes it worse. Verse 6 of our text warns us against being anxious, *"Be anxious for nothing, but in everything by prayer and supplication, with thanksgiving, let your requests be made known to God."* Based on our text, there are things we need to do in order to avoid anxiety syndrome. **First,** we should learn to rejoice in the Lord (v4). Rejoice in the Lord, not in any other thing. Joy in the Lord dispels anxiety and fear. **Second,** learn to pray over your problems (v6a). Prayer changes situations. **Third,** learn to give God thanks, even when the situation seems dire (v6b). A thankful heart is a joyous heart! When we do the above, the peace of God will guard our hearts against anxiety syndrome (v7).

Reflection: Do you live with anxiety? Christ has a cure for it!

Word for today: *An anxious mind is unstable in whatever it does*

A CONTINUUM OF GOD'S BLESSING

"For I have known him, in order that he may command his children and his household after him, that they keep the way of the LORD—that the LORD may bring to Abraham what He has spoken to him." (Genesis 18:19).

READ: 1 KINGS 3:6-9

God's blessing upon a man's life can impact those around him. For instance, Abraham's personal relationship with God spilled over to Lot, his nephew. When God wanted to destroy Sodom and Gomorrah, God made known His intention to Abraham, which prompted him to plead with God. Abraham's plea for God to spare Sodom was aimed at sparing Lot's life. Eventually, Lot and his family, except his wife, escaped the destruction of Sodom (Read Genesis chapters 18 and 19). Again, God's blessings upon Abraham spilled over to his son, Isaac. Genesis 25:11 reads, *"And it came to pass, after the death of Abraham, that God blessed his son Isaac..."* Furthermore, God's blessing upon David spilled over to his son, Solomon. When David wanted to build a house for God to dwell in, God forbade him from doing so. Instead, God told him, *"When your days are fulfilled and you rest with your fathers, I will set up your seed after you, who will come from your body, and I will establish his kingdom. He shall build a house for my name, and I will establish the throne of his kingdom forever. I will be his Father, and he shall be my son. If he commits iniquity, I will chasten him with the rod of men and with the blows of the sons of men."* (2 Samuel 7:12-14). God's blessings upon king Solomon was a spill over from David. Do you know that God's blessings upon your life can spill over to your children, if they sincerely seek after God?

In our text, we notice how God's blessings came upon King Solomon due to David's faithfulness. We read, *"And Solomon said: 'You have shown great mercy to your servant David my father, because he walked before you in truth, in righteousness, and in uprightness of heart with you; You have continued this great kindness for him, and you have given him a son to sit on his throne, as it is this day.'"* God's anointing upon a leader can also spill over to the led, as was the case of Elijah and Elisha (Read 2 Kings 2:1-15).

Reflection: Do you enjoy a continuum of God's blessings in Christ?

Word for today: *God's blessings abide with those who abide in Christ.*

A WORTHY EPISTLE

You are our epistle written in our hearts, known and read by all men (2 Corinthians 3:2).

READ; 2 CORINTHIANS 3:1-3

Another word for an epistle is, a formal letter, written to an individual or a group of people. Apostle Paul wrote about thirteen of such letters, entitled epistles. Paul used the analogy of an epistle to remind the Corinthian Christians of his ministry and relationship with them. Since an epistle is a visible and readable document, Paul urged them to see the evidence of his ministry among them in that light. In other words, "they didn't need any other letter of commendations" from them, but to rely on the result of his ministry among them to authenticate his apostleship. Verse 2 of our text reads, *"You are our epistle written in our hearts, known and read by all men."* An epistle is usually written on paper, with human hands. But, Paul speaks of an epistle written by God Himself in the human heart, indelible. The Corinthian Christians were Paul's "epistle written in his heart, known and read by all men." In other words, Paul's ministry among them brought about a change in their lives with a glaring evidence that was a matter of public record. In addition, the people were an *"epistle of Christ, not written with ink, but by the Spirit of the living God, not written on tablets of stone but on the tablets of flesh, that is of human heart."* (v3) (See Exodus 24:12)

Paul must have been very honest, loving and devoted to his audience, so much so, that he was willing to present his ministry as an epistle to be read by all. As a believer in Christ, can people read your lifestyle and behavior as an epistle worthy of commendation? Can others see Christ through you? Unfortunately, some Christians represent dead, rather than living epistle to unbelievers through their behavior and conduct. The best way to represent Christ before the world is through our behavior. Some years ago, I saw two women who came out of a Sunday service, trading abuses with each other, in a parking lot. Only God knows what passersby had thought of them, and how much shame they had brought to the name of Christ Jesus.

Reflection: How well do you represent Christ before unbelievers?

Word for today: *Become a worthy epistle of Christ today.*

LIFE'S PRIORITY

"What does the LORD your God require of you, but to fear the LORD your God, to walk in all His ways and to love Him, to serve...with all your heart and with all your soul" (Deuteronomy 10:12).

READ: MATTHEW 6:31-34

Just as our human faces and personalities differ, so do our human needs and priorities differ in life. Some priorities are spiritual and Christ-centered, while others are physical and self-centered. Whatever your priority in life may be, don't lose sight of the most important thing in life—where you will spend eternity. Life is like a journey and like every journey, it has a beginning and an end. Everyone begins his or her journey of life the moment he or she is born into this world. Then, the journey continues into eternity. The destination of one's journey is based on one's choice and priority in life. If one's priority in life is to know Christ and serve God, one will end one's journey in heaven, where Christ is. But, if on the other hand, a person chooses to forsake God, he or she will end up in hell, where Satan is. So, we see that one's priority in life defines one's behavior and consequently determines where one spends eternity.

God has not created anyone without a purpose in life. In other words, there is nothing like a purposeless life. However, the only way to know one's purpose in life is to align oneself with the Giver of life. Just like an airplane needs guidance in the air to get to its destination, so does one's life need God's guidance in order to reach one's potential and fulfil God's purpose in one's life. Life is meaningless without God's guidance. Any wonder why some people without Christ hate others and themselves and then commit suicide as a way of exiting the world that had welcomed them the day they were born? Our Lord Jesus stressed the need for us to get life's priority right. He warns, *"Seek you first the Kingdom of God and His righteousness, and all these things will be added to you."* (Matthew 6:33). God's Kingdom should be our priority in life; every other thing is an addition. **Ecclesiastes 12:13** sums up the issues of life very well, *"Fear God and keep His commandments, for this is man's all."*

Reflection: What are your priorities in life? Are they temporal or eternal?

Word for today: *A life void of good priority makes living purposeless.*

AVENGE NOT!

But I say to you, love your enemies, bless those who curse you, do good to those who hate you, and pray for those who spitefully use you and persecute you (Matthew 5:44).

READ: ROMANS 12:14-21

There is a saying that is very popular among unbelievers. It goes like this: *"If you do me evil and I do you evil, God will not be angry."* Some people prefix this statement with, "God says", making it sound like it is a quotation from the Bible. This saying which has a retaliatory tone is not in the Bible; it comes for the pit of hell. There is no where in the Bible that God says we should retaliate or seek revenge against those who have wronged us. In fact, the opposite is the case. Christ says, *"But I say to you, love your enemies, bless those who curse you, do good to those who hate you, and pray for those who spitefully use you and persecute you."* Matthew 5:44).

In our text, Paul reminds believers in Christ to avoid the sin of vengefulness. Based on our text, there are seven ways we should react to our enemies or those who persecute us:
1. We should bless them (v14b). This means we should wish them well, not evil. **2. We should not curse them** (v14b). This means that we should not wish them evil, but good. **3. We should repay no evil for evil** (v17a). This means that we should not be vengeful. Indeed, "repaying evil for evil makes us partakers of evil." **4. We should have regard for good things** (v17b). This means that we should seek after godliness and do what is right, even when no one is watching us. **5. We should live peacefully with others** (v18). This means that we should do everything within us to live in peace with those who hate us. **6. We should not be vengeful** (v19). This means that we should not be on the lookout for an opportunity to even scores with those who have wronged us. 7. **We should overcome evil with good** (v21). This means that each evil deed meted to us should be overcome with good deed from us. God has promised to take care of those who hate, persecute and treat us with evil. Let God avenge for us! Doing otherwise makes us disobedient to God's Word.

Reflection: Do you live a vengeful life? If so, ask God for forgiveness.

Word for today: *A vengeful heart wears an evil hat.*

KNOWN BY THEIR FRUITS

A good tree cannot bear bad fruit, nor can a bad tree bear good fruit (Matthew 7:18).

READ: MATTHEW 7:15-20

An apple fruit, they say, doesn't fall far away from an apple tree. In other words, it is easy to tell the kind of fruit a tree bears. While physically on earth, our Lord Jesus Christ warned His audience against false prophets. Verse 15 of our text reads, *"Beware of false prophets, who come to you in sheep's clothing, but inwardly they are ravenous wolves."* Christ's warning is still very relevant today. There are false prophets all over the place, who put on the outer garments of holiness, but inwardly, they are ravenous wolves of greed and falsehood—agents of Satan. Some years ago, a Christian brother was very much troubled by some bad news from a so-called man of God. After reviewing the contents of the message and weighing them against the Word of God, I noticed a lot of inconsistencies. God cannot contradict Himself. Any prophecy that contradicts the Bible is not from God. So, after some prayers, I encouraged the brother to trash the message from the so-called man of God and move on. Already the relatives of this brother were beginning to get worried over the contents of the message. Many years have passed and not one of the messages from the so-called man of God has come to pass, because they are not from God.

Our Lord Jesus Christ tells us how to identify false prophets. We read, *"You will know them by their fruits. Do men gather grapes from thorn bushes or figs from thistles? Even so, every good tree bears good fruit, but a bad tree bears bad fruit. A good tree cannot bear bad fruit, nor can a bad tree bear good fruit. Every tree that does not bear good fruit is cut down and thrown into the fire. Therefore by their fruits you will know them."* **Fruit** is a "Jewish metaphor for character and conduct." So, one way to identify a false prophet is through his character and conduct. **Fruit** also means doctrine. When a false prophet dishes out false doctrines, such doctrines become the fruits he bears. Therefore, "a good tree (good prophet) cannot bear bad fruit, nor can a bad tree (false prophet) bear good fruit." **Character** and **doctrine** define who a false prophet is.

Reflection: What is the source of your doctrine?

Word for today: *False doctrines often produce fake prophets. Beware!*

128

MAY

DEVOTIONALS

NOT FORGOTTEN!

So God heard their groaning, and God remembered His covenant with Abraham, with Isaac, and with Jacob (Exodus 2:24).

READ: GENESIS 19:27-29

The lyrics of a popular Christian song by Israel Houghton is quite uplifting and encouraging. It reads, *"I'm not forgotten, I'm not forgotten, God knows my name"* Indeed, God knows your name and therefore, you cannot be forgotten! God can remember you for good or for bad. After four hundred years of Egyptian slavery, the LORD remembered the children of Israel for good and sent Moses to deliver them (Read Exodus 3:7-9). He had earlier told Abraham that his descendants would be in a foreign land and that they would be afflicted for four hundred years, and thereafter, He would judge the nation responsible for their afflictions, before delivering them (Read Genesis 15:13-14). God allowed the children of Israel to undergo afflictions for that length of time, because the *"iniquity of the Amorites,* whose land they were to occupy *was not yet complete"* (v15). God is patient and loving. He gives a sinner enough time to repent and turn away from his sins, after which He rains down His judgment. God did not forget Rachel, in her state of barrenness. The Bible records that *"God remembered Rachel and listened to her and opened her womb."* (Genesis 30:22). God also remembered Hannah after a long period of barrenness (1 Samuel 1:19-20).

In a negative way, God remembered the sins of the people of Amalek and sent king Saul to destroy them (Read 1Samuel15:1-5). God always remembers! Verse 29 of our text reads, *"And it came to pass, when God destroyed the cities of the plain, that God remembered Abraham, and sent Lot out of the midst of the overthrow, when He overthrew the cities in which Lot had dwelt."* God did not forget Abraham and as a result, He delivered Lot from the cities doomed for destruction (v29). As long as you are in good relationship with the LORD, He will always remember you and your family members for good; He will not allow anything that will harm or hurt you come your way. After the deluge, God remembered Noah and delivered from him the floating ark (Genesis 8:1).

Reflection: Are you going through tough times? God knows it all.

Word for today: *Don't forget God; He has not forgotten you.*

SANCTIFICATION

As you sent me into the world, I also have sent them into the world. And for their sakes I sanctify myself, that they also may be sanctified by the truth (John 17:18-19).

READ: 1 THESSALONIANS 4:1-8

The word, **Sanctification**, is derived from the Greek word, *Hagaizo* meaning, "to separate from profane and defile state to pure and holy use"; "to consecrate self wholly to God and His service." Different ideas and interpretations have been given to the word, Sanctification. Some have interpreted it to mean sinless perfection; while others have refused to accept the idea that a human being can be sanctified.

In Biblical context, what is Sanctification? In order to define Sanctification, it is very important that we know what Sanctification is not.

What Sanctification is not:
Sanctification is not based on physical appearance
Sanctification is not based on what or how you eat
Sanctification is not based on the kind of clothes you put on
Sanctification is not a one time experience.
Sanctification is not achieved by how much time you spend praying.
Sanctification is not based on the number of spiritual gifts you posses.

What Sanctification is:
Sanctification is a progressive spiritual experience in a believer, which takes place as he or she walks with God and yields in obedience to God's Word. This means that sanctification is progressive in nature; it is not a one time experience.

Instruments of sanctification:
1. The Word of God. A daily intake and obedience to the Word of God help to sanctify the believer in Christ (John 17:17; Ephesians 5;26; 1 Timothy 4:4-5) **2. Faith in Christ** (Acts 26:18). **3. The Holy Spirit** (Romans 15:16; 1 Peter 1:2). **4. The blood of Jesus Christ** (Hebrews 10:29). **5. God Himself** (Jude 1). God wants His children to live sanctified lives.

Reflection: Are you living a sanctified life for Christ?

Word for today: *Salvation is a gift; sanctification its evidence.*

MYSTERY OF DEATH REVEALED

"The LORD God commanded the man....of every tree of the garden you may freely eat; but of the tree of the knowledge of good and evil you shall not eat, for in the day that you eat of it you shall surely die." (Genesis 2:16-17).

READ: HEBREWS 9:27-28

Death is a subject no one likes to talk about; yet it is something everyone has to face. Verse 27 of our text reads, *"And as it is appointed for men to die once, but after this the judgment."* So, we see that death is an appointment every human being has to keep. Death is a mystery! A mystery is something that defies human knowledge and understanding. Death came into being as a result of man's disobedience to God's Word. God had commanded Adam, *"Of every tree of the garden you may freely eat; but of the tree of the knowledge of good and evil you shall not eat, for in the day that you eat of it you shall surely die."* (Genesis 2:16-17). So, when Adam disobeyed God's command, death set in. Whenever and wherever death occurs, it brings with it sorrow, anguish, pain and sadness. Right from the day Adam sinned, death has remained a mystery. But, all that changed with Christ's advent. Christ, who came from heaven to earth, died and rose from the dead has given us some insight into what death looks like.

In His revelation about death, our Lord Jesus Christ told a story of what took place between two sets of people—the rich and poor man—in relation to death (Read Luke 16:19-31). From Christ's story you will notice at least five-fold truths about death. **1. There is life after death** (Luke 16:22). Death is not annihilation of life, but a transformation of life into a spiritual plane. In other words, life continues after death. **2. There is a destination after death** (v23). The rich man was in hell, while Lazarus was in paradise—a place of rest for believers in Christ. Note: The rich man did not go to hell because he was rich, but, because he did not have God in his life. **3. There is joy or pain after death** (v24-25). Lazarus and the rich man had different experiences after death. **4.There is no crossing over after death** (v26). **5. There is no repentance after death** (v27-29). Repentance takes place prior to death.

Reflection: You have known what happens after death; check your life.

Word for today: *The mystery of death is revealed in Christ.*

DIVINE INTERVENTION

So they said, "Has the LORD indeed spoken only through Moses? Has He not spoken through us also?" And the LORD heard it (Numbers 12:2).

READ: DANIEL 6:18-23

When God decides to intervene on your behalf, those who are after you will be in big trouble. On two occasions, God intervened on behalf of Moses. First, He intervened when Aaron and Miriam— Moses' siblings spoke against Moses. They told Moses, *"Has the LORD indeed spoken only through Moses? Has He not spoken through us also."* And *the LORD hear it* (Numbers 12:2). The statement of Aaron and Miriam borders on spite towards Moses and pride about themselves. Interestingly, God heard what they said about Moses and decided to intervene. Do you know that as a Christian leader, God hears every false accusation and spiteful statement made against you? At the appropriate time, He will intervene. When God intervened on behalf of Moses, Miriam paid dearly for it—she became leprous (v9-10). On another occasion, God intervened on behalf of Moses, when Korah, Dathan and Abiram organized a group of two hundred and fifty leaders in Israel to rebel against Moses and Aaron. They said to Moses, *"You take too much upon yourselves, for all the congregation is holy, every one of them, and the LORD is among them. Why then do you exalt yourselves above the assembly of the LORD?"* (Numbers 16:3). Moses, a man *"who was very humble, more than all men who were on the face of the earth"* was completely devastated, disappointed, distraught and fell down on his face. (12:3, 16:4). Due to God's intervention, Korah and his company were buried alive (Read Numbers 16:20-35).

In our text, we notice how God intervened on behalf of Daniel by delivering him from the lion's den. When God intervenes on your behalf, four things will happen: **First,** you will have testimony to give, like Daniel did (v21-22). Daniel testified to God's goodness. **Second,** your enemies will be surprised at what God has done (v23). **Third,** your enemies will become the victims of their plot against you (v24). **Fourth,** God's name will be glorified (v25-27). **Fifth,** prosperity will become your portion (v28). Just like Daniel, you will prosper.

Reflection: Can you remember when God intervened on your behalf?

Word for today: *When God intervenes, the impossible becomes possible.*

A MEASURED LIFE SPAN

LORD, make me to know my end, and what is the measure of my days, that I may know how frail I am (Psalm 39:4)

READ: PSALM 90:10-12

Everyone in this world has a measured life span, called Age—Aggregate Growth Expectancy. Prior to the deluge, the Aggregate Growth Expectancy of people used to be really long. For instance, Adam lived nine hundred and thirty years (Genesis 5:5), Methuselah lived nine hundred and sixty-nine years (v27). Indeed, the Average Life Expectancy of people prior to the deluge was about nine hundred years. But, all that changed due to man's evil ways. God reduced the human Life Expectancy to one hundred and twenty (120) years. Genesis 6:3 reads, *"And the LORD said, 'my Spirit shall not strive with man forever, for he is indeed flesh; yet his days shall be one hundred and twenty years."* So, we notice how sin has drastically reduced the human life span from nine hundred to one hundred and twenty years.

Still, man's rebellion against God continued—which caused God to further reduce human life span to seventy years. Verse 10 of our text reads, *"The days of our lives are seventy years; and if by reason of strength they are eighty years, yet their boast is only labor and sorrow; for it is soon cut off, and we fly away."* You can see that you and I live a measured life—with an Aggregate Growth Expectancy of seventy years. Understandably, with strength and the benefits of medical science, people can add twenty to thirty years to their life expectancy. This is good, but that notwithstanding, we all still live under a measured-life-span curse. Hence the writer of our text prayed, *"[LORD], teach us to number our days, that we may gain a heart of wisdom."* (v12). The understanding that God has apportioned to each of us a specific life span should make us have some wisdom as how to live. Like David we should learn to pray, *"LORD, make me to know my end, and what is the measure of my days, that I may know how frail I am."* (Psalm 39:4). May God grant us the grace to know how frail and measured our lives are, because *"certainly, everyman at his best state is but vapor."* (v5).

Reflection: How do you live your life—for God or for worldly pleasure?

Word for today: *Life is like vapor, commit it to God.*

SOUGHT, FOUND & FOLLOWED

Then they came to Philip, who was from Bethsaida of Galilee, and asked him, saying, "Sir, we wish to see Jesus." (John 12:21).

READ: JOHN 1:35-42

One of the last pieces of advice from king David to Solomon concerning how to walk with God reads as follows, *"If you seek Him, He will be found by you; but if you forsake Him, He will cast you off forever."* (1 Chronicles 28:9b). What does it mean to seek God? It means to have a passion to serve God in obedience to His Word. God wants us to seek after Him. Jeremiah 29:13 records God's statement to the children of Israel during their captivity relative to how He could be sought. We read, *"And you will seek me and find me, when you search for me <u>with all your heart.</u>"* Again, in Deuteronomy 4:29 we read, *"But from there you will seek the LORD your God, and you will find Him if you seek Him <u>with all your heart and with all your soul.</u>"* So, we see that the issue of seeking after God lies with heart attitude. We must seek God with all our hearts and souls. God does not accept a lip-service or a divided loyalty. Our commitment to God must be total. Indeed, if we seek after God with our whole hearts, we will find Him.

In the New testament, Christ reiterated the need for us to have the desire to seek after God, when He told His audience to seek first the Kingdom of God and His righteousness, and all things that pertain to life will be added to them (Matthew 6:33). Christ's statement runs true today. In deed, all those who sincerely seek the Lord will find Him; the incident recorded in our text being a classic example. John the Baptist, on seeing Jesus passing by, told his audience *"Behold, the Lamb of God!"* (v36). When two of John's disciples heard it, they left him and followed Jesus. John testified that he was not even worthy to loose the straps of Jesus' sandals (John 1:27). Jesus accepted the two disciples of John who demanded to know where He was staying. He took them in and they stayed with Him that day (v38-39). Andrew, one of the two disciples, went and told his brother Simon and took him to Jesus. Any wonder why they left all and followed Jesus when they were eventually called? (Matthew 4:18-20).

Reflection: Have you found Jesus and what have you left to follow Him?

Word for today: *Seek after Christ and you will find Him.*

HE'S FROM ABOVE

And He said to them, "You are from beneath; I am from above. You are of this world; I am not of this world." (John 8:23).

READ: JOHN 3:31-36

Verse 31 of our text reads, *"He who comes from above is above all; he who is of the earth is earthly and speaks of the earth. He who comes from heaven is above all.."* John speaks of two distinct places of origin. **Above**—meaning heaven, and Earth. He referred to heaven as Christ's place of origin, and the earth as man's place of origin. In addition, he testified to Christ preeminence and superiority over himself, when said, "He [Christ] must increase, but I must decrease." (v30). Christ Himself confirmed John's testimony about Him, when He told the unbelieving Jews, *"You are from beneath; I am from above. You are of this world; I am not of this world."* (John 8:23). Since Christ is from above, He only can tell us what goes on in heaven. Hence, during His conversation with Nicodemus, Christ told him, *"Most assuredly, I say to you, We speak what We know and testify what we have seen, and you do not receive our witness. If I have told you earthly things and you do not believe, how will you believe if I tell you heavenly things? No one has ascended to heaven but He who came down from heaven, that is, the Son of Man who is in heaven."* (John 3:11-13). Christ made it clear to Nicodemus about His place of origin—heaven. In another occasion, Christ told the Jews about Himself and His place of origin, *"I am the living bread which came down from heaven. If anyone eats of this bread, he will live forever; and the bread that I shall give is my flesh, which I shall give for the life of the world."* (John 6:51). Since Christ is from above, He makes those who believe in Him to be born again from above.

Christ came down from heaven as the last Adam: He came to undo the damage done by the first Adam. Just as Adam "was a living being" because he was earthly; so was Christ a "life-giving Spirit." because He was from heaven (1 Corinthians 15:45,47). Today, Christ is in heaven and all those who believe in Him will be in heaven with Him on the resurrection day (John 17:24).

Reflection: Do you want to be in heaven? Seek after heavenly things.

Word for today: *Christ who is from above, is above all.*

137

AN UNEARNED INHERITANCE

"Now as He was going out on the road...one asked Him, 'Good Teacher, what shall I do that I may inherit eternal life?'" (Mark 10:17).

READ: MARK 10:17-22

Anything that is earned is invariably something for which one must have worked so hard. For instance, when people go to work, they earn wages or salaries. But, when they stop working, they stop earning wages or salaries. Furthermore, when someone pursues an academic study in the University, he or she ends up earning a degree. Thank God that in salvation, things are different! One doesn't have to work at all to earn salvation; Salvation is free! In Ephesians 2:8-9 we read, *"For by grace you have been saved through faith, and that not of yourselves; it is the gift of God, not of works, lest anyone should boast."* In spite of the fact that salvation is free, a lot of people spend time trying to work for it. This is probably due to the fact that after the fall of Adam and Eve in the Garden of Eden, human beings have always tried to work their way back to God. When Adam and Eve sinned, they worked so hard to correct their mistakes in order to look good before God. In doing so, the Bible records that they sowed fig leaves to cover their nakedness (Genesis 3:7). The human race is a fallen race, due to Adam's sin. As a fallen race, it cannot help itself, how much more working its way back to God. As a result of humankind's fallen condition, God sent His Son—Jesus Christ to redeem it (Luke 19:10).

The story contained in our text illustrates the futility of trying to work for one's salvation. A young man approached Jesus with this question, *"Good Teacher, what must I do that I may inherit eternal life."* (Mark 10:17b). Since this guy wanted to earn his salvation, Christ told him what he needed to do: *"Go your way, sell whatever you have and give to the poor, and you will have treasure in heaven; come, take up the cross, and follow me."* (v21). Jesus gave him a four-fold command that doesn't go well with the ungodly rich. **1.** Sell all you have. **2.** Donate the proceeds to the poor. **3.** Carry your cross. **4.** Follow me. This guy failed Christ's test of self-righteousness —went away sad and sorrowful

Reflection: Do you work so hard to be saved? You don't need to; just believe.

Word for today: *Salvation is a free gift from God; it is not earned.*

DON'T GET HOOKED UP!

"You shall make no covenant with them...nor shall you make marriages with them" (Deuteronomy 7:2-3).

READ: GENESIS 24:1-9

When God called Abraham, He asked him to get out of his country and from his family and his father's house (Genesis 12:1). The purpose of asking Abraham to come out of his kindred, was to bless him and to bless the families of the earth through him (v2-3). By calling out Abraham from his heathen family, God started painting a picture of the Church— the called out ones from the world. At the fullness of time, God sent Jesus Christ to complete the picture that He started painting when He called Abraham (Read Galatians 4:4).

A time came when Isaac was ready to marry. So, Abraham made all necessary arrangements to ensure that Isaac did not get hooked up in marriage with the heathen nations around him. Our text reads, *"So Abraham said to the oldest servant of his house, who ruled over all that he had, 'Please, put your hand under my thigh, and I will make you swear by the LORD, the God of heaven and the God of the earth, that you will not take a wife for my son from the daughters of the Canaanites, among whom I dwell; but you shall go to my country and to my family, and take a wife for my son Isaac.'"* (Genesis 24:2-4). By making his servant swear under oath, Abraham was trying to accomplish three things. **First,** he was trying to ensure that Isaac did not marry a heathen woman. Marrying a heathen woman would have caused Isaac some problems down the road. What happened to king Solomon would have happened to him (Read 1 Kings 11:1-8). **Second,** Abraham was trying to ensure that Isaac did not return to the land of Ur of the Chaldeans, from where God brought him out. **Third,** Abraham was trying to ensure that Isaac, had a godly family. Even though Abraham wanted to connect to his roots, by getting a wife for Isaac from there, he definitely did not want Isaac to abandon God's call in his life. Two spiritual lessons from our text: **1.** Don't get hooked up in marriage with an unbeliever. **2** Don't go back to the world, from where God had called you out.

Reflection: Have you been saved? Don't go back!

Word for today: *The saved don't get hooked up with the unsaved.*

A MOTHER'S GREATEST GIFT

Train up a child in the way he should go, and when he is old he will not depart from it (Proverbs 22:6).

READ: 2 TIMOTHY 1:1-7

A mother's greatest gift to her child is pointing the child to God and bringing him or her to the knowledge of Christ Jesus. This means that such a mother would have known the Lord Jesus Christ herself. A material gift will perish, but the gift of salvation to a child will last forever. Timothy was a young adult, whose grandmother's and mother's faith impacted his life. Timothy's grandmother, Lois and her daughter Eunice were Jewish, while his father was Greek (Acts 16:1). Lois and Eunice may have gotten converted to Christianity, through Paul's ministry in Lystra. Their strong Christian faith impacted the life of Timothy, so much so, that Timothy was *"well spoken of by the brethren who were in Lystra and Iconium."* As a result, Paul was willing to take him along on his missionary journey (v2,3).

As a Christian mother or grandmother, ask yourself these questions: ***What spiritual impact have I made in my children or grandchildren? What will be my legacy in their lives?*** As you celebrate mother's day today, endeavor to help in molding the character of your children. Learn to inculcate in them Christian virtues and values as Timothy's mother and grandmother did. Raise them up in the fear of the Lord. That will be the greatest gift you can ever give them to enable them successfully navigate through this crooked and adulterous world. Consider these seven **"P"** values as you do so: **1.** Have a **principle**. Teach them the principles of God's Word. **2.** Show them a **pattern** to follow. Children need direction. 3. Be **persistent** in your approach. Firmness and fairness are the best ways to train up a child. **4.** Try to **participate** in what they do. Be involved in their daily lives. **5.** Learn to **praise** them when they do well. Children like to be appreciated. **6. Pray** with them and teach them how to pray. **7.** Have a **plan** to make them succeed in life. May God grant you the grace and courage to impact your children with Christian values. Happy Mother's day!

Reflection: Can you reflect on the impact you have made on your children?

Word for today: *The gift of salvation is the greatest gift in life.*

WEEP BEFORE HIM IN PRAYER

I cry out to the LORD with my voice; with my voice to the LORD I make my supplication (Psalm 142:1).

READ: 1 SAMUEL 1:8-11

Need calls for prayer, but Burden prompts weeping in prayer. Whenever the soul is burdened and overwhelmed, the right person to turn to should be the LORD. Unfortunately, this is not always the case. When people are overwhelmed with problems, instead of crying out to God, they cry out to individuals, who also have their own problems.

Prayers offered from a burdened heart is hardly ignored by God; Hannah was a good example. She had been taunted by Peninnah, her colleague over her barrenness for years. Peninnah *"provoked her severely to make her miserable, because the LORD had closed her womb."* (1 Samuel 1:6). But one day, Hannah decided to do something different. She had been praying, but this time, she decided to do what she had never done before—she cried and wept before the LORD. The Bible records that, *"she was in bitterness of soul and prayed to the LORD and wept in anguish."* (v10). Hannah's 'weeping-prayer' ascended to the throne of God and she got results. Even though Hannah did not cry out aloud, God saw the anguish in her soul and answered her prayer by giving her Samuel. Many years ago, a beloved Christian sister faced the same dilemma that Hannah went through. She was barren for many years. Many men of God, including pastors and evangelists had prayed over her for the fruit of the womb, but to no avail. But, one afternoon, this Christian sister locked herself up in her room, spent sometime praying and weeping before the LORD over her condition. According to her, she wept for over an hour before the LORD— praying that the LORD would remove her shame. By her next menstrual circle, she noticed that she was pregnant. Nine months later, she gave birth to a bouncing baby boy, who is now an adult. Sometimes, God answers our prayers directly based on our open-heartedness towards Him. Our 'weeping-prayer' touches the heart of our gracious God.

Reflection: Are you going through tough times? Weep before Him in prayer.

Word for today: *A burdened heart prayerfully weeps before the LORD.*

FAITH CONTENDERS

And from the days of John the Baptist until now the kingdom of heaven suffers violence, and the violent take it by force (Matthew 11:12)

READ: JUDE 1:3-4

Jude, the author of the epistle of Jude, was the half-brother of the Lord. He deliberately avoided a personal identification with Christ Jesus, possibly, due to the superstitions surrounding the 'holy family', in the years following Christ's resurrection. Rather, Jude chose to mention James as his brother, instead of the Lord to avoid attracting the attention. The purpose of Jude's letter was to warn the believers in Christ against false teachers and prophets. In so doing, he reminded them of the need *'to contend earnestly for the faith which was once for all delivered to the saints."* (v3). The word **contend** means "to defend", "fight against" and "protect." According to The Life Application Bible, "All Christians should stand ready to defend the faith as they would defend any prized possession." This means that the truth of the Bible must not be compromised, twisted or manipulated.

What does it take to contend earnestly for the faith? It takes four important things:
1. Sound Bible doctrine. The knowledge of, intake of and abiding in sound Bible doctrine are crucial in contending for the faith. The devil uses false teachers and doctrines to attack the Christian faith and anyone who is not grounded in the truth of God's Word cannot earnestly contend for the faith.
2. Faith
Having faith in Christ Jesus means believing everything the Bible says about Him. If you decide to choose and pick what you want to believe about Christ, you will expose yourself to the danger of false teachers.
3. Courage.
Courage is not the absence of danger, but the ability to withstand it. Remember, *"God has not given us a spirit of fear, but of power and of love and of a sound mind."* (2 Timothy 1:7).
4. Prayerfulness. Prayer connects you to God—the Source of all power.

Reflection: Do you contend for the faith and how strong is your faith?

Word for today: *Faith contenders are usually well grounded in faith.*

GIFTED FOR SERVICE

But the manifestation of the Spirit is given to each one for the profit of all (1 Corinthians 12:7).

READ: ROMANS 12:3-8

Serving the Lord is likened to a musical band, in which everyone is gifted to play his instrument to produce a melodious tune. Though the players play different instruments, the purpose is one—to produce sweet, harmonious melody. Just like every instrument is important to a musical band, so is everyone important in the body of Christ. In the same vein, no one should consider himself more important than others as we serve . According to apostle Paul, no one *"should think himself more highly than he ought to think, but to think soberly, as God has dealt to each one a measure of faith."* (1 Corinthians 12:3). Our giftedness should humble us, rather than puff us up. We are what we are through God's grace (v6).

Apart from the nine Spiritual gifts mentioned in 1 Corinthians 12:1-11, our text contains additional seven gifts for service in the body of Christ. **1. Gift of Prophecy**—the ability to speak with insight through the guidance of the Holy Spirit. Those with the gift of prophecy should prophesy in proportion to their faith. In other words, every prophetic utterance must be true and in accordance to the tenets of the Christian faith. **2. Gift of Ministry.** Another word for ministry is **serving**. This is the ability to serve in the body of Christ. Regarding the gift of ministry or serving, one should use it where and when needed. **3. Gift of Teaching**. This gift refers to the gift of teaching God's Word; it has nothing to do with academic scholarship. **4. Gift of Exhortation.** The word exhortation means **encouragement** . Some Christians are not good in teaching God's word, but very good in exhorting and motivating others to action. **5. Gift of giving**—contributing to the needs of others. There are those who like to give, not because they have more than enough, but because they like to give to meet the needs of others. **6. Gift of leadership**—supernatural ability to organize and manage things. **7. Gift of showing mercy**—the ability to see others through suffering. The exercise of these gifts demand thoroughness and humility.

Reflection: Are you gifted? Do you use the gifts in serving God?

Word for today: *Spiritual gifts are for service, not for show.*

DEMONSTRATING GOD'S POWER

"My speech and my preaching were not with persuasive words...but in demonstration of the Spirit and of power, that your faith should not be in the wisdom of men but in the power of God." (1 Corinthians 2:4-5).

READ: 1 CORINTHIANS 4:18-21

In 2 Chronicles 16:9a we read, *"For the eyes of the LORD run to and fro throughout the whole earth, to show Himself strong on behalf of those whose heart is loyal to Him..."* These were the words of Hanani, the seer, to king Asa of Judah for relying on the king of Syria, instead of trusting in the LORD for military victory (v7). Indeed, God likes to demonstrate His power through his people. For instance, God demonstrated His power to Pharaoh through His servant Moses. When approached by Moses to let the children of Israel go, Pharaoh specifically asked for some demonstration of power from Moses to convince him to agree to his demand. Exodus 7:9 reads, *"When Pharaoh speaks to you, saying, 'Show a miracle for yourselves,' then you shall say to Aaron, 'Take your rod and cast it before Pharaoh, and let it become a serpent.'"* In obedience to God's command, when Aaron threw down *"his rod before Pharaoh and his servants, it became a snake."* (v10). Pharaoh called on his magicians who through enchantments produced their own snakes by throwing down their rods. Snakes don't usually swallow themselves alive, but in this particular case, something unusual happened: Aaron's snake swallowed up the snakes of Pharaoh, alive (v12). In addition, God used Moses to judge Egypt through ten plagues (Read Exodus 7:14-11:10).

Just as God chose Moses through whom He demonstrated His power in the land of Egypt, so has He chosen the Church through whom He demonstrates His power to the spiritual Egypt—the world. In our text Paul wrote, *"For the kingdom of God is not in word but in power"* (v20). If power demonstration weren't necessary, Christ wouldn't have told His disciples, *"But you shall receive power, when the Holy Spirit has come upon you..."* (Acts 1:8). The early Church demonstrated God's power. God's power struck Ananias and his wife dead for lying. Today's Church lacks God's power due to sin and unbelief.

Reflection: Are you being used of God to demonstrate His power?

Word for today: *God's power is for God's people to demonstrate.*

144

THE VIRTUE OF PATIENCE

And you will be hated by all for my name's sake. But not a hair of your head
shall be lost. By your patience possess your souls (Luke 21:19).

READ: 1 SAMUEL 13:8-15

Patience is one of the fruit of the Holy Spirit (Galatians 5:22). A Christian who lacks patience, lacks an essential ingredient for spiritual growth and maturity. Our text is a classic example of how lack of patience can ruin someone's career. Saul was not supposed to offer a burnt offering; that was Samuel's responsibility. Kings don't offer sacrifices; the priests do. King Saul gave a very good reason for offering the burnt offering. He had waited seven days for Samuel's arrival and his fighting men were in disarray, so he went ahead and offered the burnt offering, preparatory to going to war against the Philistines (v9). Verse 10 records that *"as soon as he had finished presenting the burnt offering, that Samuel came."* How I wish Saul had exercised some patience and waited a little bit longer for Samuel! He would have avoided acting foolishly. Samuel called Saul's indiscreet burnt offering a foolish act, because he violated God's command. Impatience ruined Saul's career as a king (v13-14). As a user of this devotional, may impatience never cause you to do things that will ruin your relationship with God. King Saul, like many people today, was a character who loved offering sacrifices to God, while living in sin. For instance, he spared the sheep and beasts of the Amalekites doomed for destruction in order to offer sacrifices to God with them. But, Samuel rebuked him (Read 1 Samuel 15:21-22). "Are you one of those who donate huge sums of money to Churches, but live in rebellion against God?

Patience is a virtue every believer in Christ must have, because it produces character (Romans 5:3). Another word for **patience** is endurance. Without patience, there will be no character, and without character, we cannot run the race that is set before us (Hebrews 12:1c). God will not accept any excuses for being an impatient Christian. Do you know that lack of patience has been the undoing of many Christians, who have fallen into the hands of unbelievers in marriage? Such people often live to regret their actions.

Reflection: Has impatience robbed you of God's blessings lately?

Word for today: *A patient Christian eats God's fattest 'bone of blessing.'*

MY TIMES ARE IN GOD'S HAND

*Make your face shine upon your servant; save me for your mercies' sake
(Psalm 31:16).*

READ: PSALM 31:14-18

In 1824, W. F. Lloyd wrote the hymn, ***"My times are in your hand; My God, I wish them there."*** Lloyd must have been overwhelmed by the compelling truth of life's uncertainty outside of God. Indeed, life is uncertain and meaningless without God's benevolence, love and protection. Man at his best is nothing, but in Christ he is something (Read Colossians 2:9-10). God the Giver of life is the only One who has the ability and capability to handle the human life. Not too long ago, I heard a woman on the phone yelling at someone on the other end with these words, *"You cannot tell me how to live my life; I'll take control of my own life."* "Taking control of her life" implies that she is capable of dealing with issues that affected her life. Throughout her ranting, this woman never mentioned God. The life she claimed was hers, was actually God's, but on loan to her. Unfortunately, we live in a culture where people think that bringing God into the picture in their daily lives, shows weakness. If anything, the opposite is the case. When God is on your side, you are strong and able to overcome the forces of darkness operating in the atmosphere. Do you know that God can liberate you from the powers of Satan and sin? For divine protection, the best thing to do is to handover your times to the mighty and everlasting hand of God.

David, the writer of our text knows the benefits of handing over his life to God's mighty Hand. Verses 14-15 of our text read, *"But as for me, I trust in you, O LORD; I say, 'You are my God.' My times are in your hand; deliver me from the hand of my enemies, and from those who persecute me.'"* David was severely persecuted and haunted by king Saul. Most of the time, he spent sleepless nights in the caves to escape from Saul (Read 1 Samuel 22:1-22). But, he trusted in the LORD for divine protection when he said, *"My times are in your hand."* No matter the plot and plan of your enemies, if you learn to commit your times into God's mighty hand, it shall be well with you.

Reflection: On whom or what do you base your life's security?

Word for today: *The future is secure, if you are anchored in Christ.*

STAY ON THE RIGHT LANE

Therefore, my beloved brethren, be steadfast, immovable, always abounding in the work of the Lord, knowing that your labor is not in vain in the Lord (1 Corinthians 15:58).

READ: 2 PETER 3:14-18

Sometime last week, as I was driving along the highway, I noticed a sudden slowing down of vehicles in front of me. I later realized that the cause of the traffic slow-down was due to some motorists on the wrong lane—far left lane trying to change to the far right lane, in order not to miss their exit ramps. In doing so, these motorists caused a huge slowing down of the traffic. This could have been avoided if the motorists involved had stayed on the right lane as they approached their exit routes. They lost focus, stayed on the wrong lanes until it was too late. A similar thing can happen to a believer's spiritual journey. Every believer in Christ is on a spiritual journey. Unfortunately, due to worldly distractions, believers in Christ tend to lose their spiritual bearing. Like motorists who fail to stay on the right lane, they cause unnecessary traffic hold- up for others, by trying to change lanes when it is too late. Staying on the right lane is the key to a successful spiritual journey. Doing so requires spiritual focus and discipline.

In our text, Apostle Paul admonishes us as believers in Christ to stay on the right lane as we journey to heaven, so that when Christ returns, we can *"be found by Him in peace, without spot and blameless."* (v14). He warns against being led astray with the "error of the wicked." (v17). A motorist who drives from one lane to another with little or no regard for other fellow motorists is considered a dangerous driver. Similarly, in Christendom, any one who disregards the Word of God and the wise counsel of mature Christians is driving on the wrong lane into eternity. As a reader or user of this Devotional, ask the Lord to make you stay on the right lane as you drive to eternity, through the intake of sound doctrine, living a life of righteousness, holiness, faithfulness and obedience to the Word of God. As you journey to heaven, don't allow worldly allurements to steer your spiritual attention off course.

Reflection: Are you on the right lane in your spiritual journey?

Word for today: *On heaven's journey, there is no careless driving.*

GOD'S 'ALERT' MECHANISM

"Then those who heard it, being convicted by their conscience, went out one by one, beginning with the oldest even to the last…" John 8:9).

READ: ROMANS 2:12-16

Adam and Eve were innocent—devoid of the knowledge of good and evil (Genesis 3:5). But, when they sinned, God's hidden mechanism within them, called consciences set in. They automatically felt guilty in their conscience for their acts of disobedience. In order to deal with their shame and guilt, Adam and Eve, *"sewed fig leaves together and made themselves coverings."* and went and *"hid themselves from the presence of the LORD God among the trees of the garden."* (v7,8). Due to Adam's and Eve's sin, human conscience replaced human innocence. Ever since, human beings have lived with conscience which alerts them when they do wrong. Therefore, it is right to define the human conscience as a "place in the soul where norms and standards for right and wrong are established."

Not long ago, during our door-to-door evangelism, a young man who thought he was too smart posed a question to me, "Sir, you said that if someone is not born again, he will not enter the Kingdom of God. Ok! What about our great grand-parents who were not born again before they died. Are they in heaven or hell now?" The Holy Spirit prompted me to read and explain Romans 2:14-15 to him. The text makes it clear that our great grand-patents who lived and died without the knowledge of the Scripture, had God's alert mechanism in them called conscience, which condemned or commended their deeds. Those who died without knowing the Scripture will be judged according to their conscience. After my explanation, the young man felt convinced about the power of human conscience. The Bible tells us about five kinds of human conscience. **1. Clear conscience**—void of evil thoughts (Acts 24:16). **2. Seared conscience**—insensitive to godliness and the Word of God (1 Timothy 4:2). **3. Defiled conscience**—full of defiled thoughts (Titus 1:15). **4. Condemned conscience**—dented with guilt (1 John 3:20). **5. Un-condemned conscience**—void of guilt (1 John 3:21).

Reflection: How sensitive is your conscience?

Word for today: *Christ-centered conscience leads to godliness.*

ADAM THE DUST

And the LORD God formed man of the dust of the ground, and breathed into his nostrils the breath of life; and man became a living being (Genesis 2:7).

READ: GENESIS 3:17-19

Every organism originates from the dust, otherwise, known as the soil. The Bible records that God created the land, sea and vegetation on the third day, while on the fifth day, He created sea and air mammals (Genesis 1:9-13, 20-23). Since every organism, including man, originates from the soil, it makes sense to return to its place of origin when it dies. Any wonder why fallen trees, dead mammals, including human beings, decay and become dust? God's pronouncement upon Adam says it all: *"You [will] return to the ground, for out of it you were taken; for dust you are. And to dust you shall return."* Indeed, after nine hundred and thirty years, Adam died and returned to the dust from where he came. After Christ's death and resurrection, He did not remain on the earth, rather He returned to heaven—His place of origin.

Every human being, in spite of his or her good looks, is nothing but, a mound of sand bearing the Spirit of God, which makes it a living soul. Hence, it is safe to refer to a human being as **Mr. Clay**, if a man, or **Miss Clay**, if a woman. Having this understanding that we are nothing, but clay, should keep us humbled and dependent on God who made clay to become a living soul. What differentiates humans from other organisms is the presence of God's Spirit and soul in human beings. God spoke every living creature into being. But, in creating a human being, He imparted His breath of life into him. As a human being, you possess a part of God, called life. Hence, no human being can run away from God. As long as you live and wherever you go, you are a possessor of life from God. Whenever that life departs from the body, the body returns to its place of origin—soil, while the soul which is spirit goes before God to give an account of its deeds and relationship with Christ Jesus, while on earth. Remember, *"It is a fearful thing to fall into the hand of the living God."* (Hebrews 10:31). Consider seriously today, where you want your soul to spend eternity—in Heaven or Hell.

Reflection: Whatever you are, don't forget your place of origin—the dust

Word for today: *Life is vanity without Christ.*

LIGHT AND SALT

"I am the light of the world. He who follows Me shall not walk in darkness, but have the light of life." (John 8:12).

READ: MATTHEW 5:13-16

How would you feel to experience a sudden black out, especially at night? I mean being in a total darkness that leaves you having to grope around to find a candle or a lantern to light the room? No one really likes being in the dark, except the demons. Prior to creation, the Bible records that the entire universe was covered with darkness. We read, *"The earth was without form, and void; and darkness was on the face of the deep. And the Spirit of God was hovering over the face of the waters."* (Genesis 1:2). In the midst of chaos and darkness, God did something: He created light. Genesis 1:3-4 reads, *"Then God said, 'Let there be light'; and there was light. And God saw the light, that it was good; and God divided the light from the darkness.'"* After creating light, God saw that it was good and therefore, divided the light from the darkness. By creating light, God introduced life into the universe and by separating the light from the darkness, He introduced the sequence of opposites: Light and darkness; good and evil, life and death, etc. Ever since God created light, light has always represented **life** and **righteousness,** while darkness has represented **death** and **evil**. Apostle John could not have put it more clearly, *"God is light and in Him is no darkness...if we say that we have fellowship with Him and walk in darkness, we lie and do not practice the truth...walk in the light as He is in the light."* (1 John 1:5,6,7). John used the symbolism of light to describe God's divine attribute of righteousness.

In the New testament, Christ used the symbolisms of **light** and **salt** to define who His followers are. Our text reads, *"You are the salt of the earth; but if the salt loses its flavor, how shall it be seasoned? It is then good for nothing but to be thrown out and trampled underfoot by men. You are the light of the world. A city that is set on a hill cannot be hidden."* (v13-14). Light shines for people to see and salt adds taste to food. Christ wants His followers to do what light and salt do—to light the dark world and season people's tasteless lifestyle.

Reflection: How bright does your light shine, as a Christian?

Word for today: *They that live for Christ are light and salt for Him.*

BIBLE IN ONE YEAR
PSALM 96-98; JOHN 6

DESPISED AND REJECTED

He was in the world, and the world was made through Him, and the world did not know Him. He came to His own, and His own did not receive Him (John 1:10-11).

READ: ISAIAH 53:1-3

Around 712 B.C, prophet Isaiah prophesied about salvation to the remnants of the nation of Israel. In our text, Isaiah's salvation prophecy contains a portrait of the suffering Messiah, who will be unattractive (Isaiah 53:2), despised and rejected (v3). The degree at which Christ was despised and rejected by some of the Jews was unprecedented! Things have not changed much. Even today, many still despise and reject Christ. Some people hate to hear the name of Jesus Christ, while others vehemently reject the idea that He died for their sins. The world has rejected Christ and refused to acknowledge Him as Lord, even though the world was made through Him (John 1:10; Colossians 1:16-17). Furthermore, the Jews through whom Christ came into the world, widely despised and rejected Him (Read John 1:11; 12:37,38 and Luke 23:13-24).

Verse 3 of our text reads, *"He is despised and rejected by men, A Man of sorrows and acquainted with grief. And we hid, as it were, our faces from Him; He was despised, and we did not esteem Him."* That the prophecy about Christ's suffering and rejection came seven decades prior to His incarnation and fulfilled to the letter, shows how accurate God's Words are. Indeed, Christ was a Man of sorrows: He was betrayed by a close confidant (Mark 14:10-11); falsely accused by those who hated Him (Matthew 26:59-61), despised and beaten by those He came to save (v65-68) and crucified for the sins He did not commit (John 1:29). If you are a true and faithful follower of Christ, it is not unlikely that you will experience the same despising and rejection that Christ suffered, probably not on the same scale. As a believer in Christ, how do you react when people despise and reject you due to your faith in Christ Jesus? Do you feel dejected and disheartened? Remember, Christ was despised and rejected by men, and yet, He never felt dejected.

Reflection: Do you struggle with people's rejection of who you are?

Word for today: *To know Christ is to know how to deal with rejection.*

FAITH

But without faith it is impossible to please Him, for he who comes to God must believe that He is, and that He is a rewarder of those who diligently seek Him (Hebrews 11:6).

READ: HEBREWS 11:1-8

The Christian life is one of faith; whatever we do in our service to God must be done by faith. The Bible records that "without faith, it is impossible to please God" (Hebrews 11:6). Romans 1:16-17 read, *"For I am not ashamed of the gospel of Christ, for it is the power of God to salvation for everyone who believes, for the Jew first and also for the Greek. For in it the righteousness of God is revealed from faith to faith; as it is written, 'The just shall live by faith.'"* What Paul is saying is simply this: The gospel is preached by faith, received by faith and lived out by faith. Faith is defined as *"being sure of what we hope for and certain of what we do not see."* (NIV). It is the confident expectation of what we hope for. Remove faith from Christianity, and you would have succeeded in destroying it. Faith is believing that God will do what He says He will do. Remember, believing before you see is of God, while seeing before you believe is of the devil.

There are three kinds of faith:
1. Saving faith—the kind of faith that brings salvation to the human soul by believing in Christ Jesus (Read John 3:16; Acts 16:31; 1 Peter 1:8-9).
2. Operational faith—the kind of faith needed to operate as a child of God (Read 2 Corinthians 5:7; James 1:5-6; 2:14-18).
3. Gift of faith—the kind of faith that produces miracle (Read 1 Corinthians 12:9).
How can we acquire faith? We acquire faith through:
1. The intake of God's Word (Romans 10:17).
2. Self-denial in following Christ (Luke 9:23-24).
3. Praying in the Holy Spirit (Jude 20).
4. Testimonies of other Christian believers (John 4:39).

Reflection: Do you have faith in Christ?

Word for today: *Faith is the spiritual oil that greases the wheel of our salvation.*

CROWNED WITH GLORY & HONOR

What is man, that you should exalt him, that you should set your heart on him, that you should visit him every morning, and test him every moment? (Job 7:17 -18).

READ: PSALM 8:3-9

A group of deer do graze around my compound and each time I try to draw close to them, they often flee. Animals don't often run away from fellow animals, except when they see predatory animals. No matter how huge and dangerous an animal may be, it's immediate reaction on seeing a human being is to run away. This makes sense! Even as a human being, whenever you see something that is greater than you, you are more likely to run away to safety. That is what happens to non-domestic animals whenever they see human beings. What makes an animal to flee from a human being is the glory, dominion and honor with which God has crowned him. After creation, the Bible records that Adam gave names to all the animals. We read, *"Out of the ground the LORD God formed every beast of the field and every bird of the air, and brought them to Adam to see what he would call them. And whatever Adam called each living creature, that was its name. So Adam gave names to all cattle, to the birds of the air, and to every beast of the field..."* (Genesis 2:19-20). For Adam to have been able to name these animals meant that he was very close to each of them. Adam's closeness to these animals without being hurt, underscored the power and dominion he exercised over them.

David, the writer of our text was quite overwhelmed by the power, dominion and glory with which God has crowned humans. After considering the magnificence of God's creative works—the heavens, moon and stars, and the dominion God gave humans over them, David wondered aloud, *"What is man that you are mindful of him, and the son of man that you are mindful of him. For you have made him a little lower than the angels, and have crowned him with glory and honor...and have made him to have dominion over the works of your hands; you have put all things under him"* (Psalm 8:4-6).

Reflection: You are a human being, not a specie of the animal kingdom.

Word for today: *Don't undermine God's glory and honor in your life.*

153

SINLESS, EMPATHETIC HIGH PRIEST

For such a High Priest was fitting for us, who is holy, harmless, undefiled, separate from sinners, and has become higher than the heavens (Hebrews 7:26)

READ: HEBREWS 4:14-16

In the Old Testament, the high priest was like an intermediary between God and man. He played dual roles in people's worship to God. **First,** he received their sacrifices and offered such sacrifices to God. **Second,** he was the only person charged with the responsibility of pronouncing God's blessings upon the people, if and when their sacrifices were acceptable to God. In spite of these enviable roles, the high priest was not sinless. In fact, on the day of atonement before entering the holy of holies, he had to first of all, offer a sacrifice of sin offering on behalf of himself and his entire family before attending to the people (Hebrews 7:27). Leviticus 16:6 reads, *"Aaron shall offer the bull as a sin offering, which is for himself, and make atonement for himself and for his house."* The high priest had his own problems to deal with, therefore, he hardly had the time, power and resources in dealing with other people's problems, how much more empathizing with them.

But in the New Testament, all that changed! The human high priest gave way to the heavenly High Priest—Jesus Christ, the Son of God. The human high priest could only offer sacrifices, but had no power to save the human soul. But Jesus Christ, our heavenly High Priest offered Himself as a sacrifice to cleanse our sins and to save us from eternal doom. Since, *"He Himself has suffered, being tempted, He is able to aid those who are tempted."* (Hebrews 2:18). This means that no matter your suffering as a believer in Christ, our Lord Jesus, is empathetic with your suffering and is able to see you through, having been through sufferings Himself. Verse 15 of our text reads, *"For we do not have a High Priest who cannot sympathize with our weaknesses, but was in all points tempted as we are, yet without sin."* The knowledge that we have a sinless and empathetic High Priest in the Person of Christ Jesus, should prompts us to *"come boldly to the throne of grace that we may obtain mercy and find grace to help in time of need."* (v16).

Reflection: What is your relationship with our heavenly High Priest?

Word for today: *Jesus has replaced God's wrath with the throne of grace.*

THANK HIM IN ADVANCE

Pray without ceasing, in everything give thanks; for this is the will of God in Christ Jesus for you (1 Thessalonians 5:17-18).

READ: JOHN 11:41-44

It is customary to thank someone after he or she has done a thing for you. What is not customary though, is to thank someone prior to him or her doing a thing. This means that offering of thanks is what people do as a compliment for a good deed received from someone. In our Christian faith, we are enjoined to give thanks to God in advance as we pray for everything that He is about to do. In Philippians 4:6 we read, *"Be anxious for nothing, but in everything by prayer and supplication, with thanksgiving, let your requests be made known to God."* 1 Thessalonians 5:18 says, *"In everything, give thanks; for this is the will of God in Christ Jesus for you."*

During His earthly ministry, our Lord Jesus always thanked His Father in advance each time He made a request. For example, in our text, we notice that Jesus thanked His Father in advance while praying for Lazarus to come back to life. We read, *"Then they took away the stone from the place where the dead man was lying. And Jesus lifted up His eyes and said, 'Father, I thank you that You have heard me. And I know that you always hear me...'"* (v41-42). After praying and giving of thanks to his Father, Jesus called back Lazarus from the dead with a loud voice (v43). Again, following the successful evangelical mission of His disciples, our Lord Jesus thanked His Father. We read, *"In that hour Jesus rejoiced in the Spirit and said, 'I thank you, Father, Lord of heaven and earth, that you have hidden these things from the wise and prudent and revealed them to babes. Even so, Father, for so it seemed good in your sight."* (Luke 10:21). Before eating the last supper with His disciples, Jesus took the cup and gave thanks; He also *"took bread, gave thanks and broke it and gave it to them"* (Luke 22:17,19). May we learn to emulate Christ by giving thanks to God in advance as we pray. Giving God thanks in advance for answered prayer enables us to develop faith and intimacy in our daily walk with Him.

Reflection: Do you thank God in advance for answer to your prayers?

Word for today: *Thanking God in advance guarantees answer to prayer.*

155

THE LORD—MY STRENGTH

In God is my salvation and my glory; the rock of my strength, and my refuge, is in God (Psalm 62:7).

READ: PSALM 46:1-3

Verse 1of our text reads, *"God is our refuge and strength, a very present help in trouble."* There is something special about "refuge" and "strength" In time of trouble or in the face of challenges and difficulties, these two words become very relevant. **Refuge** *speaks* of protection—a hiding place, while **strength** *speaks* of power to overcome. In time of trouble, God is indeed, "an abundantly available Help." In times of crisis, some helps are not always available, while others are available, but limited in provision. Since God is an abundantly available Help in time of trouble, "we will not fear" The writer of our text painted a three-fold worse case scenario of human crisis. **First,** he painted a scenario where "the earth is removed." (v2a). Whenever the earth is removed, especially during an earthquake, there is bound to be devastation. However, in the midst of this, the writer says we should not fear, because God is with us. **Second,** he painted a scenario where "the mountains are removed and carried into the midst of the sea." like landslides and volcanic eruptions. Again, we should not fear, because He who created the mountains knows how to withhold the mountains from harming His people. **Third,** he painted a scenario where, "waters roar and be troubled and the mountain shake with swelling." (v3). In the face of the above natural disasters, God is asking us not to fear, but to trust Him. As we run into Him by faith, we are protected.

Running into God demands three important things:
1. It demands faith. Faith propels you to trust God for protection in the time of danger. You can do all you want to in times of danger, but without God's hand of protection, all your efforts are bound to fail (Read Jeremiah 17:5-8).
2. It demands obedience to God's Word. Disobedience to God's Word spells disaster for the people of God (Read Isaiah 1:19-20).
3. It demands action. God does not accept lip service, but heart service. Heart service for God goes with action, for faith without works is dead (James 2:17).

Reflection: Who is your source of strength—the LORD or the world?

Word for today: *Real strength comes from God—the Source of strength.*

SHUN DISORDERLY BEHAVIOR

"[Do not] keep company with anyone named a brother, who is sexually immoral, or covetous, or an idolater, or a reviler, or a drunkard, or an extortioner—not even to eat with such a person (1 Corinthians 5:11).

READ: ROMANS 16:17-18

Our text reads, *"Now I urge you, brethren, note those who cause divisions and offenses, contrary to the doctrine which you learned, and avoid them. For those who are such do not serve our Lord Jesus Christ, but their own belly, and by smooth words and flattering speech deceive the hearts of the simple."* Those were the inspired Word of God from Paul to the Christians in Rome, in which there were reported cases of disorderly conduct among them. The same strong words of admonition holds true for today's Church. Indeed, many sycophants in the guise of servants of God, have crept into the body of Christ, who "do not serve our Lord Jesus Christ, but their own belly, and by smooth words and flattering speech deceive the hearts of the simple" (Romans 16:18), and "whose end is destruction, whose god is their belly, and whose glory is in their shame—who "set their mind on earthly things" (Philippians 3:19).

Have you ever run into some so-called believers in Christ, who are fond of borrowing money from the brethren and not paying back; who prefer to live on other people's benevolence, rather than work to earn a living; whose stock in trade is to gossip and slander. Such behaviors are considered disorderly and the Bible warns against them. Many years ago, a Christian brother borrowed some amount of money from another brother to meet a pressing financial need. He promised to repay the loan within a specific time frame as agreed upon by the two parties. The deadline for the loan repayment passed and still the loan was not repaid. The lender brother who understandably became very worried, approached the debtor brother several times to make do on his promise to repay the loan. But, all his effort was in vain! When other brethren stepped in and urged him to repay the loan he borrowed, the brother became agitated and left the Church without repaying the loan. Such a behavior is unchristian.

Reflection: Do you have disorderly behaved Christians round you?

Word for today: *Promise breakers are disorderly in their ways, avoid them.*

157

THE BLOOD OF JESUS CHRIST

And they overcame him by the blood of the Lamb and by the word of their testimony, and they did not love their lives to the death. (Revelation 12:11).

READ: REVELATION 12:10-12

Irrespective of modern gigantic medical and scientific strides, no one has been able to produce human blood in the laboratory. One can produce blood plasma, but not real blood. There are two powerful elements, hidden from the human eyes, present in the human blood. One is the power that sustains life; the other is life itself. The Bible tells us that there is life in the blood, hence we are forbidden from eating it. To eat blood is to eat life (Read Leviticus 17:14; Deuteronomy 12: 23-24). Unknown to Cain, after he murdered his brother, Abel, the Bible records that Abel's blood cried to God. God told Cain, *"The voice of your brother's blood cries out to me from the ground."* (Genesis 4:10). If there were no life in the human blood, Abel's blood would not have cried to God. Inanimate objects don't cry out.

Since there is power and life in the human blood, you can imagine the tremendous amount of power and life that is in the blood of Jesus Christ. The human blood has been contaminated with sin, due to the sin-gene of Adam. But, Christ's blood is sinless. It has no sin-gene in it, because His conception was not through human relationship (Read Luke 1:34-35). Verse 11 of our text reads, *"And they overcame him by the blood of the Lamb and by the word of their testimony, and they did not love their lives to the death."* Indeed, believers in Christ are victorious over the devil and his cohorts through the power that is in the blood of Jesus Christ. If you have ever pleaded the blood of Jesus Christ over the forces of darkness, you will notice the tremendous power that is in it. As a believer in Christ, His blood does five important things in your life. **1.** It redeems your soul from destruction and hell fire (Colossians 1:14). **2.** It grants you peace before God (v20). **3.** It justifies you before God (Romans 5:8-9). **4.** It cleanses you from sin (1 John 1:7). **5.** It enables you to overcome the devil (Revelation 12:11).The blood of Jesus is powerful in dealing with our sins; we don't need animal blood any more.

Reflection: Do you still offer animal sacrifices for your sins?

Word for today: *The sinless blood of Jesus Christ cleanses the sinner.*

EXTERNAL APPEARANCE

*Charm is deceitful and beauty is passing, but a woman who fears the LORD,
she shall be praised (Proverbs 31:30).*

READ: 1 SAMUEL 16:1-7

E very human being has two parts to his or her appearance: One is external, the other is internal. Unfortunately, a lot of attention is given to the external appearance, while little or no attention is given to the internal appearance. Since human beings are incapable of seeing the internal appearances of others, the devil capitalizes on this weakness to make people concentrate more on external, than internal appearance. External appearance can be deceptive! Today, it is not difficult to notice that people do their best to have a good external appearance through make-up. The women spend a lot of money and time at hair salon, put on some cosmetics on their faces, wear earrings and necklaces and adorn themselves with nice, expensive dresses—all in an attempt to beautify their looks. The men also try to improve their looks through nice body build up, good hair cut and well trimmed moustaches. Why do people engage in make–up? The answer is simple: Human beings like to look good externally, to be admired. Unfortunately, little or nothing is being done to address our internal appearance, because no one sees it.

However, God sees it! He sees both our internal and external appearances. God is not so much interested in our external appearance as He is with our internal appearance. The incident recorded in our text is a good example of this. God rejected king Saul from reigning over His people, due to his rebellion against His commands. In order to replace king Saul, God asked Samuel to go to the house of Jesse and anoint one of his sons to be a king. On getting there, and seeing the external appearance of Eliab, one of Jesse's sons, Samuel thought he was the right candidate and said, "Surely the LORD's anointed." (1 Samuel 16:7). But God who looks on the inside, saw Eliab differently and told Samuel, *"Do not look at his appearance or his physical stature, because I have refused him. For the Lord does not see as man sees; for man looks at the outward appearance, but the LORD looks at the heart."*

Reflection: Do you make choices based on external appearances only?

Word for today: *"We cannot read hearts, but the Lord can"*

159

MY ROCK AND MY SALVATION

Truly, in vain is salvation hoped for from the hills, and from the multitude of mountains; truly, in the LORD our God is the salvation of Israel (Jeremiah 3:23).

READ: PSALM 62:5-7

In trying times, there is the tendency to lose heart and confidence in the Lord. When this happens, the people of God start operating in the flesh, rather than, in the spirit; they respond more to what the Lord has not given, than what He has made available. When the children of Israel left the land of Egypt for the Promised Land, there was no doubt in their minds that the mighty hand of the LORD was upon them. They saw how the LORD punished the Egyptians with ten kinds of plagues—how the LORD turned their water into blood, rendering it undrinkable (Exodus 7:14-18); how the LORD brought down frogs into the Egyptian households and infected with lice and flies (8:1-24); how the Egyptian livestock died, while theirs were spared. In addition, they saw the mighty hand of the LORD upon the invading army of Pharaoh—how the LORD dried up the Red sea and made them cross over on foot, while drowning Pharaoh's army in the Red sea. But, "on the fifteenth day of the second month after they departed from the land of Egypt," they started questioning God's divine benevolence towards them. They complained against Moses and Aaron and said, *"Oh, that we had died by the hand of the LORD in the land of Egypt, when we sat by the pots of meat and when we ate bread to the full! For you have brought us out into this wilderness to kill this whole assembly with hunger."* (Exodus 16:3). Some of us, sometimes behave like these children of Israel, who rather than be grateful for God's deliverance from Egyptian bondage, complained about missing the worldly pleasure in the land of Egypt.

In difficult times, instead of complaining and whining, we should learn to say, like the Psalmist, *"My soul, wait silently for God alone. For my expectation is from Him. He only is my rock and my salvation. He is my defense; I shall not be moved."* (Psalm 62:5-6). Make God your rock and salvation now.

Reflection: Are you going through tough times? How do you handle it?

Word for today: *When things get tough, get toughened in the Lord.*

GOD'S UNSEARCHABLE WAYS

For both He who sanctifies and those who are being sanctified are all of one, for which reason He is not ashamed to call them brethren (Hebrews 2:11).

READ: ROMANS 11:33-36

God's ways are unsearchable! The Bible declares, *"For as the heavens are higher than the earth, so are my ways higher than your ways, and my thoughts than your thoughts."* (Isaiah 55:9). Indeed, God's ways and thoughts are higher than ours. Who would have thought that Elijah could be fed by birds and that a poor widow could provide for him in a time of severe famine (Read 1 Kings 17:1-16). It defies human knowledge and understanding that God should redeem mankind by sending His innocent Son to die for sinners. Furthermore, it is difficult to understand why God should choose to allow Joseph to be thrown into the pit, and from the pit to the prison before taking him to the palace, in order to save lives. Since God's ways are unsearchable, it becomes impossible for the human mind to rationalize how God works.

Our text reads, *"Oh, the depth of the riches both of the wisdom and knowledge of God! How unsearchable are His judgments and His ways past finding out!"* (v33). God's ways are beyond human understanding, hence we lack the capability to know His mind, or give Him counsel (v34). He is God, but we are mortal. Verse 36 reads, *"For of Him and through Him and to Him are all things, to whom be glory forever."* In this verse, we see God's triple-play tittle. Let's take a look at what each of them represent: The phrase, *"For of Him"* speaks of God as the **Creator** of all things and as the Creator, our lives are in His mighty hand (Psalm 31:14-15). The phrase, *"Through Him"* speaks of God as the **Sustainer** of all things and the phrase, *"To Him"* speaks of God as the End of all things. God is the Creator, the Sustainer and the End of all things. *"All things were created through Him and for Him. And He is before all things, and in Him all things consist."* (Colossians 1:16,17). Knowing that God's ways are unsearchable and His wisdom and knowledge too deep to understand, should compel us to glorify Him always.

Reflection: Have you been trying to know God through searching?

Word for today: *Our incomparable God is incomparable in all His deeds.*

JUNE

DEVOTIONALS

HE'S GREATER THAN ALL!

You are of God, little children, and have overcome them, because He who is in you is greater than he who is in the world (1 John 4:4).

READ: JOHN 10:27-30

Our text records what Jesus Christ told His disciples, *"My sheep hear my voice, and I know them, and they follow me. And I give them eternal life, and they shall never perish; neither shall anyone snatch them out of my hand. My Father, who has given them to me, is greater than all; and no one is able to snatch them out of my Father's hand."* (v27-29). Indeed, God is greater than all! The word "All" denotes everything in heaven and on earth. God is greater in power than Satan and his cohorts. Hence any of Satan's attempt to snatch a believer away from God's hand is doomed for failure. A believer's position is secure in Christ; only sin can separate him or her from God. Do you know that God's greatness encompasses every facet of your life, including your problems? In other words, God is greater than your problems, no matter how huge they are? For example, the woman with an issue of blood had a huge problem of terminal illness for 12 years. The Bible records that she *"had spent all her livelihood on physicians and could not be healed by them."* (Luke 8:43). But, the woman *"came from behind and touched the border of Christ's garment. And immediately her flow of blood stopped."* (v44). Stop carrying the load of your problem around. Bring them to the throne of God's grace; for God is greater than your problems.

The evidence of God's greatness can is noticeable in the following aspects of our human existence: **1. In creation:** God single-handedly created all things through the power of His spoken Word (Read Genesis 1:3,6,9,11,14, 20,24). **2. In recreation:** God initiated and executed the plan of salvation for man kind (Genesis 3:15 and Matthew 1:21-23). **3. In Provision:** God provides rain, sun and food for all living creatures (Matthew 6:26-28). **4. In Protection:** God protects and preserves those who trust in Him (Read Isaiah 54:17; Psalm 91:1-16). May God grant you the grace to know that He is greater than all your problems.

Reflection: Come to God today and enjoy the greatness of His power, mercy and grace.

Word for today: Our God is the Greatest!

BEAUTY FOR ASHES

[God] turned the cities of Sodom and Gomorrah into ashes, condemned them to destruction, making them an example to those who afterward would live ungodly (2 Peter 2:6).

READ: ESTHER 4:1-4

Verse 1 of our text reads, *"When Mordecai learned all that had happened, he tore his clothes and put on sackcloth and ashes, and went out into the midst of the city. He cried out with a loud and bitter cry."* Why did Mordecai put on sackcloth and ashes? He did so to lament over Haman's plot to exterminate all the Jews, including himself. Haman had already agreed to pay into king Ahasuerus' treasury, ten thousand talents of silver—equivalent of twenty million dollars ($20, 000,000.00). Sackcloth and ashes *represented* shame, defeat and sorrow. So, for Mordecai to come out in the public dressed in sackcloth and ashes, meant that he was in a deep state of sorrow. But, God who knows how to exchange ashes for beauty turned things around for Mordecai. He made Mordecai exchange his ashes for beauty by turning Haman's plot against himself and caused him to be hanged in the gallows he had prepared for Mordecai (Read Esther 7:7-10).

In the New testament, a man named Zacchaeus exchanged his ashes for the beauty of Christ Jesus. Luke 19:2-4 read, *"Now behold, there was a man named Zacchaeus who was a chief tax collector, and he was rich. And he sought to see who Jesus was, but could not because of the crowd, for he was of short stature. So he ran ahead and climbed up into a sycamore tree to see Him, for He was going to pass that way."* From the above text, we notice that Zacchaeus had a four-fold problem that brought him to Christ. In the end, he exchanged all of them for the beauty of Christ and went home a happy, changed man. **First,** Zacchaeus was **diminutive** in stature. After his encounter with Christ, he felt tall inside. **Second,** he was a **dubious** character. As a tax collector, he was fraudulent. **Third**, he was **despised** in the society. Going to dine with Zacchaeus drew anger from the Jewish religious leaders (v7). **Fourth,** he was a **desperate** man in nature. He climbed a tree to see Jesus, defying shame.

Reflection: Are there ashes in your life? Exchange them for Christ's beauty.

Word for today: *Christ's beauty deals with the ashes and dents of the past.*

THE PRINCE OF LIFE & PEACE

But you denied the Holy One and the Just, and asked for a murderer to be granted to you, and killed the Prince of life, whom God raised from the dead, of which we are witnesses (Acts 3:14-15).

READ: ACTS 3:11-16

In his epic-making sermon following his arrest for healing a man born lame, Peter who was afraid to identity with Jesus during His trial, was extraordinarily bold to glorify His Master. Interestingly, Peter spoke to the same audience that he was afraid of during Christ's trial. This time around, Peter chided the Jewish religious leaders for their intransigence. He accused them of a four-fold criminal act. **First,** he accused them of denying Christ, the Holy One of God (Acts 3:13a). **Second,** he accused them of delivering Christ to be crucified, even when Pilate was willing to set Him free (v13b). **Third,** he accused them of preferring to set a murderer free, instead of innocent Jesus (v14). **Fourth,** Peter accused them of killing the Prince of life (v15). Peter told them that in spite of their murderous act of killing Jesus, God raised Him up and that they were witnesses to His resurrection. He added, *"And His name, through faith in His name, has made this man strong, whom you see and know. Yes, the faith which comes through Him has given him this perfect soundness in the presence of you all."* (Acts 3:16). Peter's sermon which was full of facts stunned his audience. The Jewish religious leaders tried to kill the Prince of Life, but failed. The word Prince speaks of **"Originator"** Jesus is the Originator of Life. Peter's sermon was delivered under the anointing of the Hoy Spirit. As a result, the Jewish religious leaders were *"greatly disturbed that Peter taught the people and preached in Jesus the resurrection from the dead."* (4:2).

Jesus is not only the Prince of life; He is also the Prince of peace. (Isaiah 9:6). Indeed, Jesus is the Prince of life and peace. If you let Him into your heart, He will give you eternal life and peace. Jesus said, *"Peace I leave with you, my peace I give to you; not as the world gives do I give to you. Let not your heart be troubled, neither let it be afraid."* (John 14:27). To know Jesus is to know peace, but to deny Him is to deny peace and eternal life.

Refection: Have you experienced the life and peace of Christ?

Word for today: *No Jesus, no eternal life and peace.*

THE SPIRIT OF UNBELIEF

Therefore I said to you that you will die in your sins; for if you do not believe that I am He, you will die in your sins (John 8:24).

READ: 2 KINGS 7:1-2

Have you ever tried to pray and only to find that your mind kept wandering from one thing or place to another. Under such a condition, you cannot offer and effective prayer to God. The devil is behind such a wandering thought—aimed at creating doubt and unbelief in your mind. You have one soul and by wandering in thought while praying, your mind is not agreeing with what you are uttering. Since your utterance and mind are not in agreement, it becomes very difficult for you to connect heaven, talk less receiving an answer to your prayers. Your mind and utterance must be in agreement, if you want your prayers to be effective. The Scriptures must be fulfilled: It says that if two do not agree they cannot walk together (Amos 3:3). The devil will do everything to make people doubt God. He tried it against Adan and Eve and it worked, so he uses the same strategy today to deny people of God's blessings.

The spirit of unbelief is a horrible spirit; it robs people of divine blessings. Our text is a classic example of that. The children of Israel had been through a time of severe and crushing famine as a result of total besiegement of Samaria by the Syrian army. The famine was so severe that two women agreed to boil their infant children, in turns, for food (Read 2 Kings 6:24-29). God in His mercy decided to intervene to elevate the suffering of His people. In doing so, God spoke to the people through His spokesperson—Prophet Elisha. He said, *"Hear the word of the LORD. Thus says the LORD: 'Tomorrow about this time a seah of fine flour shall be sold for a shekel, and two seahs of barley for a shekel, at the gate of Samaria.'"* Read the response of the king's bodyguard in v2. *"If the LORD God would make windows in heaven, could this thing be?"* But, Elisha's reply sealed this guy's fate, *"In fact, you will see it with your eyes, but you shall not eat of it."* For the fulfilment of God's Word and Elisha's pronouncement upon this guy, read v3-16,17-20). Don't mess with God's Word!

Reflection: Are you in the habit of doubting God and His Word?

Word for today: *Faith saves, unbelief kills.*

BE DIFFERENT!

In regard to these, they think it strange that you do not run with them in the same flood of dissipation, speaking evil of you (1 Peter 4:4).

READ: 1 PETER 4:1-6

A Christian is someone who behaves like Christ, whose speech, behavior and values are different from that of the world. Any wonder why the Bible warns every Christian *"Do not love the world or the things in the world. If anyone loves the world, the love of the Father is not in him. For all that is in the world--the lust of the flesh, the lust of the eyes, and the pride of life--is not of the Father but is of the world. And the world is passing away, and the lust of it; but he who does the will of God abides forever."* (1 John 2:15 -17). The **world** refers to the norms, practices and sinful pleasures of the world. Worldliness and sensual desires should not be part of your Christian life. *"Come out from them and be separate, says the Lord. Do not touch what is unclean, and I will receive you"* (2 Corinthians 6:17).

In our text, apostle Paul reminds believers in Christ that their identity is no longer in the world, but in Christ. We read, *"Since Christ suffered for us in the flesh, arm yourselves also with the same mind, for he who has suffered in the flesh has ceased from sin, that he no longer should live the rest of his time in the flesh for the lusts of men, but for the will of God. For we have spent enough of our past lifetime in doing the will of the Gentiles—when we walked in lewdness, lusts, drunkenness, revelries, drinking parties, and abominable idolatries."* Christ suffered in the flesh for our sins, therefore, anyone who identifies with Him should be prepared to suffer in the flesh through self-denial. In other words, he or she must be prepared to forsake all the sinful lifestyles of the past, such as sexual immorality, lust, wild parties, drunkenness and idolatry. A true child of God must be different from unbelievers. If you claim to be born again and still retain your old lifestyle of lustfulness and immoral behavior, you are not telling yourself the truth; you need a change. In fact, you need the touch of God. Be sincere with God. Ask Him to help you live a life of holiness and be willing to give up those things that lure you to sin and it will be well with you.

Reflection: Ever since you accepted Christ, has there been a change in you?

Word for today: *Worldliness and righteousness do not blend.*

GOD CONFOUNDS THE WISE

Where is the wise? Where is the scribe? Where is the disputer of this age? Has not God made foolish the wisdom of this world? (1 Corinthians 1:20).

READ: 1 CORINTHIANS 1:26-31

An excerpt from one of Charles Spurgeon's sermons reads as follows, "I expect to be amazed by three things when I first arrive in heaven. I will be delighted by those I find are actually there. I will be shocked to note who isn't there whom I assumed I would see. And then I will be speechless with wonder as I realized that by God's grace I am there!" In effect what Spurgeon is saying is that, God sees things differently from the way we see things. Christ made this very clear when He said, *"What is highly esteemed among men is an abomination in the sight of God"* (Luke 16:15b). The wise and the powerful are no match for God. In fact, He confounds them. In the Old Testament, God confounded king Nebuchadnezzar and his wise men, as they struggled without success, to interpret the night dream given to him by God (Daniel 2:1-13). But, Daniel who was full of God's wisdom was the only person able to interpret Nebuchadnezzar's dream (v27-45). In the New Testament, God again confounded the wise in executing His salvation plan. He chose to save mankind through the suffering and death of His Son—Christ Jesus. It defies human wisdom for the sinless Son of God to die in order to save sinners, but God chose to do this in order to confound the wise.

In our text, Paul reminded his readers of God's wisdom and urged them to remember their lowly calling in Christ. We read, *"For you see your calling, brethren, that not many wise according to the flesh, not many mighty, not many noble, are called"* (v26). Paul used three words descriptive of the wise and powerful in his days. The **Wise** refers to the Greek Philosophers, who sought to use wisdom to answer questions about God and life; the **Mighty** refers to the influential and politically powerful people; the **Noble** refers to the aristocratic upper class. God in His wisdom, has chosen the lowly to preach His Word, so that "no flesh would glory in His presence." (v29).

Reflection: Are you called and being used of God?

Word for today: *God of wisdom still confounds the wise and powerful.*

THE 'MODERATION' CLICHÉ

Rejoice in the Lord always. Again I will say, rejoice! Let your gentleness be known to all men. The Lord is at hand (Philippians 4:4-5).

READ: PHILIPPIANS 4:4-7

I t is amazing how some people easily try to twist the Word of God to suit their selfish motives and end up in self-destruction. In a conversation, such people are fond of interject the Word of God to muddle up facts. For instance, those who are fond of drinking alcohol defend their alcohol intake, because according to them, Jesus turned water into wine. They are quick to quote John 2:1-12. Those who don't want to give up their sinful behaviors, resort to moderation lifestyle and preach 'moderation' cliché of moral behavior. They even quote Philippians 4:5, which says, "Let your moderation be known to all men." Not only do they take the word, "moderation" in the text, out of context, they apply the verse in a negative way. They apply this verse wrongly to their perdition. To such people, moderation is good, while excessiveness is bad. According to them, it is not bad to engage in extra-marital sexual behavior; it is not evil to steal, lie, hate, drink, quarrel and even fight, as long as it is done in moderation. Their moderation cliché is dangerous and poisonous to the moral fabrics of our society. Beware!

The Bible teaches total, not partial holiness. God does not measure holiness the way humans do. Humans measure holiness in percentage. In other words, people score themselves on a moral score card and try to compare their moral behaviors to that of others. If they think that their moral behavior is better than that of others, they feel good and continue with their sinful lifestyles. God does not measure righteousness in percentages. Rather, He measures righteousness in the light of our faith in Christ through the efficacy of His shed blood. Remember how sorrowful and disappointed the rich guy who wanted to follow Jesus was, after he failed the test of self-righteous (Read Matthew 19:16-22). Moderation cliché in regard to sinfulness is not Biblical; it is a teaching from the pit of hell, promoted by the New Age theology.

Reflection: How do you live—in total or percentage holiness?

Word for today: *Righteousness measured in percentage is self made.*

SOUL-WINNING OPPORTUNITY

But you be watchful in all things, endure afflictions, do the work of an evangelist, fulfill your ministry (2 Timothy 4:5).

READ: ACTS 17:16-21

Whenever the Spirit of God prompts you to share the gospel with someone, don't miss such an opportunity. Refusal to obey the Holy Spirit's prompt in soul-wining, amounts to grieving Him and letting sinners go to hell. Remember the warning, *"Do not grieve the Holy Spirit of God, by whom you were sealed for the day of redemption."* (Ephesians 4:30). We are enjoined to be ready to "preach the Word in season and out of season." (2 Timothy 4:2). Another word for the phrase, *"in season and out of season"* is "Always". We are to preach the gospel always—when it's good and when it's bad, when it's convenient and when it's inconvenient. Even if you cannot preach, depending on where you are, you can give out tracts. But, make sure that any tract you give out has been read by you.

A story was told of how God used a tract to bring about the conversion of a young man in his early twenties, who later became a renown evangelist in Nigeria. A Christian group had conducted a three-day evangelical crusade in a village. Before the commencement of each day's crusade, people went about in the village giving out tracts. Two days after the crusaded had ended, a young man was walking across the field where the crusade was held. He saw a leaflet and picked it up, which turned out to be one of the tracts given out during the crusade. As this young man read the tract, the Holy Spirit convicted him of his sinful lifestyle, so much so, that he cried out to God for help. He immediately contacted the Church that organized the crusade for spiritual help and growth and went ahead to become one of Nigerians renowned evangelists. In our text, we notice how Paul was provoked in spirit on seeing the idolatrous lifestyle of the Athenians. Then Paul went into the Synagogue and reasoned with both the Jewish and Gentile worshippers (v16-17). He used the opportunity given to him to share the gospel of Christ. Since the pastime of the Athenians was to hear about something new, Paul gave them the risen Christ.

Reflection: How committed are you in soul-winning?

Word for today: *He who wins souls is wise (Proverbs 11:30).*

172

LOST, FOUND AND RESTORED

"For the Son of Man has come to seek and to save that which was lost." (Luke 19:10).

READ: GENESIS 3:6-11

Adam and Eve were lost, ashamed and afraid after they sinned against God by eating the fruit from the forbidden tree. They were found, because God came looking for them. Verse 9 of our text reads, *"The LORD God called to Adam and said to him, "Where are you?"* Indeed, Adam's reply was that of a lost man: "I heard your voice in the garden, and I was afraid because I was naked; and I hid myself." (v10). Adam tried to hide from God, but couldn't, because he had God's divine 'chip', called the Spirit of God inside of him. In fact, no one can hide from God, due to this divine chip. After creating Adam, Adam was lifeless, until God imparted His breath into Adam. The Spirit of God in a human being monitors and knows everything about him, therefore, it is impossible to hide or run away from God. (Read Psalm 139:7-12).

Adam and Eve were lost and found, but not restored; human restoration took place in Christ Jesus. There are five things human beings lost in Adam, which were restored in Christ.
1. Divine relationship. Adam had a close relationship with God, but lost it due to disobedience. But, that relationship was restored in Christ (Read Galatians 3:13-14; Colossians 2:14-18). **2. Peace of God.** Adam had the peace of God, but his disobedience stole away that peace from him (Genesis 3:10). Thank God, the lost peace has been restored in Christ (Read John 14:27; Philippians 4:7). **3. Boldness.** Adam's boldness was replaced with fear due to his disobedience (Genesis 3:10). But, thank God, that lost boldness has been restored in Christ (Read 2 Timothy 1:7). **4. Victory over Satan.** Adam became a servant to Satan by disobeying God. But, through Christ, victory over Satan was restored (Read Genesis 3:15; Romans16:16-18). **5. Victory over death.** God did not create Adam to die, but due to disobedience, Adam became subject to death (Genesis 3:19). God replaced death with eternal life in Christ (John 3:16).

Reflection: As a lost sinner, has Christ found and restored you?

Word for today: *Except a sinner is found and restored, he is lost for ever.*

THE BETTER COVENANT

In that He says, "A new covenant," He has made the first obsolete. Now what is becoming obsolete and growing old is ready to vanish away.

READ: HEBREWS 7:20-28

A covenant is *a pact, treaty, alliance, or agreement between two parties of equal or of unequal authority.* There are about five important covenants in the Bible as follows: **1. Adamic covenant** (Genesis 1:26-29; 2:15-17). **2. Noahic covenant** (Genesis 6:18-22; 9:8-17). **3. Abrahamic covenant** (Genesis 15:18; 17:1-14). **4. Mosaic—Old covenant** (Exodus 19:5-6; 24:6-8) **5. New covenant** (Jeremiah 31:31-34; Matthew 26:28; Hebrews 8:6,13). God made His covenant with Noah, which extended to all animals (Genesis 9:9-17). The *covenant with Noah involve a righteous man* (Genesis 6:8-9), while the *covenant with Abraham involved a man of faith* (Genesis 15:6). Of all the above covenants, the New covenant is better. It is *better because, it allows us to go directly to God through Christ. We no longer need to rely on animal sacrifices and mediating priests to obtain God's forgiveness. In addition, while all human priests die, Christ, our High Priest lives forever.*

From our text, we notice that the Priesthood of our Lord Jesus Christ was with an oath from God, while the priesthood of other priests were without an oath from God. Verse 20-21 of our text reads, "And in as much as *He was* not *made priest* without an oath (for they have become priests without an oath, but He with an oath by Him who said to Him: *"The LORD has sworn and will not relent, 'You are a priest forever according to the order of Melchizedek'").* As a result, Christ has become a *surety for a better covenant* for as many as put their trust in Him (v22). Other priests offered continuous sacrifices to God, which could not bring salvation to anyone. But, Christ, our High Priest, offered Himself once for the sins of the whole world and for the salvation of humankind (John 1:29; Hebrews 9:14-15, 28). Thank God, Christ our High Priest has ushered in a better covenant , which is *fitting for us,* because He *is holy, harmless, undefiled, separated from sinners* and seated *higher than the heavens* (Hebrews 7:26).

Reflection: Which of the covenants do you identify with—the Old or the New?

Word for today: *The eternal Lord makes the better covenant permanent.*

DIVINELY COMMISSIONED

Now therefore, go, and I will be with your mouth and teach you what you shall say (Exodus 4:12).

READ: ISAIAH 6:8-10

God's call comes with a mandate and a commission. The mandate is an authoritative command, while the commission is the empowerment that goes with such mandate. When God called Moses, He gave him a two-fold mandate—one to Pharaoh, the king of Egypt and the other to the children of Israel. God's mandate to Moses for Pharaoh reads as follows: *"Come now, therefore, and I will send you to Pharaoh that you may bring my people, the children of Israel, out of Egypt."* (Exodus 3:10). Verse 16 tells us of God's mandate to Moses for the children of Israel. After giving Moses the mandate, God commissioned (empowered) him for the task ahead. Prior to his commissioning ceremony, Moses asked a relevant and legitimate question, *"Suppose they (the children of Israel) will not believe me to listen to my voice; suppose they say, 'The LORD has not appeared to you.'"* (4:1). In commissioning Moses, the LORD did two miracles before him. In the first miracle, the LORD said to Moses "What is that in your hand? And Moses replied, "A rod" (v2). Then the LORD asked Moses to cast the rod on the ground. When Moses did, the rod became a serpent (snake) (v3). Then the LORD asked Moses to take the snake by the tail. So, when Moses "reached out and caught it, it became a rod in his hand." (v4). Furthermore, the LORD asked Moses to put his hand in his bosom. When he did, his hand became leprous. Again the LORD asked him to put back his hand in his bosom and when he did, his hand was restored, "like his other flesh" (v6-7). At Moses' commissioning ceremony before Pharaoh, the LORD asked him to tell Aaron to cast his rod before Pharaoh. When Aaron did, his rod became a snake.

In our text, we notice how God commissioned and mandated Isaiah to serve as a prophet. First of all, the LORD sanctified Isaiah's mouth with a touch of live coal taken from the altar (v6-7). Secondly, the LORD mandated him, "Go and tell this people…" (v9). When God calls, He mandates and commissions.

Reflection: Has the LORD called, mandated and commissioned you?

Word for today: *Divine commission is different from an earthly commission.*

TEMPLE NOT MADE WITH HANDS

Jesus answered and said to them, "Destroy this temple, and in three days I will raise it up." (John 2:19).

READ: 2 CORINTHIANS 5:1-8

During the trial of Jesus Christ before the Sanhedrin, one of the false accusations brought against Him by the unbelieving Jews reads as follows: *"We heard Him say, 'I will destroy this temple made with hands, and within three days I will build another made without hands.'"* (Mark 14:58). Christ's accusers referred to Christ's statement in John 2:19, which reads in part, *"Destroy this temple, and in three days I will raise it up."* Christ's statement came in response to a request for a sign from the unbelieving Jews. In effect, Christ answered their request for a sign by telling them that His body (temple) will be destroyed and that He would raise it up after three days. Christ was referring to His death and resurrection, not the physical temple building in Jerusalem. Being ignorant of God's Word and bereft of spiritual understanding, the Jewish religious leaders took Christ's statement out of context by saying, *"It has taken forty-six years to build this temple, and will you raise it up in three days?* (John 2:20) John noted that Christ was speaking of the temple of His body (v21). Any wonder why the Bible says, *"The natural man does not receive the things of the Spirit of God, for they are foolishness to him; nor can he know them, because they are spiritually discerned."* When told, *"Except a man be born again, he cannot see the Kingdom of God."* (John 3:3). Nicodemus' question sounded like that of the Jews, *"How can a man be born again when he is old? Can he enter a second time into his mother's womb and be born again.?"* (v4). Indeed, it takes the Spirit of God to understand God!

In verse 1 of our text, apostle Paul speaks of a house not made with hands. It reads, *"For we know that if our earthly house, this tent, is destroyed, we have a building from God, a house not made with hands, eternal in the heavens."* Paul was referring to the resurrection body of a believer who died in Christ. Every true believer in Christ will *be clothed with the habitation from heaven."* (v2), the same body that Christ has.

Reflection: Do you look forward to a temple not made with hands?

Word for today: *Earthly temple is temporal; heavenly temple is eternal.*

SIN—A DYSFUNCTIONAL GENE

"For all have sinned and fall short of the glory of God, being justified freely by His grace through the redemption that is in Christ Jesus." (Romans 3:23-24).

READ: ROMANS 5:12-14

Sin is a debilitating spiritual sickness; it is a dysfunctional gene passed on from Adam to every human being. Everyone born into this world has a sin gene in him or her. It is only a matter of time before it begins to manifest in such an individual. Even if you put away a newborn from having contact with others, you will discover that sooner or later, the child will begin to exhibit the characteristics of his sinful nature, due to the sin gene in him. The sin gene in humans cannot be treated by any human being. Attempting to do so will look like a doctor who is sick of an illness for which he is incapable of treating, trying to treat someone else with a similar illness. No human being can treat the sin gene in humans; only Christ, the Son of God can.

Our text reads, *Therefore, just as through one man sin entered the world, and death through sin, and thus death spread to all men, because all sinned—* (v12). Indeed, Adam got the sin gene through disobedience and then passed it on to all humankind. The effect of Adam's sin gene is death (Romans 6:23). Thanks be to God that Christ Jesus through His obedience has gotten rid of the effects of sin gene passed on to humankind by Adam. Romans 5: 17, 18 and 19 are introduced by the phrase, "As by one man". Each of these verses contrasts what Adam and Jesus did. Verse 17 tells us how through Adam's offence, death reigned to humankind. In contrast, through Christ's righteousness, life is restored to mankind. In verse 18, we notice that through Adam's offence, leading to condemnation, judgment befell mankind. In contrast, through Christ's righteous act, "free gift of salvation came to all men, resulting in justification of life." Verse 19 tells us that by Adam's "disobedience many were made sinners." In contrast, by Christ's obedience, "many will be made righteous." This means that whoever believes in Christ, automatically gets cured of the effects of sin-gene. On the other hand, whoever rejects Christ will continue to suffer the effects of a dysfunctional gene—called sin and spend eternity in hell.

Reflection: Has your sin-gene been treated by Christ yet?

Word for today: *Only Christ without a sin-gene can treat the sickness of sin.*

BEWARE!

Beware of dogs, beware of evil workers, beware of the mutilation!
(Philippians 3:2).

READ: DEUTERONOMY 8:11-17

I am sure that when you see a sign with an inscription, **Beware!**, you will instinctively feel a sense of danger, risk and insecurity, even though, the sign does not tell you what to beware of. In our text, the children of Israel were warned by Moses to beware not to forget the LORD their God. We read, *"Beware that you do not forget the LORD your God by not keeping his commandments, his judgments, and his statutes which I command you today."* (v11). Moses' warning to the children of Israel is relevant to everyone of us today. From our text, we notice three reasons why we should beware not to forget God. **First,** there is the tendency to forget God in time of plenty (v12-13). **Second,** there is the tendency to forget God due to pride of life (v14). **Third,** there is the tendency to forget God when you become powerful in the society (v17).

The Bible tells us **ten** things we should beware of as believers in Christ:
1. We should beware not to forget the LORD our God (Deuteronomy 8:11)
2. We should beware not to forget the poor among us (Deuteronomy 15:9).
3. We should beware of false prophets (Matthew 7:15). **4.** We should beware of evil men (Matthew 10:17). **5.** We should beware of the leaven of the Pharisees and Sadducees, alias, **false doctrine** (Matthew 16:6). **6.** We should beware of covetousness (Luke 12:15) **7.** We should beware of the Scribes—the learned theologians of our days, who turn the Bible upside down; who display head knowledge of the Bible without heart knowledge of Christ (Luke 20:46-47). **8.** We should beware of dogs—evil workers in the Church (Philippians 3:2) **9.** We should beware of the mutilation—those who depend on works to gain salvation (Ephesians 2:8-9; Philippians 3:2). **10.** We should beware of philosophical arguments about Christ (Colossians 2:8). Failure to beware of the above mentioned traits, could land someone in a big spiritual mess. Remember, the kind of spiritual food you eat determines your spiritual well-being.

Reflection: Carefully go through the above traits and see how you measure up.

Word for today: *The negligence of danger is the height of foolishness.*

178

COMMANDMENTS & DOCTRINES

[You] should not give heed to Jewish fables and commandments of men who turn from the truth (Titus 2:14).

READ: COLOSSIANS 2:18-23

Commandments are imperative directives and orders, while doctrines are teachings that flow from such directives. This makes commandments and doctrines inseparable. In the Bible we read of two kinds of commandments and doctrines. One is the commandments and doctrines of God; the other is the commandments and doctrines of men. Our Lord Jesus Christ chided the Scribes and Pharisees for superimposing their human tradition over the commandment of God. Jesus told them that God's commandment says, "Honor your father and your mother; and he who curses father or mother, let him be put to death." (Matthew 15:4). But, the Scribes and Pharisees came up with their own version of commandment regarding how a person should honor his or her parents. Their command to the people was, *"Whoever says to his father or mother, 'Whatever profit you might have received from me is a gift to God"— then he need not honor his father or mother.'"* (v5). By such a command, they provided an escape route for those who didn't want to honor their parents with their gifts. In other words, if someone decided to deny his parents certain gifts, all he needed to do was to tell the parents that the gifts due them had become the gifts given to God. In so doing, the Scribes and Pharisees *"made the commandment of God of no effect by their tradition."* (v6).

The Bible warns against the doctrines of men which are inspired by demons (Read 1 Timothy 4:1-3). Some of these doctrines are with us today. Any wonder why the Church is operating without the power of God. From what is going on in the Church today, you will agree that these doctrines are causing a lot of havoc in the Church of God. In our text, we are warned not to touch, taste or handle these commandments and traditions of men. Otherwise, those who practice them will perish with them (Colossians 2:21-22). Self abasement and imposed humility without Christ are counterproductive. All who indulge in them cannot bear the fruit of the Holy Spirit.

Reflection: Which do you obey: God's or man's commandment and doctrine?

Word for today: *Human commandments produce wrong doctrines.*

TIME IS RUNNING OUT!

"Today, if you will hear His voice, do not harden your hearts." (Hebrews 4:7).

READ: 2 CORINTHIANS 6:1-2

Have you ever found yourself in a life and death situation? I mean a situation, where time is of the essence—where if nothing is done, lives could be lost. You probably have. But, just in case you haven't, the recent mysterious disappearance of a Malaysian plane is a classic example of the urgency of time. This plane's mysterious disappearance was a tragic and heartbreaking incident to the families of the victims and to the entire world. Two weeks after the disappearance of the plane, the world's oceanic search engine swung into action in an attempt to find the missing plane. Two weeks of search produced no positive result. Then, it became necessary to turn attention of the search to the plane's black-box in order to know what transpired prior to the plane's disappearance. Meanwhile, time was running out on the search team, because the battery of the black box sensor could only last for 30 days. The United States, Britain, Australia and other countries joined in the search effort, because time was running out on the possibility of retrieving the black-box. Since every effort to locate the missing plane or retrieve its black-box seemed to have failed, it is safe to conclude that time has run out on the search team and the wreckage of the plane and the victims may never be found.

The Malaysian plane's disappearance and the time sensitive nature of its search has a spiritual lesson for everyone. The lesson is that those who are lost—who live daily under the bondage of sin and Satan, need urgent rescue effort. The Bible warns that time is running out on such people. We read, *"Behold, now is the acceptable time; behold, now is the day of salvation."* (2 Corinthians 6:2b). Failure to heed this warning will result in spending eternity in hell with Satan (Read Revelation 20:10, 12-15). Our Lord Jesus made an open declaration, *"The Son of Man has come to seek and to save that which was lost."* (Luke 19:10). Christ contrasts the work of Satan and His: Satan's work is to "steal, and to kill, and to destroy", but Christ's work is to save and give eternal life to all who believe in Him (John 10:10).

Reflection: Don't let time run out on you in seeking salvation in Christ.

Word for today: *Salvation is a time sensitive issue; be urgent about it.*

SALVATION—A REVEALED MYSTERY

"And without controversy great is the mystery of godliness…" (1 Timothy 3:16).

READ: 1 TIMOTHY 3:14-16

The American Heritage English Dictionary defines the word, **"mystery"** as *something not understood or eluding the understanding.* In Biblical context, Nelson's New Illustrated Bible Dictionary defines **mystery** as *the hidden, eternal plan of God that is being revealed to God's people in accordance with His plan.* Both the English and Biblical definitions of mystery agree on one thing—a mystery cannot be understood, unless it is revealed. In the secular world, a mystery is something that eludes understanding, but in God's Kingdom, a mystery is an "open-secret"—a secret that is revealed by God to His servants through His Spirit. Many demon worshippers, like the mystics, feed their victims with falsehood and demonic mysticism

Verse 16 of our text reads, *"And without controversy great is the mystery of godliness: God was manifested in the flesh, justified in the Spirit, seen by angels, preached among the Gentiles, believed on in the world, received up in glory."* The salvation of humankind will continue to be a mystery to the rational mind. But to the faithful in Christ, it is an open-secret. Based on our text, the mystery of godliness is revealed by a six-fold testimony. **First,** God was manifested in the flesh. This refers to Christ's incarnation (John 1:14; 1 John 1:1-2). **Second,** God was justified in the flesh. This refers to Holy Spirit's *work in Christ's ministry and resurrection* (Matthew 3:16-17; Romans 1:3-4). **Third,** God was seen by angels. This refers to *the angelic witness of Christ's ministry and resurrection* (Matthew 28:2). **Fourth,** God was preached among the Gentiles. This refers to *the proclamation of Christ to the nations (*Acts 10:42; Colossians 1:23). **Fifth,** God was believed in the world. This refers to *the response of individuals to God's salvation plan* (1 Corinthians 1:18-25). **Sixth,** God was received up in glory. This refers to Christ's Ascension and being seated in the presence of God in heaven (Acts 1:9; Ephesians 4:10)

Reflection: Is salvation in Christ still a mystery to you?

Word for today: *In Christ—no mystery or mysticism, but the revealed truth.*

WITNESSING/SOUL WINNING

"...And you shall be witnesses to me in Jerusalem, and in all Judea and Samaria, and to the end of the earth." (Acts 1:8).

READ: 2 CORITNTHIANS 5:18-20

Evangelism, Witnessing/Soul-wining are the same, except that in Witnessing/Soul-wining, after planting the seed of God's Word in the heart of a sinner, you personally water the seed in prayer, watch it germinate, grow and bear fruit. Evangelism is seed sowing which can result in soul saving, while Soul-wining is soul harvesting. To be an effective witness/soul winner, you must have witnessed a transformed life in Christ. You cannot be a soul-winner for Christ, if Christ has not won you to Himself. The Bible makes it clear, *"He who wins souls is wise."* (Proverbs 11:30). The negative version of this verse will read like this, "He who does not win souls is foolish." This means that whoever refrains from soul-wining for Christ, is foolish.

From our text, we notice that the objective of soul-wining is to reconcile sinners to God. We read, *"Now all things are of God, who has reconciled us to Himself through Jesus Christ, and has given us the ministry of reconciliation, that is, that God was in Christ reconciling the world to Himself, not imputing their trespasses to them, and has committed to us the word of reconciliation."* (v18-19). When you are reconciled to God by believing the gospel, you should carry that message of reconciliation to others as well. In witnessing/soul -wining, you should preach Christ, not Church denomination (Read Acts 8:4-5, 35). You should also preach the message of forgiveness of sins in Christ, not in any other (Read Acts 5:31; 13:38-39 and Ephesians 1:7). As a witness/soul-winner, you should preach salvation in Christ only. Acts 4:12 reads, *"Neither is there salvation in any other, for there is no other name under heaven given among men by which we must be saved."* (See also 2 Timothy 2:10). Five golden qualities of a true witness/soul winner for Chris are: **1.** A life of purity (2 Timothy 2:20-21). **2.** A good knowledge of God's Word (2 Timothy 2:15). **3.** Obedience to Holy Spirit's leading (Acts 16:6-10). **4.** Commitment to service (Acts 20:17-21). **5.** Willingness to endure hardship (2 Timothy 2:3-4).

Reflection: How involved are you in witnessing/soul-wining for Christ?

Word for today: *Be a soul-winner; be wise.*

TALK LESS; PRAY MORE

Whoever guards his mouth and tongue keeps his soul from troubles (Proverbs 21:23).

READ: PSALM 141:1-4

As humans, there is the tendency for people to share their problems and that of friends and loved ones with others. Some do this to help find solutions; others do it to create forum for gossip. As a believer in Christ, it is proper to first of all, take your problems to God in prayers, before sharing it with other people. If you must talk about your problems to others, let it be trusted, mature Christians, who will help you in prayers. Sharing your problems with others, before taking it to the Lord in prayers is counter-productive. It opens you up to the whims and caprices of the devil. Make God the first port of call with your problems. If you call upon God and cry to Him about your problem, He will bring a solution to it. He may choose to use someone you least expect to solve such a problem. A problem is like a bag, which everyone carries around. You will be stunned with the magnitude of problem people have when their bags are laid open. No human being is immune to problems, except that the magnitude differs from person to person. This means that the person you are talking to about your problems has his or her own problems as well. If you learn to take your problems to God, rather than man, you will never be put to shame (Romans 10:11).

How do you react to your problems? Do you complain, talk to people or pray to God about it? It is better to go to God and talk to Him about your problems first, before sharing it with others. If it means crying to God, do so. After all, kids do cry out to their fathers for help. So, it is not a bad thing to cry out to your heavenly Father regarding your problems. Verse 1-2 of our text read, *"LORD, I cry out to you; make haste to me! Give ear to my voice when I cry out to you. Let my prayer be set before you as incense, the lifting up of my hands as the evening sacrifice."* David saw the need to cry out to God in prayer for help and to ask Him to guard his mouth and watch the door of his lips" in time of problem. May God grant us the grace to do the same.

Reflection: How do you handle your problem? Pray or talk to people about it?

Word for today: *In the face of difficulties, talk less and pray more.*

PRAISE & DANCE BEFORE HIM

Praise the LORD! For it is good to sing praises to our God; for it is pleasant, and praise is beautiful (Psalm 147:1).

READ: PSALM 145: 1-3

Verse 1-2 of our text read, *"I will extol you, my God, O King; and I will bless your name forever and ever. Every day I will bless you, and I will praise your name forever and ever."* David, the writer of Psalm 145, was a man who knew how to really praise the LORD. In one occasion, David was very much engulfed in praising and dancing before the Almighty God, in celebration of the return of the ark of God. We read, *"Then David danced before the LORD with all his might; and David was wearing a linen ephod. So David and all the house of Israel brought up the ark of the LORD with shouting and with the sound of the trumpet."* (2 Samuel 6:14). As David was praising and dancing before the LORD, his wife, Michal was at home feeding her eyes through her house window, rather than join the praise and dance team. As Michal looked out through her house window, she saw David, her husband, praising and dancing before the LORD—*leaping and whirling before the LORD.* Michal did not like the excitement and exhilaration shown by David. The Bible records that *she despised him (David) in her eyes.* (v16). In other words, Michal looked down on David with disrespect for dancing so joyfully unrestrained before the LORD. On David's return to his house, Michal greeted him with these unkind words, *"How glorious was the king of Israel today, uncovering himself today in the eyes of the maids of his servants, as one of the base fellows shamelessly uncovers himself."* (v20). David was quick to respond to Michal's accusations (Read v21-22). As a pay back for despising David, because he danced before Him, the LORD closed the womb of Michal; she died childless (v23).

Are you one of those who despise others, who dance before the LORD during praise and worship service in your Church? Learn a lesson from what happened to Michal. Those who find it hard to dance before the Lord end up dancing before Satan through worldly music, which glorifies the flesh.

Reflection: How do you praise the LORD?

Word for today: *Learn to dance before the LORD, as you praise Him.*

GODLY FATHERHOOD

"The LORD was with Jehoshaphat, because he walked in the former ways of his father David; he did not seek the Baals, but sought the God of his father..." (2 Chronicles 17:3-4).

READ: 2 CHRONICLES 17:1-6

It takes a man to be a father, just as it takes a father to be a man. This means that only a man can possess the characteristics of fatherhood, and that fatherhood qualities are visible in a man. A woman can only play the role of a mother in a child's life, not that of a father. Hence, a child needs a father and a mother in his or her life. Today, as we celebrate the father's day, let's not forget the importance of godly fatherhood in the family. A godly father is both the physical and spiritual head of the family. If a father is godly, there is every likelihood that his family will be godly also. But, if on the other hand, a father is ungodly, his family will tend to be ungodly, unless God intervenes. That was what happened to Jehoshaphat, who followed in the footsteps of his father David. Godliness begets godliness and sinfulness begets sinfulness! God saw in Abraham the qualities of a godly father, even when he was still childless, and testified this about him, *"I have known him, in order that he may command his children and his household after him, that they keep the way of the LORD, to do righteousness and justice..."* (Genesis 18:19). As a father, can God testify positive things about you?

Fatherhood is a calling that must be taken very seriously. Here are seven tips for a godly fatherhood: **(1) Do not provoke your children to anger.** To do so will discourage them from fulfilling God's purpose in their lives (Colossians 3:21). Learn to speak encouraging words to them. **(2) Do not be bitter with your wife.** To do so will eventually alienate your children from you (v19). **(3) Learn to discipline your children** (Proverbs 13:24). **(4) Train up your children in the way of the LORD** (21:6). **(5) Learn to provide for your family** (1 Timothy 5:8). **(6) Teach your children the Word of God** (6:6-7). **(7) Be courageous in the face of adversity** (Proverbs 24:10). Be the good father that God wants you to be.

Happy father's day!   Happy father's day!! Happy father's day!!!

Reflection: Can you truly say that you are a godly father?

Word for today: *A godly father has God inside of him.*

SOW IN TEARS; REAP IN JOY

For His anger is but for a moment, His favor is for life; weeping may endure for a night, but joy comes in the morning (Psalm 30:5).

READ: PSLAM 126:5-6

Nothing good comes easy in life! Anything done in this world to survive, demands effort, suffering and hard work. The reason for this can be found n the Bible. When Adam sinned against God, the ground which the LORD had earlier blessed (Genesis 2:26-28) became cursed by God Himself (Read 3:17-19). Ever since, humanity has been engulfed in suffering and toiling in order to get by in life. Whatever you are or aspire to become, there is an element of suffering (tears) associated with your endeavor. Even if someone chooses stealing as a means of livelihood, there is still an element of suffering (tears) associated with it. Anything we do to succeed in life involves suffering. Just like a farmer who sows in tears during the planting season, goes reaping in joy during the harvest season, so does anyone who sows time, talent, effort, energy, money, etc. in tears, expect to reap in joy. Although, seed sowing involves hard work and risk-taking, nonetheless, during the harvest season, the hardworking farmer smiles home with an abundant harvest.

As believers in Christ, we should learn to sow in tears, so that we may reap in joy. **"Sowing in tears"** *speaks* of making some self-sacrifices in order to advance God's Kingdom agenda. For instance, sowing the seed of God's Word in people's lives is not an easy thing to do. Sometimes, you get insulted, rejected and ridiculed in the process. However, when in due season, the seeds sown bring transformation in people's lives, it echoes unspeakable joy in heaven and the heart of the sower (Read Luke 15:7). Joy of reaping dispels the pain of tears. Jesus told a parable to drive home the lesson of sowing in tears and reaping in joy. We read, *"A woman, when she is in labor, has sorrow because her hour has come; but as soon as she has given birth to the child, she no longer remembers the anguish, for joy that a human being has been born into the world."* (John 16:21). Learn to sow in tears that you may reap in joy as you make your time, talent and resources available to God.

Reflection: When last did you share the gospel with an unbeliever?

Word for today: *In Christ, tears become joy when we sow diligently.*

SPIRITUAL PARENTAGE

"For whoever does the will of My Father in heaven is My brother and sister and mother." (Matthew 12:50).

READ: PHILEMON 1:10-16

Spiritual parentage is a term used in describing the relationship that exists between two individuals, as a result of one leading the other to Christ. Usually, the one who leads the other person to Christ, being a more mature Christian, assumes the responsibility of spiritual parentage to the new convert. During His earthly ministry, our Lord Jesus Christ alluded to the principle of spiritual parentage. During one of His teachings, someone came and said to Him, *"Look, your mother and your brothers are outside seeking you"* In response Jesus said, *"Who is my mother, or my brothers?' And He looked around in a circle at those who sat about Him, and said, 'Here are my mother and my brothers! For whoever does the will of God is my brother and my sister and mother.'"* (Mark 3:32-35). By Christ's statement, spiritual parentage is centered on being a follower of Christ.

Apostle Paul played the role of spiritual parenting to a good number of people in the Bible, whom he led to Christ. He referred to the Corinthian Christians as his, *"beloved children"* whom he had begotten through the gospel (I Corinthians 4:14,15). He called the Galatian Christians, his *"little children, for whom he labored in birth.."* (Galatians 4:19), and commended Timothy in his letter to the Philippian Church, as his son (Philippians 2:22-23). In our text, we notice how Paul again played the role of spiritual parenting in the life of Onesimus—a runaway slave. Onesimus, is a Greek name which means, **"useful"** In the time of Paul, most slave masters liked to give the name, Onesimus to their nameless slaves in the hope that such a slave will be useful to them. Philemon a convert through Paul's ministry was a rich landowner and like most landowners had a slave, named Onesimus. The Bible did not tell us how Onesimus got into jail, except that he was Paul's convert. In his letter to Philemon, Paul referred to Onesimus as his son, whom he begot in chains. (Philemon 1:10). As a good spiritual father, Paul sent Onesimus back to Philemon, his master.

Reflection: If you were in Paul's shoes, what would you have done?

Word for today: *Spiritual parenting is a serious spiritual responsibility.*

A 'SLAVERY' SWITCH

*And having been set free from sin, you became slaves of righteousness
(Romans 6:18).*

READ: ROMANS 6:15-23

By definition, a slave is *one bound in servitude as the property of a person or household; one who is abjectly subservient to a specified person or influence.* After Adam sinned in the Garden of Eden, he became subservient to Satan, sin and death. Satan is the originator of sin and sin is an act of disobedience, while death is the result of such an act. So, we see that Satan, sin and death are interwoven. Ever since Adam sinned against God, by believing Satan, instead of God, humanity has been under the bondage of Satan, sin and death. So, in order to get rid of death—both physical and eternal death, one has to get rid of Satan and sin.

Our text gives us a very good insight into servitude and obedience in relation to slavery. Verse 16 reads, *"Do you not know that to whom you present yourselves slaves to obey, you are that one's slaves whom you obey, whether of sin leading to death, or of obedience leading to righteousness?"* In fact, just as a slave is bound to obey his master, so is someone under Satanic bondage bound to obey him. In life, there are two parallel masters to be obeyed—Christ or Satan—no middle ground. Due to Adam's disobedience, humanity has been enslaved by Satan and sin. But thanks be to God, who sent Christ Jesus to destroy that condition of being slaves to Satan and sin. By believing in Christ, one makes a slavery switch—from being a slave of Satan and sin to becoming the slave of righteousness and God (v22). If you have not made that slavery switch yet, you are certainly under the bondage of Satan and sin, and therefore, not yet saved. Salvation is freedom from bondage. Until this takes place in one's life, one is still in bondage of Satan and sin. Just as a slave seeks to please his master, so does someone who is a slave to Satan and sin, seek to please them. Hence, someone without Christ finds it hard to please Him. It is written, *"No servant can serve two masters; for either he will hate the one and love the other, or else he will be loyal to the one and despise the other..."* (Luke 16:13).

Reflection: Have you made a slavery switch from Satan to Christ?

Word for today: *Switch over to Christ and experience abundant life.*

188

THE POWER OF INFLUENCE

My son, if sinners entice you, do not consent (Proverbs 1:10).

READ: 1 KINGS 12:6-11

The Bible cautions, *"Do not be deceived: 'Evil company corrupts good habits.'"* (1 Corinthians 15:33). An opposite rendition of this verse would look like this, "Do not be deceived, 'Good company improves bad behavior.' There is power in influence. If you keep a godly company, your behavior will tilt towards godliness. But, if on the other hand, you keep a bad company, you will learn bad behaviors. This means that the kind of company you keep can influence your behavior.

Our text contains a classic example of the power of influence. After the death of king Solomon, his son, Rehoboam reigned in his place. Then the elders of Israel approached him with these words of appeal, *"Your father made our yoke heavy; now therefore, lighten the burdensome service of your father, and his heavy yoke which he put on us, and we will serve you."* (v4). As Rehoboam asked for three days to ponder over their request, he consulted those who served under his father for advice. Their advice was simple and clear, *"If you will be a servant to these people today, and serve them, and answer them, and speak good words to them, then they will be your servants forever."* (v5-7). Rather than heed the wise counsel of the elders, Rehoboam sought an advice from his youthful peers, who said to him, *"Thus you should speak to this people who have spoken to you... 'My little finger shall be thicker than my father's waist! And now, whereas my father put a heavy yoke on you, I will add to your yoke; my father chastised you with whips, but I will chastise you with scourges!'"* (v10-11). The advice of Rehoboam's peers influenced his decision making, which led to the divided kingdom of Israel (v16-19). Jezebel had a negative influence on king Ahab to act wickedly. How dearly they both paid for their wickedness (Read 1 Kings 21:24-26). King Ahaziah's mother had a negative influence on him "to do wickedly." (2 Chronicles 22:3). On the positive side, apostle Paul influenced Timothy to become a vessel in the hand of God (Read Acts 16:1-3; 1 Timothy 1:2, 18).

Reflection: How do you influence others—negatively or positively?

Word for today: *Positive influence comes from the influence of God's Word.*

RETURN TO YOUR GOD

Let the wicked forsake his way, and the unrighteous man his thoughts; let him return to the LORD, and He will have mercy on him; and to our God, for He will abundantly pardon ((Isaiah 55:7).

READ: HOSEA 6:1-3

There is an African adage which says that a loving mother often beats her child with one hand, and draws him closer with the other hand. No matter how deplorable a child's behavior may be, no mother ever disowns her child. No mother ever throws away her baby together with the dirty bath water. This is the spiritual lesson to be learnt from our text. Hosea 5:14-15 painted an angry picture of God towards the children of Israel with the promise to receive them back, if they repented. Based on that promise, Hosea asked the people to return to the LORD. Our text reads, *"Come, and let us return to the LORD; for He has torn, but He will heal us; He has stricken, but He will bind us up. After two days He will revive us; On the third day He will raise us up, That we may live in His sight. Let us know, Let us pursue the knowledge of the LORD. His going forth is established as the morning; He will come to us like the rain, like the latter and former rain to the earth."* (Hosea 6:1-3). Even though the LORD has torn them like a lion does, He would *heal them*, and *bind them up*, if they repented. The phrase, "After two days he will revive us; on the third day He will raise us up." refers to how quickly the LORD will restore His people, if they truly repent. God is so merciful and caring! Just like the proverbial mother who beats her child with one hand and draws him closer with the other hand, so is the Lord willing to restore and reestablish His relationship with any offending child of His who truly repents and returns.

Unfortunately, some Christians take God's mercy and grace for granted. Even when rebuked for their sins, rather than repent and ask God for His forgiveness, they proudly mount oppositions against any attempt towards genuine repentance. Rather than lament over their sins, they behave as if God owes them something. Like the children of Israel, such people end up rebelling against God, His Word and His Church (Read Jeremiah 44:15-18).

Reflection: No matter how far you may have drifted, God is waiting for you.

Word for today: *Repent and return to your God and it shall be well with you.*

AN ABORTED MINISTRY

"Be diligent to come to me quickly; for Demas has forsaken me, having loved this present world..." (2 Timothy 4:9-10).

READ: JUDGES 16:21-27

I n his letter to young Timothy, Paul warned against an aborted ministry. It reads, *"But you be watchful in all things, endure afflictions, do the work of an evangelist, fulfill your ministry."* (2 Timothy 4:5). An unfulfilled ministry is a let-down on God's grace and calling. In our text, we notice how Samson aborted his ministry—due to careless brinkmanship. Samson was born as a child of destiny. Prior to his conception, God had chosen Samson as a vessel through which He would deliver the children of Israel from their oppressors. An Angel of the LORD had appeared to Samson's mother, who was barren, with these words, *"Behold, you shall conceive and bear a son. And no razor shall come upon his head, for the child shall be a Nazirite to God from the womb; and he shall begin to deliver Israel out of the hand of the Philistines."*(Judges16:5). Indeed, God brought Samson into this world to fulfil a divine purpose. After Samson was born, his ministry started. But, unfortunately, he aborted his ministry. Rather than deliver the children of Israel out of the hand of the Philistines, Samson played into the hand of the Philistines and died a miserable death. After the disclosure of the source of his power and subsequent arrest by the Philistines, Samson was made a laughing spectacle. The Philistines jubilated and thanked their god for delivering Samson into their hands (Judges 16:23-24). How disappointed the LORD must have felt to see Samson abort the ministry for which he was born!

In the New Testament, we learn of another person who aborted his ministry; his name was Demas. In his letters to the Colossian Church and Philemon, Paul cited Demas as one of the brethren who sent their greetings (Colossians 4:14; Philemon 24). But, by the time Paul wrote his second letter to Timothy, Demas had aborted his ministry and gone back into the world (Read 2 Timothy 4:10). May God never allow you to abort your God-given ministry, in Jesus name.

Reflection: How faithful have you been in your ministry?

Word for today: *An unfulfilled ministry leads to an unfulfilled life.*

SLOW DOWN!

"When Jesus heard it, He departed from there by boat to a deserted place by Himself..." (Matthew 14:13).

READ: MARK 6:30-32

In Genesis 2:1-3 we read, *"Thus the heavens and the earth, and all the host of them, were finished. And on the seventh day God ended His work which He had done, and He rested on the seventh day from all His work which He had done. Then God blessed the seventh day and sanctified it, because in it He rested from all His work which God had created and made."* God rested on the seventh day—meaning He ceased from the work of creation. One of God's commandments to the children of Israel was the observance of the Sabbath (Exodus 20:8). By asking them to keep the Sabbath, God was trying to teach them the importance of rest. In principle, the Sabbath is synonymous with rest, and rest is synonymous with the Sabbath. It is not uncommon to hear of "burnt out pastors" these days. These "bunt out pastors" are the pastors who by virtue of their busyness in the vineyard become stressed out to a breaking point. It is good to work hard, but it is foolhardy to think that you can get everything done without having some rest. The human body is like a machinery, which needs some maintenance from time to time. Just as a machinery needs a periodic maintenance, so does the human body need a physiological maintenance called, rest. A lack of maintenance leads to a breakdown, be it a machinery or the human body.

In our text, we notice the importance Jesus places on rest. On their return from an evangelical outreach, Christ's disciples reported to Him *"all things; both what they had done and what they had taught."* (v30). In response, He knew they needed rest and told them, *"Come aside by yourselves to a deserted place and rest a while. For there were many coming and going, and they did not even have time to eat."* (v31). Christ's disciples obeyed and *departed to a deserted place in the boat by themselves [and rested]* (v32). All work and no play, they say, makes Jack a dull and sick boy. Slow down, take a break and get rested.

Reflection: Have you been a busy bee—going without a rest?

Word for today: *God slows us down, when we refuse to slow down.*

BRIGHTEN UP!

*Anxiety in the heart of man causes depression, but a good word makes it glad
(Proverbs 12:25).*

READ: PROVERBS 15:13-14

A survey conducted in 2012 about the happiest people on earth revealed an unbelievable result! It picked Mexico and Nigeria as the happiest countries in the world. Paradoxically, Mexico and Nigeria have something in common—poverty, corruption and crime. Yet, it turned out that the happiest people on the planet are in these two countries. Poverty, corruption and crimes are vices that should make people sad, not happy. The survey indicated that these two countries share a common belief that things would get better. In other words, they look at the sunny-side of life, in the face of abject poverty, corrupt leadership and crime infested society. They share a philosophical belief that tomorrow will be better than today, which gives them hope and brightens their spiritual countenance. Challenges, difficulties, failures and disappointments in life can dampen one's spirit and prevent one from expressing any hope for the future. As believers in Christ, we should never allow this to happen. Rather than wear sad countenance, we should brighten up in our spirit by putting our trust and confidence in God. In God, there is no disappointment. The Bible records, *"Whoever believes on Him will not be put to shame."* and *"Whoever calls on the name of the LORD shall be saved."* (Romans 10:11, 13).

Our text reads, *"A merry heart makes a cheerful countenance, but by sorrow of the heart the spirit is broken."* (v13). When we put our trust in God, sadness will give way to cheerfulness. The Bible records how Nehemiah's sad countenance brightened up because the LORD was with him. Nehemiah was a cupbearer to king Artaxerxes of Persia, as a slave. One day, the news about the dilapidated condition of Jerusalem saddened Nehemiah's countenance before the king. The LORD brightened up Nehemiah's countenance through king Artaxerxes (Read Nehemiah 2:1-10). The solution to sad countenances is not found in night clubs, drinking bars or wild parties; it is found in Christ.

Refection: When sad and disappointed, what do you do?

Word for today: *A sad countenance brightens up in Christ Jesus.*

CHRISTIANITY, NOT RELIGIOSITY

Woe to you! For you build the tombs of the prophets, and your fathers killed them (Luke 11:47).

READ: MATTHEW 23:25-28

Christianity is coming to God through faith in His Son, Christ Jesus, while Religiosity is coming to God through a religious founder, human effort and observance of Church rites. While Christianity honors God, religiosity promotes self. In our text, we notice Christ's indictment of the Scribes and Pharisees for their religiosity. We read, *"Woe to you, scribes and Pharisees, hypocrites! For you cleanse the outside of the cup and dish, but inside they are full of extortion and self-indulgence."* (v25). Our Lord Jesus Christ compared the religiosity of the Scribes and Pharisees to someone who cleanses the outside of a dirty cup and dish, while leaving the inside full of rotten stuff—extortion and self indulgence. The Scribes and Pharisees were more interested in external and ceremonial cleanliness than inner purity. Their mistaken perception as being the epitome of holiness made them blinded to the truth and salvation in Christ. Christ called them hypocrites and pronounced woe on them—a curse that still haunts those Jews who have refused to receive Christ as their expected Messiah.

Verse 27 of our text reads, *"Woe to you, scribes and Pharisees, hypocrites! For you are like whitewashed tombs which indeed appear beautiful outwardly, but inside are full of dead men's bones and all uncleanness. Even so you also outwardly appear righteous to men, but inside you are full of hypocrisy and lawlessness."* In their religiosity, the Scribes and Pharisees were compared to a whitewashed tomb, which looked beautiful outside, but contained rotten human bones inside. Christ accused them of putting up an outward appearance of righteousness, while inwardly they were *"full of hypocrisy and lawlessness."* (v28). In the Church, it is not difficult to find some people who behave like the Scribes and Pharisees, whose outward appearance contradicts their moral standard. Today, fashion competition goes on secretly in the Body of Christ. On Sundays, people are evaluated by what they wear to Church.

Reflection: Which do you embrace—Christ or religion?

Word for today: *Christ makes Christianity meaningful and purposeful.*

JULY

DEVOTIONALS

I CALLED & HE ANSWERED

In my distress I cried to the LORD, and He heard me (Psalm 120:1).

READ: PSALM 118:5-9

Whenever someone is in distress, he or she needs help. Hence, in most developed countries, an emergency response system is in place whereby people can call in time of emergency for help. Law enforcement agencies, the firefighters and medical emergency personnel are usually quick to respond to any distress call from people, if they call in time of emergency. But, sometimes, people fail to call and as a result they suffer loss of property and human lives. In a similar way, God has set up a distress call response system in heaven to deal with distress calls from the people of God. In Jeremiah 33:3 we read, *"Call to me, and I will answer you, and show you great and mighty things, which you do not know."* Those were God's Words to Jeremiah in his time of distress, when he *"was shut up in the court of the prison."* (v1). God's promise to Jeremiah is relevant to us today. If you align yourself with God and live in obedience to His Word, He will respond whenever you make a distress call to Him. What hinders heaven's response to our distress calls is sin. Sin is always a barrier between us and God (Read Proverbs 15:8; 21:27 and Isaiah 59:1-3).

The Psalmist understood very well God's promise in responding to distress calls from His people when he said, *"I called on the LORD in distress; the LORD answered me and set me in a broad place."* (Psalm 118:5). Faith in God and the understanding that He has promised to respond to your distress calls will make you to declare like the Psalmist, *"The LORD is on my side; I will not fear. What can man do to me?"* (v6). When God responds to your distress call, you can confidently say, "It is better to trust in the LORD, than to put confidence in man or princes (v8-9). Last winter, the weather forecast called for a severe snowfall on the week-end of an important event in our Church. Since it was too late to postpone the event or make alternative arrangements, a distress call (prayer) was made to heaven. God responded by moving the snowstorm from Baltimore area to neighboring cities and the event was held.

Reflection: In your time of distress, who do you call?

Word for today: *A distress call receives an urgent response from the LORD.*

HOLY SPIRIT BAPTISM

"But you shall receive power when the Holy Spirit has come upon you..." (Acts 1:8).

The word, baptism is derived from the Greek word *baptisma*, which is "a process of submersion or immersion." When you receive water baptism, you get submerged or immersed in water. Similarly, when you receive Holy Spirit baptism, you get submerged or immersed in the power of the Holy Spirit. Therefore, Holy Spirit baptism is an experience of being submerged or immersed in the power of the Holy Spirit. It takes place subsequent to salvation (Read Acts 2:1-4; 19:1-6). At salvation, you are baptized into Christ (Romans 6:4; 1 Corinthians 12:13)—-**Indwelling** experience; at Holy Spirit baptism, you are baptized (immersed) into the power of the Holy Spirit—**Infilling** experience (Acts 2:4).

WHO IS THE HOLY SPIRIT? The Holy Spirit is not an influence, a concept or a force. He is a Personality—the third Person of the Godhead (Matthew 28:19b; 1 John 5:7).Since the Holy Spirit is a Person, He can be **grieved** (Ephesians 4:30); He can be **blasphemed** against (Matthew 12:31-32) and **sinned** against (Acts 5:3,9).

HOW CAN ONE EXPEREINCE THE HOLY SPIRIT BAPTISM?
1. You must be born again. In order to be filled with the Holy Spirit, you must belong to Jesus (Read Romans 8:9-10). **2. You must have the desire for the Holy Spirit baptism.** God does not force any thing on anyone. Just as God does not force salvation on anyone, so does He not force Holy Spirit baptism on anyone (Read John 7:37-39). **3. You must ask in prayer**. Luke 11:13 reads, *"If you then, being evil know how to give good gifts to your children, how much more will your heavenly Father give the Holy Spirit to those who ask Him."* **4. You must be willing to obey the Holy Spirit** (Read Acts 5:32).
WHAT ARE THE EVIDENCES OF HOLY SPIRIT BAPTISM? **1. Speaking in tongues** (Read Acts 2:4; 10:44,46; 19:6). Simon, the sorcerer saw the evidence of speaking in tongues and tried to purchase Holy Sprit baptism (Read Acts 8:13-20). **2. Spiritual giftedness** (Read 1 Corinthians 12:7-11).

Reflection: Have you ever considered being baptized in the Holy Spirit?

Word for today: *Holy Spirit baptism endows you with power for service.*

198

EXCEEDINGLY ABUNDANT GRACE

Moreover the law entered that the offense might abound. But where sin abounded, grace abounded much more (Romans 5:20).

READ: 1 TIMOTHY 1:12-17

Many years ago, a young Christian sister in the Lord had a hard time understanding how God's grace worked. The aspect of God's grace that was too difficult for this sister to understand was that of God's forgiveness. She asked, "How can someone murder an innocent person, and after several years become a believer in Christ with his sins forgiven? What will happen to the innocent person that has been killed? I tried my best to answer this sister's question by pointing out three facts of life. **First,** God's ways are not our ways, and His thoughts are not our thoughts. In fact, God's ways and thoughts are beyond our human understanding (Isaiah 55:8-9). The way we look at something is not the way God looks at it. Second, God does not guarantee anyone how and when one would die. Hence, we find that an innocent as well as a guilty person can die anytime. Sometimes, bad things do happen to good people. **Third,** it is important to be born again, because no one knows when death will strike.

In our text, Paul referred to God's act of forgiveness of one's sinful past an exceedingly abundant grace. Paul remembered his own dark past and how God forgave him and called me xto serve. We read, *"And I thank Christ Jesus our Lord who has enabled me, because He counted me faithful, putting me into the ministry, although I was formerly a blasphemer, a persecutor, and an insolent man; but I obtained mercy because I did it ignorantly in unbelief. And the grace of our Lord was exceedingly abundant, with faith and love which are in Christ Jesus."* (v12-14). Just like Paul, we all have our sinful past, yet, it pleased God to chose us in Christ. Paul regarded himself as chief of sinners, due to his persecution of Christians. After all, he masterminded the killing of Stephen (Read Acts 7:57-60; 8:1). If you are born again you need to thank God for His exceedingly abundant grace in your life. If on the other hand, you are not born again, know that you are wasting God's abundant grace.

Reflection: How do you handle God's abundant grace in your life?

Word for today: *To waste God's grace is to waste one's life.*

THE PRICE OF FREEDOM!

You were bought at a price; do not become slaves of men (1 Corinthians 7:23).

READ: JOHN 10:15-18

No freedom ever comes without a price (Read Leviticus 25:47-52). Three hundred and thirty nine (239) years ago, the United States of America secured her freedom from Britain. This freedom did not come without the human price. In fact, the United States is still paying the human price to sustain her freedom. Today, as we celebrate the freedom of this great country, let us not forget those who paid the utmost price with their lives to obtain and sustain the freedom. Any nation that enjoys freedom today, must have in one way or the other paid the human price for such a freedom.

There is another kind of freedom unknown to many: It's spiritual, not political; personal, not national; eternal, not temporal and heavenly, not earthly. Verses 15 and 17 of our text read, *"As the Father knows me, even so I know the Father; and I lay down my life for the sheep. Therefore my Father loves me, because I lay down my life that I may take it again."* In these verses, our Lord Jesus Christ was referring to His impending death for the redemption of humankind. Indeed, Christ paid a huge price to secure our freedom from satanic bondage. Right after the fall of Adam, the entire human race came under the bondage of Satan, and ever since, every person born into this world has been held in spiritual captivity by Satan and his cohorts. Since, a captive cannot free himself from captivity without the help of someone, God decided to send His son, Jesus Christ to free the human race from the bondage of Satan. In doing so, Christ paid a price with His life and blood to secure such a freedom (Read Matthew 20:28; 26:28). Based on the death and triumphant resurrection of Christ, every human being now has the opportunity to enjoy real freedom in Christ. Unfortunately, many are still in Satanic bondage, in spite of the freedom Christ has made available to all. They prefer to be enslaved by Satan, rather than be set free in Christ. As you enjoy political freedom, for which you should be grateful to God, don't forget to enjoy spiritual freedom as well. To enjoy spiritual freedom, you must believe in the Lord Jesus Christ.

Reflection: Are you really free from Satan and sin?

Word for today: *Real freedom is in Christ, receive Him today.*

KEEPING THE WORLD AT BAY

I have given them your word; and the world has hated them because they are not of the world, just as I am not of the world (John 17:14).

READ: JOHN 17:15-19

Prior to His death on the cross, our Lord Jesus Christ had this to say to His Father regarding His disciples: *"I do not pray that you should take them out of the world, but that you should keep them from evil. They are not of the world, just a I am not of the world."* (John 17:15-16). Two truths are obvious from the above prayers by the Lord. **First,** every believer in Christ is kept from the power and domination of the devil. Although the devil is the prince of this world, he has no power over the children of God. In fact, he ceases to be their master, the moment they put their trust in Christ. Every believer in Christ has passed from the kingdom of Satan to the Kingdom of God (Colossians 1:13). **Second,** every believer in Christ is not of this world, just as Christ is not of the world. Just as the devil used worldly things to tempt Christ in order to derail His salvation plan for humankind, so does the devil use worldly things to tempt the believer in Christ in order to derail his salvation in Christ. Worldly things are opposed to heavenly things. Anyone who holds tenaciously to worldly things will find it very hard to grow spiritually as a Christian. The only way to grow spiritually is to keep the world at bay—at a distance (Read 1 John 2:15 -17).

Although we are in the world, it is not impossible to keep the world at bay. **Here are some tips: 1.** Don't be unequally yoked together with unbelievers (2 Corinthians 6:14). An unbeliever is of the world, while you as a follower of Christ are not. Therefore, to become unequally yoked with an unbeliever, especially in marriage, is like Christ being yoked with the devil.
2. Do not love the world (1 John 2:15). You cannot love God and the world at the same time. To keep the world at bay is to love God.
3. Constantly feed on and obey the Word of God (John 17:17) The more you feed on the Word of God and do what God says, the more likely you are to keep the world at bay.

Reflection: How close is the world to you? And how close are you to Jesus?

Word for today: *To keep the world away, keep Christ within you.*

BRIBERY & CORRUPTION

Righteousness exalts a nation, but sin is a reproach to any people (Proverbs 14:34).

READ: PROVERBS 17:22-23

Bribery and corruption are two deadly vices that can destroy a society. The Bible declares, *"Righteousness exalts a nation, but sin is a reproach to any people (Proverbs 14:34).* Any society that promotes bribery is under God's reproach. Another word for reproach is **curse**. Wherever there is bribery, God's curse is not lacking. When people take bribes, they do so in order to cover up the truth or gain something that they really don't merit, hence those who take bribes are corrupt and prone to telling lies. Verse 23 of our text reads, *"A wicked man accepts a bribe behind the back to pervert the ways of justice."* Whenever people take bribes, they do so behind closed doors to hide their evil deeds from the human eyes. But, they forget that there is an **Eye** in heaven which sees every hidden thing. God hates bribery and warns people against it. In Exodus 23: 8 we read, *"And you shall take no bribe, for a bribe blinds the discerning and perverts the words of the righteous."* Any wealth made through bribery is ill-gotten and all those who engaged in bribery will be consumed by the fire of God (Job 15:34). Bribery destroys a person's heart as well as his household (Proverbs 15:27; Ecclesiastes 7:7). It is unfortunate that the word, bribery has been refined and renamed, **'gift'** Today, people tend to call bribes gifts.

Bribery helps to suppress the truth while promoting lies. For example, Jezebel bribed those in authority to lie against Neboth in order to kill him and deprive him of his vineyard (Read 1 Kings 21:9-14). Delilah took bribe to uncover the source of Samson's strength to destroy him (Judges 16:5). Judas took a bribe of thirty pieces of silver to betray Jesus (Matthew 26:14-16). The soldiers who witnessed Christ's triumphant resurrection, took bribe from the Jewish religious leaders to suppress the truth regarding what they saw (Matthew 28:11-15). Felix, the governor, sought bribe from Paul during his trial, but got none (Acts 24:26-27).

Reflection: Do you give or take bribes? Beware!

Word for today: *Corrupt minds are corrupt through bribery and corruption.*

LOSING A GOOD NIGHT'S SLEEP?

It is vain for you to rise up early, to sit up late, to eat the bread of sorrows; for so He gives His beloved sleep (Psalm 127:2).

READ: ECCLESIASTEES 5:11-12

A good night's sleep is a blessing from God; unfortunately, not every one enjoys this blessing. Whenever you wake up in the morning, after a good night's sleep, it is good that you give thanks to God. A bad night's sleep can be scary, tormenting and frustrating. There are those who can't even sleep at night due to some medical conditions. Apart from medical issues, there are several things that can deprive one of a good night's sleep, one of which is highlighted in v12 of our text. It reads, *"The sleep of a laboring man is sweet, whether he eats little or much; but the abundance of the rich will not permit him to sleep."* (v12). Indeed, the riches of a man can cause him to lose sleep. Whenever this happens, such riches become a source of torment, rather than a thing of blessing. Unfortunately, a lot of rich people are worried about losing their wealth and as a result, they lose sleep over such wealth. Anyone who loses a good night's sleep over his or her wealth, should have a reflection of how he or she got the wealth in the first place. An ill-gotten wealth can cause someone to lose sleep, because the Word of God makes it clear that *"there is no peace for the wicked."* (Isaiah 57:21). When God blesses you with material wealth, He does not add sorrow to it. Proverbs 10:22 reads, *"The blessing of the LORD makes one rich, and He adds no sorrow with it."* But, when Satan gives a person material wealth, he always adds sorrow to it (Read John 10:10).

Besides an ill-gotten wealth, a sad news can cause someone to lose a good night's sleep. For instance, when someone receives some sad news, his or her spirit becomes depressed and when a person's spirit is depressed, he or she loses appetite and sleep. Scary dreams can also cause someone to lose a good night's sleep. Sometimes, the devil scares people by giving them terrible dreams. When this happens, such people wake up and become scared to even venture to sleep again. If you are frequently losing a good night's sleep due to scary dreams, you need some serious prayers from gifted men of God.

Reflection: Do you lose sleep at night? Are you scared to even sleep?

Word for today: *God gives His beloved a good night's sleep*

LORD: SHOW, LEAD AND TEACH ME

Teach me your way, O LORD; I will walk in your truth; unite my heart to fear your name (Psalm 86:11).

READ: PSALM 25:4-5

Our text reads, *"Show me your ways, O LORD; teach me your paths. Lead me in your truth and teach me, for you are the God of my salvation; on you I wait all the day."* (v4-5). David, the writer of Psalm 25, used three key words in our text: **"Show"**, **"Teach"** and **"Lead"**. **First**, David prayed that the LORD would **show** him His ways. There are ways of men; there are also ways of the LORD. The ways of men may seem good, but they lead to destruction (Psalm 14:12). David preferred the ways of God to the ways of men. The ways of the LORD *speak* of the characters of God. When we know the ways (characters) of God, we will be able to serve Him more faithfully. **Second**, David asked the LORD to **teach** him His paths. The paths of the LORD *speak* of the salvation of God. The path of the LORD is often a narrow path, but it certainly leads to eternal life. **Third**, David prayed that the LORD would **lead** him in His truth. The truth refers to the Word of God— sound Bible doctrines. Being led by God's truth is the key to knowing God. Knowledge of the truth sets people free from the bondage of Satan and sin. Our Lord Jesus told the Jews who believed in Him, *"And you shall know the truth, and the truth shall make you free."* (John 8:32). As a believer in Christ, develop the desire to be taught the truth—sound Bible doctrines.

The LORD has promised to *"instruct and teach you in the way you should go and to guide you with His eyes"* (Psalm 32:8). He can teach and guide you through His Word, the Holy Spirit and events in your life. Many years ago, I tried to embark on a small business venture in Nigeria and spent a lot of time praying about it. It looked a promising business since the capital, equipment, human resources and expertise were available. From a human stand point, it looked a lucrative business to venture into. Then one night, as I was praying, God told me not to start that business, because the devil would use it to attack me down the road. I thanked the Lord that I heeded His warning.

Reflection: Are you led and taught by God?

Word for today: *God leads those who want to be led by Him.*

THE MYSTERY OF LIFE

The fear of the LORD is a fountain of life, to turn one away from the snares of death (Proverbs 14:27).

READ: LUKE 12:22-23

Life is a mystery and no human being can fully comprehend it. Life means different things to different people. For instance, to the atheist, life is wind; to the naturalist, life is beauty; to the biologist, life is the particle of energy in a microbe and to the physicist, life is an embodiment of DNA. Yes, DNA helps us to understand the structure of human genetics, but it is not the source of life, nor does it tell us how life originated. Since life has been in existence before the discovery of DNA, science can only discover something about life, but cannot truly tell us how life originated.

The Bible is the only Book that has an answer about the mystery of life. Genesis records that prior to creation, there was no life and that God brought life into existence through His creative Words (Read Genesis 1:20-24). In addition, God created a human being in His image; He formed him "out of the dust of the ground and breathed into his nostrils the breath of life and man became a living being." (2:7). God is the Originator of life and He only knows the mystery of life. John 1-4 gives us some insight into the mystery of life. We read *"In the beginning was the Word, and the Word was with God, and the Word was God. He was in the beginning with God. All things were made through Him, and without Him nothing was made that was made. In Him was life, and the life was the light of men. And the light shines in the darkness, and the darkness did not comprehend it."* What the Spirit of God is saying through John is that, in creation, God through His spoken Word, who is Christ, brought life into existence. This means that Christ is the Source of life. Any wonder He said, *"I am the Way, the Truth and the Life...?"* (John 14:6). Life is God's investment of eternal value in humans. He takes care of it, if only humans can faithfully depend on Him. In our text, our Lord Jesus Christ warns us, *"Do not worry about your life....life is more than food, and the body is more than clothing."* (Luke 12:22-23).

Reflection: What is life to you?

Word for today: *One of life's mysteries is that you don't own your life.*

205

DIVINELY AMBUSHED

"When the three hundred blew the trumpets, the LORD set every man's sword against his companion throughout the whole camp..." (Judges 7:22).

READ: 2 CHRONICLES 20:22-24

In a physical ambush, you secretly lay in wait for your enemy. But, the opposite is the case with a divine ambush. In a divine ambush, God does not launch His attack in secret, but in the open. Our text tells us how God ambushed the people of Ammon, Moab and Mount Seir, who conspired to attack Jehoshaphat and his people. Jehoshaphat had set up singers as they matched to the battle field, having been given an assurance of a divine victory (2 Chronicles 20:15). The lyrics of their song was reflective of God's mercy (v21). As Jehoshaphat and his men sang praises to the LORD on their way to the battle field, God did the fighting for them: He sent divine ambushes against their enemies (v22). Isn't it amazing how God can send an ambush against your enemies when you offer a spirit-filled praise and worship to Him? What the LORD did to Jehoshaphat, He can still do today. All He wants from us is faith and total obedience to His Word. Saul was divinely ambushed on his way to the city of Damascus to persecute the believers in Christ. Fortunately for Saul, he was not killed, but transformed.

Whenever God sends an ambush into the camp of your enemy, five things will take place: **1.** Confusion will engulf them. Verse 23 of our text reads, *"For the people of Ammon and Moab stood up against the inhabitants of Mount Seir to utterly kill and destroy them. And when they had made an end of the inhabitants of Seir, they helped to destroy one another."* The people of Ammon, Moab and Mount Seir went into confusion mode and ended up destroying one another. **2.** There will be no escape route for your enemy (v24). **3.** You will rejoice and praise God for the victory (v27-28). **4.** Fear will overtake those who witness what God has done for you (v29). **5.** The peace of God will become your portion (v30). As a user of this devotional, learn to trust in the LORD as Jehoshaphat did and it shall be well with you.

Reflection: Don't make yourself the target of divine ambush

Word for today: *God can ambush your known and unknown enemies.*

206

TRANSFORMATION & RENEWAL

"Put off, concerning your former conduct, the old man which grows corrupt according to the deceitful lusts, and be renewed in the spirit of your mind" (Ephesians 4:22-23).

READ: ROMANS 12:1-2

Verse 1 of our text reads, *"I beseech you therefore, brethren, by the mercies of God, that you present your bodies a living sacrifice, holy, acceptable to God, which is your reasonable service."* In an animal sacrifice, the priest first of all, kills the animal before placing it on the altar. But, in a spiritual sacrifice, the believer in Christ offers himself to God, not as a dead, but living sacrifice. The difference between a dead and living sacrifice is that a dead sacrifice is dead in sin and does not please God, while a living sacrifice is dead to sin, but alive in Christ and pleases God. Verse 2 reads, *"And do not be conformed to this world, but be transformed by the renewing of your mind, that you may prove what is that good and acceptable and perfect will of God."* Every believer in Christ is reminded not to be "conformed to this world"—not to yield to the sinful pressure of the world system, but to "be transformed" through mind renewal.

The mind is "the seat of all reflective consciousness, comprising the faculties of perception, understanding, feelings and judgment." This means that what goes on in one's mind controls one's behavior. In this verse, there are three reasons why as a believer in Christ, your mind should be renewed. First is the ability to prove what is good before God. Someone whose mind is screwed up with worldliness cannot prove what is good before God. Second is to know what is acceptable to God. Things that are acceptable to the world are usually not acceptable to God, because the world is at variance with the Word of God. Third is the ability to be in the perfect will of God. God has His will for everyone, but until a person is transformed and renewed in his mind, he cannot operate in God's will. The human mind needs a daily renewal, because Satan uses fear, unbelief, doubts, worldly lusts and sinful pleasures to constantly attack it. The Word of God and Prayer are mind renewal tools.

Reflection: Can you tell of how God has transformed and renewed you?

Word for today: *Transformation and renewal—keys to knowing God's will.*

MIGHTY AND STRONG

For His eyes are on the ways of man, and He sees all his steps (Job 34:21).

READ: 2 CHRONICLES 16:7-10

God is mighty and strong. He has proven over and over that, that is who He is. In deed, God is mightier than the mightiest and stronger than the strongest of men. For instance, when God sent Moses and Aaron to Pharaoh with this message: *"Let my people go, that they may hold a feast to me in the wilderness."* (Exodus 5:1). At the time Moses and Aaron met Pharaoh to deliver God's message to him, Pharaoh was considered a demi-god—adored and worshipped by all. Therefore, it was not surprising that Pharaoh answered Moses and Aaron the way he did. He told them, *"Who is the LORD, that I should obey His voice to let Israel go? I do not know the LORD, nor will I let Israel go."* (v2). How stupid Pharaoh must have been! He failed to acknowledge that God was stronger and mightier that he. This is what happens to a number of bigots today. They feel the world revolves around them. In their ignorance, they fail to acknowledge and respect God, who created them. Just last Sunday, our Church went for a door-to-door evangelism outreach in the neighborhood. Then, we met a middle-aged man who said to us, "I don't need your preaching. I have been a member of the church of Satan for 20 years. I believe in Satan; that is my belief." When told that God loved him, the man became agitated and asked us to leave his premises. People who think the way this man does, behave like Pharaoh and unless they repent, they will end up the way Pharaoh did—hardened and hell bound.

Verse 9 of our text reads, *"For the eyes of the LORD run to and fro throughout the whole earth, to show Himself strong on behalf of those whose heart is loyal to Him. In this you have done foolishly; therefore from now on you shall have wars."* These were the words of Hanani to king Asa of Judah for despising the power of God Almighty, while relying on the king of Syria for deliverance in time of war. Hanani's indictment of king Asa holds true to all who claim to be God's children, yet, fail to rely on Him for help in times of need. God is mighty and strong on behalf of those who trust in Him.

Reflection: Do you rely on God or men in times of need?

Word for today: *Our mighty God strengthens the weak and the feeble.*

208

GOD'S MERCY & COMPASSION

For I am the LORD, I do not change; therefore you are not consumed, O sons of Jacob. (Malachi 3:6).

READ: LAMENTATION 3:22-23

There is as a popular chorus that I love so much. It tells us about the enduring power of God's faithfulness, mercy and compassion. There is no doubt that the composer of this chorus got the lyric from our text, Lamentation 3:23. The lyric of the chorus is as follows:

The steadfastness of the LORD never ceases;
His mercy never come to an end.
They are new every morning, new every morning;
Great is your faithfulness, O, LORD,
Great is your faithfulness.

God's mercy **saves** us; His compassion **sustains** us. Without God's mercy and compassion, human beings are done. Psalm 78:38-39 underscore why God's mercy and compassion fail not. We read, *"But He, being full of compassion, forgave their iniquity, and did not destroy them. Yes, many a time He turned His anger away, and did not stir up all His wrath, for He remembered that they were but flesh, a breath that passes away and does not come again."* Indeed, there are times that our iniquities pile up to the high heavens to warrant God's wrath. But God who understands our frailty, withholds His anger and wrath, while expecting genuine repentance from us. Sometimes, people abuse God's mercy and compassion by continuing in sin. No wonder the Scripture says, *"Because the sentence against an evil work is not executed speedily, therefore the heart of the sons of men is fully set in them to do evil."* (Ecclesiastes 8:11).

Verse 22 of our text reads, *"Through the LORD'S mercies we are not consumed, because His compassions fail not."* Indeed, the LORD's mercy and compassion fail not. Who would have thought that Paul who masterminded the killing of Stephen for preaching that salvation was through Christ, would be the one to spread the same message for which he persecuted and killed Stephen. God's mercy and compassion made this possible!

Reflection: What have you done with God's mercy and compassion?

Word for today: *God's mercy and compassion are ingredients of salvation.*

A LIFE JOURNEY

Where do wars and fights come from among you? Do they not come from your desires for pleasure that war in your members? (James 4:1).

READ: 1 PETER 2:11-12

Life is a journey and like every journey, it has a beginning and an end. One's life journey begins the very moment he or she is born and continues after death into eternity. In our text, Peter reminds the believers in Christ of who they are. We read, *"Beloved, I beg you as sojourners and pilgrims, abstain from fleshly lusts which war against the soul."* (v11). Peter used two words in our text in reference to a believer's life journey. One is a **sojourner**—*one who resides temporarily in a place;* the other is a **pilgrim**—*one who is on a journey or a traveler.* These two words are associated with someone who is not a citizen of a country. A life journey has two destinations: One is **Heaven**, while the other is **Hell**. It is when one is alive that one chooses the destination of one's journey. If one chooses Christ, one ends up in heaven. But, if on the other hand one chooses Satan, one will end up in hell.

As believers in Christ, our life journey should end in heaven, not in hell. Hebrews 12:22-23 read, *"But you have come to Mount Zion and to the city of the living God, the heavenly Jerusalem, to an innumerable company of angels, to the general assembly and church of the firstborn who are registered in heaven, to God the Judge of all, to the spirits of just men made perfect."* Based on our text, we should do two important things during our life journey. **First,** we should *"abstain from fleshly lusts which war against the soul."* (1 Peter 2:11). It is the soul that journeys from earth to either heaven or hell at death. Therefore, it is very important to abstain from anything that will prevent it from making heaven. Read **Galatians 5:19-21** and you will have an insight into what fleshly lusts are. The **second** thing we should do during our life journey is to have a good and honorable conduct among the unbelievers (1 Peter 2:12). To claim to be a heavenly citizen, while portraying worldly characteristics makes mockery of heaven. Heaven is a prepared place for a prepared people. It is not what we say that matters, it is what you and I do that counts.

Reflection: How is your life journey coming up?

Word for today: *Life is a journey; journey safely with Christ.*

GOD'S GLORIOUS LANDSCAPE

"Truly, as I live, all the earth shall be filled with the glory of the LORD." (Numbers 14:21).

READ: PSALM 72:18-19

Our God is God of beauty and how beautiful and glorious is His creative landscape called the earth. By His Word, the earth and everything in it were created. During creation, God saw that everything He had created was good and beautiful. Five verses in the first chapter of Genesis testify to this fact. In Genesis 1:12 we read, *"And the earth brought forth grass, the herb that yields seed according to its kind, and the tree that yields fruit, whose seed is in itself according to its kind. And God saw that it was good."* When God spoke natural vegetation into existence, He saw that it was good and beautiful. Today, you and I can testify to the beauty of nature at spring time. In Genesis 1:16-18 we notice that after creating the sun, moon and stars, God saw that they were also good and beautiful. When God pronounces something as being beautiful, you cannot add to or take away anything from it. You and I enjoy the sun in the day, and the beauty of the moon and stars at night. Genesis 1: 25 tells us that *"God made the beast of the earth according to its kind, cattle according to tis kind, and everything that creeps on the earth according to its kind. And God saw that it was good."* Whenever you go to the Zoo, try to take a close look at the beauty of those animals; then, you will appreciate the beauty of God, who made those animals to be beautiful. At the completion of His creative work, the Bible records that, *"God saw everything that He had made and indeed it was very good."* (Genesis 12:31).

The mountains, hills, valleys, oceans, seas, rivers, all display God's glory. Ironically, every creature displays God's glory, except human beings who are created in God's image. For instance, when a man marries a fellow man as a wife, and a woman marries a fellow woman as a husband, hasn't God's glory in manhood and womanhood been desecrated and dishonored? Verse 19 of our text reminds us to bless the glorious name of the LORD for ever and to let the whole earth be filled with His glory (Psalm 72:19).

Reflection: How appreciative are you to God about His creation?

Word for today: *God created you to add beauty to His creation.*

GOD'S MYSTERIOUS WAY

Oh, the depth of the riches both of the wisdom and knowledge of God! How unsearchable are His judgments and His ways past finding out! (Romans 11:33).

READ: ACTS 16:6-9

When William Cowper penned the lyrics of the famous hymn, "God moves in a mysterious way", he was reflecting on God's wonderful deeds, which surpassed human understanding. The first stanza of this hymn tells it all:

God moves in a mysterious way; His wonders to perform.
He plants His footsteps in the sea; And rides upon the storm.

As humans, we are incapable of understanding God's mysterious way of doing things. In fact, we are limited in knowledge as to why bad things happen to good people; why God allowed innocent Stephen to be stoned to death, before arresting Paul to preach the gospel. Joseph suffered in the hands of his siblings by being sold into slavery. On getting to Potiphar's house as a slave, Joseph was falsely accused of attempted rape by Potiphar's wife—a very serious accusation that landed Joseph in prison (Genesis 39:1-23).

In our text we notice how God directed Paul and his team to take the gospel to the province of Macedonia. On their arrival at the foremost city of Macedonia called Philippi, they were imprisoned for casting out the spirit of divination from a slave girl (Acts 16:16-24). Due to God's mysterious way of doing things, He turned their adverse circumstance into an opportunity to advance His Kingdom. While in jail, God saved the jailer and his household through the ministry of Paul and Silas (v25-34). If Paul and Silas hadn't gone to Macedonia, they wouldn't have been imprisoned; and if they hadn't been imprisoned, the jailer wouldn't have had the opportunity to hear the gospel; and if the jailer hadn't heard the gospel, he and his household wouldn't have been saved. God knows how to turn disappointments into appointments and disadvantages into advantages. As a believer in Christ, pray that God will use your current circumstances to glorify His name and advance His Kingdom.

Reflection: Have you experienced God's mysterious way lately?

Word for today: *God's mysterious way is wrapped up in His mysterious love.*

GOD—MY HELP AND HOPE

Blessed is the man who trusts in the LORD, and whose hope is the LORD (Jeremiah 17:7).

READ: PSALM 146:5-10

Verse 5 of our text reads, *"Happy is he who has the God of Jacob for his help, whose hope is in the LORD his God."* There are two words in this verse that tell us about the Omnipotence of God. One is **help** and the other is **hope.** It is good to make God your help and hope in times of difficulties. As your **Help**, God provides the solution to your problems; as your **Hope**, He keeps you trusting in Him.

Our text gives us ten (10) reasons why we should make God our Help and Hope:
1. He "made heaven and earth", including "the sea and all that is in them." (v6a). As the Creator, God has the capability of taking care of His creatures. **2. He "keeps truth forever"**—meaning God does not lie (v6b). What He said a thousand years ago, stands true to date. **3. He "executes justice for the oppressed"** (v7a). If you are oppressed, have hope in the LORD. He will not forsake you; very soon, you will have a testimony. **4. He "gives food to the hungry"** (v7b). The LORD "satisfies the longing soul and fills the hungry with goodness." (Psalm 107:9). **5. He "gives freedom to the prisoners"** (v7c). The LORD sets free those who are in spiritual bondage (Read John 8:36).
6. He "opens the eyes of the blind." (v8a). The LORD opens the eyes of the physically and spiritually blind (Read Matthew 9:27-31).
7. He "raises those who are bowed down." (v8b). Read Luke 13:10-13.
8. He "loves the righteous." (v8c). The LORD loves righteousness and will never forget the righteous. **9. He "watches over the strangers."** (v9a). As a child of God, if you are a stranger in your environment. He will take care of you. Read Deuteronomy 10:18. **10. He "relieves the fatherless and widow."** (v9b). As you read this Devotional, bring all your problems to the LORD. Call upon Him by faith and He will surely deliver you. Make Him your Help and Hope and He will never disappoint you.

Reflection: Is God your Help and Hope?

Word for today: *God of hope, provides hope in a hopeless situation.*

213

AN ALTAR TO THE LORD

"Then the LORD appeared to Abram and said, 'To your descendants I will give this land.' And there he built an altar to the LORD, who had appeared to him.'" (Genesis 12:7).

READ: GENESIS 12:4-9

Basically, an altar is a platform on which sacrifices are offered. In the Old Testament, when animal sacrifices were the norm, altars were built for such sacrifices. As there were altars to the LORD, so were there altars to Satan, because Satan likes to mimic God in worship. Therefore, it was not uncommon to find the altars of Baal in which animals and even human beings were sacrificed to Satan (2 Chronicles 33:3). To date, some people still offer animal sacrifices to Satan, through idol worship. The Bible records the first altar built by Noah after the flood (Genesis 8:20-22). In our text, we notice that Abraham built an altar to the LORD, after he was asked to leave his kindred. We read, *"Then the LORD appeared to Abram and said, 'To your descendants I will give this land.' And there he built an altar to the LORD, who had appeared to him. And he moved from there to the mountain east of Bethel, and he pitched his tent with Bethel on the west and Ai on the east; there he built an altar to the LORD and called on the name of the LORD.'"* (Genesis 12:7-8). Abraham's purpose for building an altar to the LORD was for him to recognize and appreciate God's favor and goodness upon his life. Later, Abraham built an altar on which he wanted to offer Isaac as a sacrifice to the LORD (Genesis 22:9).

In the New Testament, the LORD has done away with every man-made altar and animal sacrifice. In fact, He no longer delights in "burnt offerings and sacrifices" but in a "broken spirit and contrite heart." (Psalm 51:16,17). Today, you don't need to build a temple or erect an altar in order to offer sacrifices to God. Your body is the temple of God and your heart is the altar on which an acceptable sacrifice of praise and worship should take place (Read 1 Corinthian 3:16, 17; 6:19; 2 Corinthians 6:16). Therefore, your heart needs a daily cleansing with the Word of God.

Reflection: Is your heart God's altar of praise and worship?

Word for today: *The altar of the human heart needs a daily purification.*

214

THE "WHY" QUESTION

And Jesus answered and said to them, "Do you suppose that these Galileans were worse sinners than all other Galileans, because they suffered such things?" (Luke 13:2).

READ: JOHN 9:1-5

As humans, due to our inquisitive nature, we like to know why things happen. For instance, we like to know why bad things happen to nice people; why bad people seem to live longer than good people; why God allows evil to thrive; why God doesn't destroy those who perpetrate evil, and the list goes on and on. It is good though, to ask God questions, but not all the questions receive His response. Sometimes, God's answer to our question may not be what we like or expect to hear. For instance, during a discussion regarding divorce, our Lord Jesus made it clear that it was bad for someone to divorce his wife (Matthew 19:3-6). But, Jesus' answer came to His Jewish audience as a surprise. In fact, they did not like His answer. So, they fired a follow-up question, *"Why did Moses command to give a certificate of divorce, and to put her away?"* (v7). Based on their follow-up question, Christ then went ahead to explain why Moses permitted them to divorce their wives and warned, *"Whoever divorces his wife, except for sexual immorality, and marries another, commits adultery; and whoever marries her who is divorced commits adultery."*(Matthew 19:9). The answer Jesus gave to their question regarding divorce was so strong that His disciples concluded by saying, *"If such is the case of the man with his wife, it is better not to marry."* (v10). The lesson from this divorce discussion is this: Better be careful when you ask God questions, because the answer you will get might surprise you.

In our text, Christ's disciples asked Him why a man was born blind. They asked, "Rabbi, who sinned, this man of his parents, that he was born blind" (v2). Again, Christ's answer to the **"why"** question must have taken His disciples by surprise. Jesus answered, *"Neither this man nor his parents sinned, but that the works of God should be revealed in him."* (v3). If God were to answer all our **"why"** questions, we would be so scared to live.

Reflection: Do you ask God the **"why"** questions? Do you get answers?

Word for today: *God's answer to your questions can eclipse your mind.*

NO SWEARING!

They have spoken words, swearing falsely in making a covenant. Thus judgment springs up like hemlock in the furrows of the field (Hosea 10:4).

READ: 1 KINGS 19:1-3; 20:10

Swearing is an act of *"making a solemn declaration, invoking a deity, a sacred person or thing."* The reason why people swear is to validate or authenticate their truthfulness regarding an issue or a course of action being taken. In the Old Testament, swearing by the name of the LORD was acceptable, even though there were instances of people swearing falsely in the name of the LORD (Read Isaiah 48:1; Jeremiah 5:2; 7:9-10). But, in the New Testament, that changed. Our Lord Jesus, in His teaching, forbids His followers from swearing. Matthew 5:33-37 read, *"Again you have heard that it was said to those of old, 'You shall not swear falsely, but shall perform your oaths to the Lord.' But I say to you, do not swear at all: neither by heaven, for it is God's throne; nor by the earth, for it is His footstool; nor by Jerusalem, for it is the city of the great King. Nor shall you swear by your head, because you cannot make one hair white or black. But let your 'Yes' be 'Yes,' and your 'No,' 'No.' For whatever is more than these is from the evil one."* As a believer in Christ, do you swear? If you do, you are sinning against the Lord.

Idol worshippers swear a lot to appease their gods. In our text, we notice how Jezebel swore in the name of her gods to deal with Elijah after four hundred and fifty prophets of Baal suffered a humiliating defeat and were killed by Elijah, the prophet of God (1 Kings 18:20-40). Verses 1-2 of our text read, *"And Ahab told Jezebel all that Elijah had done, also how he had executed all the prophets with the sword. Then Jezebel sent a messenger to Elijah, saying, 'So let the gods do to me, and more also, if I do not make your life as the life of one of them by tomorrow about this time."* By Jezebel swearing in the name of her gods, she was determined to carry out her evil plans. When Elijah learnt about Jezebel's threat, he ran for his life (v3). In the book of James, the Holy Spirit reiterated the Lord's warning, *"Do not swear, either by heaven or by earth...but let your "Yes" be "Yes", and your "No,..."No"* (James 5:12).

Reflection: Are you fond of swearing to make a point? Don't anymore!

Word for today: *By swearing, you expose yourself to the devil.*

A FINAL WARNING

"And Jesus said to her, 'Neither do I condemn you; go and sin no more.'" (John 8:11).

READ: JOHN 5:8-15

When someone is given a final warning in a given situation, be it in a learning institution or a place of employment, it means that something serious is bound to follow, if the individual concerned doesn't take care. The same warning applies to our walk with the Lord. Yes, God is gracious and forgiving, but we should not take His grace for granted. Let's not forget that the God who is gracious, is also the same God who is a consuming fire (Read Deuteronomy 4:24 and Hebrews 12:29). One cannot continue to live in sin and keep confessing and asking God for forgiveness over the same sin over and over. The Bible says, *"He who covers his sins will not prosper, but whoever confesses and forsakes them will have mercy."* (Proverbs 28:13). Romans 6:1 asks, *"Shall we continue in sin that grace may abound?"* The answer is a resounding, "No." *"How can we who died to sin live any longer in it."* (v2).

Our Lord Jesus Christ met a man with an infirmity at a pool, who was bedridden for thirty-eight years. Jesus said to him, *"Rise, take your bed and walk. And immediately, the man was made well, took up his bed, and walked."* (John 5:8-9). Since the man's healing took place on the Sabbath, the Jewish religious authority was angry to see him carry his bed on the Sabbath, in spite of his being healed of his infirmity—looks like more emphasis was on the Sabbath observance than the man's healing. So, the man was queried, *"Who is the man who said to you, 'Take up your bed and walk?'"* (v12). Incidentally, the guy did not know that it was Jesus who healed him (v13). Eventually, Jesus met the man who was healed in the temple, and said to him, *"See, you have been made well. 'Sin no more, lest a worse thing come upon you.'"* (v14). This man received his last warning from our Lord. Most people, unknown to them, have received their last warning regarding their sinful lifestyles. Unless they repent, God's wrath is hovering and will soon descend upon them.

Reflection: Are you still waiting for God's final warning?

Word for today: *God's final warning starts right now!*

217

CHRIST IS OUR PEACE

These things I have spoken to you, that in Me you may have peace (John 6:33).

READ: EPHESIANS 2:14-18

The opposite of peace is trouble. The word **peace** appears three times in our text v14, 15, 17 and the word, **enmity** appears twice verses15 and 16. Christ who is our peace, *"broke down the middle wall of separation"* that had existed between God and man as a result of the sin of Adam (Ephesians 2:14). **How did Christ do it?** Christ did it by *"abolishing in His flesh, the law of commandments contained in ordinances."* (v15). In other words, Christ offered His body as an acceptable sacrifice to His Father through His death on the cross. In doing so, Christ's substitutionary sacrifice took care of all the animal sacrifices contained in the law of Moses, once and for all. The old man—our sinful nature in Adam and the new man—our new nature in Christ culminate in *"the peace of God, which surpasses all understanding."* (Philippians 4:7). Since Christ is our peace, the enmity no longer exists between the believers in Christ and God the Father. The gospel is that of reconciliation. Therefore, as many as receive it are not only reconciled to God, but *"have access by one Spirit to the Father"* (v18).

The Bible makes it clear that Christ is the Prince of peace (Read Isaiah 9:6). Since Christ is the Prince of peace, the word **peace** defines His earthly ministry. He spoke peace to the raging winds and storms (Mark 4:39); He told his fearful and disappointed disciples, who were hiding behind closed doors, "Peace be with you." (John20:19). As a user of this Devotional, who is in the midst of problems and difficulties, Christ is saying to you, *"Peace I leave with you, my peace I give to you; not as the world gives do I give to you. Let not your heart be troubled, neither let it be afraid."* (John 14:27). May you dwell in Christ's peace all the time. Only Jesus Christ can grant peace to the troubled heart. Through Christ's death and triumphant resurrection, anyone who believes in Him will experience a three-fold peace. First is **Peace with God** (Romans 5:1). Second is the **Peace of God** (Philippians 4:7; Colossians 3:15). Third is **Peace from God** (Romans 1:7; 2 Corinthians 1:2; 1 Corinthians 1:3).

Reflection: Do you enjoy peace? Who is your source of peace?

Word for today: *Peace is priceless; it's a gift from God.*

WHAT A HORRIBLE ENDING!

Now Ahab the son of Omri did evil in the sight of the LORD, more than all who were before him (1 Kings 16:30).

READ: 1 KINGS 22:37-40

The beginning of one's life or career is just as important as the end of it. Hence, it is crucial to ensure that one ends one's career or life on a good and positive note. Some people who had lived good lives are today being remembered by the bad behaviors that either terminated their careers or ended their lives. News about bad behaviors don't often go away that easily. The lives of king Ahab and his wife Jezebel exemplify the bad behavior that won't go away easily. The Bible records that both "sold themselves to do evil in the sight of the LORD God." (Read 1 Kings 21:25-26). It is therefore, not surprising that Ahab ended his reign and life the way he did. From the word go, king Ahab took three dangerous steps that led him astray. **First,** he married a woman called Jezebel, the daughter of Ethbaal, king of the Sidonians (v31) in violation of God's injunction not to marry from the heathen nations (Deuteronomy 7:3; 1 Kings 11:1-2). **Second,** king Ahab *"served and worshipped Baal."* He *"set up an altar for Baal in the temple of Baal, which he had built in Samaria."* (1 Kings 16:31). **Third,** Ahab made a wooden image (v32). The Bible records that *"Ahab did more to provoke the LORD God of Israel to anger than all the kings of Israel who were before him."* (v33). King Ahab with the help of his wife Jezebel, masterminded the killing of innocent Naboth in order to take away his vineyard (1 Kings 21:1-16). This murderous act prompted God to send Elijah to pronounce a two-fold judgment upon king Ahab and Jezebel his wife (v17-19, 23-24).

In our text, we notice the fulfilment of God's judgment upon king Ahab. The wound he sustained on the battle field led to his death. While Ahab's chariot was being washed at the pool in Samaria, dogs came and licked his blood (v38). The remains of Jezebel was never buried; rather, it was eaten up by dogs after she was thrown down from a story building (Read 2 Kings 9:10, 30-37). What a horrible way to end up as a king and a queen!

Reflection: How have you been living your life?

Word for today: *The way one lives defines the way one ends up.*

219

LIVING A DISGUISED LIFE?

"Do not fear them, for there is nothing covered that will not be revealed, and hidden that will not be known." (Matthew 10:26).

READ: 1 KINGS 14:1-6

When someone decides to disguise his or her appearance, the reason for such an action is to conceal his or her real identity. Usually, those who conceal their identities have something to hide. One may succeed in disguising oneself from human beings, but not from God. He already knows who we are. That was the truth king Jeroboam and his wife did not know. King Jeroboam asked his wife to disguise herself in order to obtain something from the LORD. Jeroboam's child was very sick and he needed the help of the prophet of God (1 Kings 14:1). Then, he said to his wife, *"Please arise, and disguise yourself, that they may not recognize you as the wife of Jeroboam, and go to Shiloh. Indeed, Ahijah the prophet is there, who told me that I would be king over this people."* (v2). King Jeroboam knew that he was living in rebellion against God and that if his wife went to Jeroboam undisguised, Ahijah, the prophet of God would indict him of his sins. So, he decided to disguise his wife's appearance in order to get what he would otherwise, not have gotten, if she came plain and undisguised. In addition, king Jeroboam asked his wife to take some food items along with her—probably to appease Ahijah. We read, *"Also take with you ten loaves, some cakes, and a jar of honey, and go to him; he will tell you what will become of the child."* (v3). It is not uncommon to find some men of God who are bought over by the rich and wealthy in order to applaud them, instead of condemning their evil ways.

God who sees and knows everything that is done in secret, exposed king Jeroboam's wife to Ahijah. The LORD said to him, *"Here is the wife of Jeroboam, coming to ask you something about her son, for he is sick. Thus and thus you shall say to her; for it will be, when she comes in, that she will pretend to be another woman.'"* (v5). Not only did God expose Jeroboam's wife, He told her what the fate of the sick child would be (v12). There is no hidden or disguised sinful lifestyle or behavior that will not be revealed over time.

Reflection: It is good to judge oneself than being exposed by God.

Word for today: *A disguised life disqualifies one from having eternal life.*

SAFETY IN THE LORD'S PRESENCE

I will both lie down in peace, and sleep; for you alone, O LORD, make me dwell in safety (Psalm 4:8).

READ: PSALM 91:1-8

Verse 1 of our text reads, *"He who dwells in the secret place of the Most High shall abide under the shadow of the Almighty."* The *secret place of the Most High*, speaks of God's presence, and *The shadow of the Almighty* speaks of His divine power, protection and provision. Indeed, there is safety in the presence of the LORD. Although the presence of the LORD is everywhere, not everyone dwells in His presence. To dwell in the presence of the LORD is to be in communion and fellowship with Him. Unfortunately, not all children of God *dwell* in the secret place of the Most High. They "run to it at times, and enjoy occasional approaches, but they do not habitually reside in the mysterious presence of God"

From our text, we notice that there are some blessings promised those who dwell in the secret place of the Most High. They enjoy the "security that is based on God's faithfulness" (v3-4), which include being delivered from the "snare of the fowler"—*Satan's trap and craftiness;* from "the perilous pestilence"—*deadly epidemic* (v3). In addition, they are covered with *His feathers*, under *His wings* they take refuge and His *truth is their shield.* (v4). The Psalmist used an anthropomorphic expression in reference to God having feathers and wings. His expression is analogical to birds that protect their young ones under their feathers and wings. According to The Unger's Bible commentary, "Feathers and wings *represent* the security of the animal world, while the shield and buckler *represent* the security of human devices." Those who put their confidence in God are assured of His protection based on His faithfulness, which include protection **at nighttime**, **in darkness** and **at noonday**. In times of grave calamities, thousands may perish. But, those who "abide under God's shadow" will not be affected. Rather, with their eyes they will *"look and see the reward of the wicked."* (v8). May God grant you the grace to trust in Him in a world fraught with danger and uncertainty.

Reflection: In whom do you put your trust and hope?

Word for today: *The safest place to be is in God's presence.*

CHRIST—OUR ADVOCATE

"He is also able to save to the uttermost those who come to God through Him, since He always lives to make intercession for them." (Hebrews 7:25).

READ: 1 JOHN 2:1-2

C hrist is the Redeemer of humankind; He is also the Advocate of those who believe in Him. Through Christ's death and the shedding of His blood, redemption was accomplished. Now, in His exalted position in heaven, He advocates for every believer in Him. In verse 2 of our text we read, *"And He Himself is the propitiation for our sins, and not for ours only but also for the whole world."* Christ is not only our Advocate; He is also our Propitiation. In the court of law, an advocate is someone who argues in favor of someone or pleads on another's behalf. No advocate ever serves as a propitiator. In order to become a propitiator, one must be willing to offer himself as a sacrifice to avert God's anger toward sin. Hence, propitiation is an "offering that turns away the wrath of God directed against sin," In the Old Testament, an animal sacrifice 'covered sin' and tempered God's anger towards a sinner. But, in the New Testament, Christ's sacrifice on the cross, 'cleanses sin' and removes God's wrath upon the sinner.

In Hebrews 9:24-26 we read, *"For Christ has not entered the holy places made with hands, which are copies of the true, but into heaven itself, now to appear in the presence of God for us; not that He should offer Himself often, as the high priest enters the Most Holy Place every year with blood of another— He then would have had to suffer often since the foundation of the world; but now, once at the end of the ages, He has appeared to put away sin by the sacrifice of Himself."* From these verses, we notice that Christ—our Advocate truly qualifies as our Propitiator. A high priest entered the Most Holy Place in the temple yearly with the blood of an animal to appease God. But, Christ offered Himself as a sacrifice on the cross once, and has entered the holy place not made with human hands, into heaven—in the presence of God, where *"He lives to make intercession for us."* (Hebrews 7:25). Jesus pleads our cause before His Father daily.

Reflection: Have you made Christ your eternal Advocate?

Word for today: *Without Christ's Advocacy, it is impossible to appease God.*

WHAT A LOWLY TITLE!

The voice of one crying in the wilderness: "Prepare the way of the LORD;
make straight in the desert a highway for our God." (Isaiah 40:3).

READ: JOHN 1:19-23

We live in the day and age when people are title driven. In some African countries, some people pay huge sums of money to acquire traditional titles to elevate their socio-political status. Failure to address them by their titles attract venom from such people. Even in the Christendom, tittle-driven mentality has eaten deep into some so-called Church leaders. To such people, calling their names without adding their titles makes them feel disrespected. Today, it is not uncommon to find people who graduate from Pastor to Reverend, to Bishop, to Archbishop, to Apostle, then back to Bishop. Acquisition of titles does not produce God's anointing; faithful obedience to God's calling does. Don't be title-driven; be Spirit-filled.

In our text we notice how John the Baptist refused to be drawn into a title contention. The Jewish religious leaders came to find out from John the Baptist about his identity. They asked him, "Who are you?" (v19). From their question, it looked like they were looking for an Anointed One. John's reply was truthful and forceful, **"I am not the Christ."** (v20). The people were not satisfied as they continued with their questions. **"What then? Are you Elijah?"** In the Old Testament, Malachi had predicted that Elijah would come to prepare the way of the Lord. These Jewish leaders who knew the Scriptures too well, wanted to find out from John the Baptist if he was Elijah due to the nature of his ministry. But, unknown to them, John the Baptist came in the spirit of Elijah (Read Luke 1:17; Matthew 11:14). Again, John's reply was, **"I am not."** Then they asked, **"Are you the Prophet?"** The Scripture contains Moses' prediction about a Prophet to come (Deuteronomy 18:15). So, the people wanted to know if John the Baptist was that expected Prophet. Then John revealed his identity and title, " I am the voice of one crying in the wilderness." (John 1:23). What a title! Just as John was the voice in the wilderness, let's be God's voices to the world by proclaiming the gospel of salvation in Christ Jesus.

Reflection: Are you title driven?

Word for today: *The greatest title is to be called a child of God.*

223

THE ROCK HIGHER THAN I

For You have been a shelter for me, a strong tower from the enemy (Psalm 61:3).

READ: PSALM 61:1-8

The writer of a very popular Christian song derived his lyrics from verses 1 and 2 of our text. *"Hear my cry, O God; attend to my prayer; from the end of the earth I will cry to you. When my heart is overwhelmed; lead me to the rock that is higher than I."* It is believed that David, the author Psalm 61, wrote it after he had ascended the throne, most likely during his forced exile following Absalom's rebellion (Read 2 Samuel chapter 15).

The first sentence of our text reflects the depth of David's agony, *"Hear my cry, O God, attend to my prayers."* (v1). David cried to the God as he presented his request. It is not a bad thing to cry to the LORD in time of need and difficulties. If we don't cry to the LORD, to whom else should we cry? God who hears the cry of the needy will certainly hear your cry. Verse 2 of our text reads, *"From the end of the earth I will cry to you. When my heart is overwhelmed; lead me to the rock that is higher than I."* King David understood the Omnipresence of God. Even though he was far away from Jerusalem, he knew that God was there with him. Distance is really no barrier to God! David's heart was overwhelmed with the grief of being overthrown by his son, Absalom. While in exile, David hoped in his God, whom he described as the Rock higher than he. As a believer in Christ, in spite the difficulties and challenges you may be facing today, always remember to call upon God—the Rock that is higher than you. But, if you have not experienced a personal relationship with God, come to Jesus now by accepting Him as your Lord and Savior, after which, He will come and live in you and become the Rock of your salvation. Then you can confidently say, *"He only is my rock and my salvation; He is my defense; I shall not be greatly moved."* (Psalm 62:2). God indeed is the Rock higher than every hiding place to those who have put their truth in Him. Anyone who runs into God is secure and safe.

Reflection: Have you run into God yet? If not, what are you waiting for?

Word for today: *Our God is an unseen Rock of salvation and protection.*

THE LEGACY OF WOES

"Woe to you, scribes and Pharisees, hypocrites! For you shut up the kingdom of heaven against men...you neither go in yourselves, nor...allow those who are entering to go in." (Matthew 23:13).

READ: ISAIAH 5:8-12

Another word for **woe** is **cursed.** When God pronounces woe upon a person, it means that such a person is cursed and therefore, doomed. Our Lord Jesus pronounced woes upon the Scribes and the Pharisees during His earthly ministry. It was a pronouncement that has had some ripple effect on their descendants.

During Isaiah's ministry, God pronounced woes upon the children of Israel who lived in rebellion against His Word. Isaiah chapter 5 contains seven woe legacies for seven categories of people.

Category 1. *The Greedy (v8).* Those who are greedy of material wealth are under a divine curse, because they enrich themselves at the expense of the poor.

Category 2: *The Debauchees (v11-12).* Those who engage in a debased lifestyle are under a divine curse.

Category 3: *The unbelieving (v18-19).* Those who practice iniquity and are devoid of the fear of God are under a divine curse.

Category 4: *The perverse (v20).* Those who suppress the truth and lead others astray are under a divine curse.

Category 5: *The Arrogant (v21).* Those who are proud and arrogant, who think that they have no need for God are under a divine curse.

Category 6: *The drunkards (v22).* Those who are given to alcoholism are under a divine curse.

Category 7: *The unjust (v23).* Those who practice injustice in their dealings with others are under a divine curse.

It's unfortunate that many people today engage in behaviors and lifestyles that produce woe legacies in their lives, which will continue to haunt their families. Leave legacies of blessings, not woes to your posterity.

Reflection: Leaving a good or bad legacy depends on what you do today.

Word for today: *In order to avoid woe legacies, come to Jesus today.*

GOING AHEAD OF GOD?

Wait on the LORD; be of good courage, and He shall strengthen your heart; wait, I say, on the LORD! (Psalm 27:14).

READ: EXODUS 2:11-15

God knows everything about us and sees what goes on in our lives. He sees our passion, zeal and commitment to service. He also sees our weaknesses, like doing things at the wrong time or going ahead of Him in some of the steps we take in life. Naturally, a child who goes ahead in doing things, without parental advice and guidance is more likely to hit a road block in life. What makes us think that things will be different when we go ahead and do things on our own without seeking the guidance of our heavenly Father? Going ahead of God in whatever we do is a recipe for failure. Rebekah went ahead of God in trying to enthrone Jacob over Esau. Before Esau and Jacob were born, God knew what would become of two of them. In fact, while they were still in Rebekah's womb, the LORD said to Rebekah, *"Two nations are in your womb, two peoples shall be separated from your body; one people shall be stronger than the other, and the older shall serve the younger."* (Genesis 25:23). In turned out that Rebekah assisted Jacob in tricking his father Isaac in order to receive his blessings. Granted that Jacob was destined to serve Esau. That notwithstanding, Rebekah went ahead of God in its timing (Read Genesis chapter 27:1-40). Rebekah's action led to a bad blood existing between two siblings—Esau and Isaac (v41-46). Abraham and his wife, Sarah in their bid to have a son also went ahead of God. With Sarah's advice and consent, Abraham took Hagar as a wife in order to bear him a son. The product of that relationship was Ishmael—the progenitor of the Arabs who are today Israel's enemies. Going ahead of God in anything does not always end well.

Our text is a classical example of going ahead of God in doing something. Moses went ahead of God in trying to deliver the children of Israel from their Egyptian bondage by killing an Egyptian—an act that sent him into exile (Exodus 2:11-15). But, at the appointed time, God appeared to him with the mandate to deliver His people. (3:7-12).

Reflection: Do you go ahead of God in your plans?

Word for today: *Don't go ahead of God; wait for His timing.*

226

THE CHURCH—OUTSIDE & WITHIN

For the time has come for judgment to begin at the house of God; and if it begins with us first, what will be the end of those who do not obey the gospel of God? (1 Peter 4:17).

READ: 1 CORINTHIANS 5:9-13

I n his letter to the Church in Corinth, Apostle Paul outlined how to deal with two categories of people—those **outside** of the Church and those **within** the Church. Our text reads, *"I wrote to you in my epistle not to keep company with sexually immoral people. Yet I certainly did not mean with the sexually immoral people of this world, or with the covetous, or extortioners, or idolaters, since then you would need to go out of the world."* (v9-10). Paul instructed the Church in Corinth *"not to keep company with any sexually immoral people."* In the above text, Paul asked the Church not to concern herself with the sexually immoral in the world at the exclusion of the sexually moral in the Church. Both are important! We read, *"But now I have written to you not to keep company with anyone named a brother, who is sexually immoral, or covetous, or an idolater, or a reviler, or a drunkard, or an extortioner—not even to eat with such a person."* (v11). When someone engages in sexual immorality and perversion, the Church should not condone it; rather it should condemn it—whether or not such an individual is outside or within the Church.

Those who are sexually immoral and perverse often defend themselves by quoting what our Lord Jesus said in Matthew 7:1, *"Judge not, that you be not judged."* In doing so, they take what Jesus said out of context. Jesus did not say we should not condemn sin. Rather, He was addressing the hypocritical attitude of the Scribes and Pharisees who were fond of condemning others for the same sin they were guilty of. The same Jesus who said, "Do not judge" pronounced woes on the Scribes and Pharisees for their hypocrisy. In Paul's time, do you think that the kind of sexual immorality and perversion going on in the Church today would have been tolerated? Certainty not! God judges the sexually immoral outside and within the Church. The Church should do the same.

Reflection: Are you in the Church or outside the Church?

Word for today: *God expects holiness within and outside the Church.*

227

AUGUST

DEVOTIONALS

RIVERS OF LIVING WATER

"Whoever drinks of the water that I shall give him will never thirst..." (John 4:14).

READ: JOHN 7:37-39

Isaiah 44:3 reads, *"For I will pour water on him who is thirsty, and floods on the dry ground; I will pour my Spirit on your descendants, and my blessing on your offspring."* This statement was made by prophet Isaiah, but fulfilled in Christ Jesus. According to the Mosaic law, the children of Israel were to hold an annual Feast of Tabernacles (Read Leviticus 23:33-35). During His earthly ministry, our Lord Jesus attended this Feast and made a proclamation in fulfilment of Isaiah's prophecy. Our text reads, *"On the last day, that great day of the feast, Jesus stood and cried out, saying, 'If anyone thirsts, let him come to me and drink. He who believes in me, as the Scripture has said, out of his heart will flow rivers of living water."* (John 7:37-38). Verse 39 throws some light as to the water our Lord Jesus Christ was speaking about—the Holy Spirit. How this Scripture has been fulfilled in the life of every Spirit filled believer in Christ! The upwelling of the Holy Spirit which you experience whenever you are filled with the Holy Spirit testifies to this fact. Indeed, the Holy Spirit is a river of water springing up in the heart of every Spirit-filled Christian. Has that been your experience?

John chapter 4 contains a discussion that took place between our Lord Jesus Christ and a Samaritan woman who came to the well to draw water. Jesus asked the woman for some water. Noticing that Jesus was a Jew and she a Samaritan, the woman quickly played the race card to avoid giving Jesus a drink, because the Jews and Samaritans never got along. She told Jesus, *"How is it that you, being a Jew, ask a drink from me, a Samaritan woman? For Jews have no dealings with Samaritans."* (John 4:9). Jesus replied her, *"If you knew the gift of God, and who it is who says to you, 'Give me a drink,' you would have asked Him, and He would have given you living water."* (v10). Rivers of living water *speaks* of the Holy Spirit; Living water, *speaks* of eternal life. Both have **life** in them! The Holy Spirit flows from having eternal life in you.

Reflection: Do you have eternal life? Are you filled with the Holy Spirit?

Word for today: *No eternal life outside of the Holy Spirit.*

WHAT A HAPPY MAN!

Blessed is the man who trusts in the LORD, and whose hope is the LORD (Jeremiah 17:7).

READ: PSALM 146:5-10

Another word for **Happy** is **Blessed.** Verse 5 of our text reads, *"Happy is he who has the God of Jacob for his help, whose hope is in the LORD his God."* If we were to replace the word **Happy** with the word **Blessed,** the text would read as follows, "**Blessed** is he who has the God of Jacob for his help, whose hope is in the LORD his God."

There are ten reasons why you are blessed, if you have the God of Jacob as your LORD and Hope.
Reason #1: He is the Maker of heaven and earth and all that is in them (v6a). As the Maker of heaven and earth, God is in control of everything in heaven, on earth and beneath the earth. **Reason #2:** He "keeps truth forever" (v6b). God does not lie; whatever He says, abides forever. **Reason #3:** He "executes justice for the oppressed." (v7a). God is just and provides justice to those who are oppressed. **Reason #4:** He "provides food for the hungry." (v7b). God feeds those who are spiritually and physically hungry. All you need to do is to come to Him by faith through Jesus Christ. **Reason #5:** He "gives freedom to the prisoners." (v7c). God sets those who are in spiritual bondage free (Read Luke 4:18; John 8:36). **Reason #6:** He "opens the eyes of the blind." (v8a). Our Lord Jesus opened the eyes of both the physically and spiritually blind (Read Matthew 9:27 -31). **Reason #7:** He "raises those who are bowed down." (v8b). The physically and spiritually lame receive their healing from the Lord. See Luke 13:10-13. **Reason #8:** He "loves the righteous" (v8c). All those who are in right-standing with God through Christ are loved by Him.
Reason #9: He "watches over the strangers." (v9a). Everyone of us is a stranger here on earth; God watches over us if we align ourselves with Him.
Reason #10: He "relieves the fatherless and widow." (v9b). God has a very good track record of faithfulness; put your trust in Him.

Reflection: Are you being blessed or being lucky?

Word for today: *Blessedness comes from God, luck comes from chance.*

232

CHRIST'S MAJESTIC GLORY

And when I saw Him, I fell at His feet as dead. But He laid His right hand on me, saying to me, "Do not be afraid; I am the First and the Last." (Revelation 1:17).

READ: REVELATION 19:11-16

Christ's incarnation was for a purpose; He came to seek and to save that which was lost (Luke 19:10). God's verdict on a sinner is death. But, in His love God sent His son, Jesus Christ to die a substitutionary death for humankind. This means that by virtue of Christ's death, a sinner can be spared the eternal death, if he or she appropriates Christ's death. Prior to Christ's incarnation, prophet Isaiah painted a very horrible picture of His suffering, rejection and death (Read Isaiah 53:1-12). Indeed, Christ was rejected, brutalized, and crucified by the same people that He came to deliver from eternal death. But, after His triumphant resurrection and ascension into heaven, Christ took on His majestic and glorious appearance, which He had with His Father. While in the Island of Patmos, John had a revelation of Christ's majestic glory (Read Revelation 1:10-16). Christ's majestic and glorious appearance so dazzled John that he had to fall to the ground as one who was dead. But, Christ laid His right hand on John and said to him, *"Do not be afraid; I am the First and the Last. I am He who lives, and was dead, and behold, I am alive forevermore. Amen. And I have the keys of Hades and of Death."* Those who make caricature of the Person of Christ are blind to His glorious and majestic appearance. If their eyes were to be opened, they would not be able to behold the glory of Christ. Paul, on his way to Damascus to persecute the Christians had a little tip of Christ's glory (Acts 9:3-4). After that encounter with Christ, Paul was never the same. He changed from being a persecutor to becoming a persecutee.

Based on our text, John saw Christ on a white horse—symbol of victory, "clothed on a robe dipped in blood"—a symbol of His atoning death for humankind. On Christ's robe and thigh were written this name, "KING OF KINGS AND LORD OF LORDS" (v16). Indeed, Christ is the KING OF KINGS AND LORD OF LORDS. He's the Alpha and Omega—the Beginning and the End.

Reflection: What is your view about Christ?

Word for today: *The spiritually blind cannot behold the glory of Christ.*

THE LORD WAS WITH JOSEPH

The LORD was with Joseph, and he was a successful man; and he was in the house of his master the Egyptian (Genesis 39:2).

READ: GENESIS 39:1-6

Joseph was the youngest son of Jacob. At the age of seventeen, the LORD revealed to him in a dream, what he was going to be in life. When Joseph shared with his siblings his God-given dream, they hated him and as a result, sold him into slavery. As a slave, Joseph found himself in the land of Egypt. But, the LORD was with him (Genesis 39:2). In Genesis chapter 39, the phrase, "The LORD was with him." was used three times to emphasize how the hand of the LORD was upon Joseph (v2, 21, 23). After listening to Joseph's dream, his siblings sold Joseph into slavery because they were jealous of his bright future. There are many dream killers out there; be careful how you share your God-given dream with people. With the presence of Joseph in Potiphar's house, Potiphar was never the same. God's blessing upon Joseph was extended to Potiphar. As a child of God, do you know that the LORD can bless your boss or workplace due to His blessings upon your life? Before long, Joseph was elevated to the position of an overseer in the house of Potiphar, because the LORD was with him. Since the LORD was with Joseph, being sold into slavery did not stop the fulfillment of God's purpose for his life. In fact, it advanced the achievement of his destiny, rather than stop it.

As the LORD was with Joseph, so has He promised to be with you. Matthew 28:20b reads, *"Lo, I am with you always, even to the end of the age."* Based on the Bible, there are certain pointers to ascertain if God is with you.
1. If God is with you, He will bless you. Isaac was blessed, because the LORD was with him (Read Genesis 26: 23-24). 2. If the LORD is with you, it will be visible to those who don't know the LORD (Read Genesis 26:27-28). 3.If the LORD is with you, He will guide you in all your ways (Read Genesis 28:15-16). 4. If the LORD is with you, He will make you successful (Read Genesis 39:2). The seed of success was in Joseph because the LORD was with him.

Reflection: Do you experience God's favor?

Word for today: *God's favor comes with His presence in one's life.*

WHEN HEAVEN COMMUNICATES

Hear, O heavens, and give ear, O earth! For the LORD has spoken: "I have nourished and brought up children, and they have rebelled against me (Isaiah 1:2).

READ: JOHN 12:27-30

The Bible records three occasions during Christ's earthly ministry in which a voice thundered from heaven. The first was during Christ's baptism in River Jordan. Matthew 3:13, 16-17 read, *"Then Jesus came from Galilee to John at the Jordan to be baptized by him. When He had been baptized, Jesus came up immediately from the water; and behold, the heavens were opened to Him, and He saw the Spirit of God descending like a dove and alighting upon Him. And suddenly a voice came from heaven, saying, 'This is My beloved Son, in whom I am well pleased."* The second was at Christ's transfiguration on the Mount. *"He was transfigured before them and His face shone like the sun, and His clothes became as white as the light. And behold, Moses and Elijah appeared to them, talking with Him...a bright cloud overshadowed them; and suddenly a voice came out of the cloud, saying, 'This is my beloved Son, in whom I am well pleased. Hear Him!"* Matthew 17: 2-5). The voice from heaven was so loud that Christ's disciples—Peter, James and John *"fell on their faces and were greatly afraid."* (v6). The third occasion was when Christ predicted His death. We find this in our text. Jesus prayed, *"Father, glorify your name."* Then a voice came from heaven, saying, *'I have glorified it and will glorify it again.'* (v28). On these three occasions, the purpose for the voice from haven was to authenticate Christ's Messiah-ship and to urge the hearers to believe in Him. Do you believe in Christ?

What we hear, where we hear and how we hear are very crucial to our eternal destiny. We should check what we hear and be eager to hear the Word of God. Since the source of any information is just as important as the information itself, let's be willing to hear the undiluted Word of God from sanctified vessels of God. A polluted source can defile. Our attitude after hearing the Word of God should be to do it (James 1:19,22).

Reflection: What you hear and how you hear prepare you for eternity.

Word for today: *Ears that are open to God's Word hear God's Word.*

235

TRUE & EFFECTIVE DISCIPLESHIP

Then Jesus said to those Jews who believed Him, "If you abide in my word, you are my disciples indeed." (John 8:31).

READ: ISAIAH 6:1-10

The word "discipleship" is from the root word, "discipline" , which means "the training expected to produce specific character or pattern of behavior." A disciple is a learner, someone who is trained to behave like his master. Every believer in Christ is a disciple. How dearly Christ wants us to be true and effective disciples of His!

In order to be a true and effective disciple of Christ, there are some imperatives you must adhere to. **1.**You must respond to the call of the Master (Matthew 11:28). Christ has made a universal call and only those who respond to this call can become His disciples. **2.** You must be chosen by the Master (Matthew 22:11-14). Indeed, many are called, but few are chosen based on their attitude in responding. A guy responded to Christ's call with a pre-condition and as a result, was not chosen (Luke 9:61). Do you give Christ a pre-condition before you can serve Him? **3.** You must be prepared by the Master (John 15:16). A plant that is not well prepared and nourished does not bear much fruit. Every believer in Christ needs a four-fold preparation: First, is **Heart preparation** (Ezra 7:9-10); Ezra prepared his heart "to seek the law of the LORD and to do it and to teach the statutes." God cannot use an unprepared heart for His work. Second is **Eye preparation** (Isaiah 6:1-3). The vision that Isaiah saw prepared him for service. Isaiah recognized his filthiness after he saw the Lord. Third is **Lip preparation** (v6-7). Isaiah's lips were prepared with a coal of fire. Defiled lips don't become God's mouthpieces. May Holy Spirit fire prepare and sanctify our lips to speak God's Word. Fourth is **Ear preparation** (v8a). Isaiah was able to hear the voice of God, because his ears had been prepared. Unless our ears are prepared by God, it becomes difficult to hear from Him. What we hear conditions the way we think. **4.** You must make yourself available for the Master (v8b). Isaiah made himself available, when he said, "Here am I! Send me." Are you available for the Master?

Reflection: Are you a true and effective disciple of Christ?

Word for today: *When God calls, He chooses and prepares the individual.*

CHRIST IN YOU IS GREATER

Who is he who overcomes the world, but he who believes that Jesus is the Son of God? (1 John 5:5).

READ: 1 JOHN 4:1-6

Verse 4 of our text reads, *"You are of God, little children, and have overcome them, because He who is in you is greater than he who is in the world."* Even though the world was made through Christ, He does not operate by the world's system, nor does He dwell in those who have rejected Him in their lives. Rather, He lives in those who have accepted Him as their Lord and Savior. The world's system is often at variance with God's Word because of Satan's influence over people. The person our text refers to "he who is in the world" is none other than Satan. He manipulates the mind of people to hate God and His Word. In so doing, they reject Christ and the salvation He offers for the redemption of their souls. 2 Corinthians 4:3-4 reads, *"But even if our gospel is veiled, it is veiled to those who are perishing, whose minds the god of this age has blinded, who do not believe, lest the light of the gospel of the glory of Christ, who is the image of God, should shine on them."* So, we see that Satan's main task is to blind people's eyes and minds from receiving the gospel. It is right to say that those who hate the gospel do so under the influence of Satan. However, God has given human beings the freedom of choice. If one chooses to serve God, Satan's influence over such an individual will give way to the Spirit of God. But, if on the other hand, someone chooses to reject Christ, then Satan will have dominion over such a person.

To those who have accepted Christ as their Lord and Savior, Apostle John reminds them that Christ living in them is greater and more powerful than Satan who is in the world (1 John 4:4). There are practical ways to know if Christ is in you. Here are just a few of them:
1. You will love to obey God's Word (John 14:15). 2. There will be the witness of God's Spirit in you (Romans 8:16). 3. You will not deny Christ (1 John 2:23; 4:15). 4. You will love Christ and the brethren (1 John 4: 7-8). 5. You will be heavenly minded (Colossians 3:1-2)

Reflection: Are you sure that Christ is in you? If not, why not?

Word for today: *Christ is far greater than Satan and the world.*

DUTIFUL MARTHA

"Do not labor for the food which perishes, but for the food which endures to everlasting life, which the Son of Man will give you..." (John 6:27).

READ: LUKE 10:38-42

Ecclesiastes 3:1 reads, *"To everything there is a season, a time for every purpose under heaven."* Doing the right thing at the wrong time manifested so well in the incident that took place when our Lord Jesus Christ visited the home of Mary and Martha. During Christ's visit, Mary sat at Jesus' feet and heard His Word (Luke 10:39). Verse 40 records that *"Martha was distracted with much serving."* Due to the distraction occasioned by much serving, Martha was not able to listen to the teaching of Jesus. Dutiful Martha was so overwhelmed by the task of serving the guests that she went and complained to Jesus about her sister Mary not helping out with serving. But Jesus answered her, *"Martha, Martha, you are worried and troubled about many things. But one thing is needed, and Mary has chosen that good part, which will not be taken away from her."* (v41-42). Jesus did not condemn Martha for serving, but He rebuked her for doing the right thing at the wrong time. In other words, Martha was mindful of physical food, when she was supposed to be feeding on spiritual food at the feet of Jesus. As Life Application Bible Commentary rightly put it, "Fixing and serving a meal wasn't intrinsically wrong, but it wasn't the best, at that moment. Spending some time quietly listening to Christ's Word could empower Mary to serve many other days, to many other guests."

There are three lessons to deduce from this story. **1.** One's priorities determine the way one responds to the issues of life. Mary's priority was to listen to Christ's teaching. She might have been hungry for physical food, but chose to feed on spiritual food, instead. **2.** We should learn to choose what is best. Mary chose what was best for her life—hearing the Word of God. God's Word is the best thing in life. **3.** There is time for everything in life. We should develop the habit of setting aside a time every day and listen to God speak to us by reading the Bible in combination with the daily Devotional.

Reflection: Does your busy schedule prevent you from reading the Bible?

Word for today: *Busyness without God's Word makes for spiritual indolence.*

THE WEAPON OF PRAISE

They went out before the army and were saying: "Praise the LORD, for His mercy endures forever." (2 Chronicles 20:21).

READ: 2 CHRONICLES 20:21-23

There is power in praise! From our text, we notice how Jehoshaphat went to the battle field with an army of praise team and came home victorious. After an assurance from God that He was going to fight his battle, Jehoshaphat appointed those who should sing to the LORD, and who should praise the beauty of His holiness as they went out before the army. The lyric of Jehoshaphat's song was aimed at showering praises to God and reminding Him of His everlasting mercy. Verses 22-23, tell us of the effect of Jehoshaphat's praises upon his enemies. We read, *"Now when they began to sing and to praise, the LORD set ambushes against the people of Ammon, Moab, and Mount Seir, who had come against Judah; and they were defeated. For the people of Ammon and Moab stood up against the inhabitants of Mount Seir to utterly kill and destroy them. And when they had made an end of the inhabitants of Seir, they helped to destroy one another."* The praises of Jehoshaphat and his men, brought down the power of God to vanquish his enemies. Our God is a Man of war and can use any weapon in fighting. In this instance, the LORD used the weapon of praise to defeat Jehoshaphat's enemies.

During the invasion of Jericho, the weapon of praise was used in bringing down the walls of Jericho. Joshua and his men in obedience to the LORD's command, marched round the city of Jericho with trumpet blasts and praises rending the air. The Bible records that on the seventh day, as they marched round the city seven times, the priests blew the trumpet and the people shouted with a loud voice as the walls of Jericho came tumbling down. Indeed, God inhabits the praises of His people (Psalm 22:3). Some years ago, a group of Christians gathered during a Church fellowship. As they sang and praised God, God released the power of healing to heal those who were sick in their midst without any prayer being offered.

Reflection: Do you know how to praise God? If so, in what way do you praise Him?

Word for today: *If prayer fails, try praises.*

THE GOD OF PROVISION

"And Abraham said, 'my son, God will provide for Himself the lamb for a burnt offering..." (Genesis 22:8).

READ: GENESIS 22:7-14

As Abraham journeyed with Isaac to the place where God wanted him to offer Isaac as a burnt offering, a dialogue ensued between Isaac and Abraham, his father. Isaac being familiar with the way Abraham used to offer burnt offerings, noticed that something was missing—the lamb for the burnt offering. Unknown to him, Isaac was actually the lamb for the burnt offering. Isaac asked his father, *"Look at the fire and the wood, but where is the lamb for the burn offering?"* Abraham replied, *"My son, God will provide for Himself the lamb for a burnt offering."* (Genesis 22:7-8). Indeed, God did provide for Himself the lamb for the burnt offering in an unusual way (see v9-13). On their way to the Promised Land, the children of Israel complained of water, because the only water available was bitter. But, God of provision provided them with water by turning the bitter water into good water (Exodus 15:22-25). On another occasion, the children of Israel complained of food (16:2-3). God of provision rained food from heaven for them to eat.

God provided meal for prophet Elijah during a time of severe famine and draught. God told Elijah, *"Get away from here and turn eastward, and hide by the Brook Cherith, which flows into the Jordan. And it will be that you shall drink from the brook, and I have commanded the ravens to feed you there."* (1 Kings 17:3-4). In fact, it is unheard of that birds should feed a human being. It should be the other way round—the human being feeding birds. But, since God can provide through unlikely sources, this impossibility became possible! Moreover, when the water from the brook dried up, God relocated Elijah to the house of a widow in order to provide for him. (Read 1 Kings 17:9). In the same vein, God provided water for Hagar when her son was about to die of thirst, by opening her eyes to see a nearby well of water, from which she filled the skin with water and gave the lad a drink. (Genesis 21:19). In all thee situations, God proved Himself as the God of provision. He still does the same today.

Reflection: How has God provided for you lately?

Word for today: *The God of provision is also God of salvation.*

240

STIR UP ONE ANOTHER

[Bear] with one another, and [forgive] one another... even as Christ forgave you, so you also must do (Colossians 3:13).

READ: HEBREWS 10:23-25

Verse 24 of our text reads, *"And let us consider one another in order to stir up love and good works."* As believers in Christ, we are encouraged to stir up one another. The word **stir up** means to spur, to provoke, to prompt to action. In the military, trainee soldiers chant motivational songs and get some pep-talks from their trainers, especially during their early morning jogging. The purpose for chanting these songs and dishing out the pep-talks is to stir up the minds of the trainee soldiers to enable them take their training seriously in order to perform well on the battle field. Similarly, the same principle applies to soldiers of the cross—followers of Christ. Every believer in Christ needs some spiritual stirring up in order to be spiritually fit to fight the daily spiritual battles he or she faces.

Five areas in which every believer needs to be stirred up spiritually include: **1. Prayer:** We should pray for one another. The Bible enjoins us to "confess our trespasses to one another and to pray for one another." (James 5:16). **2. Love:** As believers in Christ, we ought to stir up love in others. In other words, we should encourage others to love by demonstrating our love towards them. Love attracts. When you love, you are stirring up others to love as well (Read John 13:34-35). **3. Faith:** People differ on their level of faith. Some are strong in faith, while others are not that strong. Those who are strong in faith, should stir up those who are weak, by bearing with them in love (Read Galatians 6:1-2). **4. Serving:** One of the ways to stir up someone to serve is by yourself serving. People like to imitate good examples. When Christ washed the feet of His disciples, He demonstrated how to serve others (Read John 13:14-15). So, if you want others to serve, be an example to them. **5. Exhortation:** Another word for **exhortation** is admonition. We should admonish one another as believers in Christ. By so doing, we prompt one another to action for Christ (Read Romans 15:14; Colossians 3:16).

Reflection: How stirred up are you for the Lord's work?

Word for today: *A spiritual stir up steers you towards godliness.*

241

CHRIST—THE BREAD OF LIFE

For my flesh is food indeed, and my blood is drink indeed (John 6:55).

READ: JOHN 6:48-51

Every human being is dual in nature—the physical and the spiritual. The physical and spiritual components of our being are sustained by different kinds of food. While the physical component of our being feeds on physical food, the spiritual component feeds on spiritual food, which is the Word of God. This means that the spirit of someone who does not feed on the Word of God is constantly being starved. When a being is starved, it becomes very difficult for such a being to function properly. This is what happens to those who fail to feed on the Word of God daily. Such people steal, cheat, kill and commit all sorts of atrocities. Whatever happens in the physical has a spiritual origin. Since the spirit of those who refuse to feed on the Word of God are weak and feeble, the devil manipulates them to do evil. Spiritual strength stems from the intake of spiritual food. If you fail to take in the Word of God, you will definitely be spiritually weak and therefore incapable of resisting the devil (Read James 4:7-8).

In one of His teachings, our Lord Jesus Christ made a statement that bewildered His Jewish religious audience and which continues to be misunderstood by some members of the body of Christ to date. Our text reads, *"I am the bread of life. This is the bread which comes down from heaven, that one may eat of it and not die. I am the living bread which came down from heaven. If anyone eats of this bread, he will live forever; and the bread that I shall give is my flesh, which I shall give for the life of the world."* (John 6:48-51). Jesus described Himself as the Bread of Life, which came down from heaven. Christ's audience was too familiar with the manna that their fathers ate in the wilderness and later died. But, whoever eats the flesh of Christ will never die. Jesus is the Word of God that became flesh (John 1:14) and whoever feeds on Him will never die (6:50). Unfortunately, like the Jewish religious leaders, some people today have misinterpreted Christ's statement to mean eating the Lord's super. The Lord's supper does not give eternal life; Christ Jesus does.

Reflection: Do you feed on Christ—the living Word of God daily?

Word for today: *Christ is the Bread of life; the Lord's supper, a sacrament.*

TRYING TIMES!

"A man's enemies will be those of his own household." (Matthew 10:36).

READ: MICAH 7:5-7

Around 704 BC, prophet Micah prophesied about God's impending judgment upon Jerusalem and her inhabitants—a prophecy which came to fulfilment during the fall of Jerusalem in 587 BC. In his prophecy, Micah highlighted some of the evils that would prevail during the fall of Jerusalem. Verses 5-6 of our text read, *"Do not trust in a friend; do not put your confidence in a companion; guard the doors of your mouth from her who lies in your bosom. For son dishonors father, daughter rises against her mother, daughter-in-law against her mother-in-law; a man's enemies are the men of his own household."* The siege and fall of Jerusalem ushered in trying times for the inhabitants of Jerusalem. True to Micah's prophecy, there were lots of mistrust and deception: "Neighbors and friends turned to be traitor to one another; even husbands and wives became untrustworthy." But, in spite of all the mistrust, Micah declared, *"I will look to the LORD; I will wait for the God of my salvation; my God will hear me."* (Micah 7:7). Let this be your prayer.

Our Lord Jesus Christ made similar pronouncement in His teaching regarding the division His message of salvation will create in families and hosueholds. We read, *"Do not think that I came to bring peace on earth. I did not come to bring peace but a sword. For I have come to 'set a man against his father, a daughter against her mother, and a daughter-in-law against her mother-in-law'; and 'a man's enemies will be those of his own household.'"* (Matthew 10:34-36). Today, it is not uncommon to find parents hating their children and vice versa, as a result of commitment to follow Christ. The times in which we live are indeed trying times: Children are rebellious against their parents to a point of killing them to have their way; husbands hate their wives and cause them to be murdered. Our society is infested with terrible crimes ever heard. In fact, one would have expected the society to be kind, loving and peaceful due to the vast knowledge that people have acquired through education. But unfortunately, the opposite is the case!

Reflection: What kind of challenges do you face? Spiritual or physical?

Word for today: *If you are going through trying times, try Jesus.*

THE INWARD BEAUTY

"In like manner also, that the women adorn themselves in modest apparel, with propriety and moderation, not with braided hair or gold or pearls or costly clothing, but, which is proper for women professing godliness, with good works." (1 Timothy 2:9-10).

READ: 1 PETER 3:1-6

Women are created to be admired, hence, there is the natural tendency and desire in them to look beautiful and attractive (Read Genesis 2:20-23). In doing so, some women like to be fashionable in order to look beautiful, making fashion and outward beauty twin brothers—inseparable. The quest for <u>fashion and beauty drives the way people dress and look</u> There is nothing wrong in looking fashionable and beautiful. But, there is everything wrong in making fashion and beauty your god.

In our text, Apostle Peter advises every woman who professes to be a child of God on how to dress. In other words, Peter stipulates in his letter, a godly dress code for a Christian sister. Verse 3-6 of our text read, *"Do not let your adornment be merely outward—arranging the hair, wearing gold, or putting on fine apparel—rather let it be the hidden person of the heart, with the incorruptible beauty of a gentle and quiet spirit, which is very precious in the sight of God. For in this manner, in former times, the holy women who trusted in God also adorned themselves, being submissive to their own husbands, as Sarah obeyed Abraham, calling him lord, whose daughters you are if you do good and are not afraid with any terror."* The summary of Peter's dress code for women professing to be Christians is this: ***Chastity with gentle spirit is better than outward beauty.*** Peter is not saying that the Christian woman should dress shabbily and look unattractive. What he is saying is that the primary goal of a Christian woman should center on the inner beauty of godliness and gentleness, rather than the outward beauty without Christian character. The same thing applies to men. Dropping his pant to the buttock while exposing his underwear is bad for a man who professes to be a Christian believer. Christ wouldn't dress that way. Don't dress in a way that makes heaven ashamed.

Reflection: Which is more important to you—inward or outward beauty?

Word for today: *Christ's beauty is the best; seek after it.*

THE INVINCIBLE GOD

"A prophet approached Ahab king of Israel, saying, 'Thus says the LORD: Have you seen all this great multitude? Behold, I will deliver it into your hand today, and you shall know that I am the LORD.'" (1 Kings 20:13).

READ: 1 KINGS 20:23-30

After their defeat by the army of Israel, the Syrians reorganized themselves to launch an offensive in the spring of the year (1 Kings 20:22). In doing so, the military advisers of king Ben-Hadad of Syria encouraged him with the following statement, *"Their gods are gods of the hills. Therefore they were stronger than we; but if we fight against them in the plain, surely we will be stronger than they."* Ben-Hadad heeded the advice of his military officers to fight the children of Israel in the valley, instead of on the hills. Verse 26 of our text reads, *"So it was, in the spring of the year, that Ben-Hadad mustered the Syrians and went up to Aphek to fight against Israel."* In their ignorance, the Syrians tried to compare their gods to the Almighty God. God is not the God of the mountain, or the valley, or the forest, or the rivers; He is God of the entire universe. This means that He has power over every creature. To prove the Syrians wrong, God sent his servant to the king of Israel with these words, *"Thus says the LORD: 'Because the Syrians have said, 'The LORD is God of the hills, but He is not God of the valleys,' therefore I will deliver all this great multitude into your hand, and you shall know that I am the LORD.'"* (v28). God fought for the children of Israel to rout the Syrian army in the plains. The children of Israel "killed one hundred thousand foot soldiers of the Syrians in one day." God caused the wall of the city to collapse and kill those who fled into it, while king Ben-Hadad hid himself in the inner chamber – an equivalent of today's bunker (v30).

The invincibility of God does not wane; it is the same yesterday, today and forever. Sin and doubt often hinder the manifestation of God's power amongst His people. Remember, "The LORD is a Man of war" (Exodus 15:3) and He "shows Himself strong on behalf of those whose heart is loyal to Him." (2 Chronicles 16:9).

Reflection: How do you view Almighty God? Does He fight your battles?

Word for today: *The vincible gods are no match to our invincible God.*

245

BECOMING BRAND-NEW IN CHRIST

It is the Spirit who gives life; the flesh profits nothing. The words that I speak to you are spirit, and they are life (John 6:63).

READ: 2 CORINTHIANS 5:16-17

The God who created, is the same God who recreates. God created Adam through whom every human being emanated. In other words, God created every human being through the first Adam. But, through the second Adam—Christ Jesus, God recreates those who come to Him. This means that through Christ, every human being has the opportunity to be recreated by God. Our text reads, *"Therefore, from now on, we regard no one according to the flesh. Even though we have known Christ according to the flesh, yet now we know Him thus no longer. Therefore, if anyone is in Christ, he is a new creation; old things have passed away; behold, all things have become new."* (v16-17). A new creation is someone who has been recreated by God—a renewed humanity. As a new creation, you become a brand-new person. Christ gives you a new life and you are not the same anymore. In the process of new creation, you are not reformed, rehabilitated or reeducated; you are **recreated** to "live in vital union with Christ." (Read Colossians 2:6-7, 9-10). When this happens, all things will become new (2 Corinthians 5:17). Your life changes because of the transformation that has taken place in you.

When a car is brand-new, it looks different from old cars and drives better. The same thing happens to someone who is a new creation in Christ. Such a person looks different from the world and serves God better. He or she looks at the world through the prism of God's Word. With the Spirit of God living inside of a new creation, he or she is able to communicate with God and serve Him more effectively. Without a new creation experience in someone, it is impossible to relate with God, talk less of pleasing Him. The Bible declares, *"God is Spirit, and those who worship Him must worship in spirit and truth."* (John 4:24). Trying to worship God in the flesh is an exercise in futility. It is sad to note that many troop to the Church Sunday after Sunday without a personal relationship with Christ, who is the Head of the Church.

Reflection: Have you experienced a brand-new life in Christ?

Word for today: *God makes an old life to become new in Christ.*

ASLEEP, NOT DEAD

"He said to them, Our friend Lazarus sleeps, but I go that I may wake him up." (John 11:11).

READ: MARK 5:37-43

During His earthly ministry, our Lord Jesus Christ on two occasions, referred to death as sleep. First was in reference to the daughter of a Synagogue ruler, named Jairus (Matthew 9:24), the second was in reference to Lazarus (John 11:11). On both occasions, the individuals involved were brought back to life by Jesus.

From a human view point, the arrival of Christ to Jairus' house would be considered late. In fact, the news from Jairus' house indicated so. The messengers said to him, *"Your daughter is dead. Why trouble the Teacher any further.?"* (Mark 5:35). To them all hope of recovery has been lost, since the girl was dead. But, little did they know that Christ has power over death. By the time Jesus arrived at Jairus' house, mourners were already busy doing what they loved most—crying and wailing. At the time of Jesus, mourners were hired and paid to mourn at funerals to keep the spirit of sorrow alive. On arrival, our Lord Jesus took Peter, James and John with Him as He entered the room where the dead girl was lying. Then an interesting dialogue ensued: Jesus told the mourners, *"Why make this commotion and weep? The child is not dead, but sleeping."* (v39). In response the mourners, "ridiculed Jesus" But, Jesus put them all outside, took the father and the mother of the girl and those with Him—most likely Peter, James and John, and entered where the child was lying (v40). Jesus took the girl by the hand and said to her, "Talitha, cumi." an Aramaic statement which means, *"Little girl, I say to you, arise."* (v41). The restoration of this little girl by Jesus brought a lot of amazement to the crowd (v42). Paul in his letter to the Corinthian Christians also referred to those who died in Christ as being asleep (1 Thessalonians 4:13-15). In deed, every believer who dies in Christ, is not dead, but asleep. Death means separation, while sleep means rest. One day, Christ will wake up all those who are asleep in Him with a shout of triumph (v16).

Reflection: Are you alive in Christ? Do you expect to hear the trumpet?

Word for today: *One who is alive in Christ will be asleep at death.*

COVENANT BREAKERS

They did not keep the covenant of God; they refused to walk in His law (Psalm 78:10).

READ: 2 KINGS 17:15-18

A covenant is "an agreement between two people or two groups that involves promises on the part of each to the other." In the Old Testament, human covenants were usually made between equals or between a superior and an inferior. In Biblical context, a divine covenant is between God, who is superior and humans, who are inferior; covenant is more than a contract or agreement. While a contract has an expiration date, a covenant does not—it is permanent. Whenever God enters into a covenant with someone, there is always a sign to seal such a covenant. For instance, after the deluge, God made a covenant with Noah. In that covenant, God said to Noah, *"I establish my covenant with you: Never again shall all flesh be cut off by the waters of the flood; never again shall there be a flood to destroy the earth."* (Genesis 9:11). God made the rainbow to be the sign of that covenant. Verses 12-13 read, *"This is the sign of the covenant which I make between me and you, and every living creature that is with you, for perpetual generations: I set my rainbow in the cloud, and it shall be for the sign of the covenant between me and the earth."* Today, when there is a rainbow in the sky, it reminds us of the covenant between God and Noah on behalf of human kind. When God made a covenant with Abraham to multiply his seed, He commanded him to circumcise every male child. In this covenant, God made the circumcision to be the sign of the covenant between Him and Abraham (Read Genesis 17:2,10-11).

God gets disappointed whenever His people break His covenant with them. Our text reads, *"And they rejected His statutes and His covenant that He had made with their fathers, and His testimonies which He had testified against them; they followed idols, became idolaters, and went after the nations who were all around them, concerning whom the LORD had charged them that they should not do like them."* (v15). There is a price to pay for breaking God's covenant (Read v18). Through His death, we now have a new covenant in Christ.

Reflection: God is a covenant Keeper. What about you?

Word for today: *Those who break Christ's covenant will be broken to pieces.*

SIN—A SPIRITUAL BARRIER

When you spread out your hands, I will hide my eyes from you; even though you make many prayers, I will not hear. Your hands are full of blood (Isaiah 1:15)

READ: ISAIAH 59:1-3

Our text reads, *"Behold, the LORD'S hand is not shortened, That it cannot save; nor His ear heavy, that it cannot hear. But your iniquities have separated you from your God; and your sins have hidden His face from you, so that He will not hear."* (v1-2). Right after the fall of Adam and Eve, sin became a spiritual barrier between God and man. The Bible records that Adam and Eve made fig leaves to cover themselves and then went and hid among the trees of the garden in order to get away from God. Just as Adam's sin created a spiritual barrier between him and God, so does one's sin create a spiritual barrier between him and God. God is Spirit and relates to us through His Spirit. Sin stalls such relationship.

God told the children of Israel that His hand was not shortened, that it could not save them, nor His ears heavy that He could not hear their cry and prayer. God pointed out that sin was the barrier to their deliverance and answer to their prayers. At the time of Isaiah's writing, shedding of innocent blood was common among the children of Israel, for which they were warned (Read Isaiah 1:15; 59:7; Ezekiel 7:23-24). God also indicted the people for their lives of falsehood and deception (Isaiah 59:13). God's Word to the children of Israel is relevant to us today. In the cities and villages around the world, we hear news of innocent blood being shed on daily basis; falsehood has now become the norm in business deals. Yet, the same people who perpetrate all these atrocities are emboldened to lift up their hands to God in prayer. Today, it is not uncommon to find politician who are rogues, donate money to Churches to make them look like saints, in order to hide their evil practices. The Word of God makes it clear, *"Do not be deceived, God is not mocked; for whatever a man sows, that he will also reap. For he who sows to his flesh will of the flesh reap corruption, but he who sows to the Spirit will of the Spirit reap everlasting life."* (Gal. 6:7).

Reflection: Are you connected to God? If not, why not?

Word for today: *Christ deals with the spiritual barrier of sin; come to Him.*

HOW TO KNOW A FOOL

The fool has said in his heart, "There is no God." They are corrupt, and have done abominable iniquity; there is none who does good (Psalm 53:1)

READ: PSALM 14:1-3

Being called a fool is an insult, because it paints a picture of someone who is unintelligent, deficient in understanding and unwise in a given situation. No one likes to be called a fool; everyone wants to be identified as being wise. Unfortunately, some people by choice , behave like fools.

How to identify a fool?
The Bible tells us about seven ways to identify a fool:
1. A fool is someone who says there is no God (Psalm 14:1). If you know of someone who says that there is no God, regard such a person as a fool, no matter his or her academic achievement. **2. A fool is someone who is materialistic** (Read Luke 12:20-21). Being rich in material things without knowing Christ makes someone a fool, because at death, he or she leaves all the riches behind to spend eternity in hell. **3. A fool is someone who despises wisdom** (Proverbs 1:7). How seriously do you take the instructions from the Word of God?
4. A fool is someone who gossips (Proverbs 10:18). Anyone who is in the habit of gossiping and backbiting is a fool. **5. A fool is someone who makes mockery of sin** (Proverbs 14:9). Mocking at sin comes in various ways, such as calling good evil and evil good; loving what God hates (Isaiah 5:20). **6. A fool is someone who folds his hands and refuses to work** (Ecclesiastes 4:5). If you ever run into someone who refuses to work, such a person is a fool.
7. A fool is someone who is hearer, but not a doer of the Word of God (Matthew 7:26-27; James 1:22). Those who hear the Word of God and refuse to do it, for whatever reason, are fools.
What to do about fools.
1. We should lead them to Christ. The Bible declares, *"He that wins souls is wise."* (Proverbs 11:30).
2. We should pray for them. If you know of anyone who fits the above profile, he or she is a fool and needs a lot of prayer.

Reflection: Do you have or know of any fool around you?

Word for today: *It takes spiritual enlightenment for a fool to find his way.*

GOD'S JUDGMENT UPON THE LAND

"The more they increased, the more they sinned against me; I will change their glory into shame" (Hosea 4:7).

READ: HOSEA 4:1-3

God is just and righteous. He never pronounces judgment upon anyone or group of people without first of all, letting such people know about their sins and wrong doings. This was what happened to the children of Israel. Verse 1-2 of our text reads, *"Hear the word of the LORD, you children of Israel, for the LORD brings a charge against the inhabitants of the land: 'There is no truth or mercy or knowledge of God in the land. By swearing and lying, killing and stealing and committing adultery, they break all restraint, with bloodshed upon bloodshed.'"* Those were the words of God's indictment on the children of Israel for their sinfulness. In the days of Hosea, people suppressed the truth; failed to show mercy to their neighbors; stole and swore falsely; committed sexual immorality and shed innocent blood. The sins for which God pronounced judgment upon the children of Israel are very much with us today. Things have not changed; rather, they have gotten worse, instead. In verse 3 of our text, we read of God's punishment for the sins of the children of Israel. *"Therefore the land will mourn; and everyone who dwells there will waste away with the beasts of the field and the birds of the air; even the fish of the sea will be taken away."* This verse paints a horrific picture of destruction in the land of Israel. Have you wondered why there is so much commotion and devastation all over the world? On a daily basis, people are murdered all over the world; women are raped; married couples divorce before the celebration of their fifth anniversary; families are torn apart, leaving the innocent children to suffer. The answer to all these is simple: People have turned their backs on God their Maker.

In Proverbs 8:35-36, the Word of God tells us what happens to those who love God and those who hate Him: *"Whoever finds me finds life, and obtains favor from the LORD; but he who sins against me wrongs his own soul; all those who hate me love death."* As long as people live in rebellion against God, they will have no peace in their lives, as well as in the land in which they live.

Reflection: Has your life been dented by the sinful culture of our society?

Word for today: *Sinners cannot escape the wrath of God.*

LOVE IN ACTION

This is my commandment, that you love one another as I have loved you (John 15:12)

READ: LUKE 10:30-37

Love is an action word; if not put to work, it becomes an abstract word—dead and unfruitful. The Bible enjoins that *"you love the Lord your God with all your heart, with all your soul, with all your strength, and with all your mind, and your neighbor as yourself."* (Luke 10:27). Matthew 5:44 reads, *"But I say to you, love your enemies, bless those who curse you, do good to those who hate you, and pray for those who spitefully use you and persecute you."* Mark 12:31 also declares, *"You shall love your neighbor as yourself."* Our Lord Jesus said to His disciples, *"A new commandment I give to you, that you love one another; as I have loved you, that you also love one another."* (John 13:34). Apostle Paul had this to say, *"Husbands, love your wives, just as Christ also loved the church and gave Himself for her."* (Ephesians 5:25). In all of the above texts, we notice that love is the key word as well as the action word. It tells us what we need to do about love.

Our text is a classic example of putting love in action. The fact that our Lord Jesus told this story underscores the importance of demonstrating love. A certain man who was travelling from Jerusalem to Jericho was robbed by thieves after being thoroughly beaten and left for dead. As the man laid by the road side longing for help, a priest walked by and on seeing him, "passed by on the other side." (v30-31). Again, a Levite saw the man and "passed by on the other side." (v32). But, when a Samaritan arrived, he "had compassion on the injured man", treated him and took him to an inn for further treatment and care (v33-34). In the epistle of James, we read about the need of putting love in action (James 2:14-17). Although James wrote about the need to do good to others vis-à-vis our faith in Christ, his letter has an undertone of love in it. The surest way to demonstrate a genuine love toward a hungry brother or sister in the Lord who happens to visit you is to give him or her food, among other things. Sending him or her away hungry makes love inactive.

Reflection: When last did you put in action your love for someone?

Word for today: *An indemonstrable love is a dead love.*

LOSE TO GAIN

He who loves his life will lose it, and he who hates his life in this world will keep it for eternal life (John 12:25).

READ: LUKE 9:23-26

At one of His teachings, during His earthly ministry, our Lord Jesus Christ told His audience, *"Whoever desires to save his life will lose it, but whoever loses his life for my sake will save it."* (Luke 9:24). Christ's statement sounds contradictory. How can you gain something by losing it? But, it is not contradictory at all! Verse 25 throws some light on Christ's statement. We read, *"For what profit is it to a man if he gains the whole world, and is himself destroyed or lost?"* Indeed, it is foolishness to exchange an eternal life for a temporal worldly pleasure. Whoever that is unwilling to sacrifice his life for the service of our Lord Jesus Christ, will find it hard to gain eternal life. In other words, the road to eternal life starts by surrendering your life to Christ in exchange for eternal life in Him. To forsake the world is to gain Christ, but to gain the world is to forsake Christ. You cannot have both at the same time. Anyone who is unwilling to forsake worldly pleasure to have Christ, is really not ready for heaven.

Apostle Paul was willing to lose all that he had in order to gain Christ. In His letter to the Church in Philippi, he wrote, *"But what things were gain to me, these I have counted loss for Christ. Yet indeed I also count all things loss for the excellence of the knowledge of Christ Jesus my Lord, for whom I have suffered the loss of all things, and count them as rubbish, that I may gain Christ."* (Philippians 3:7-8). Wouldn't it be wise for us to follow Christ's example, who laid down His life that He might gain many souls into eternal life? We read, *"As the Father knows me, even so I know the Father; and I lay down my life for the sheep. And other sheep I have which are not of this fold; them also I must bring, and they will hear my voice; and there will be one flock and one shepherd."* (John 10:15-16). A farmer who fails to part with his seedlings during planting season, cannot reap during the harvesting season. You have to lose something in order to gain something of greater importance.

Reflection: What have you lost in order to gain Christ?

Word for today: *Remember, nothing lost; nothing gained.*

253

STUBBORN & REBELLIOUS SPIRIT

"Thus says the LORD: 'Stand in the ways and see, and ask for the old paths, where the good way is, and walk in it'... but they said, 'We will not walk in it.'" (Jeremiah 6:16).

READ: JEREMIAH 44:11-14

Stubbornness and rebellion are closely related. Someone who is stubborn is more likely to be rebellious. The evil spirit that makes someone to be stubborn, makes him also to be rebellious. Stubbornness borders on unreasonableness, while rebellion borders on effrontery. A combination of these two vices produces stubbornness and rebellion. Stubbornness and rebellion have spirits behind them. This means that those who are stubborn and rebellious are infested with the spirit/spirits of rebellion and stubbornness. Unfortunately, many people have these spirits living inside of them, without their knowing of it. The devil makes such people to live under the illusion that they are strong and assertive, when in fact, they are being stubborn and rebellious.

In our text, we notice how, even in the face of God's impending judgment, the children of Israel were hell bent on being stubborn and rebellious. Through prophet Jeremiah, God told them what would happen to them if they failed to repent. Our text tells us of such pronouncements (Read v11-14). In spite of all the warnings of Jeremiah, the people insisted on carrying out their evil actions. Read their response to him, *"As for the word that you have spoken to us in the name of the LORD, we will not listen to you! But we will certainly do whatever has gone out of our own mouth, to burn incense to the queen of heaven and pour out drink offerings to her, as we have done, we and our fathers, our kings and our princes, in the cities of Judah and in the streets of Jerusalem. For then we had plenty of food, were well-off, and saw no trouble." (v16-17).* Their response smacks of pride, stubbornness and rebellion against God, His Word and His messenger. May we never be stubbornly rebellious against God. Doing so amounts to foolhardiness, because all those who rebelled against God in the past did not end well at all. For an example, read 1 Samuel 2:27-36; 3:10-14. and know how Eli and his sons ended.

Reflection: Have you been resisting the Holy Spirit in your life?

Word for today: *The stubborn and rebellious often end up disastrously.*

WHAT A GREAT SALVATION!

"Of how much worse punishment, do you suppose, will he be thought worthy who has trampled the Son of God underfoot...and insulted the Spirit of grace?" (Hebrews 10:29).

READ: HEBREWS 2:1-4

Salvation is a gift from God to humankind that have been sold into spiritual slavery through the sin of Adam (Genesis 3:1-12). But, thanks be to God who has provided us with redemption through His Son, Jesus Christ (Read Romans 3:23-24; 5:17-19). Anyone who fails or neglects to seek salvation in Christ is lost forever. The Bible declares, *"Neither is there salvation in any other, for there is no other name under heaven given among men by which we must be saved."* (Acts 4:12). It is not what you think, but what God says that matters. Jesus Christ is God's Gift of salvation to humankind, to which God testified from heaven (Read Matthew 17:5).

The author of Hebrews reminds us of the need to put our confidence in the salvation that God has provided in Christ. He warns us *"to pay earnest heed to the things we have heard, lest we drift away."* (Hebrews 2:1). Indeed, we should pay attention to the intake of sound Bible doctrine, so that we will *"no longer be children, tossed to and fro and carried about with every wind of doctrine, by the trickery of men, in the cunning craftiness of deceitful plotting, but, speaking the truth in love, and grow up in all things into Him who is the head— Christ."* (Ephesians 4:14-15). We are warned that *"in latter times some will depart from the faith, giving heed to deceiving spirits and doctrines of demons, speaking lies in hypocrisy, having their own conscience seared with a hot iron."* (1 Timothy 4:1-2). That latter times which Paul wrote to Timothy about is here with us. Today, many find it hard to adhere to sound Bible doctrine; rather, they go to places where they hear what they want to hear, not what God wants them to hear (Read 2 Timothy 4:3-4). Without experiencing salvation in Christ, humankind is doomed. Verse 4 of our text tells us how God has borne witness to the message of salvation through *"signs and wonders, with various miracles, and the gifts of the Holy Spirit."* Hence, we should not neglect God's salvation.

Reflection: Have you embraced God's salvation of your soul?

Word for today: *Our great God has given us a great salvation in Christ.*

A SPIRITUALLY HEALTHY HEART

Blessed are the pure in heart, for they shall see God (Matthew 5:8).

READ: PROVERBS 4:20-23

The heart is considered the most vital organ of the human body. Without it, there can be no life. In fact, whenever the heart stops beating, life stops existing. This means that the beating of the heart sustains life. No wonder why people often ensure that they have healthy hearts? Unfortunately, some people's hearts may be medically healthy, but spiritually sick. Hence, the spiritual diagnosis of the human heart by God looks horrible! We read, *"The heart is deceitful above all things, and desperately wicked; Who can know it?"* (Jeremiah 17:9). After His diagnosis of the human heart, God says that the human heart has two spiritual problems: **Deceit** and **wickedness.** As a result, God *"searches the heart and tests the human mind to give every man according to his ways, according to the fruit of his doings."* (v10). God rewards the deceitfulness and wickedness of man. In Genesis 6:5,7 we read, *"Then the LORD saw that the wickedness of man was great in the earth, and that every intent of the thoughts of his heart was only evil continually. So the LORD said "I will destroy man whom I have created from the face of the earth, both man and beast, creeping thing and birds of the air, for I am sorry that I have made them."*

The spiritual sickness in the human heart comes from Satan. It is made worse by man heeding the deception of Satan, rather than, trusting and obeying God. God was not sorry, rather He was disappointed that He made man (Gen. 6:6). To be sorry meant that God was apologetic. So, the word **sorry** in our text is improperly rendered. Cain committed the first murder by killing his brother Abel, because his heart was spiritually sick. While they were both in the field, Cain exhibited his sick heart condition, "As he talked with his brother, he rose up and murdered him." (Genesis 4:8). When confronted by God about Abel's where about, Cain tried to be smart in his reply. He told lies, *"I do not know"* and then queried God, *"Am I my brother's keeper?" (v9).* Sin causes the heart to be spiritually sick and only Christ has the cure for it.

Reflection: Is your heart spiritually healthy?

Word for today: *A spiritually healthy heart is spiritually wealthy.*

NOT BY WORKS!

For by grace you have been saved through faith, and that not of yourselves; it is the gift of God, not of works, lest anyone should boast (Ephesians 2:8-9).

READ: JOHN 6:28-30

During Christ's earthly ministry, a group of Jews who were zealous about the Kingdom of God met Him and asked, *"What shall we do, that we may work the works of God?"* (John 6:28). The word, **work** appears four times in   our text (v28,29,30). Works *speak* of human effort and self-righteousness, while faith *speaks* of God's grace. Apparently, these Jews by their question, were trying to attain eternal life through works. But, in reply our Lord Jesus said to them, *"This is the work of God, that you believe in Him whom He sent."* Have you been making an effort to be a good Christian by trying to do good? If the answer is yes, you will not be able to become a good Christian through your own effort; you need to believe in Christ Jesus and accept Him into your life. Works do not save, faith in Christ does! The Bible declares, *"But as many as received Him, to them He gave the right to become children of God, to those who believe in His name* (John 1:12). Unsatisfied with the answer Christ gave to them and still bent on works, the Jews asked Christ another question, *"What sign will you perform then, that we may see it and believe you? What work will you do?"* (v30). These guys wanted to see before believing, rather than believing before seeing. We have to believe in Christ in order to experience the good works of God in our lives.

Prior to his conversion, Apostle Paul tried to attain eternal life through good works, alias, self-righteousness. He prided himself on keeping the law (Philippians 3:4-6). On the contrary, after his conversion, Paul had this to say, *"What things were gain to me, these I have counted loss for Christ. Yet indeed I also count all things loss for the excellence of the knowledge of Christ Jesus my Lord, for whom I have suffered the loss of all things, and count them as rubbish, that I may gain Christ and be found in Him, not having my own righteousness, which is from the law, but that which is through faith in Christ, the righteousness which is from God by faith."* (v7-9).

Reflection: Are you a moralist, a good person, but, without Christ?

Word for today: *Good morals outside of Christ are like filthy rags to God.*

TOUGH LOVE!

For what will it profit a man if he gains the whole world, and loses his own soul? Or what will a man give in exchange for his soul? (Mark 8:36-37).

READ: MARK 10:17-22

Love is an act of kindness towards others. But, when the word love is preceded with the word tough, love assumes a deeper meaning. It becomes an act of kindness aimed at correcting the recipient—trying to make him or her a better person. The phrase **Tough love** was "evidently coined by Bill Milliken when he wrote the book *Tough Love* in 1968. In most cases, practicing tough love may force someone to treat others harshly with the intent to making such an individual a better person in the long run. As a believer in Christ, if you really love someone, you need to practice tough love in order to help such a person get rid of bad habit or sinful lifestyle.

We notice in our text, how Christ demonstrated tough love on a guy who came to Him to inquire how he would inherit eternal life. The guy's question was concise and direct: "Good Teacher, what shall I do that I may inherit eternal life?" (17). Since the guy wanted to do something in order to inherit eternal life, in reply, Christ pointed him to the commandment: *"You know the commandments: 'Do not commit adultery,' 'Do not murder,' 'Do not steal,' 'Do not bear false witness' 'Do not defraud,' 'Honor your father and your mother.'"* The guy said to Jesus, *"Teacher, all these things I have kept from my youth."* (v20). The fact that Christ did not dispute this guy's claim, meant he was telling the truth. Since the guy was telling the truth, Jesus loved him and demonstrated tough love toward him. We read, *"Then Jesus, looking at him, loved him and said to him, One thing you lack: Go your way, sell whatever you have and give to the poor, and you will have treasure in heaven; and come, take up the cross, and follow me."* (v21). The guy's reaction to what he was told by Christ was that of dejection and abandonment. Verse 22 reads, *" But he was sad at this word, and went away sorrowful, for he had great possessions."* People react to tough love differently. In this case, the guy who wanted to know what he would do to inherit eternal life refused to accept the truth of tough love.

Reflection: How do you react to tough love? Avoid and abandon the source?

Word for today: *Tough love sometimes mellows the human heart.*

"EVEN THE WINDS...OBEY HIM"

All things were made through Him, and without Him nothing was made that was made (John 1:3).

READ: LUKE 8:22-25

Whenever a boat encounter windstorms on the high seas and are in danger of shipwreck, the sailors do something to save the lives of those on board. As Jesus and His disciples sailed across the lake of Galilee, our text tells us that *"the windstorm came down on the lake and their boat began to be filled with water, and they were in jeopardy."* (Luke 8:23). Noticing that Jesus was asleep, His disciples came to Him with this frightening news, *"Master, Master, we are perishing."* Then Jesus *"arose and rebuked the wind and the raging of the water. And they ceased, and there was a calm."* (v24). Christ's disciples had witnessed unclean spirits leave their victims in obedience to His command, but, they had never witnessed nature obey His command. No wonder why they exclaimed, *"Who can this be? For He commands even the winds and water, and they obey Him!"* (v25). As a user of this Devotional, I want to assure you that as long as you have Christ in the boat of your life, you will never sink (Read Isaiah 54:17). The storms of life will always obey the voice of Master Jesus. In order to experience this, endeavor to do the following: **First,** recognize the presence of God in your life. **Second,** put your trust in Him and don't waver in your faith, nor be afraid of the storms. **Thirdly,** remain faithful to Him. God honors and rewards faithfulness.

In Book of Jonah, we learn of how the sailors lightened their ship in the face of a severe windstorm. Jonah 1:5 reads, *"Then the mariners were afraid; and every man cried out to his god, and threw the cargo that was in the ship into the sea, to lighten the load. But Jonah had gone down into the lowest parts of the ship, had lain down, and was fast asleep."* The lightening of the ship did not help matters, nor did the consultation of their gods. So, it was not surprising that Jonah was approached by the captain of the ship to call on his own God (v6). Just as motor vehicular accident is akin to the road, so is shipwreck akin to the sea.

Reflection: How obedient are you to the command of the Lord?

Word for today: *Christ is willing to calm the storm; call on Him.*

DOWN THE MEMORY LANE

"This may be a sign among you when your children ask in time to come, saying, 'What do these stones mean to you?'"

READ: ACTS 13:16-23

Sometimes it is good to go down the memory lane regarding the issues of life. The purpose for this, is to take a stock of the past to enable us face the future better. This was exactly what Paul did as he spoke to his Jewish brethren during his missionary journey from Perga to Antioch in Pisidia. On his arrival at Antioch, Paul and his team *"went to the synagogue on a Sabbath day and sat down."* (Acts 13:15).

In the time of Paul, there were Synagogues wherever the Jews lived. Unlike the temple, the synagogue was easy to establish. About ten Jewish males could start a synagogue, which served as an assembly for prayer. The Jews met at the synagogue every Sabbath day. So, it was not surprising that Paul attended one of the synagogue meetings on the Sabbath day. Verse 15 of our text reads, *"And after the reading of the Law and the Prophets, the rulers of the synagogue sent to them, saying, 'Men and brethren, if you have any word of exhortation for the people, say on.'"* After the traditional reading of the Tura—the law and the Prophets, an opportunity was given to anyone who had a word of exhortation for the people. Paul seized the opportunity to present to the people, Christ Jesus. In doing so, he took them down the memory lane. **First,** he reminded them of God's choice of their fathers and their deliverance from Egyptian bondage (v17). Read Deuteronomy 7:6-8. **Second,** Paul reminded his audience of their wilderness experience—how for forty years, God *"put up with their ways in the wilderness."* (v18). Paul's statement sounded more like an indictment, than a commendation. **Thirdly,** Paul reminded them of how God destroyed the *"seven nations in the land of Canaan"* and distributed to them the land as an inheritance. From time to time, it is good to go down the memory lane by reflecting on God's goodness in our lives; what He has done, what He is doing and what He will do. This will enable us appreciate Him more and serve Him even better.

Reflection: How often do you reflect on God's goodness in your life?

Word for today: *A reflective heart is a thoughtful and thankful heart.*

DON'T STANDBY AND GAZE

Now it came to pass, while He blessed them, that He was parted from them and carried up into heaven (Luke 24:51).

READ: ACTS 1:9-11; 2:1-4

Something dramatic took place as Christ delivered what looked like a farewell address to His disciples on Mount Olivet during His last moment on earth. We read, *"Now when He had spoken these things, while they watched, He was taken up, and a cloud received Him out of their sight. And while they looked steadfastly toward heaven as He went up, behold, two men stood by them in white apparel, who also said, 'Men of Galilee, why do you stand gazing up into heaven? This same Jesus, who was taken up from you into heaven, will so come in like manner as you saw Him go into heaven.'"* (Acts 1:9-11). After Christ had spoken to His disciples, He was lifted up and the clouds received Him out of their sight. But, while the disciples kept gazing into heaven in bewilderment, two angels appeared and said to them, *"Men of Galilee, why do you stand and gaze up into heaven? This same Jesus who was taken up from you into heaven, will so come in like manner as you see Him go into heaven"* (v11). The disciples of Christ must have felt a sense of loss and disappointment as they watched Jesus disappear into the clouds, but after the angelic announcement, they picked up courage and took a step in the right direction.

Christ's disciples' reaction to the angelic announcement.
1. They stopped gazing and obeyed the Lord's command.
"He commanded them not to depart from Jerusalem, but to wait for the Promise of the Father...you shall be baptized with the Holy Spirit not many days from now." (Acts1: 4-5). The disciples obeyed the Lord by going back to Jerusalem to wait for the Holy Spirit. **2. They stopped gazing and went into prayer session**. *"Then they returned to Jerusalem from the mount called Olivet...and continued with one accord in prayer and supplication..."* **3. They stopped gazing and prepared themselves for the great commission** (v8). One cannot be gazing and fulfilling the great commission at the same time. So, stop gazing and start serving to fulfil the great commission.

Reflection: How committed are you to the great commission?

Word for today: *Those who stand and gaze are not obedient disciples.*

SEPTEMBER

DEVOTIONALS

FAITH AND COURAGE

"Moreover David said, 'The LORD, who delivered me from the paw of the lion and from the paw of the bear, He will deliver me from the hand of this Philistine.'" (1 Samuel 17:37).

READ: 1 SAMUEL 17:40-47

The story of David versus Goliath is an interesting one: It is a story often told in Sunday school classes and preached from the pulpits. What makes David versus Goliath story so interesting was the way a youthful David was able to kill Goliath a renown warrior.

When king Saul learnt of David's willingness to fight Goliath, he made two attempts to discourage him. **First,** he tried to talk David out of it by saying, *"You are not able to go against him; for you are a youth, and he a man of war from his youth."* (v33). But, David insisted that he was able to fight and defeat Goliath, citing God's deliverance in the past (v34-37). **Second,** king Saul *"clothed David with his armor, and put a bronze helmet on his head; he also clothed him with a coat of mail."* (v38). After being clothed with Saul's war gear, David considered it a stumbling block, rather that an asset in fighting Goliath. So, David took them off with this comment, *"I cannot walk with these, for I have not tested them."* (v39). Thereafter, David prepared to fight against Goliath in an unusual way. We read, *"Then he (David) took his staff in his hand; and he chose for himself five smooth stones from the brook, and put them in a shepherd's bag, in a pouch which he had, and his sling was in his hand. And he drew near to the Philistine."* (v40). David went against Goliath with a sling and a stone without any armor and was disdained by Goliath (v41-42). Goliath said to David, *"Am I a dog, that you come to me with stick? And he cursed David by his gods."* (v43). David's reply was that of faith and courage: *"You come to me with a sword, with a spear, and with a javelin. But I come to you in the name of the LORD of hosts, the God of the armies of Israel, whom you have defied."* (v45). Faith in God prepared David, while courage made him to act. Without courage, it is difficult to put your faith to work. As a believer in Christ, learn to combine faith and courage in whatever you do.

Reflection: How faithful and courageous are you?

Word for today: *Faith promotes trust; courage promotes action.*

BLOOD MONEY

"[Judas] was remorseful and brought back the thirty pieces of silver and said, 'I have sinned by betraying innocent blood.'" (Matthew 27:3-4).

READ: MATTHEW 27:3-10

Money is a useful and dependable means of exchange, for without it buying and selling will be difficult. There is nothing bad in having money, but there is every thing bad in having money that is tinted with human blood. In other words, when someone acquires wealth through the shedding of human blood, such wealth is known as blood money. This was what happened to Judas Iscariot. Judas went to the Jewish religious leaders and specifically asked for money to betray Jesus Christ. Matthew 26:14-16 read, *"Then one of the twelve, called Judas Iscariot, went to the chief priests and said, 'What are you willing to give me if I deliver Him to you?' And they counted out to him thirty pieces of silver. So from that time he sought opportunity to betray Him."* Judas knew the game he was playing, but did not understand the full consequences of his action. He got blood money by betraying His Master.

After our Lord Jesus had been condemned and was being manhandled, Judas realized his mistake. Our text reads, *"Then Judas, His betrayer, seeing that He had been condemned, was remorseful and brought back the thirty pieces of silver to the chief priests and elders, saying, 'I have sinned by betraying innocent blood.' And they said, 'What is that to us? You see to it.' Then he threw down the pieces of silver in the temple and departed, and went and hanged himself.'"* (Matthew 27:3-5). The fact that the Jewish leaders refused to accept the same money that they had given to Judas, showed how blood tinted that money had become. Unfortunately, they failed to realize the blood in their hands for killing Jesus. Those who make a living through kidnapping and armed robbery, as well as those who enrich themselves by denying the poor of their only means of livelihood, are by implication living on blood money. Sooner or later, the wrath of God will descend upon such people, unless they repent and ask God for His forgiveness. Just as Judas did not get away with blood money, so will anyone who lives on blood money not go unpunished.

Reflection: How do you make your wealth?

Word for today: *Don't allow your wealth to be tinted with blood.*

DENIERS OF REALITY

But Peter and the other apostles answered and said: "We ought to obey God rather than men" (Acts 5:29).

READ: ACTS 5:26-29

Trying to deny reality is a difficult thing to do. For instance, to deny the reality of Christ as the son of God, the Jewish religious leaders tried thrice, without success. **First** was their refusal to heed God's two-fold testimonies about Christ (Read Matthew 3:17; 17:4-5). **Second** was their denial of the reality of Christ's triumphant resurrection. A day after Christ was buried, the chief priests and the Pharisees came to Pilate and demanded that His tomb be sealed (Matthew 27:62-63). Their request was granted by Pilate who said to them, *"You have a guard; go your way, make it as secure as you know how."* In obedience to Pilate's command, *"they went and made the tomb secure, sealing the stone and setting the guard."* (v65-66). But, on the early hours of Sunday morning—the first day of the week, Christ rose triumphantly from the dead, in spite of the sealing of the tomb and setting of guards (Matthew 28:2-8). Rather than accept the reality of Christ's resurrection, the Jewish leaders decided to bribe the guards to suppress the truth (v11-15).

The **third** attempt by the Jewish religious leaders to deny reality is recorded in our text. Peter and his colleague, John had been imprisoned for healing a man born lame at the beautiful gate of the Temple. But, at night God sent his angel to bring them out of the prison, with the following command, *"Go, stand in the temple and speak to the people all the words of this life."* (Acts 5:19-20). Later Peter and John were rearrested and brought before the high priest, who queried them, *"Did we not strictly command you not to teach in this name? And look, you have filled Jerusalem with your doctrine, and intend to bring this Man's blood on us!"* (v27-28). Based on the statement of the high priest, it was evident that the Jewish leaders were worried about the spread of the gospel and being held responsible for the blood of Jesus. How short their memory must have been! At Christ's trial, they openly told Pilate, *"Let His blood be on us and on our children."* (Matthew 27:25). Denial of reality doesn't make sense.

Reflection: Are you among those who deny the reality of God's Word?

Word for today: *Reality is a fact that cannot be hidden or denied.*

TESTIMONIES ABOUT CHRIST

"The Father Himself, who sent me, has testified of me. You have neither heard His voice at any time, nor seen His form." (John 5:37).

READ: JOHN 8:13-20

Deuteronomy 19:15 reads, *"One witness shall not rise against a man concerning any iniquity or any sin that he commits; by the mouth of two or three witnesses the matter shall be established."* That was the LORD's command to Moses in relation to adjudicating a case involving. There must be two or three witnesses before someone could be considered guilty of an accusation brought against him. There is no doubt that the laws of the secular courts evolved from God's law, as such, witnesses are usually required in judicial cases. In our text, we notice that the Pharisees accused Christ of being His own witness and that His witness was false (John 8:13) But, Jesus refuted their accusation by saying, *"My witness is true, for I know where I came from and where I am going."* (v14).

There are **seven-fold testimonies about the Person of Christ: 1. Testimony of God, the Father.** During Christ's baptism, God testified, *"This is my beloved Son, in whom I am well pleased."* (Matthew 3:17). At the transfiguration, God testified again, *"This is my beloved Son, in whom I am well pleased, Hear Him!"* (17:5). Since God cannot give a false testimony, we need to listen to Him. **2. Testimony of Christ Himself.** John 8:18 reads, *"I am one who bears witness of myself...."* Christ cannot tell lies, and has no need to do so. His testimony about Himself is aimed at letting us believe that He came from the Father to save mankind. **3. Testimony of His works.** In John 10:25 we read, *"Jesus answered them, 'I told you, and you do not believe. The works that I do in my Father's name, they bear witness of me.'"* Read also Matthew 11:2-6. 4. **Testimony of Peter.** Peter said, *"You are the Christ, the Son of the living God."* (Matthew 16:16). **5. Testimony of the Samaritan woman:** *"Come, see a man who told me all things that I ever did. Could this be the Christ?"* (John 4:29). **6. Testimony of the centurion and the guards** (Matthew 27:54) **7. Testimony of the multitude** (Read Matthew 21:9-11).

Reflection: Can you give a testimony about Christ's Lordship in your life?

Word for today: *Testimonies about Christ are timeless and limitless.*

GOD OUR FATHER

The field is the world, the good seeds are the sons of the kingdom, but the tares are the sons of the wicked one (Matthew 13:38).

READ: JOHN 8:37-44

Fatherhood springs from having an offspring. When God changed the name of Abram—*exalted father* to Abraham—*father of multitude,* He said to him, *"I have made you the father of many nations. I will make you exceedingly fruitful; and I will make nations of you, and kings shall come from you."* (Genesis 17:5-6). Abram and Sarah were hundred and ninety years old respectively when the LORD made this promise to Abraham (v17). The LORD's promise to Abraham has been fulfilled to the letter: the nation of Israel being the biological offspring of Abraham, while the nation of believers in Christ has also become the spiritual offspring of Abraham (Read Romans 4:11; Galatian 3:29). Christ taught His followers to address God as their Father in their prayers (Matthew 6:9). The reason for this is simple: They have been begotten by God as children through faith in Christ. John 1:12-13 read, *"But as many as received Him, to them He gave the right to become children of God, to those who believe in His name: who were born, not of blood, nor of the will of the flesh, nor of the will of man, but of God."* God recognizes all those who believe in Christ as His children, and they are eligible to call Him Father. Anyone who is not born of God, and claims to be a child of His or calls God his or her Father is living in a fool's paradise. Yes, God is the Creator of all, but He is not the Father of all. There are two kinds of fathers in the world (1 John 3:10).

Our text makes this issue clearer. Our Lord Jesus Christ told the unbelieving Jews, *"I speak what I have seen with my Father, and you do what you have seen with your father."* (John 8:38). Christ's statement of the Jews having another father other than Abraham was surprising to them. So, they quickly replied, *"Abraham is our father"* and then added, *"We are not born of fornication; we have one Father—God."* (v39,41). But, Christ made it clear to them that they had the devil as their father and not God, because they do exactly what the devil does—murder and lying (v44) Read also 1 John 3:8,9,15.

Reflection: Who is your father? Can you truly say that God is your Father?

Word for today: *Those born of God are His children, and He is their Father.*

THE NEED FOR STILLNESS

"Stand still, and see the salvation of the LORD, which He will accomplish for you today..." (Exodus 14:13).

READ: PSALM 46:8-11

Not long after their departure from Egypt, the children of Israel were faced with a dilemma—they had the Red sea in front and the Pharaoh's army behind them. From a human standpoint, they were done. If they moved forward, they would all be drowned in the Red sea, and if they moved backward, they would be consumed by Pharaoh's advancing army. Since the LORD was with them, they needed to be still in order to see His salvation. Therefore, Moses told them, *"Stand still, and see the salvation of the LORD....the LORD will fight for you, and you shall hold your peace."* (Exodus 14: 13-14). No matter the situation you are facing right now, remember that as a believer in Christ, the God you are serving is the same God who fought for the children of Israel. Be still—don't be afraid, stop panicking and just put your trust in Him for He will fight for you and deliver you.

Verse 10 of our text reads, *"Be still, and know that I am God; I will be exalted among the nations, I will be exalted in the earth!"* The sons of Korah who authored Psalm 46 spoke the mind of God to His people by reminding them of the need to be still. The phrase, **"Be still"** means, **to be calm** in the face of difficulties, challenges and persecutions, if you are a child of God. It also means **"to stop striving"** against God, if you are an enemy of God; for He "will be exalted among the nations and in the earth." There is need for stillness in our lives as God's children, because He (God) who has begun a good work in us—the work of salvation, transformation, restoration, provision and protection, will never abandon us; He will bring what He has started to a perfect completion (Philippians 1:6). Based on our text, there are good reasons why we should be still and know that the LORD is God. For instance, *"He makes wars cease to the end of the earth; breaks the bow and cuts the spears in two and burns the chariots in the fire."* (Psalm 46:9). God knows how to cause wars to cease in people's lives.

Reflection: Do you experience stillness or turbulence in your life?

Word for today: *Only God can infuse stillness in a turbulent heart.*

THE COMPASSIONATE DOCTRINE

Do not be overcome by evil, but overcome evil with good (Romans 12:21).

READ: ROMANS 12:14-21

Compassionate doctrine is a divine command that enjoins us to show compassion to our enemies—to love and not hate them; pray and not curse them; feed and not starve them. Our text commands us to practice compassionate doctrine in dealing with our enemies. It reads, *"Bless those who persecute you; bless and do not curse."* (v14); *"Repay no evil for evil."* (v17); *"Do not avenge yourselves."* (v19); *"If your enemy is hungry, feed him; if he is thirsty, give him a drink; for in so doing you will heap coals of fire on his head."* (v20).

A practical act of compassionate doctrine took place after Elisha had single-handedly captured a band of Syrian soldiers, who had come to arrest him in Dothan. Elisha had requested that God should strike them with blindness, and God did. 2 Kings 6:18 reads, *"So when the Syrians came down to him, Elisha prayed to the LORD, and said, 'Strike this people, I pray, with blindness.' And He struck them with blindness according to the word of Elisha.'"* After a wave of divine blindness had visited the Syrian army, they became helpless and hopeless. So, Elisha led them into the city of Samaria—a city of their enemy—Israel. Elisha told them, *"Follow me, and I will bring you to the man whom you seek.' But he led them to Samaria* (v19). On arriving Samaria, Elisha prayed, *"LORD, open the eyes of these men, that they may see. And the LORD opened their eyes, and they saw; and there they were, inside Samaria!"* . When the king of Israel saw a bunch of Syrian soldiers in his territory, he requested permission to kill them all. But, Elisha turned down his request and reminded him of the compassionate doctrine. He said to him, *"You shall not kill them. Would you kill those whom you have taken captive with your sword and your bow? Set food and water before them, that they may eat and drink and go to their master.* The king of Israel heeded Elisha's advice and practiced the compassionate doctrine by feeding his enemies. As a result, the Syrian army never returned to bother him again (v23).

Reflection: How compassionate are you to your enemies?

Word for today: *Compassionate doctrine comes from a compassionate heart.*

THE JUDGMENT SEAT OF CHRIST

"...God will judge the secrets of men by Jesus Christ, according to my gospel." (Romans 2:16).

READ: 2 CORINTHIANS 5:9-11

In His first advent, Christ came principally to deal with the sin of our Adamic nature. By so doing, He became a sacrificial Lamb—died to pay the penalty for sin through the death of the cross. Prior to His birth, there was an angelic announcement to the effect that Mary would bring forth a Son and that His name should be called Jesus, for He would save His people from their sins. (Matthew 1:21). From the outset of John the Baptist's ministry, he had this to say when he saw Christ, *"Behold! The Lamb of God who takes away the sin of the world!"* (John 1:29). Although Christ is God, He never sat on any judgment seat during His earthly ministry. When a man approached Christ to adjudicate in a family dispute between himself and his siblings, Christ replied, *"Man, who made me a judge or an arbitrator over you?"* (Luke 12:14). Christ could have pronounced judgment on the matter, but chose not to, because He did not come as a **Judge**, but as a **Lamb.** During one of His teachings, Christ even told the Pharisees, *"You judge according to the flesh; I judge no one."* (John 8:15).

However, during His second advent, Christ will sit on His throne of glory to judge the world (Read John 5:22; Acts 10:42; 2 Timothy 4:1 and 1 Peter 4:5). In Romans 14:10, and 12 we read, *"But why do you judge your brother? Or why do you show contempt for your brother? For we shall all stand before the judgment seat of Christ. So then each of us shall give account of himself to God."* God has committed to Christ the judgment of the world (John 5:22). Therefore, every person's work is being recorded in the Book of records and everyone will be rewarded accordingly (Read Matthew 16:27; Revelation 20:12). In our text, Paul addressed the issue of Christ's judgment seat. We read, *"For we must all appear before the judgment seat of Christ, that each one may receive the things done in the body, according to what he has done, whether good or bad."* (v10). The knowledge that we must all appear before Christ's judgment seat, should prompt us to live in holiness, serve, and live in obedience to God's Word.

Reflection: What are your expectations hereafter?

Word for today: *Christ, the Advocate is also Christ the Judge and Rewarder*

THE IMMUTABLE GOD!

Your kingdom is an everlasting kingdom, and your dominion endures through-out all generations (Psalm 145:13).

READ: MALACHI 3:6-7

Nothing is constant in this world! Times change, days change, weathers change, kings change, kingdoms change, behaviors and attitudes change, laws change. In fact, virtually everything is subject to change. There are two things that do no change—God and His Word. Numbers 23:19 reads, *"God is not a man, that He should lie, nor a son of man, that He should repent. Has He said, and will He not do? Or has He spoken, and will He not make it good?"* Those were the words of Balaam—testifying of the immutability of God Almighty. From everlasting to everlasting, God remains the same. The Bible declares, *"Jesus Christ is the same yesterday, today, and forever."* (Hebrews 13:8).

Verse 6 of our text reads, *"For I am the LORD, I do not change; therefore you are not consumed, O sons of Jacob."* The LORD was very disappointed with the changing attitude of the children of Israel towards Him: They served Him and yet turned around and served Baal. Under this kind of unstable loyalty came God's indictment through Malachi, telling them that He has not changed, even though they have changed. God reminded them of their disloyalty to Him which was an extension of their fathers behavior. We read, *"From the days of your fathers you have gone away from my ordinances and have not kept them. Return to me, and I will return to you,"* says the LORD of hosts. *"But you said, 'In what way shall we return?'"* (v7). Since God does not change, He stands to punish those who rebel against Him. Many Christians behave like the children of Israel who Malachi addressed in our text. They have turned away from the truth and gone after fables and doctrines of the devil—replacing God's Word with human traditions, suppressing the truth by feeding the people with prosperity sermons, instead of undiluted Word of God. If you are in such a condition, God is extending the same appeal He made to the children of Israel to you: *"Return to me and I will return to you."* (v7).

Reflection: How do you view God? Is He real to you?

Word for today: *Our unchanging God can change your situation.*

A WRONG MOTHERLY ADVICE

But his mother said to him, "Let your curse be on me, my son; only obey my voice, and go, get them for me." (Genesis 27:13).

READ: 2 CHRONICLES 22:1-4

Children love their mothers as well as their fathers, but are emotionally attached to their mothers. The reason for this is simple: The nine months incubation period a child undergoes in the mother's womb helps to establish a strong affinity between the child and the mother. In addition, throughout his infancy, the maternal care a child enjoys strengthens the bonding that exists between him and the mother. A child is usually emotionally attached to whoever stays close by and spends much time with him.

Our text contains a classic example of how a mother's advice can influence a person's judgment and action. We read, *"Ahaziah was forty-two years old when he became king, and he reigned one year in Jerusalem. His mother's name was Athaliah the granddaughter of Omri. He also walked in the ways of the house of Ahab, for his mother advised him to do wickedly."* (v2-3). Ahaziah like some people today, must have been so emotionally attached to his mother that she was able to influence his thinking and judgment, at his age. Due to king Ahaziah's wrong motherly advice, *"he did evil in the sight of the LORD, like the house of Ahab; for they were his counselors after the death of his father, to his destruction."* (v4). As a mother reading this Devotional, what kind of advice do you give to your children? The kind of advice you give to your children can make or mar them. If you give them a godly advice, they will gravitate towards God and be successful in life. But, if on the other hand, you give them ungodly advice, they will gravitate towards the devil to their destruction. It is said, "An apple does not fall far away from the tree." Athaliah, Ahaziah's mother was the daughter of Ahab and Jezebel, who sold themselves to do evil (Read 1 Kings 21:25; 2 Chronicles 21:6). She gave her son what she learned from her parents. King Ahaziah's reign was short-lived—only one year, before his untimely death, due to his mother's wrong advice.

Reflection: What kind of advice do you get from your mother?

Word for today: *A wrong motherly advice can ruin one's future.*

CHRIST—THE CHIEF CORNERSTONE

"[You have] been built on the foundation of the apostles and prophets, Jesus Christ Himself being the chief corner stone." (Ephesians 2:20).

READ: PSALM 118:22-24

Cornerstones hold a building together. In ancient Israel, "a cornerstone was placed at the joint of two walls of a building. By uniting two intersecting walls, a cornerstone helped to align the whole building and tie it together." In our text, Paul compares a cornerstone of a building to Christ, the Author and Finisher of our faith (Hebrews 12:2). Our Lord Jesus Christ is not just a cornerstone; He is the chief Cornerstone of our salvation and the Foundation of the Church.

The author of our text, inspired by the Spirit of God, was prophetic about Christ's rejection. He referred to Him as the *"stone that the builders rejected which has become the chief corner stone."* (Psalm 118:22). Yes, the Jewish religious authority rejected Christ as the Messiah, but God ordained Him the chief Cornerstone of their salvation. Since Christ's Messiah-ship is of the LORD, *"it is marvelous in our eyes."* (v23). Christ Himself cited our text as He chided the Jews for their rejection of His Messiah-ship. We read, *"Jesus said to them, 'Have you never read in the Scriptures: 'The stone which the builders rejected Has become the chief cornerstone. This was the LORD'S doing, and it is marvelous in our eyes.'"?* (Matthew 21:42). Peter in his defense before the Sanhedrin, also cited our text to prove the Messiah-ship of Christ (Read Acts 4:11). Peter also cited our text to underscore the truth regarding Christ's Messiah-ship (1 Peter 2:7). Indeed, Christ is the *"living stone, rejected by men, but chosen by God and precious."* (v4).Through the eyes of the Spirit, the writer of our text beheld the day Christ would go the cross to consummate the salvation of humankind and exclaimed, *"This is the day that the LORD has made; we will be glad and rejoice in it."* (Psalm 118:24). As the chief Cornerstone of our salvation, joy and gladness heralded the day of Christ's birth and His triumphant resurrection (See Luke 2:8-14 and Matthew 28:1-8). Anyone who builds on Christ, the chief Cornerstone, will not be disappointed.

Reflection: Do you build your life on Christ—the chief Cornerstone?

Word for today: *To reject Christ is to reject a solid foundation of one's life.*

GREAT IS HIS FAITHFULNESS!

"The LORD your God, He is God, the faithful God who keeps covenant and mercy for a thousand generations with those who love Him and keep His commandments." Deuteronomy 7:9)

READ: LAMENTATION 3:22-26

Faithfulness is an act of "dependability, loyalty and stability" and it is one of God's divine attributes. God never slacks in His faithfulness. For instance, from the beginning till date, His covenant with Abraham still holds (Read Genesis 12:2-3; 13:16). God is faithful to keep His covenant and to fulfil His promises to those who love and obey Him (Deuteronomy 7:9). The divine attribute of faithfulness is ascribed to Christ, as the Son of God. He is clothed in faithfulness (Isaiah 11:5); He is the "true and faithful witness" (Revelation 1:5; 3:14); He is called the "Faithful One" (19:11); the "faithful High Priest" (Hebrews 2:17). God's faithfulness is the source of our strength and deliverance as followers of Christ. God's faithfulness delivers us from temptation (1 Corinthians 10:13); guarantees the assurance of our salvation and forgiveness of our sins (Hebrews 10:23; 1 John 1:9)

As His children, God expects us to be faithful in serving Him (Matthew 25:21;1 Corinthians 4:1-2). God's faithfulness to save and bless is unshakeable (Read Romans 10;13;1 Corinthians 15:58), and He is faithful in fulfilling His promises. Many years ago, as a new convert, the Lord revealed to me about His calling upon my life and everyone of those revelations has come to pass. When God makes a promise to you, He will definitely fulfil such a promise, as long as you align yourself with Him. God spoke these words to me many years ago, *"From today, I will show you the mysteries in my Word. Whenever you open the Bible, I will open your eyes to see hidden things in it."* Ever since, the hidden things that I see when I read or study the Bible have blown my mind. Hence, it has been possible to write the Heavenly Banquet Devotional of over 400 pages yearly, amidst my tight Pastoral schedule. Only God's grace and His divine illumination could have made this possible. For this, I give Him all the glory and adoration. God is faithful in keeping covenants and promises!

Reflection: Reflect on God's faithfulness and write them down.

Word for today: *Our faithful God demands faithfulness from us.*

PARDONED—NOT GUILTY

"God did not send His Son into the world to condemn the world, but that the world through Him might be saved (John 3:17)

READ: JOHN 8:7-11

During Christ's earthly ministry, *"the Scribes and Pharisees brought to Him a woman caught in adultery...and said, 'Teacher, this woman was caught in adultery, in the very act. Now Moses in the law, commanded us that such should be stoned. But what do you say?'"* (John 8:3-5). The purpose for bringing this woman to Jesus was to test Him in order to lay an accusation against Him. But, Jesus did not answer them a word. Rather, He *"stooped down and wrote on the ground with His finger, as though He did not hear them."* (v6). Verse 7-8 read, *"So when they continued asking Him, He raised Himself up and said to them, 'He who is without sin among you, let him throw a stone at her first.' And again He stooped down and wrote on the ground."* Our Lord Jesus challenged those who brought the woman caught in adultery to Him to cast the first stone if they were without sin. Since none of them was without sin, "they were convicted by their conscience and went away one after the other—beginning with the oldest even to the last." (v9).

There are three important spiritual lessons to learn from this story:
1. No one has the moral right to accuse someone else of the same sin of which he or she is guilty. The crowd that brought this woman to Jesus included the Scribes and Pharisees. But, when Jesus asked whoever was sinless among them to cast the first stone on this woman, they all went away, including the Scribes and the Pharisees, who exhibited the a sanctimonious attitude. (Read Matthew 7:3, 5). **2.** Don't try to ask questions in order to test God or raise argument about the authenticity of the Scriptures. The crowd came to test Jesus with their questions, but they felt very stupid and disappointed at the end.
3. Christ does not condone sin, but pardons the sinner. He told the woman, "Go and sin no more." (John 8:11).

Reflection: Are you dealing with any sinful habit? Turn to Jesus today for solution.

Word for today: *Christ condemns sin, but pardons the sinner.*

GOD'S DWELLING PLACE

"He who is joined to the Lord is one spirit with Him." (1 Corinthians 6:17).

READ: 1 CORINTHIANS 6:15-20

When king David conceived in his heart the idea of building a house for the LORD, he must have envisaged a place where God would dwell. But, *"at night, the word of the LORD came to Nathan, the prophet, saying, "Go and tell my servant David, 'Thus says the LORD; 'Would you build a house for me to dwell in? "* (2 Samuel 7:2-5). God pronounced his blessings upon David for the very thought of building Him a house. But, such a house would not be for Him to dwell in, but for His name. We read, *"When your days are fulfilled and you rest with your fathers, I will set up your seed after you, who will come from your body, and I will establish his kingdom. He shall build a house for my name, and I will establish the throne of his kingdom forever."* (v12-13). The Old Testament speaks of different kinds of pagan gods, such as **Chemosh**—*the pagan god of the Moabites* (Judges 11:24); **Ashtoreth**—*the pagan god of the Sidonians*; **Milcom**—*the pagan god of the Ammonites* and **Baal**—*the pagan god of the Midianites* (2 Kings 23:13). Each of these pagan gods had a temple in which it was housed. God Almighty is not a man-made god and therefore cannot be housed by man. No house can contain God, because He fills heaven and earth.

However, God dwells in people—the believers in Christ through the Holy Spirit. Verse 19 of our text reads, *"Do you not know that your body is the temple of the Holy Spirit who is in you, whom you have from God, and you are not your own?"* As a Christian believer, your body is God's; He wants to dwell in your body, therefore, you must not defile it (v20; see also Leviticus 19:27-28). There are three reasons why God wants to dwell in you as a believer in Christ. **First,** He created and recreated you. In Adam, He created you to live here on earth; in Christ Jesus, He recreated you to live with Him in heaven. **Second,** He has the deposit of His breath in you—called soul (Genesis 2:7). **Third,** He wants to fellowship with you (2 Corinthians 6:16). Do you know that God sees you as an inheritance to Himself? (Read Ephesians 1:18).

Reflection: Are you sure that God lives in you? If not, why not?

Word for today: *God lives in those who are alive in Christ.*

DEMONIC UTTERANCES

And suddenly they cried out, saying, "What have we to do with you, Jesus, you Son of God? Have you come here to torment us before the time?" (Matthew 8:29).

READ: MARK 3:7-12

One day, a large crowd gathered before Christ and He *"healed many, so that as many as had afflictions pressed about Him to touch Him* (Mark 3:10). But, as the healing ministration was taking place, the unclean spirits (demons) saw Christ and fell down before Him and cried, *"You are the Son of God."*, but Jesus sternly warned them that they should not make Him known." (v11-12). The evil spirits knew and testified to who Jesus was, but Jesus warned them to stop such a testimony. Our Lord Jesus Christ wanted His audience to hear from Him and not from the demons, even though what they were saying about Him was correct. Do you know that Satan and his cohorts like to transform themselves into angels of light, while indeed, they are angels of darkness? Demons like to operate as God's messengers in order to deceive the people of God (Read 2 Corinthians 11:14-15).

In the Book of Acts 16:16-18, we read of an incident in which a demon-possessed slave girl made some utterances that sounded correct. *"Now it happened, as we went to prayer, that a certain slave girl possessed with a spirit of divination met us, who brought her masters much profit by fortune-telling. This girl followed Paul and us, and cried out, saying, 'These men are the servants of the Most High God, who proclaim to us the way of salvation.' And this she did for many days. But Paul, greatly annoyed, turned and said to the spirit, 'I command you in the name of Jesus Christ to come out of her.' And he came out that very hour."* If it were today, this girl with the spirit of divination would have easily been ordained a prophetess in the Church. No wonder, a lot of people operate with the spirit of divination as men and women of God in Churches today. As a child of God, there is need to be discerning regarding the sources of revelations and prophecies from people. To accept demonically-induced revelation is tantamount to agreeing with the devil.

Reflection: Do you go about seeking revelations and prophecies from people?

Word for today: *Not all revealed utterances are from God. Be careful!*

279

GOD'S WORD IS INDESTRUCTIBLE

Heaven and earth will pass away, but my words will by no means pass away (Matthew 24:35).

READ: JEREMIAH 36:20-26

I t is no secret that the gods, temples, words, documents and all the paraphernalia of ancient pagan gods have been destroyed over the centuries, as a result, the worshippers of these pagan gods have diminished, courtesy of the power in the gospel! Several attempts have been made by kings and kingdoms to destroy the Word of God, but to no avail. The reason why the Word of God cannot be destroyed is because God is in His Word. In order to destroy the Word of God, one has to first of all, destroy God, which is impossible. For centuries, the Church of the living God has gone through severe persecutions aimed at eradicating Christianity. With these persecutions came the burning of Scriptures which were at times, written on papyrus scrolls. During the 300 years of persecution, God in His divine wisdom preserved the Scriptures from total eradication. With the advent of printing press, the Scripture received a boost by being put into a booklet form, as we see it today.

In our text, we notice an attempt by Jehoiakim, king of Judah to destroy the Scriptures. Jeremiah had instructed Baruch to read the Word of God to the people, including the king's advisers. After listening to the Words of LORD and His impending judgment, king Jehoiakim's advisers requested that the writing be read to the king (Read Jeremiah 36:9-19). So, as they all gathered in the king's court, the Scripture was read to the hearing of king Jehoiakim, who heard the truth he didn't want to hear: *"Babylon will certainly come and destroy this land and cause man and beast to cease from here."* (v29). To demonstrate his hatred for the truth, king Jehoiakim, *"cut the scrolls with the scribe's knife and cast it in the fire that was on the hearth, until the scroll was consumed in the fire that was on the hearth."* (v23). After the destruction of the first scroll, God instructed Jeremiah to write another scroll with a stiffer punishment upon Jehoiakim. Indeed, Jehoiakim tried to destroy the Word of God, but ended up destroying himself, his destiny and posterity (v27-31).

Reflection: Do you behave like Jehoiakim towards God's Word?

Word for today: *Hatred of God's Word leads to self-destruction.*

280

CHRIST'S EVER-ABIDING PRESENCE

"Do not be afraid, but speak, and do not keep silent; for I am with you, and no one will attack you to hurt you; for I have many people in this city." (Acts 18:9 -10).

READ: MATTHEW 28:19-20

T he last sentence in the Lord's article of the Great Commission reads, *"And lo, I am with you always, even to the end of the age."* (Matthew 28:20b). Indeed, Christ has always been with His followers! He was with His disciples on their way to Emmaus from Jerusalem. A group of them engaged in a conversation while returning from Jerusalem to a nearby village called Emmaus. Their conversation which centered on the death of Christ evoked some deep emotions of sadness and disappointment. But, *"while they conversed, and reasoned, Jesus Himself drew near and went with them."* (Luke 24:15). As Christ joined them, He asked, *"What kind of conversation is this that you have with one another as you walk and are sad."* Ttghey replied, *"Are you the only stranger in Jerusalem, and have you not known the things which happened there in these days?"* Jesus in His sense of humor asked, *"What things?"* (v17-19). Then, the disciples narrated how the chief priests and rulers masterminded the crucifixion of Jesus and how certain women amongst them reported of seeing a vision of Him being alive. All this while, they never knew that they were talking to Jesus Himself. What an abiding presence! The Lord's promise of His abiding presence with His followers holds true today. You may not see Him, but He is always with you. If you are sensitive in the spirit, you will know and feel His presence.

Let's consider what it takes to experience the Lord's presence:
1. You must have an exchanged identity. When you accept Christ into your life, God replaces your Adamic identity with that of Christ. You go from being a child of Satan to becoming a child of God (Read John 1:12-13). Thereafter, you begin to experience Christ's presence in your life. **2. You must obey God's Word** (Isaiah 1:19-20). **3. You must live a life of holiness**. Christ does not dwell in sin (1 Peter 1:15-16).

Reflection: Do you truly feel Christ's presence in your life?

Word for today: *Christ is an unseen Guest in all that we say and do.*

THE MYSTERY OF GODLINESS

Behold, I tell you a mystery: we shall not all sleep, but we shall all be changed— (1 Corinthians 15:51).

READ: 1 TIMOTHY 3:14-16

Verse 16 of our text reads, *"And without controversy great is the mystery of godliness: God was manifested in the flesh, justified in the Spirit, seen by angels, preached among the Gentiles, believed on in the world, received up in glory."* There are two key words in the above text: **Mystery** and **Godliness**. The word *Mystery* is defined by the Nelson's New Illustrated Bible Dictionary as, "the hidden eternal plan of God that is revealed to God's people in accordance with His plan." and the word *Godliness* is defined as, "a piety or reverence toward God; the reality and power of a vital union with God."

In v16 of our text, we notice **six** action words which define the greatness of the mystery of godliness: First is **Manifested**: God was manifested in the flesh. John 1:14 reads, *"And the Word became flesh and dwelt among us, and we beheld His glory, the glory as of the only begotten of the Father, full of grace and truth."* Christ, who is God, took the form of man in order to save humankind (Philippians 2:5-8). Second is **Justified**: Christ was justified in the Spirit. Matthew 3:16 reads, *"When He had been baptized, Jesus came up immediately from the water; and behold, the heavens were opened to Him, and He saw the Spirit of God descending like a dove and alighting upon Him."* The descent of the Spirit of God upon Christ testified His Son-ship of God. Read Romans 1:4. Third is **Seen**: Christ was seen by angels. *An angel of the Lord descended from heaven, and came and rolled back the stone from the door, and sat on it."* An angel that was in attendance at Christ's resurrection, saw Him and was a witness to what took place. Fourth is **Preached**: Christ was peached among the Gentiles. (Read Acts 8:4-5). Fifth is **Believed**: That you and I believe in Christ today is a mystery (Read Ephesians 1:13). Sixth is **Received**. Christ was receive into heaven (Read Luke 24:51; Acts 1:9). Indeed, great is the mystery of God's plan for humankind.

Reflection: Have you become a beneficiary of the mystery of godliness?

Word for today: *Godliness is a mystery that puzzles the ungodly.*

THE NAME OF JESUS

Then Peter said, "Silver and gold I do not have, but what I do have I give you: In the name of <u>Jesus Christ of Nazareth,</u> rise up and walk." (Acts 3:6).

READ: LUKE 1:30-33

There is power in name! A name is a mark of identity and defines who you are. Prior to His incarnation, a name was carved out by God for His Son. Hence, during an announcement to Mary, the angel of the LORD said to her, *"Behold, you will conceive in your womb and bring forth a Son, and shall call His name JESUS."* (Luke 1:31). Matthew 1:21 put it more explicitly, *"And she will bring forth a Son, and you shall call His name JESUS, for He will save His people from their sins."* The name Jesus means a Savior, a Deliverer. As His name implies, Jesus came into the world and died to save humankind from the bondage of Satan and sin. Jesus has a title attached to His name—the **Messiah**, (Hebrew) and **Christ** (Greek), meaning the anointed One. There is a lot of power in the name of Jesus. During His earthly ministry, Jesus sent out His disciples on an evangelical outreach. On their return they reported to Him, *"Lord, even the demons are subject to us in your name."* (Luke 10:17). After His resurrection and prior to His ascension, Jesus encouraged His disciples to make use of His name, due to the tremendous power attached to it. We read, *"And these signs will follow those who believe: In my name they shall cast out demons."* (Mark 16:17).

The first demonstration of the power in the name of Jesus is recorded in the Book of Acts. One day, as Peter and John were going to the temple for a prayer meeting, they met a man lame from his mother's womb, who sat at the gate of the temple, called Beautiful, begging for alms from those who entered the temple (Acts 3:1-2). When this man saw Peter and John, he asked for alms. But, Peter told him, "Look at us...silver and gold I do not have, but in the name of Jesus Christ of Nazareth, rise up and walk." As Peter lifted him up, immediately, his feet and ankle bones received strength." He stood up and leapt for joy (v3-7). The power in the name of Jesus brought about the healing of this guy. It is still the same today. Praise God!

Reflection: What does the name of Jesus mean to you?

Word for today: *There is power in the name of Jesus; make use of it.*

HE IS ON TIME!

*He will not allow your foot to be moved; He who keeps you will not slumber.
Behold, He who keeps Israel shall neither slumber nor sleep (Psalm 121:3-4).*

READ: GALATIANS 4:1-7

God walks with time and since He is eternal, time is no constraint to Him. The Bible is full of incidents of God being on time in situations and in the lives of people. For instance, Sarah, the wife of Abraham was barren, yet God was on time in her situation regarding child-bearing. In spite of Sarah's old age, God promised Abraham, *"At the appointed time, I will return to you, according to the time of life, and Sarah shall have a son."* (Genesis 18:14). Indeed, God fulfilled His promise to Abraham regarding Sarah. In Genesis 21:1-2 we read, *"And the LORD visited Sarah as He had said, and the LORD did for Sarah as He had spoken. For Sarah conceived and bore Abraham a son in his old age, at the set time of which God had spoken to him.* Rachel, the sweetheart wife of Jacob was barren, but at an appointed time, God remembered her and she conceived and bore a son and called his name Joseph (Genesis 30:22,24). God did not forget Rachel and then suddenly remember her. Rather, God acted on time in her situation based on His divine plan for Rachel. God has a divine plan for every child of His, just as you and I would have a plan for our beloved children. Therefore, if you are a child of God, no matter what you are going through, be rest assured that God has not forgotten you. At the appointed time, He will visit you.

Our text contains Paul's admonition regarding God's plan of salvation for us. He reminds us that prior to the coming of Christ, we were all slaves to the law, *"but when the fullness of time had come, God sent forth His Son born of a woman, born under the law, to redeem those who were under the law, that we might receive the adoption as sons."* (v1-5). In deed, God is a Master Planner who is always on time and works with time. God has a timetable (Read Genesis 15:13-16). Remember, there was a time you and I were unsaved, but at the appointed time, God visited us with the gift of salvation; there was a time we had no hope, but at the appointed time, God gave us hope in Christ.

Reflection: Do you think the answer to your prayer is delayed?

Word for today: *God is never late; He is always on time.*

THE POWER OF CONSCIENCE

Then Paul, looking earnestly at the council, said, "Men and brethren, I have lived in all good conscience before God until this day." (Acts 23:1).

READ: ROMANS 2:14-16

Conscience is a *"place in the human soul, where norms and standards for right and wrong are established."* When God created Adam and Eve, He left their conscience dormant and as a result, they were innocent beings. Then came Satan's temptation through the serpent, *"Has God indeed said, 'You shall not eat of every three of the garden?'* (Genesis 3:1). Eve did her best to correct Satan about what God did not say. She told the serpent *"We may eat the fruit of the trees of the garden; but of the fruit of the tree which is in the midst of the garden, God has said, 'You shall not eat of it, nor shall you touch it, lest you die.'"* (2-3). Satan tried to plant doubt in Eve's heart by telling her, *"You will not surely die. For God knows that in the day you eat of it your eyes will be opened, and you will be like God, knowing good and evil."* Eve agreed with Satan and then ate the fruit of the forbidden tree and also gave it to her husband, Adam. Adam and Eve disobeyed God and as a result, activated their conscience to know right and wrong. Hitherto, they had lived in innocence, but with their conscience activated, they started becoming aware of good and evil. Consequently, they became aware of its consequences—death, fear and shame (Read Genesis 3:7-10). While Adam and Eve remained in the state of innocence, they were not subject to death, fear and shame. But, the moment they committed sin of disobedience, their conscience was activated and they went from being innocent to becoming conscientious human beings. Without the power of conscience, there would be no knowledge of sin, fear and shame.

Our text explains the power of the human conscience. For instance, people who do not know or have the Scripture have conscience within them which tells them of what is good and bad.(v14-15). On the day of judgment, such people will be judged by their conscience. Therefore, there will be no excuse for those who died without the knowledge of the Bible.

Reflection: Does your conscience condemn or excuse you?

Word for today: *Conscience is God's alert button in the human soul.*

285

THE POWER OF CORPORATE PRAYER

"When they had prayed, the place where they were assembled together was shaken..." (Acts 4:31).

READ: MATTHEW 18:19-20

There is power in corporate prayer! Our text reads, *"Again I say to you that if two of you agree on earth concerning anything that they ask, it will be done for them by my Father in heaven. For where two or three are gathered together in my name, I am there in the midst of them."* Wherever there is corporate prayer, our Lord Jesus Christ has guaranteed to be there to answer such a prayer. Although there is nothing wrong in praying individually, but corporate prayer will definitely be more damaging to the kingdom of Satan.

The Book of Acts contains some examples of the power of corporate prayers. We find the **first** example in Acts 4:31 which reads, *"And when they had prayed, the place where they were assembled together was shaken; and they were all filled with the Holy Spirit, and they spoke the word of God with boldness."* After being threatened by the Jewish religious authority to stop preaching in the name of Jesus Christ, the disciples entered into a session of corporate prayer. They prayed so much that the place where they were staying was shaken. Not only was the place shaken, the disciples were filled with the Holy Spirit. What an individual prayer cannot do, corporate can! The **second** example is recorded in Acts 12:1-19. When Herod arrested James, the brother of John, the Bible did not record that the Church prayed. As a result, Herod went ahead and killed James with the sword. After that, Herod arrested Peter and kept him in prison with the intent to kill him after the Jewish Passover feast. This time around, the Church embarked on intense corporate prayer (Acts 12:5-6). The corporate prayer of the Church touched the throne of God and He sent an angel to release Peter from the prison cell (v7-11). The **third** example is in Acts 16:24-26. Paul and Silas were arrested, beaten and imprisoned (v23-24). But at midnight, they embarked on a praise and prayer session (v25). Then God sent an earthquake to open the prison doors and break loose their chains—an incident that led to the conversion of the jailer and his family (v27-34).

Reflection: How much do you value corporate prayers?

Word for today: *Don't under-rate the power of corporate prayers.*

THE FOUNTAIN OF LIVING WATER

He who believes in me, as the Scripture has said, out of his heart will flow rivers of living water (John 7:38).

READ: PSALM 36:7-9

A water fountain is a device or structure from which a jet or stream of water emanates. Water fountains can be natural or artificial; some of which are installed in walls, tables and cisterns. Although a good water fountain conveys an imagery of nature, beauty and serenity, it does not produce water of life. There are many natural and artificial water fountains, but none can be compared to the Fountain of living water—who is Christ. During a dialogue with a Samaritan woman, who came to Jacob's well to fetch water, Christ said to her, *"Whoever drinks of this water [from the well] will thirst again, but whoever drinks of the water that I shall give him will never thirst. But the water that I shall give him will become in him a fountain of water springing up into everlasting life."* (John 4:13-14. Indeed, Christ is the Fountain of living water. Anyone who drinks from Him will be satisfied.

Water and life are inseparable; without water there can be no life. Christ—the Fountain of living water gives life to as many as come to Him. Christ declared, *"I am the bread of life. He who comes to me shall never hunger, and he who believes in me shall never thirst."* (John 6:35). Have you ever been hungry and thirsty? If you have, you will agree with me that under such a condition, nothing else matters in life, than **food** and **water**. In fact, nothing satisfies hunger and thirst like food and water. Christ, the Word of God that became flesh, satisfies our spiritual hunger and thirst (John 1:1,14). Therefore, we need to feed on Him daily (John 6:51). In our text, the Psalmist reminds us that those who put their trust in God will be abundantly satisfied with the fullness of His house. In addition, they will drink from the river of His pleasure, because with Him is the fountain of life and in Him is light (v7-9). Are you looking for satisfaction in life? Are you experiencing a missing link in your life? The missing link and satisfaction are in Christ Jesus. Come to Him with an open heart and ask Him to point you to the right direction in life. You will be glad you did.

Reflection: From what kind of spiritual fountain do you drink?

Word for today: *Christ—the Fountain of living water never dries up.*

287

CHRIST—THE CURE FOR SIN

The wicked are like the troubled sea, when it cannot rest, whose waters cast up mire and dirt. "There is no peace," says my God, "for the wicked." (Isaiah 57:20-21).

READ: JOHN 8:21-24

In treating a patient, a doctor will first of all come up with a diagnosis of his illness. A wrong diagnosis leads to an ineffective treatment, while a right diagnosis results in a successful treatment. The same principles applies to the issues of life. Every human problem, both physical and spiritual, originate from sin. Sickness, crimes, poverty, stealing, etc. are the side effects of the disease of sin. In His diagnosis of human problem, God declared, *"All have sinned and fall short of the glory of God."* (Romans 3:23).

Having diagnosed the problem of mankind, God offered a cure in His Son, Jesus Christ. In John 3:16-17 we read, *"For God so loved the world that He gave His only begotten Son, that whoever believes in Him should not perish but have everlasting life. For God did not send His Son into the world to condemn the world, but that the world through Him might be saved."* God sent His Son, Jesus Christ into the world to deal with the disease of sin that has plagued mankind (Read Romans 5:12,14,17-19). In dealing with the disease of sin, God prescribed an eternal treatment: Faith in Christ heals the disease of sin. Christ died on the cross and paid the penalty for sin against God by shedding His blood to cleanse us from our sins—making us righteous before God. Apostle Paul buttressed this fact in his letter to the Church in Rome (Read Romans 3:24-26). Just as a sick patient who refuses treatment will eventually die, so does a sinner who rejects Christ eventually die and end up in hell. Sin is a spiritual disease that needs spiritual cure. No one goes to heaven with it. Hence, the Word of God declares, *"He who believes in Him is not condemned; but he who does not believe is condemned already, because he has not believed in the name of the only begotten Son of God."* Again, *"He who believes in the Son has everlasting life; and he who does not believe the Son shall not see life, but the wrath of God abides on him."* (John 3:18,36).

Reflection: Has Christ cured you of the disease of sin? Any evidence?

Word for today: *Sin kills, therefore, get cured today in Christ!*

288

A MAN UNDER AUTHORITY

Then Jesus said to the centurion, "Go your way; and as you have believed, so let it be done for you." And his servant was healed that same hour (Matthew 8:13).

READ: MATTHEW 8:5-13

In our text, we notice that when our Lord Jesus Christ entered into the city of Capernaum, He was met by a centurion who begged Him saying, *"Lord, my servant is lying at home paralyzed and dreadfully tormented."* (v5-8). To which Jesus replied, " I will come and heal him." (v7), but the centurion made a profound statement about the exercise of authority. He said, *"Lord, I am not worthy that you should come under my roof. But only speak a word, and my servant will be healed. For I also am a man under authority, having soldiers under me. And I say to this one, 'Go,' and he goes; and to another, 'Come,' and he comes; and to my servant, 'Do this,' and he does it.'"* (v8-9). Apparently, the centurion knew what authority meant. Under the Emperor's authority he could issue orders which were obeyed. In a similar way, since Jesus had God's authority backing His words, He too could order the demons responsible for his servant's sickness to leave and they will obey. Our Lord Jesus Christ commended the centurion for his faith and said, *"Go your way; and as you have believed, so let it be done for you. And his servant was healed that same hour."* (v13).

There are four important spiritual lessons in this story.
1. Distance is not a barrier to God. The centurion knew that distance would not stop Christ from healing his servant, so he told Him, "Speak a word, and my servant will be healed." (v8). Today, God still heals from a distance.
2. God honors faith. Jesus marveled at the centurion's faith and said to those who followed Him, "Assuredly, I have not found such a great faith, not even in Israel!" Jesus classified the centurion's faith as "great" **3. God does not discriminate.** The centurion was a gentile, yet Christ's response to his request was positive (v7). **4. There is power in word.** God can speak to your situation.

Reflection: Under whose authority are you?

Word for today: *The believer's authority stems from being under God's authority.*

BEARING GOD'S PRESENCE

Behold, the ark of the covenant of the Lord of all the earth is crossing over before you into the Jordan (Joshua 3:11).

READ: JOSHUA 3:14-17

The ark of the LORD *represented* His presence. Wherever the ark was taken to, the LORD's presence went with it. For instance, when the Philistines captured the ark of the LORD and took it to the house of their god— Dagon, they literally brought the presence of God face to face with their idol. We notice that Dagon could not stand in the presence of God. We read, *"And when the people of Ashdod arose early in the morning, there was Dagon, fallen on its face to the earth before the ark of the LORD. So they took Dagon and set it in its place again. And when they arose early the next morning, there was Dagon, fallen on its face to the ground before the ark of the LORD. The head of Dagon and both the palms of its hands were broken off on the threshold; only Dagon's torso was left of it. Therefore neither the priests of Dagon nor any who come into Dagon's house tread on the threshold of Dagon in Ashdod to this day* (1 Samuel 5:1-5). The presence of God sent Dagon falling headlong the first day, and the next day it broke Dagon into pieces. The presence of God can either bless or destroy. In this case, it destroyed Dagon and its worshippers (v6-12).

We notice in our text, the miracle that took place when the presence of the LORD descended on the banks of River Jordan. Verse 15-16 of our text read, *"And as those who bore the ark came to the Jordan, and the feet of the priests who bore the ark dipped in the edge of the water (for the Jordan overflows all its banks during the whole time of harvest), that the waters which came down from upstream stood still, and rose in a heap very far away at Adam, the city that is beside Zaretan. So the waters that went down into the Sea of the Arabah, the Salt Sea, failed, and were cut off; and the people crossed over opposite Jericho."* As soon as the feet of those who bore the ark of the LORD touched the banks of River Jordan, the waters dried up, because the presence of the LORD was in the ark. Every true believer in Christ bears the presence of the LORD.

Reflection: Do you bear God's presence? If yes, how?

Word for today: *God's children bear His presence wherever they go.*

THE GREATEST IS LOVE!

Beloved, let us love one another, for love is of God; and everyone who loves is born of God and knows God (1 John 4:7).

READ: 1 CORINTHIANS 13:1-8

O f all spiritual virtues, love is the greatest; love is synonymous with God for God is love. In 1 John 4:8-11 we read, *"He who does not love does not know God, for God is love. In this the love of God was manifested toward us, that God has sent His only begotten Son into the world, that we might live through Him. In this is love, not that we loved God, but that He loved us and sent His Son to be the propitiation for our sins. Beloved, if God so loved us, we also ought to love one another."* Indeed, God is the epitome of love. Love made Him to send His Son Jesus to save humankind (John 3:16). He who does not love others cannot claim to know God. The knowledge of God comes from loving others (Read 1 John 4:20). Sometimes, people mistake lust for love; both are not the same. Lust evokes sensual feelings and is selfish, while love promotes spirituality and is selfless. It is not uncommon to hear people of the opposite sex verbalize love towards each other. But, with time, it becomes obvious that what they really mean is lust, not love.

Our text tells us of twelve-fold dynamics of love:
1. Love suffers long—*meaning it is patient (v4a)*. **2.** Love is kind—*meaning it is willing to help others (v4b)* **3**. Love does not envy—*meaning it does not desire what another person has (v4c)*. **4.** Love does not parade itself—*meaning it is not boastful (v4d)*. **5.** Love is not puffed up—*meaning it is not proud and cocky (v4e)*. **6.** Love is not rude—*meaning it is polite and courteous (v5a)*. **7.** Love does not seek its own—*meaning it is not self-seeking (v5b)*. **8**. Love is not provoked—*meaning it is not easily angered (v5c)*.
9. Love thinks no evil—*meaning it does not devise evil against others (v5d)*
10. Love does not rejoice in iniquity—*meaning it's unhappy to see people live in sin (v6a)*. **11.** Love bears all things, believes all things, hopes all things, endures all things—*meaning it always protects, trusts, hopes and perseveres." (v7)*. **12.** Love never fails—*meaning it does not disappoint (v8)*.

Reflection: Do you really love God and others? How do you express it?

Word for today: *Christ is the expression of God's love.*

SPIRITUALLY THIRSTY

On the last day, that great day of the feast, Jesus stood and cried out, saying, "If anyone thirsts, let him come to me and drink." (John 7:37).

READ: PSALM 42:1-4

Whenever someone is hungry and thirsty, he craves for food and water. Just as there is hunger and thirst for physical food and water, so is there hunger and thirst for spiritual food and water. Our Lord Jesus said, *"I am the bread of life. He who comes to me shall never hunger, and he who believes in me shall never thirst."* (John 6:35). In John 7:37-39 we read, *"If anyone thirsts, let him come to me and drink. He who believes in me, as the Scripture has said, out of his heart will flow rivers of living water. But this He spoke concerning the Spirit, whom those believing in Him would receive; for the Holy Spirit was not yet given, because Jesus was not yet glorified."* From the above text, we notice that Christ is the **Bread** that satisfies our spiritual hunger and the **Water** that quenches our spiritual thirst. Through the intake of the Word of God we are spiritually fed, and through the infilling of the Holy Spirit, our spiritual thirst is quenched.

Verse 1-2 of our text read, *"As the deer pants for the water brooks, so pants my soul for you, O God. My soul thirsts for God, for the living God. When shall I come and appear before God?"* The writer of our text compared the panting for water brooks of a thirsty deer to that of his soul for God. His soul thirsted for the living God so much that he couldn't wait to appear before Him. That should be our attitude towards God! We should be hungry for His Word and thirsty for His Holy Spirit. Unfortunately, some people, including the so-called Christians are thirsty for everything, but God and His Word. They think that they are doing God a favor by going to Church. Even when they do, they go there late and without any Bible. They hardly spend time with God through personal or corporate Bible study, prayer and fellowship. John in his letter encourages us to have fellowship with the brethren, the Father and with His Son Jesus Christ. (1 John 1:3). Become spiritually thirsty for God today and it shall be well with you.

Reflection: How thirsty are you for God?

Word for today: *Spiritual thirst for God promotes fellowship with Him.*

CAUSE FOR JOY & CELEBRATION

Rejoice in the LORD, you righteous, and give thanks at the remembrance of His holy name (Psalm 97:12).

READ: LUKE 10:17-20

Luke 10:1 reads, *"After these things the Lord appointed seventy others also, and sent them two by two before His face into every city and place where He Himself was about to go."* Why did our Lord Jesus Christ send out His disciples on evangelism in pairs *"into every city and place where He Himself was about to go?"* The reason was three-fold. **First,** He wanted to test their preparedness for the great commission. Having been taught for a while, it was time for the disciples to put into practice what they had been taught. No wonder they came back with this wonderful testimony about a successful evangelism. We read, *"Then the seventy returned with joy, saying, "Lord, even the demons are subject to us in Your name.'*(v17). **Second,** Christ wanted them to demonstrate His power over satanic forces. Look at His response to the disciples' report, *"I saw Satan fall like lightning from heaven. Behold, I give you the authority to trample on serpents and scorpions, and over all the power of the enemy, and nothing shall by any means hurt you.'"* **Third,** Christ was trying to set an example for a house-to-house evangelism for His Church. In v20, Christ said something worthy of joy and celebration— far more than the demons being subject to them. It reads, *"Nevertheless do not rejoice in this, that the spirits are subject to you, but rather rejoice because your names are written in heaven."* Christ was by this statement letting His followers know that their salvation calls for joy and celebration.

In His parable of the lost and found coin, Christ said, *"There is joy in the presence of the angels of God over one sinner who repents."* (Luke 15:10). In other words, joy and celebration always greet every believer's salvation in heaven. The salvation of mankind is a thing of joy and is worthy of celebration, hence, the angelic host sang praises to God on Christ's arrival for His mission of redemption. Christians should learn to celebrate their spiritual birthdays, just as they do their physical birthdays. Spiritual regeneration is a thing of joy!

Reflection: Do you rejoice and celebrate your salvation? If not, why not?

Word for today: *No joy exceeds the joy of salvation in Christ.*

293

PHYSICAL APPEARANCE

Do you look at things according to the outward appearance? (2 Corinthians 10:7)

READ: 1 SAMUEL 16:6-13

Physical appearance is a mirage. That was the lesson the LORD tried to teach his servant Samuel. During a private coronation ceremony at the home of Jesse, Samuel was very impressed with the physical appearance of Eliab, one of Jesse's sons in becoming a king. But, the LORD thought otherwise! He told Samuel something about the mirage of physical appearance. The LORD said to Samuel, *"Do not look at his appearance or at the height of his stature, because I have refused him, for the Lord does not see as man sees; for man looks at the outward appearance, but the LORD looks at the heart."* (1 Samuel 16:6-7). As a mirage, physical appearance can be deceptive—creating a false impression of reality. God who searches the heart knew that Eliab would not make a good king, even though his physical appearance suggested otherwise. God's call to the ministry or to serve in any position in His vineyard is not dependent on one's physical appearance, social or economic status. The problem many people face today is that of making very important choices in life, including the choice of whom to befriend, whom to marry, where to live and so on, purely on physical appearance.

The Book of Genesis records the dilemma of Lot in basing his choice of where to settle on physical appearance. Before they parted ways, Abraham gave Lot the opportunity to choose where to settle down with his herdsmen. He said to Lot, *"Please let there be no strife between you and me, and between my herdsmen and your herdsmen; for we are brethren. Is not the whole land before you? Please separate from me. If you take the left, then I will go to the right; or, if you go to the right, then I will go to the left.'"* (Genesis 13:8-9). In a quick response, based on physical appearance, *"Lot lifted his eyes and saw all the plain of Jordan, that it was well watered everywhere... and chose for himself all the plain of Jordan, and "pitched his tent as far as Sodom."* (v10-12). Lot's choice landed him in three big problems (Read Genesis Chapters 14 and 19).

Reflection: On what do you base your choices? Sight or facts?

Word for today: *Physical appearance is a mirage—fades away over time.*

OCTOBER

DEVOTIONALS

REWARD FOR FAITHFULNESS

"The LORD preserves the faithful, and fully repays the proud person." (Psalm 31:23).

READ: 2 CHRONICLES 26:1-10

Proverbs 16:7 reads, *"When a man's ways please the LORD, He makes even his enemies to be at peace with him."* This was what happened to king Uzziah, who did "what was right in the sight of the LORD." "Doing what was right in the sight of the LORD" is the same as being faithful to the LORD. Our text reads, *"Uzziah was sixteen years old when he became king, and he reigned fifty-two years in Jerusalem. His mother's name was Jecholiah of Jerusalem. And he did what was right in the sight of the LORD, according to all that his father Amaziah had done* (v3-4). King Uzziah did the right thing by seeking after God. Verse 5 reads, *"He sought God in the days of Zechariah, who had understanding in the visions of God; and as long as he sought the LORD, God made him prosper."* As long as king Uzziah sought after God, the LORD made him to prosper. Do you know that God doesn't owe any person? He is a Rewarder of those who diligently seek Him (Hebrews 11:6); He is also a Rewarder of those who despise and hate Him (Read 1 Samuel 2:30; Proverbs 8:35-36). God prospered king Uzziah so much so that, "he broke the walls of Jabneh, and Ashdod, and built his cities around Ashdod and among the Philistines, while the Ammonites brought him **tributes**—another word for taxes. King Uzziah excelled in military, political and economic power (v9-15).

God excepts us to be faithful in all that we do in serving Him. Our Lord Jesus Christ emphasized the need for faithfulness in His parable of the talents. The word, **"faithful"** was used four times by the Lord in the reward process of the two servants who traded with the talents they were given by their master (Matthew 25:21;23). God honors faithfulness. Still on the issue of faithful stewardship, Christ has this to say, *"He who is faithful in what is least is faithful also in much; and he who is unjust in what is least is unjust also in much."* (Luke 16:10). Faithfulness is an attitude of the mind—total obedience, trust and dependence on God.

Reflection: Can you remember God's blessings for your faithfulness to Him?

Word for today: *Faithfulness opens the doors to divine blessings.*

THE RAPTURE

"The Lord Jesus [will be] revealed from heaven with His mighty angels, in flaming fire taking vengeance on those who do not know God, and...who do not obey the gospel of our Lord Jesus Christ.." (2 Thessalonians 1:7-8).

READ: MATTHEW 24:36-44

Speaking about His second coming, our Lord Jesus Christ painted a picture of a sudden disappearance of His followers to mark that event. Verse 40-41 of our text reads, *"Then two men will be in the field: one will be taken and the other left. Two women will be grinding at the mill: one will be taken and the other left."* From our text comes the idea of rapture. Therefore the word, **"rapture"** (Latin *rapio*, and Greek *harpazo*) means "being caught up suddenly." Although the word, "rapture" is not found in the Bible, however, it is a theological parlance that best describes the suddenness, joy and ecstasy that will mark the return of Christ to receive His followers. In v42 of our text Christ warns, *"Watch therefore, for you do not know what hour your Lord is coming."* The early Church was very expectant of Christ's return and conscious of the rapture. Paul wrote, *"If in this life only we have hope in Christ, we are of all men the most pitiable."* (1 Corinthians 15:19). Based on Paul's statement, Christ will certainly return to take His followers with Him to heaven, where they will be rewarded accordingly. Are you ready?

It is unfortunate that today's Church has become lukewarm regarding Christ's return and the rapture. Emphasis has shifted from heaven-consciousness to entanglement with the world, from spiritual preparedness for Christ's return to endless pursuit of worldly riches and pleasures. Due to the seriousness which our Lord attaches to His return and the rapture, Paul by divine revelation, had an insight into what rapture will look like. We read, *"Behold, I tell you a mystery: We shall not all sleep, but we shall all be changed—in a moment, in the twinkling of an eye, at the last trumpet. For the trumpet will sound, and the dead will be raised incorruptible, and we shall be changed."* (1 Corinthians 15:51-52). Read also 1 Thessalonians 4:16-17. The rapture should be the hope of every true believer in Christ. Is it your hope?

Reflection: How prepared are you for the Lord's return and rapture?

Word for today: *He who misses rapture is doomed forever?*

ABUNDANT LIFE EXPERIENCE

Through Him (Jesus) we have access by one Spirit to the Father (Ephesians 2:18).

READ: JOHN 10:7-10

There is a common parlance which says that 'life has no duplicate.' Since life has no duplicate, people tend to guide their lives very carefully to preserve them from danger, sickness and death. Every right-thinking person wants to have a good life and enjoy such a life to the fullest. Abundant life is the aspiration of many. Literally, an abundant life speaks of a life that is peaceful, joyous, productive and eternal. Unfortunately, not everyone experiences this kind of life. With the presence of wealth and power, some people may live happily, while others, by dint of hard work accomplish great things in life. But, none of them can boast of experiencing abundant life. Any life that is devoid of eternal value is really not abundant. An abundant life does not end here; it continues into eternity. Our Lord Jesus said, *"I am the door. If anyone enters by me, he will be saved, and he will go in and out and find pasture...I have come that they may have life and have it more abundantly."* (John 10:9-10). In order to experience an abundant life, three imperatives must be in place: **First**, you must come to Him (v9a)—meaning a total surrender to Christ's Lordship. **Second,** you must be saved (v9b). Without salvation in Christ, abundant life experience is a far cry. You may be happy due to things happening around you, but you cannot have an abundant life without Christ—the Source of life (John 14:6).**Thirdly**, one must find pasture in Christ (v9c). Feeding on Christ—the Word of God sustains abundant life (Read John 6:51,53-55).

When someone has an encounter with Christ, something happens—a life of self, struggle, misery, unproductivity gives way for an abundant life in Christ. Apostle Paul, a man who experienced an abundant life in Christ had this to say, *"I have been crucified with Christ; it is no longer I who live, but Christ lives in me; and the life which I now live in the flesh I live by faith in the Son of God, who loved me and gave Himself for me."* (Galatians 2:20). Once you surrender your life to Christ, He gives you an abundant life in exchange.

Reflection: Do you enjoy an abundant life in Christ?

Word for today: *Abundant life comes by surrendering your life to Christ.*

YOUTH SERVICE

Indeed, You have made my days as handbreadths, and my age is as nothing before you; certainly every man at his best state is but vapor (Psalm 39:5).

READ: ECCLESIASTES 11:9-10

In Nigeria, there is a program called National Youth Service. It is a program designed for graduates of tertiary institutions to serve the country for one year in a state other than their home states. In so ding, the young gradates are able to travel to different parts of Nigeria, learn and integrate with people from different cultural backgrounds. Youths are very vibrant and able to accomplish a lot, hence it is very crucial to serve God in one's youth. Our text reads, *"Rejoice, O young man, in your youth, and let your heart cheer you in the days of your youth; walk in the ways of your heart, and in the sight of your eyes; but know that for all these God will bring you into judgment. Therefore remove sorrow from your heart, and put away evil from your flesh, for childhood and youth are vanity."* (v9-10). The phrase **"Rejoice O young man"** is a cautionary warning, not an advice to indulge in sinful pleasures. The Amplified Bible gives this verse an original intent: *"Rejoice, O young man, in your adolescence, and let your heart cheer you in the days of your full grown youth. And walk in the ways of your heart and in the sight of your eyes. But, know that for all these things God will bring you to judgment."* A youth who is full of life today may be gone tomorrow. Death does not discriminate between sexes, nor does it have any age barrier. If you are a youth and a user of this Devotional, utilize your youthfulness in serving God. Take a cue from youths like Daniel, Joseph and Timothy.

Daniel was a youth when he was captured and exiled to Babylonian. In his youthful age, Daniel knew God and therefore, *"purposed in his heart that he would not defile himself with the portion of the king's delicacies, nor with the wine which he drank."* (Daniel 1:8). Daniel's decision to honor God made him an instrument of God in the land of Babylon. Joseph as a youth, served God with integrity and refused the sexual advances of Potiphar's wife (Genesis 39:7-12). Timothy was a youth when he pastored a Church (1 Timothy 4:12-16).

Reflection: Are you a youth? Do you serve God?

Word for today: *Youthful service for God attracts fruitful reward.*

300

REFLECTING GOD'S GLORY

Declare His glory among the nations, His wonders among all peoples (Psalm 96:3).

READ: PSALM 96:1-9

In Genesis 2:26-27 God said, *"Let us make man in our image, according to our likeness...so God created man in His own image; in the image of God He created him..."* An image is a resemblance or reflection of something. God the Creator is glorious, therefore, human beings whom He has created in His own image should reflect His glory. That was the case until Adam sinned and as a result, that reflection of God's image ceased. After the glory of God departed from Adam, he went and hid himself from the presence of God (Read Genesis 3:7-10). Sin caused the cessation of God's glory being reflected by man. However, to deal with this, God sent His Son into the world to die for mankind, in order to restore the broken relationship so that man could once again live to reflect His glory. Romans 8:29-30 clarifies the issue of restoration of God's image in man. We read, *"For whom He foreknew, He also predestined to be conformed to the image of His Son, that He might be the firstborn among many brethren. Moreover whom He predestined, these He also called; whom He called, these He also justified; and whom He justified, these He also glorified."* God has predestined that through His Son, Jesus Christ, every person should bear His image.

Verse 3 of our text reads, *"Declare His glory among the nations, His wonders among all peoples."* Declaring God's glory is one way of reflecting His glory among unbelievers. But, one cannot declare the glory of God until one becomes a depository of His glory, because one cannot give out what one doesn't have. Another way of reflecting God's glory is by being Christ-like in our behaviors.—loving those wo hate us and forgiving those who erred against us. During Christ's trial, Peter almost severed the head of Malchus—the servant of the high priest with a sword, but ended up cutting off his ear. Jesus could have left the guy to bleed to death, but in His love, He touched Malchus' ear and healed him. (Read Luke 22:50-51). That is how to reflect God's glory.

Reflection: Whose glory do you reflect? Is it that of God or man?

Word for today: *Reflecting God's glory comes by being Christ-like.*

301

A WORTHY COMMENDATION

"I trust in the Lord Jesus to send Timothy to you shortly...for I have no one like -minded, who will sincerely care for your state." (Philippians 2:19-20).

READ: PHILIPPIANS 2:25-30

Whatever we do for the Lord is recorded in heaven; it also draws commendation from those with whom we serve. Paul served with Epaphroditus and gave him a worthy commendation to the Church in Philippi. He wrote, *"I considered it necessary to send to you Epaphroditus, my brother, fellow worker, and fellow soldier, but your messenger and the one who ministered to my need."* (Philippians 2:25). Paul described Epaphroditus in five -fold complimentary terms: **1. My brother.** Epaphroditus was not Paul's sibling. Yet, Paul called him "my brother" because he was a fellow believer in Christ. **2. Fellow worker.** Epaphroditus was involved in the work of the Lord to the extent of being sick to death (v27). **3. Fellow soldier.** As a soldier of the cross, Epaphroditus fought honorably alongside Paul in bearing the gospel to the gentile nations. **4. Your messenger.** Epaphroditus had barely recovered from his sickness, and was willing to be sent by the Church to deliver what Paul needed. **5. A minister to Paul's need.** Epaphroditus ministered to Paul's need and was willing to be sent by Paul. He was an obedient and willing messenger of the gospel, just like Paul. As Nelson's Study Bible Commentary rightly puts it, "Paul and Epaphroditus were messengers of the gospel, but Paul's authority was greater than that of Epaphroditus. Paul had a direct commission from the Lord, while Epaphroditus was sent by the Church in Philippi."

Paul's commendation of Epaphroditus was so strong that he urged the Church to take good care of him. In v29-30 we read, *"Receive him therefore in the Lord with all gladness, and hold such men in esteem; because for the work of Christ he came close to death, not regarding his life, to supply what was lacking in your service toward me."* Similarly, Timothy sought after Christ, while others were mindful of their personal interest. Hence, Paul commended him as a man of proven character and a son (Philippians 2:21-22).

Reflection: Can others commend your service to the Lord?

Word for today: *Learn to serve in order to be commended.*

WHO IS JESUS?

"She will bring forth a Son, and you shall call His name JESUS, for He will save His people from their sins." (Matthew 1:21).

READ: JOHN 14:1-6

Jesus is the Son of God, the second Person in the Godhead. During His earthly ministry Jesus always referred to God as His Father. For example in His prayer of thanksgiving, Jesus said, *"I thank you, Father, Lord of heaven and earth, that you have hidden these things from the wise and prudent and revealed them to babes. Even so, Father, for so it seemed good in your sight. All things have been delivered to me by my Father, and no one knows who the Son is except the Father, and who the Father is except the Son, and the one to whom the Son wills to reveal Him."* (Luke 10:21-22). Read also John 5:19-21; 8:16-19; 10:29-30. By divine revelation, Paul wrote this regarding the name Jesus vis-à-vis our salvation, *"Therefore God also has highly exalted Him and given Him the name which is above every name, that at the name of Jesus every knee should bow, of those in heaven, and of those on earth, and of those under the earth, and that every tongue should confess that Jesus Christ is Lord, to the glory of God the Father."* (Philippians 2:9-11). We can see that prior to His incarnation, Christ— the second Person in the Godhead was not known by the name, Jesus. The name Jesus was given to Him just before His incarnation—a befitting name for His work of the salvation of mankind.

The name Jesus is a transliteration of the Hebrew name, Joshua, which means "Jehovah is salvation" or "is the Savior" True to His name, Jesus possesses the following divine attributes: **1. Son of God** (Luke 1:31-32). As the Son of God, Jesus and God are one (John 10:30). **2. Son of Man** (Luke 9:58). As the Son of Man, Jesus who is God, came in the form of man to redeem mankind (Philippians 2:8). **3. Messiah**—the Anointed One (John 1:41; 4:25-26). As the Anointed One, Jesus is God's choice for the salvation of mankind. **4. Prince of Peace** (Isaiah 9:6). As the Prince of peace, Jesus made peace between God and man, and between man and man (Colossians 1:19-21; 2:14). **5. Gateway to God** (John 14:6). No one comes to God without Jesus.

Reflection: Who is Jesus to you? What does His name mean to you?

Word for today: *Jesus is the Light that lights the world of darkness.*

PETITIONING WITH ASSURANCE

"Whatever you ask in my name, that I will do, that the Father may be glorified in the Son. If you ask anything in my name, I will do it.." (John 14:13-14).

READ: PSALM 20:1-5

Whenever people petition an authority or someone, they expect one thing—a **response**. Any petition that does not receive a response leaves the petitioners feeling neglected, forgotten and frustrated. The same thing happens when we petition heaven in prayer. No human petition is ever guaranteed a response. But, this is not the case with petitioning heaven. God Himself has promised to respond whenever we petition Him in prayer. In Jeremiah 33:3 we read, *"Call to me, and I will answer you, and show you great and mighty things, which you do not know."* God is interested and willing in responding our prayer petitions. If He fails to respond, it could be that sin, unbelief and un-forgiveness are responsible, not God. Our Lord Jesus promised to respond to our petitions made through prayer. Matthew 7:7-11 record such promises: *"Ask, and it will be given to you; seek, and you will find; knock, and it will be opened to you. For everyone who asks receives, and he who seeks finds, and to him who knocks it will be opened. Or what man is there among you who, if his son asks for bread, will give him a stone? Or if he asks for a fish, will he give him a serpent? If you then, being evil, know how to give good gifts to your children, how much more will your Father who is in heaven give good things to those who ask Him!"* Still on His promise to respond, Jesus said, *"Whatever you ask in my name, that I will do, that the Father may be glorified in the Son. If you ask anything in my name, I will do it." (John 14:13-14).* Read also John 16:23-24. From Jesus' statement, you can see that the answer to your prayer petition as a child of God is guaranteed.

David, the author of our text was a man familiar with petitioning God with an assurance of response from Him. Hence, he prays that God will answer, defend, help, strength you, remember all your offering to Him, grant you according to your heart's desire and fulfill all your purpose." (v1-4).

Reflection: Can you petition heaven? Do you pray?

Word for today: *Response to your heavenly petition signifies that you known there.*

A WORKER APPROVED OF GOD

Therefore, brethren, be even more diligent to make your call and election sure, for if you do these things you will never stumble (2 Peter 1:10).

READ: 2 TIMOTHY 2:14-19

Today, it is not hard to find people who claim to be God's servants, but, who are nothing short of hirelings and dupes. They parade themselves as Apostles, Prophets, Prophetesses, Bishops, Archbishops, Overseers, etc.—in flowing garments and expensive outfits. There is nothing wrong in a man of God looking well dressed. But, when a hireling or a dupe dresses in disguise to create the impression that he is genuine, it becomes very troubling. Many have been deceived by the looks and talks of the so-called men pf God. In our text, we read of Paul's injunction to young Timothy regarding being approved by God in his calling, *"Be diligent to present yourself approved to God, a worker who does not need to be ashamed, rightly dividing the word of truth."* (v15). Timothy was to be careful in ensuring that his calling and services received God's approval. Paul's injunction to Timothy is applicable to us today. As a believer in Christ, it is important that you keep abreast of God's Word, so that you can teach it to others. You don't have to be a pastor in order to invest time, money and energy in knowing God's Word. Sound knowledge in the Word of God makes you a better disciple of Christ, who is not ashamed in dispensing God's Word. You may have the opportunity to attend a Bible college or Seminary to acquire theological knowledge in order to enrich and prepare yourself in the Body of Christ, not necessarily to become a pastor or a priest. We may not all be pastors, but we must all be dispensers of God's Word to the dying world unashamedly.

What makes God's worker approved?
1. Willingness to walk in the footsteps of Christ (Read 1 Corinthians 11:1; Ephesians5:1-2).
2. Willingness to bear spiritual fruit (Read John 15:1-6). A worker who lacks spiritual fruit is not approved of God.
3. Willingness to live in obedience to God's Word (Read Isaiah 1:19-20).

Reflection: How much of a fruitful worker are you for Christ?

Word for today: *Work as unto the Lord, He will reward you accordingly.*

CREATED EQUAL BY GOD

"And He has made from one blood every nation of men to dwell on all the face of the earth..." (Acts 17:26)

READ: GENESIS 1:26-28

A part of the opening statement of the United States Declaration of Independence reads: "We hold these truths to be self-evident, that all men are created equal, that they are endowed by their Creator with certain unalienable Rights, that among these are Life, Liberty, and the Pursuit of Happiness." Jefferson, the author of this declaration, must have gotten his thought of the equality of human beings in creation from the Bible. Verse 26-27 of our text read, *"Then God said, 'Let Us make man in our image, according to our likeness; let them have dominion over the fish of the sea, over the birds of the air, and over the cattle, over all the earth and over every creeping thing that creeps on the earth.' So God created man in His own image; in the image of God He created him; male and female He created them.'"* That God created Adam and Eve in His own image meant that Adam and Eve were created equal. Both possessed the image of God. However, after creation, Adam and Eve played different roles, with Adam as the leader. For instance, it was Adam who gave names to all the animals, not Eve (Genesis 2:19-20); it was also Adam who gave name to Eve and not the other way round (2:20). We are all equal before God in creation, but not in calling and responsibility. Some people have higher calling and responsibility than others. According to Paul, God has made from *"one blood every nation of men to dwell on all the face of the earth and has determined their pre-appointed times and the boundaries of their dwellings."* (Acts 17:26).

There are three important truths which underscore the fact that all men are created equal. **1:** No one is ever born with clothes on; everyone comes into this world naked. **2:** No one ever comes into this world with any belongings; everyone comes empty-handed and will departed empty-handed. **3:** No one lives in this world forever. Everyone born into this world is subject to death Since all men are created equal by God, it will be wise to treat others humanely.

Reflection: How do you relate to others as a Christian?

Word for today: *Equal before God, but unequal before men—what a pity!*

306

FEAR GOD!

"I will show you whom you should fear: Fear Him who, after He has killed, has power to cast into hell; yes, I say to you, fear Him!" (Luke 12:5).

READ: HEBREWS 10:26-31.

Verse 31 of our text reads, *"It is a fearful thing to fall into the hands of the living God."* God ought to be feared, because it is a fearful thing to fall into His hands. It is better to fall in favor with God, rather than fall into his hands. When people fall in favor with God, He blesses them. But, if on the other hand, they fall into His hands, He punishes them. That was what happened to king Nebuchadnezzar, Daniel and Herod

King Nebuchadnezzar fell into the hands of God, while Daniel fell in favor with God. King Nebuchadnezzar was highly feared and respected by his subjects to the point of being worshipped as god. One night Nebuchadnezzar had a divinely induced dream which took away sleep from him (Daniel 2:1). After several attempts by Nebuchadnezzar's magicians to interpret his dream failed, Daniel was called to see if he could interpret the dream, otherwise he too would be killed like other wise men. But, since Daniel was in favor with God, the LORD revealed to him the meaning of the dream. As a result of the interpretation of Nebuchadnezzar's dream, Daniel and his friends were promoted (v46-49). In spite of what had taken place, Nebuchadnezzar failed to learn his lesson nor fear God. Instead, he went and made an image of gold, whose height was sixty cubits (about 90 feet), set it up in the plain of Dura, in the province of Babylon, and commanded everyone to bow down and worship the golden image. Failure to do so attracted being thrown into a fiery furnace (3:1-7). But, Shadrach, Meshach, and Abed-Nego refused to obey the orders of king Nebuchadnezzar resulting in their being thrown into the burning fiery furnace. God sent His angel to save them. By this singular act, Nebuchadnezzar fell into the hands of the living God and dwelt among animals in the bush for seven years, after which he praised and extoled the LORD God (Daniel 4:28-37). Similarly, Herod fell into the hands of God and was struck down by an angel and eaten up by maggots (Acts 12:1-4, 20-24). May you never fall into the hands of God!

Reflection: Do you fear God? Do you obey Him?

Word for today: *All who love and fear God are in favor with Him.*

JUDGED BY HIS WORD

And it shall be that whoever will not hear my words, which He speaks in my name, I will require it of him (Deuteronomy 18:19).

READ: JOHN 12:44-50

Whenever a judge sits in the law court, he judges people based on the law of the land. In other words, it is the law of the land that judges an offender and not the judge *per se.* In fact, what the judge does is to apply the laws of the land in making sound judicial decisions. God the Creator of heaven and earth, judges every human being by His Word. In God's Word (the Scripture), there are the **do's** and **don'ts** of life. Any violation of God's Word is a rebellion against Him and attracts His judgment. In the Book of Deuteronomy18:18-19, the LORD promised to raise another Prophet like Moses among the children of Israel. We read, *"I will raise up for them a Prophet like you from among their brethren, and will put my words in His mouth, and He shall speak to them all that I command Him. And it shall be that whoever will not hear my words, which He speaks in my name, I will require it of him."* This text was fulfilled in Christ. While addressing His Jewish audience, our Lord Jesus Christ alluded to the above text in indicting them for their unbelief when He said, *"He who believes in me, believes not in me but in Him who sent me. And he who sees me sees Him who sent me. I have come as a light into the world, that whoever believes in me should not abide in darkness. And if anyone hears my words and does not believe, I do not judge him; for I did not come to judge the world but to save the world. He who rejects me, and does not receive my words, has that which judges him—the word that I have spoken will judge him in the last day."* (John 12:44-48). In effect, whoever rejects Christ will be judged by the words He or she has heard about Jesus Christ.

Some people deliberately refuse to hear the gospel in order to avoid being judged by it. Unfortunately, such people forget that in the court of law, ignorance of the law does not absolve an offender from guilt. The same principle applies to the court of heaven. Ignorance of God's Word is no excuse for the sinner nor does it prevent him or her from going to hell.

Reflection: How open are you to the Word of God?

Word for today: *If we judge ourselves, God's Word will not judge us.*

SERVICE VS. OBEDIENCE

"Behold, to obey is better than sacrifice, and to heed than the fat of rams." (1 Samuel 15:22).

READ: 1 SAMUEL 15:20-23

Not only does it not make sense serving God, while disobeying Him, it is also unprofitable doing so. In our relationship with God, service must blend with obedience and partial obedience is not obedience at all. A good number of people like to answer God's children, but not all of them are willing to obey Him. Going by the name of a child of God and the semantics of being born again while living in disobedience to God's Word makes one a rebellious child. Like every rebellious child, one becomes estranged from the blessings of God. Under such a condition, no matter how hard one works, success continues to be a mirage.

Our text contains a classic example of a flagrant act of disobedience to God, while calming to serve Him. God through Samuel ordered king Saul to destroy the city of Amalek. If you compare verses of 1 Samuel 15:3 and v20, you will notice king Saul's flagrant act of disobedience to God. In verse 3, God's command was to utterly destroy everything—humans and beasts. But, verse 20 tells us how king Saul spared Agag, the king of Amelek and some best of sheep and oxen. King Saul gave an excuse why he failed to utterly destroy everything in Amalek. In verse 21 we read, *"But the people took of the plunder, sheep and oxen, the best of the things which should have been utterly destroyed, to sacrifice to the LORD your God in Gilgal."* King Saul brought back some nice looking sheep and oxen to sacrifice to God, but he did not say why he brought Agag alive. Then Samuel said to him, *"Has the LORD as great delight in burnt offerings and sacrifices, as in obeying the voice of the LORD? Behold, to obey is better than sacrifice, and to heed than the fat of rams."* (v22). Indeed, obedience is better than sacrifice and service to God. The same act of disobedience is prevalent among the people of God today. No wonder the power of God is absent from the Church, as people flout God's command and think it doesn't matter.

Reflection: Do you serve God in obedience to His Word?

Word for today: *Serving God in disobedience makes one a rebel.*

PERFECT LOVE

"If we love one another, God abides in us, and His love has been perfected in us." (1 John 4:12).

READ: 1 JOHN 4:12-19

A woman who was battered by her husband expressed her feelings about him on a public television in these words: ***"I love him, but I am scared of him."*** This woman's experience is very common among some battered and abused women. On one hand they love their husbands, but on the other hand, they are scared of them. This is what I call , 'an imperfect and scary love.' The love in which you are scared of being with the person you love is imperfect. This kind of love is different from God's perfect love, which makes you love to be with Him now and for eternity. It is a perfect love, hence it has no fear in it. Verse 16-18 of our text reads, *"And we have known and believed the love that God has for us. God is love, and he who abides in love abides in God, and God in him. Love has been perfected among us in this: that we may have boldness in the day of judgment; because as He is, so are we in this world. There is no fear in love; but perfect love casts out fear, because fear involves torment. But he who fears has not been made perfect in love."* The love of God has been perfected in us and we can boldly approach His throne of grace. Unless the love of God has been perfected in someone's life, it is scary to approach the presence of God. For instance, when Adam and Eve sinned, they became scared of God's presence and went into hiding. When God called, *"Adam, 'Where are you'?* Adam's reply was that of fear, *"I heard your voice in the garden, and I was afraid..."* (Genesis 3:9-10).

Our God is the epitome of prefect love. He demonstrated this by sending His only begotten Son to die for the sins of the world (1 John 4:9) In John 3:16 we read, *"For God so loved the world that He sent His only begotten Son, that whoever believes in Him should not perish, but have everlasting life."* God also demonstrated His perfect love in forgiving our sins (1 John 4:17) as well as giving us His Holy Spirit (v13). We were God's enemies but His perfect love changed all that.

Reflection: Have you ever enjoyed God's perfect love?

Word for today: *Perfect love seeks no revenge, but forgives.*

WHAT A FREE & DELICIOUS MEAL!

Receive my instruction, and not silver, and knowledge rather than choice gold (Proverbs 8:10).

READ: PSALM 119:97-104

Free and delicious meal is hard to find in a restaurant. In fact, it is uncommon. Some restaurants have made names for themselves due to the taste of the food they serve and the quality of service they offer. Invariably, good and delicious food cost much money, while cheap and tasteless food cost less. This means that what you pay for in a restaurant is what you get. But, there is another kind of food that is delicious, yet free! It is not physical, but spiritual and satisfies one's spiritual hunger. It is not prepared by human chefs, nor is it served in restaurants. It is called the Word of God. The Word of God is so sweet and delicious that the Psalmist has this to say, *"How sweet are your Words to my taste, sweeter than honey to my mouth."* (Psalm 119:103). Honey is very sweet and nothing surpasses it in sweetness, except the Word of God.

Based on our text, there are five benefits for feeding on the free and delicious Word of God.
1. It makes you wiser than your enemies (v98). The intake of the Word of God enables you to know the mind of God as regards how to deal with your enemies.
2. It gives you more understanding than your teachers (v99). A servant who is filled with the wisdom of God is far better than a scholar whose wisdom is based merely on human effort.
3. It gives you more understanding than the aged (v100). Usually, the aged are associated with knowledge and understanding. However, not every old person is wise. He who has God and His Word knows the secret things of God, which enable him or her to be wiser than the aged. 4. It restrains you from evil (v101). Many people get into all sorts of evil practices because they lack the knowledge of God's Word.
5. It gives you an understanding to live a successful life (v104). Let the Word of God guide you in life. If you do, you will have success in all your endeavors. Read Psalm 119:105 and reflect on how God's Word has guided you so far.

Reflection: Have you tasted the Word of God?

Word for today: *The sweetness of God's Word is in doing it.*

IMPORTANT SPIRITUAL DECISION

Now when they heard this, they were cut to the heart, and said to Peter and the rest of the apostles, "Men and brethren, what shall we do?" (Acts 2:37).

READ: JOHN 12:20-26

Whenever someone makes a decision in life, he or she lives with the consequences of such a decision. The consequences of some decisions people make have temporal effect, while others have a lasting and even eternal effect. Hence, it is very crucial to ponder very seriously on the consequences of any decision you have made or about to make, especially when it concerns your place in eternity. In the New Testament Scriptures, we read of three important decisions made by the Jews in relation to Christ and the gospel on different occasions. **First,** was their decision to hand over Christ— their Messiah to be crucified. Pilate found Christ not guilty, yet they wanted Him crucified. Even when Pilate asked, *"What evil has he done?" They cried out with one voice, 'Let Him be crucified' and then added, 'Let his blood be on us and on our children.'"* (Matthew 27:22-25). Today, the Jewish nation is suffering the consequences of their self-inflicted curses. **Second,** was their decision regarding Peter's sermon on the day of Pentecost. After Peter's sermon, his Jewish audience responded positively. We read, *"Now when they heard this, they were cut to the heart, and said to Peter and the rest of the apostles, 'Men and brethren, what shall we do?'"* Then, Peter asked them to repent and believe in Christ Jesus, which they did and about three thousand souls were saved that day (Acts 2:36-41). **Third,** was their decision to stone Stephen to death. The Jews responded to Stephen's sermon negatively. Rather than repent, they gnash at him with their teeth, cast him out of the city and stoned him to death (Acts 7:54,58).

In our text, we read about a positive spiritual decision made by some Gentile worshippers at the feast in Jerusalem. They came to Philip, one of Christ's disciples and said to him, *"Sir, we wish to see Jesus."* (John 12:21). These people had seen the temple and the Jewish religious rulers, but were not satisfied. So they wanted to see Jesus. What an important decision!

Reflection: What spiritual decision have you made in life?

Word for today: *God gives eternal life, but you make the decision to have it.*

FAITH-BASED FRIENDSHIP

But you, Israel, are my servant, Jacob whom I have chosen, the descendants of Abraham my friend (Isaiah 41:8).

READ: JOHN 15:14-15

Abraham was a friend of God, due to his faith in God. 2 Chronicles 20:7 reads, *"Are You not our God, who drove out the inhabitants of this land before your people Israel, and gave it to the descendants of Abraham your friend forever?"* Jehoshaphat in his prayer during the invasion of Jerusalem by the combined armies of Ammon, Moab and others, reminded God of His friendship with Abraham (Read Isaiah 41:8). Abraham's friendship with God was based on Abraham's faith in God. In Genesis 15:5-6 we read, *"Then He brought him outside and said, 'Look now toward heaven, and count the stars if you are able to number them.' And He said to him, 'So shall your descendants be.' And he believed in the LORD, and He accounted it to him for righteousness.'"* The LORD told Abraham that He was going to bless him in such a measure that his descendants would be like the stars of heaven in number. At the time of this promise, Abraham was about 75 years old, without a child. Twenty fives years later, God visited Abraham and his wife Sarah at the ages of hundred and ninety years respectively and enabled them to beget Isaac, as a son (Read Genesis 17:15-17). Nothing is imposable with God! Just as Abraham became the friend of God based on his faith, so are all believers in Christ God's friends due to their faith in Him.

Our Lord Jesus Christ reiterated the importance of our faith-based friendship with Him, when He said, *"You are my friends if you do whatever I command you. No longer do I call you servants, for a servant does not know what his master is doing; but I have called you friends, for all things that I heard from my Father I have made known to you."* (John 15:14-15). Based on the above text, friends of Christ obey His command and hear from Him. Conversely, foes of Christ do not obey Him nor do they hear from Him. Through faith in Christ, those who believe in Him have become children of God as well as His friends. It pays to be a friend of God.

Reflection: Are you a friend of God? Write down what makes you think so.

Word for today: *Friends and foes of God have their rewards (Prov. 8:35-36).*

313

A LAMP & A LIGHT

For the commandment is a lamp, and the law a light; reproofs of instruction are the way of life (Proverbs 6:23).

READ: PSALM 119:105-106

Verse 105 of our text reads, *"Your word is a lamp to my feet and a light to my path."* The world in which we live is full of spiritual darkness. Therefore, no amount of physical light can dispel the kind of darkness that has engulfed the entire world. As we walk through the dark paths of life, we need the lamp and light of God to brighten our paths. We need a **lamp** and a **light**, both of which speak of the Word of God. As a **lamp**, the Word of God illuminates our immediate surroundings; while as a **light,** it shines bright on our paths. During creation, amidst darkness and chaos, the LORD spoke, *"Let there be light; and there was light."* (Genesis 1:3). Christ, who is the spoken Word of God caused darkness to give way. No wonder Christ said, *"I am the Light of the world. He who follows me shall not walk in darkness, but have the light of life"* (John 8:12). Again He said, *"I have come as a light into the world, that whoever believes in me should not abide in darkness."* (12: 46). Christ, the written Word of God can cause your spiritual path to be lit, if you read and meditate on His Word (Read John 5:39 and 6:63).

The human spirit needs to walk in spiritual light, which is the Word of God. Walking in spiritual darkness will lead the human spirit to hell— a place of perpetual darkness. Just as no one can walk and have his or her bearing in a physical darkness, so can no one walk and have his or her bearing is a spiritual darkness. Darkness is bad for one's physical and spiritual life. A couple of months ago, there was a black out in our neighborhood, due to rainstorm. It was raining heavily at night and suddenly, the lights went off. Everyone was caught off guard! I had to grope in the dark to locate our emergency lantern. Looking for something in the dark as well as trying to avoid banging your head against an object is not funny. Something that I would have picked up in less than 30 seconds, if there was light, took me over 5 minutes to do in the dark. That is what happens when people walk in spiritual darkness; they stumble through life.

Reflection: Is the Word of God your lamp and light?

Word for today: *No one ever succeeds by walking or working in darkness.*

GIFTED FOR THE BENEFIT OF ALL

But one and the same Spirit works all these things, distributing to each one individually as He wills (1 Corinthians 12:11).

READ: 1 CORINTHIANS 12:7-11

Christ's injunction to His followers regarding the ministration of spiritual gifts reads as follows: *"Heal the sick, cleanse the lepers, raise the dead, cast out demons. Freely you have received, freely give."* (Matthew 10:8). What we see today is the opposite! We see people who are spiritually gifted, put a price tag on the use of such gifts. They tell you how much you will pay before you are prayed for and the cost of such a prayer depending on the severity of your problem. Some preachers tell you the kind of hotel to lodge them, including their choice of meals and how much to pay them before they accept any invitation to minister in the Church. To such people, there is nothing like free ministration. There is nothing bad in taking good care of someone who has ministered the Word of God to the flock of the Lord. After all *"the Lord has commanded that those who preach the gospel should live from the gospel."* (1 Corinthians 9:14). It is more honorable to be blessed as people are led by the Spirit of God after ministering to them, rather than put a price tag on how much you should be paid. Doing so, amounts to commercializing the gifts of God. At the same time, it amounts to stinginess, if you fail to bless someone who has ministered the Word of God to the flock in your congregation (Read Luke 10:7; 1 Corinthians 9:7-9; 1 Timothy 5:18).

In our text, Paul reiterated the fact that spiritual giftedness is not for profit, but to benefit the Body of Christ. In verse 7 we read, *"But the manifestation of the Spirit is given to each one for the profit of all."* In whatever area you are gifted, be it in the word of knowledge and wisdom, or in healing and miracles, or prophecy, you should not charge people for making use of such gifts. Remember that you will give account of your stewardship to the Lord one day. Not long ago, someone told me of the staggering amount of money he was asked to pay by a so-called man of God in order to pray a deliverance prayer for him and the members of his family in their village. What a pity!

Reflection: Are you spiritually gifted? If so, how do you make use of the gifts?

Word for today: *Spiritual gifts are meant for service, not for profit.*

IT IS THE WORK OF GRACE

"Where sin abounded, grace abounded much more." (Romans 5:20b).

READ: EPHESIANS 2:8-10

Our text reads, *"For by grace you have been saved through faith, and that not of yourselves; it is the gift of God, not of works, lest anyone should boast"* (v8-9). What the above text is saying is that our salvation from sin and eternal death is by God's grace and not by our good works. The word grace (Greek *charis*) means "an unmerited favor." No one merits eternal life, because *"all have sinned and fallen short of the glory of God."* (Romans 3:23). But, because of God's grace, everyone now has the opportunity to experience eternal life through faith in Christ Jesus. A lot of well-meaning people do good works and think that such good works will earn them a place in heaven. Unfortunately, this is not possible! Any good work outside of Christ is not good enough to earn anyone salvation, talk less of a place in heaven. ***We are saved to do good works, but we are not saved by good works.*** Another name for good works is **self-righteousness**. The Scripture has this to say about good works or self-righteousness, *"But we are all like an unclean thing, and all our righteousnesses are like filthy rags; we all fade as a leaf, and our iniquities, like the wind, have taken us away."* (Isaiah 64:6). Righteousness based on good works is like a filthy rag before God. Whatever you and I are today as believers in Christ is by God's grace. Our salvation is by His grace; our ministration is by His grace; the life we have is by His grace. Indeed, everything about us is by God's grace. This should make us appreciate God the more.

There are four things God's grace does for us as believers in Christ.
1. God's grace **saves** us. 2 Timothy 1:9 reads, *"[God] has saved us and called us with holy calling, not according to our works, but according to His purpose and grace..."* Our calling and salvation are based on God's grace.
2. God's grace **justifies** us. In Romans 3:24 we read, *"Being justified freely by His grace through the redemption that is in Christ Jesus."* Justification means being in good standing before God. That is what God's grace does for us.
3. God's grace **establishes** us in Christ (Read Romans 5:2).

Reflection: Have you accepted Christ as your Savior? If not, why not?

Word for today: *Work-based salvation is not good enough to God.*

VALUE GOD'S WORD

And afterward he read all the words of the law, the blessings and the cursings, according to all that is written in the Book of the Law (Joshua 8:34).

READ: DEUTERONOMY 6:6-9

Joshua 1:8 reads, *"This Book of the Law shall not depart from your mouth, but you shall meditate in it day and night, that you may observe to do according to all that is written in it. For then you will make your way prosperous, and then you will have good success."* In the Old Testament, the Book of the Law is the same as the Scriptures. In the New Testament, the Book of the Law unfolds into what we call the Bible today. The word Bible is derived from the Latin word, *biblio,* meaning book. So we notice that the Scripture is no longer only the Book of the Law, but the Book—consisting of the Book of the Law, the prophets, the chronicles, the gospels, the epistles and Revelation. Another name for the Bible is the Word of God.

God created the universe by his spoken Word. For instance, Genesis chapter 1 verses 3, 6, 9, 11, 14, 24, 26 and 29 are preceded with the phrase, "Then God said." Whatever God said came to pass. There are seven reasons why you should value the Word of God as follows:
1. It provides light and guidance to your spiritual pathway (Psalm 119:105). God's Word is spirit and therefore capable of providing spiritual guidance (John 6:63). 2. It is powerful and sharp (Hebrews 4:12). Only the Word of God can penetrate into the human soul.
3. It makes you successful in life, if you obey it (Joshua 1:8).
4. It makes you wiser than your enemies (Psalm 119:98).
5. It brings about a spiritual transformation (Romans 10:17). The intake of God's Word leads to the salvation and transformation of one's soul.
6. It sanctifies your soul (John 17:17). Our Lord Jesus prayed, "Father sanctify them by your truth, your word is truth.
7. It is good for doctrine, correction and reproof (2 Timothy 3:16). The Word of God serves as the manual for moral guidance and righteous living. Anyone who fails to value God's Word, fails to value his life as well as eternal life.

Reflection: Whose word do you value—God's or man's word?

Word for today: *God's Word is priceless and eternal, value it!*

REPENT AND RETURN

"Repent, for the Kingdom of heaven is at hand!" (Matthew 3:2).

READ: EZEKIEL 18:30-32

Our text reads, *"Therefore I will judge you, O house of Israel, every one according to his ways, says the Lord GOD. 'Repent, and turn from all your transgressions, so that iniquity will not be your ruin. Cast away from you all the transgressions which you have committed, and get yourselves a new heart and a new spirit. For why should you die, O house of Israel? For I have no pleasure in the death of one who dies, says the Lord GOD. Therefore turn and live!'"* (v30-32). The same problem God had with the children of Israel still persists today. People find it hard to repent of their sinful lifestyles and return to God. The devil is responsible for this kind of behavior. Through deception and lies, he prevents people from knowing the gravity of their sins, thus making them candidates for hell fire once they close their eyes in death (Read Revelation 21:8). In our text, we notice <u>four</u> important truths about repentance. **First,** repentance requires turning away from sin. Any repentance without a corresponding rejection of sin is not genuine. **Second,** God gives a new heart following a genuine repentance. **Third,** failure to repent leads to death. **Fourth,** God is not pleased when an unrepentant sinner dies.

The word, "Repent" means to "change one's mind", to change direction. No genuine repentance ever takes place without a change of direction, attitude or behavior. It is not alright to claim to have repented of your sins while still in them, nor is it proper to claim to have been born again, while still living the old lifestyle. Repentance should lead you back to your Maker, hence repentance and conversion are linked. After being convicted by the sermon they hear, some people feel sorry, but fall short of genuine repentance. Such people usually respond to an altar call, but end up going back the same way they came out, due to lack of genuine repentance. A genuine repentance leads to conversion, and conversion leads to newness of life in Christ. 2 Corinthians 5:17 reads, *"Therefore, if anyone is in Christ, he is a new creation; old things have passed away; behold, all things have become new."*

Reflection: Have you repented and returned to your Maker?

Word for today: *He who fakes repentance, fakes going to heaven.*

GOD IS MY ROCK & REFUGE

God is our refuge and strength, a very present help in trouble (Psalm 46:1).

READ: PSALM 18:1-3

David penned down Psalm 18 as a lyric of a song on the day the LORD delivered him from the hand of all his enemies and from the hand of Saul. In verse 2 of our text, David used some figurative names to illustrate the awesomeness of the LORD. We read, *"The LORD is my rock and my fortress and my deliverer; my God, my strength, in whom I will trust; my shield and the horn of my salvation, my stronghold."*

Let's consider each of these names ascribed to the LORD by David and see how they benefit us as believers in Christ.

1. Rock. A rock is a massive stone that provides some protection and security. As a Rock, the LORD provides solid foundation to all who put their trust in Him.

2. Fortress. A fortress is a "thick-walled city built on mountain top, meant to be impenetrable and intimidating to the enemies." As a Fortress, the LORD's defense system is impregnable.

3. Deliverer. The LORD is a Deliverer in times of trouble. As a Deliverer, the LORD delivers to the utmost (Read Daniel 6:16-23).

4. God. As God, the LORD is the Creator, Sustainer and Ruler of all things (Read Isaiah 45:5-7).

5. Strength. God is an epitome of power and strength. As the Source of strength, God knows how to turn our human weakness into His strength (Read 2 Corinthians 12:8-9).

6. Shield. A shield was "an ancient Near Eastern warrior's primary defensive weapon." With it a warrior warded off darts from the enemy aimed at him. As a Shield, the LORD protects you from every attack of the enemy.

7. Horn of salvation. A horn is s symbol of power and authority. As Horn of salvation, the LORD saves those who call upon Him (Romans 10:13).

8. Stronghold. As a Stronghold, the LORD is "a place of safety from the enemy, inaccessible place of refuge in times of trouble."

Reflection: Is God your Rock and Refuge? Write down how.

Word for today: *God is Rock and Refuge to all who run into Him.*

THE SPIRIT VS THE LETTER

It is the Spirit who gives life; the flesh profits nothing. The words that I speak to you are spirit, and they are life (John 6:63).

READ: 2 CORINTHIANS 3:4-6

In our text, Paul writes about being one of the *"ministers of the new covenant, not of the letter, but of the Spirit; for the letter kills, but the Spirit gives life."* (v6). There are four truths that are relevant to our salvation in this verse. **First** is the truth about the **new covenant.** Before one talks about a new covenant, there must have been an old covenant. A covenant *"is an agreement between two people or two groups that involves promises on the part of each to the other."* Speaking about the covenant, the Spirit of the LORD through Prophet Jeremiah gives us some insight into the dynamics of the old and new covenants. We read, *"Behold, the days are coming, says the LORD, when I will make a new covenant with the house of Israel and with the house of Judah— not according to the covenant that I made with their fathers in the day that I took them by the hand to lead them out of the land of Egypt, my covenant which they broke, though I was a husband to them, says the LORD. But this is the covenant that I will make with the house of Israel after those days, says the LORD: I will put my law in their minds, and write it on their hearts; and I will be their God, and they shall be my people."* (Jeremiah 31:31-33). The covenant the LORD made with the children of Israel on their way to the Promised land was an old covenant. God fulfilled the promise of a new in Christ Jesus. Through the shedding of His blood, Christ established the new covenant. He told His disciples, *"This is the cup of the new covenant in my blood."* (1 Corinthians 11:25b). **Second** is the truth about the covenant of the **letter.** "The letter" refers to the Old Testament Scriptures of the Mosaic law.

Third is the truth about covenant of **the Spirit.** This speaks of the salvation that Christ gives through the Holy Spirit to whoever believes in Him (Read 1 Corinthians 12:13). **Fourth** is the truth that "the letter kills, but the Spirit gives life." (John 6:63) No one can be saved based on the law, therefore, "trying to be saved by keeping Old Testament laws will end in eternal death."

Reflection: Do you worship God in Sprit or by 'the letters?'

Word for today: *The Spirit saves; the law binds and kills.*

THE MASTER'S VESSEL

Does not the potter have power over the clay, from the same lump to make one vessel for honor and another for dishonor? (Romans 9:21).

READ: 2 TIMOTHY 2:20-26

A vessel is a container or receptacle, sometimes made of clay. Paul used the word **vessel** five times in reference to the human body (Read Romans 9:22-23; 2 Corinthians 4:7; 2 Timothy 2:20-21). The earthen vessel has something in common with the human vessel—our physical body. For instance, just as the earthen vessel is made of clay, so is the human body made of clay (Read Genesis 2:7). An earthen vessel is a fragile object; similarly, the human vessel is fragile—prone to damage and death. The earthen vessel is a receptacle of an object; similarly, the human body is a receptacle of the human spirit. A vessel is a treasure to the owner; similarly our human vessel is God's treasure (Read 1 Corinthians 6:19-20). "Just as the clay vessel reflects the craftsmanship of its potter, so do human beings reflect the craftsmanship of God."

Paul used the word **vessel** figuratively to describe the believers in Christ vis-à-vis their relationship to and stewardship in Christ. We read, *"But in a great house there are not only vessels of gold and silver, but also of wood and clay, some for honor and some for dishonor. Therefore if anyone cleanses himself from the latter, he will be a vessel for honor, sanctified and useful for the Master, prepared for every good work."* (2 Timothy 2:20-21). There are five important truths to be deduced from Paul's vassal analogy. **1.** The "great house" *speaks* of the Church of Christ. God's invisible Church is a great and holy assembly, therefore, "let everyone who names the name of the Lord depart from iniquity." (2 timothy 2:19). **2.** The Master refers to Christ Himself. Our Lord Jesus Christ is the Master and Head of the Church (Ephesians 5:23). **3.** The golden and silver vessels refer to believers in Christ on different spiritual levels—some operate on golden level, while others operate on silver level of spirituality. **4.** The wooden and clay vessels speak of unproductive carnal believers. 5. The cleansing refers to a sanctified life in Christ.

Reflection: Are you a sanctified vessel for the Lord?

Word for today: *God does not use a defile vessel for His work.*

321

SHORT OUTSIDE; TALL INSIDE

[Zacchaeus] sought to see who Jesus was, but could not because of the crowd, for he was of short stature (Luke 19:3).

READ: LUKE 19:1-10

Someone's stature can make or mar his ability to do certain things. For instance, someone who is fat may have problem running fast . On the other hand, someone who is thin may find it difficult to lift a heavy object. Also, someone who is tall may not easily bend down, while someone who is short may find it had to reach an object that is placed high on a wall. That was the predicament that Zacchaeus faced. He was a man of short stature, which did not allow him to see Jesus as He passed by. To make up for his short stature, Zacchaeus had to do something; he climbed up a sycamore tree in order to see Jesus. Verse 3-4 of our text read, *"And he [Zacchaeus] sought to see who Jesus was, but could not because of the crowd, for he was of short stature. So he ran ahead and climbed up into a sycamore tree to see Him, for He was going to pass that way."*

Prior to meeting Jesus, Zacchaeus had a four-fold problem. **First,** he was diminutive in stature (Luke 19:3). His shortness forced him to climb a tree to see Jesus. **Second,** He was dubious in character (v2). As a tax collector, Zacchaeus lined his pocket with ill-gotten wealth. **Third,** Zacchaeus was despised in the society (v7). **Fourth,** Zacchaeus was desperate in nature. He ran ahead of everyone and climbed up a tree to see Jesus (v4). After Zacchaeus' encounter with Jesus, he became tall inside, even though, he was short outside. In other words, he became spiritually elevated in five ways:
1. He was recognized by Jesus. When Jesus saw him, He said to him, *"Zacchaeus, make haste and come down, for today I must stay at your house."* ((v5). **2. Zacchaeus joyfully received Jesus** (6). You can receive Jesus now by faith, as Zacchaeus did. **3. Jesus became Zacchaeus' guest** (v7). 4. **Zacchaeus recognized his horrible spiritual condition** (v8). **5. Zacchaeus became spiritually transformed** (v9). The salvation which Zacchaeus experienced brought joy into his heart and made him tall inside.

Reflection: Do you have the joy of salvation in your heart?

Word for today: *Salvation in the Lord takes care of our inadequacies.*

WAIT ON THE LORD!

"Rest in the LORD and wait patiently for Him...." (Psalm 37:7).

READ: ISAIAH 40:30-31

Our text reads, *"Even the youths shall faint and be weary, And the young men shall utterly fall, but those who wait on the LORD shall renew their strength; they shall mount up with wings like eagles, they shall run and not be weary, they shall walk and not faint."* (v30-31). Waiting requires patience; in fact both are intertwined. You cannot claim to be patient without waiting, nor can you really claim to be waiting without an element of patience. We live in a fast culture, where the word **patience** has become synonymous with weakness. What does waiting on the LORD mean? ***It means to be totally dependent on God for solution to problems and direction in decision making process.*** From our text we notice a four-fold benefit for those who wait on the LORD. **First,** they "shall renew their strength" as they wait on the LORD. God, the epitome of strength, knows how to renew the strength of those who wait on Him. **Second,** "they shall mount up with wings like eagles." This is a figurative statement typifying the soaring height of an eagle. If you wait on the LORD, just like as an eagle is able to see its prey from an advantageous position, so will you be able to see spiritual things from God's perspective. **Third,** "they shall run and not be weary." Spiritual race demands spiritual strength. If you wait on the LORD, He will supple you with the strength to run the Christian race. **Fourth**, "they shall walk and not faint", meaning they will not suffer from spiritual amnesia on their spiritual journey.

In the Bible we read of Simeon who patiently waited on the LORD for something, *"And behold, there was a man in Jerusalem whose name was Simeon, and this man was just and devout, waiting for the Consolation of Israel, and the Holy Spirit was upon him. And it had been revealed to him by the Holy Spirit that he would not see death before he had seen the Lord's Christ. So he came by the Spirit into the temple. And when the parents brought in the Child Jesus, to do for Him according to the custom of the law, he took Him up in his arms and blessed God..."* (Luke 2:25-28). Simeon waited patiently on the LORD and was rewarded with the honor of dedicating infant Jesus.

Reflection: Are you patient enough to wait on the LORD?

Word for today: *Waiting brings blessings, haste brings destruction.*

REWARD FOR BENEVOLENCE

"Whoever gives you a cup of water to drink in my name,...I say to you, he will by no means lose his reward." (Mark 9:41).

READ: MATTHEW 10:40-42

An act of kindness, alias, benevolence often comes with a reward. For instance, when Lot showed kindness to two unknown men who passed by his house in the evening, little did he know that he was about to entertain angels on a mission to destroy the cities of Sodom and Gomorrah. Lot urged the two men to lodge with him since it was getting dark, in order to save them from the molestation of homosexual hoodlums in the city. The angels reluctantly accepted to lodge with Lot. Then, at night, the city hooligans came banging at Lot's door to make the men available to satisfy their sensual desires. Not only did the angels blind the eyes of those hoodlums trying to force the door open, they made their mission known to Lot. They said to Lot, *"Have you anyone else here? Son-in-law, your sons, your daughters, and whomever you have in the city—take them out of this place! For we will destroy this place, because the outcry against them has grown great before the face of the LORD, and the LORD has sent us to destroy it."* (Read Genesis 19:1-15). Lot's benevolence in accommodating those angels helped to spare his family from the divine wrath and destruction upon the cities of Sodom and Gomorrah. Another example was the reward the widow of Zarephath received for her benevolence to prophet Elijah. For giving her last meal to Elijah, the widow received a four -fold reward from the LORD. **First,** her bin of flour never ran out during the famine. **Second,** she and her son ate for many days, many meals and lived, rather than eat the last meal and die. **Third,** the widow's jar of oil never dried up. **Fourth,** her dying son was restored back to life (Read 1 Kings 17:8-24).

Our text contains the Lord's promise to reward all those who are benevolent to His servants. He said, *"He who receives a prophet in the name of a prophet shall receive a prophet's reward."* A prophet's reward is a package of material and spiritual blessings. Giving a cup of water to a servant of Christ attracts God's reward. "A cup of water" *speaks* of the least amount of caring.

Refection: How benevolent are you to others, especially servants of God?

Word for today: *Benevolence to God's servants attracts divine reward.*

324

GREEDY SHEPHERDS!

"Woe to the shepherds of Israel who feed themselves! Should not the shepherds feed the flocks?" (Ezekiel 34:2).

READ: EZEKIEL 34:1-10

God pronounced "woe" to the shepherds of Israel. The word, **Shepherds** is a metaphor for the leaders of Israel. God indicted the political leaders of Israel for their failure to look after His sheep—the children of Israel. Verse 3-6 of our text read's, *"You eat the fat and clothe yourselves with the wool; you slaughter the fatlings, but you do not feed the flock. The weak you have not strengthened, nor have you healed those who were sick, nor bound up the broken, nor brought back what was driven away, nor sought what was lost; but with force and cruelty you have ruled them. So they were scattered because there was no shepherd; and they became food for all the beasts of the field when they were scattered. My sheep wandered through all the mountains, and on every high hill; yes, my flock was scattered over the whole face of the earth, and no one was seeking or searching for them."* The above text paints a pathetic picture of merciless exploitation, gross negligence and inhuman treatment of God's people by their careless leaders. Rather than feed the flock, they "fed themselves on the sheep, and clothed themselves with the wool from the sheep."

Today, in the Church of the living God, the same thing takes place. Unfortunately, some pastors behave like the shepherds of the children of Israel. Rather than feed the flock with the Word of God, they starve them of God's Word; rather than care for the flock, they care for themselves. It is not uncommon to find some pastors who live in affluence at the expense of the flock—driving three or four cars, and priding themselves of personal ownership of private jets, while the flock they are supposed to take care of, live in abject poverty. In some Churches people are levied and compelled to contribute towards buying a special kind of car for the pastor. Some of these people barely eat three square meals a day. Yet, out of fear, they manage to pay up their levies to appease the pastor. Failure to subscribe to the levy for the purchase of pastor's dream car, makes you his enemy and a target of sermon from the pulpit. What a greed!

Refection: Are you a greedy pastor or a leader? Do you feed the flock or self?

Word form today: *The way to measure greed is by being insatiable.*

ALIVE OR DEAD TO LEGALISM?

I was alive once without the law, but when the commandment came, sin revived and I died (Romans 7:9).

READ: ROMANS 7:1-6

In our text, Paul compares the freedom one experiences for not being under the bondage of the law to that of a married woman who regains her freedom after the death of her husband. We read, *"For the woman who has a husband is bound by the law to her husband as long as he lives. But if the husband dies, she is released from the law of her husband. So then if, while her husband lives, she marries another man, she will be called an adulteress; but if her husband dies, she is free from that law, so that she is no adulteress, though she has married another man."* (v2-3). In effect, what Paul is saying is that whoever lives by the law is married to the law. In other words, "just as death breaks the bond between a husband and wife, so a believer's death to old self breaks the bond with the law. The old contractual agreement with legalism has been completely repealed and replaced with the new one in Christ. A believer in Christ becomes dead to righteousness that is based on legalism, but alive to righteousness that is based on faith in Christ. Apostle Paul did not know this truth until he had an encounter with the Lord, after which his theology about God changed (Read Acts 9:1-6; Philippians 2:3-11).

A lot of folks have tried to attain salvation through legalism, but failed woefully. What is legalism? ***Legalism is an act of trying to please God by attaining eternal life through keeping the law.*** But, the Bible has made it clear that no one can attain salvation in Christ by keeping the law (Read Ephesians 2: 8-9). Let's consider some dangers of legalism:
1. It evokes a sense of pride and self-righteousness; Read Luke 18:9-14). Self-based righteousness is unacceptable to God
2. It undermines God's salvation plan in Christ Jesus (Read Acts 4:12; Galatians 5:3-6)
3. It leads to eternal condemnation (Romans 8:1-4).
4. It attracts God's wrath (John 3:36).

Reflection: Are you alive in Christ and dead to legalism?

Word for today: *Legalism is man seeking God; grace is God seeking man.*

I'M WHAT GOD SAYS I AM

Therefore, if anyone is in Christ, he is a new creation; old things have passed away; behold, all things have become new (2 Corinthians 5:17).

READ: 2 CORINTHIANS 5:16-21

There is power in what God says! What He says you will be is what you will become. In the Bible there are number of things God says about you, if you are His child. Let's consider a few of them:
1. God says you are a new creation, once you become born again (2 Corinthians 5:17). Becoming a new creature means that your old lifestyle has made way for a new life in Christ. **2.** God says you are a victor in Christ (1 John 5:4-5). As a believer in Christ, you are a victor over the forces of darkness.
3. God says you are a success in Him (Joshua 1:8). It is God who crowns your effort with success for without His divine providence, you cannot succeed in life. **4.** God says you a winner in Christ (Romans 8:37-39). In Christ, God has made you a new creation, a victor, a success and a winner. Your faith in Christ will enable you to experience all these blessings that God has provided for you.

There are three things that God wants you to know about who you are in Christ: First is the **perception** of who you are in Christ (Read Ephesians 1:15-18). Perception matters a lot! The perception of who you are in Christ will embolden you to overcome the enemy—the devil. Second is the **power** of who you are in Christ (v19-21). The power backing who you are in Christ is the same power that raised Christ from the dead. It is the power of God—far above all "principalities, power and dominions." Third is the **purpose** of who you are in Christ. The purpose of who you are in Christ is to serve the Lord (John 12:26a). Anyone who refuses to serve God will end up serving the devil; there is no neutral ground. Your purpose in Christ is to be holy and blameless before God and to be with Christ forever (Luke 1:74-75; Ephesians 1:4). Christ wants every believer in Him to be with Him in heaven (John 14:3; 17:24), and to reign with Christ in the millennium (1 Corinthians 2:9-10; Revelation 20:6). Are you who God wants you to be? Are you a child of His (John 1:12), born again (3:3) and living in obedience to God's Word? (14:15).

Reflection: It is important that you know who you are in Christ?

Word for today: *Your identity in Christ comes by identifying with Him.*

NOVEMBER

DEVOTIONALS

PEACE IN TRIBULATION

Yes, and all who desire to live godly in Christ Jesus will suffer persecution (2 Timothy 3:12)

READ: JOHN 16:32-33

The word **tribulation** comes from the Latin words, *tribulare*—"to oppress" and *tribulum*—"threshing sledge". So, tribulation means "great trial, affliction, or distress." In our text, our Lord Jesus said to His disciples, *"These things I have spoken to you, that in me you may have peace. In the world you will have tribulation; but be of good cheer, I have overcome the world."* (v33). Persecution is an aspect of tribulation. While tribulation is the package, persecution is the ingredient of trial and suffering. In our text, we notice that Christ's statement reveals two opposing words: **Persecution**—vice; **Peace**—virtue. The Lord's statement regarding persecution from the world and peace from Him is a common experience of believers who want to live for Christ. Once you become born again and want to live a godly life in Christ, be prepared to face persecution from your family members, friends and colleagues who are not born again.

In spite of all the persecutions you my face for being in Christ, the Lord has already promised you peace and victory. The world is Satan's system that is opposed to God, as such will do everything possible to oppose every Christian, who is heavenly minded. Jesus experienced the same opposition from the world, therefore, it is not surprising that believers in Christ will experience the same opposition from the world. But, just as God did not leave Jesus alone, so has Jesus promised not to abandon His followers in their conflict. Are you going through some persecution experience due to your faith in Christ? Be strong in the Lord! The persecution will not last forever. Remember, after darkness, comes light and after rain comes sunshine. The Bible declares, *"No temptation has overtaken you except such as is common to man; but God is faithful, who will not allow you to be tempted beyond what you are able, but with the temptation will also make the way of escape, that you may be able to bear it."* (1 Corinthians 10:13).In the midst of persecution the Lord will grant you strength to enable you overcome the enemy.

Reflection: Have you trials and temptation? Call upon the Lord.

Word for today: *God's peace is a cooling factor in the heat of persecution.*

HAVE THE MIND OF CHRIST

Take my yoke upon you and learn from me, for I am gentle and lowly in heart, and you will find rest for your souls (Matthew 11:29).

READ: PHILIPPIANS 2:5-8

Our text reads, *"Let this mind be in you which was also in Christ Jesus, who, being in the form of God, did not consider it robbery to be equal with God, but made Himself of no reputation, taking the form of a bondservant, and coming in the likeness of men. And being found in appearance as a man, He humbled Himself and became obedient to the point of death, even the death of the cross."* (v5-8). Paul wrote the above piece of advice in his letter to the Philippian Church, urging them to live in unity and love towards one another. Paul's advice to the Philippian Church is also relevant to today's Church. The word **mind** refers to attitude and behavior. When someone shows good attitude and behavior, the mind of such a person is considered to be right. But, if on the other hand, someone exhibits bad behavior, his or her mind is considered screwed up. In Philippians 2:3-5, Paul used the word, **"Let"** three times to express what a true believer in Christ should be doing. In v3 read we read, *"Let nothing be done through selfish ambition or conceit, but in lowliness of mind let each esteem others better than himself."* Verse 4 reads, *"Let each of you look out not only for his own interests, but also for the interests of others."* and in v5 we read, *"Let this mind be in you which was also in Christ Jesus."*

Let's reflect on the mind of Christ a bit: 1. The mind of Christ is the mind of a bondservant (v7). Christ *"took the form of a bondservant and came in the likeness of men"* even though He is God. 2. The mind of Christ is the mind of humility (v8a). Christ "humbled Himself" to become a human being in order to save mankind. 3. The mind of Christ is the mind of obedience (v8b). Christ was obedient to His Father even to the point of death. Due to His obedience Christ prayed, *"O my Father, if it is possible, let this cup pass from me; nevertheless, not as I will, but as you will." (Matthew 26:39).* 4. The mind of Christ is the mind of serving (John 13:4-7). Christ washed the feet of His disciples to demonstrate self-less service.

Reflection: Do you have the mind of Christ? If so, write down how.

Word for today: *The mind of Christ is better expressed in action, than word.*

GAIN BY LOSING

He who loves his life will lose it, and he who hates his life in this world will keep it for eternal life (John 12:25).

READ: LUKE 9:23-26

The opposite of gain is loss. But, with Christ this is not the case. Christ made it clear that whoever losses his life for His sake will gain it. In other words, the best way to make gains in Christ is to lose something. In our text we read, *"Then He said to them all, 'If anyone desires to come after me, let him deny himself, and take up his cross daily, and follow me. For whoever desires to save his life will lose it, but whoever loses his life for my sake will save it."* (v23-24). For you to become a child of God, you have to lose something. For instance, you lose Satan to gain Christ; you lose the world to gain eternal life; you lose worldly pleasures to gain heavenly bliss. In fact, no one ever serves the Lord sincerely without giving up something. Whoever desires to save his life by not following Christ will lose it. Someone may escape persecution and death by denying Christ, but that is only a temporary measure. The life which such a person is trying to save by denying Christ will be lost forever in hell. So, we notice that it is by being prepared to die for Christ's sake that one can preserve his life. Our Lord Jesus Christ wants us to give up the temporary life we live today in exchange for eternal life in Him.

It is foolhardiness trying to hold on to something that you do not own, nor can preserve. The life you and I live is from God; He alone knows how to preserve it better. Therefore, we should align ourselves with Him to make the most of it. Verse 25 of our text asks a very important question, *"For what profit is it to a man if he gains the whole world, and is himself destroyed or lost?"* Many people are willing to gain the whole world, but no one has been able to do so since the world came into existence, because the world is bigger than human beings. One may accumulate as much riches and wealth as one can in the world, yet the world will still remain as one exits from it. Unfortunately, many people lose their souls and end up in hell as they pursue material things in the world at the exclusion of Christ, the Owner and Savior of the world.

Reflection: What have you lost to gain Christ?

Word for today: *In Christ, the way to gain is to lose.*

THE POWER OF PRAYER

"Call upon me in the day of trouble; I will deliver you, and you shall glorify me." (Psalm 50:15)

READ: JAMES 5:13-18

Unknown to many, prayer is a very powerful force in the universe. Any wonder why Daniel's prayer disturbed the heathen kingdom of Persia so much that a decree aimed at stopping Daniel from praying was promulgated? We read, *"All the governors of the kingdom, the administrators and satraps, the counselors and advisors, have consulted together to establish a royal statute and to make a firm decree, that whoever petitions any god or man for thirty days, except you, O king, shall be cast into the den of lions."* (Daniel 6:7). Daniel was not disturbed by the decree forbidding him praying to His God. The Bible records that *"when Daniel knew that the writing was signed, he went home. And in his upper room...he knelt down on his knees three times that day, and prayed and gave thanks before his God, as was his custom since early days."* (v10). There is power in prayer! A prayerful Church is a powerful Church and a prayerful Christian is a powerful Christian. Conversely, a prayerless Church is a powerless Church, just as a prayer-less Christian is a powerless Christian. God has ordained prayer as the means by which human beings can receive something from Him. Our Lord set the example during His earthly ministry. He prayed all night (Luke 6:12) and woke up in the early hours of the morning to pray (Mark 1:35). He prayed for His disciples and all those who would believe in Him (John 17:20-26). Prior to His trial and crucifixion, Christ spent time to pray. As a Christian believer, do you spend time in prayer just like your Master, Jesus did? Peter's prayerlessness was the cause of his undoing. Rather than pray, Peter relied on the arm of flesh to fight a spiritual battle, and ended up denying his Master three times (Read Matthew 26:40-45, 69-75).

In our text, James enjoins us to pray when we are suffering and also for the sick. The prayer of faith can heal the sick and set the captives free (James 5:13-15). We read, *"The effective fervent prayer of the righteous avails much."* However, unconfessed sin can hinder prayers from being answered (v16).

Reflection: Do you spend time in prayer?

Word for today: *Prayer is our vertical connection to God.*

334

DUAL REBUKE!

Jesus said to him, "Away with you, Satan! For it is written, 'You shall worship the LORD your God, and Him only you shall serve.'" (Matthew 4:10).

READ: MATTHEW 16:21-23

In our text, we notice that something which started as information update by Christ regarding His death, ended up as a dual rebuke between Him and Peter. We read, *"From that time Jesus began to show to His disciples that He must go to Jerusalem, and suffer many things from the elders and chief priests and scribes, and be killed, and be raised the third day. Then Peter took Him aside and began to rebuke Him, saying, 'Far be it from you, Lord; this shall not happen to You!' But He turned and said to Peter, 'Get behind me, Satan! You are an offense to me, for you are not mindful of the things of God, but the things of men.'"* (v21-23). Peter rebuked Jesus for telling the truth, while Jesus rebuked Peter for resisting the truth about His impending death, burial and resurrection. In His rebuke to Peter, the Lord seemed to have called Peter Satan. But, that was not the case! Actually, Christ was addressing Satan who spoke through Peter. Sometimes, certain statements which people make to, or against you might be Satan motivated, and not from the individuals *per se*. Satan knows how to speak through intermediaries. For instance, He spoke to Madam Eve through the serpent (Genesis 3:1-5) and addressed Paul and Silas through a slave girl who was demon possessed (Acts 16:16-18). Sometimes, a rebuke is a good thing, especially if it is aimed at correcting a mistake.

Our Lord Jesus enjoins us to rebuke an erring brother. We read, *"If your brother sins against you, rebuke him; and if he repents, forgive him."* (Luke 17:3). Paul encouraged young Timothy to "rebuke and exhort, with all longsuffering and teaching." (2 Timothy 4:2. Also in his letter to Titus, Paul urged him to preserve the truth and guide against false doctrines by rebuking the false teachers. Titus 1:3 reads, *"This testimony is true. Therefore rebuke them sharply, that they may be sound in the faith, not giving heed to Jewish fables and commandments of men who turn from the truth."* In Titus 2:15 we read, *"Speak these things, exhort, and rebuke with all authority. Let no one despise you."*

Reflection: How do you feel when rebuked by the Word of God?

Word for today: *He that listens to a godly rebuke is wise.*

KNOW GOD, KNOW WISDOM

"Behold, the fear of the Lord, that is wisdom, and to depart from evil is understanding." (Job 28:28).

READ: DEUTERONOMY 4:5-8

If you need wisdom, make God your Source. God is the epitome of wisdom and whoever asks Him for wisdom will receive it. James 1:5 reads, *"If any of you lacks wisdom, let him ask of God, who gives to all liberally and without reproach, and it will be given to him.* In 1 Kings 4:29-32, we read of how king Solomon asked God for wisdom and God gave him so much wisdom that Solomon became the wisest man on earth: *"And God gave Solomon wisdom and exceedingly great understanding, and largeness of heart like the sand on the seashore. Thus Solomon's wisdom excelled the wisdom of all the men of the East and all the wisdom of Egypt. For he was wiser than all men—than Ethan the Ezrahite, and Heman, Chalcol, and Darda, the sons of Mahol; and his fame was in all the surrounding nations." King Solomon's wisdom enabled him to* speak three thousand proverbs, and his songs were one thousand and five (1 Kings 4:29-32). King Solomon knew God and then God gave him wisdom. Anyone who knows God, knows wisdom. Conversely, anyone who doesn't know God, does not know wisdom. Wisdom is not just the acquisition of academic knowledge, but having the fear of God (Job 28:28). God is the Giver of wisdom (Proverbs 2:6-7). Some people depend on their earthly wisdom, which is foolishness before God. Any wisdom that is void of the knowledge of Christ is sensual, earthly and leads to hell.

In our text, we notice that Moses spoke to the children of Israel about the need to know God in order to have wisdom. He reminded the people of how he had taught them *"statutes and judgments, as the LORD had commanded him."* (Deuteronomy 4:5). He added, *"Therefore be careful to observe them; for this is your wisdom and your understanding in the sight of the peoples who will hear all these statutes, and say, 'Surely this great nation is a wise and understanding people.'"* (v6). Wisdom from God does not operate in a vacuum; it comes from knowing God and living in obedience to His Word.

Reflection: Do you know God? If so, how?

Word for today: *No God, no wisdom; know God, know wisdom.*

EXCELLENCY OF THE LORD

"They shall see the glory of the LORD, the excellency of our God" (Isaiah 35:2b).

READ: ISAIAH 35:1-4

The lyric of a popular Christian chorus which addresses God as being excellent goes like this:

How excellent is your name, O Lord, how excellent is your name, O Lord;
How excellent is your name, how excellent is your name;
How excellent is your name, O Lord!

The word **"excellent"** means "exceptionally good of its kind." Based on this definition, it is safe to say that only God deserves the title, **"Excellency"** God is excellent in every ramification. He is excellent in name (Psalm 8:1,9); excellent in power (Job 37:23; Psalm 147:5); excellent in Word (Isaiah 40:8); excellent in greatness (Psalm 150:2). Unfortunately, most dignitaries, especially presidents and governors in some African countries go by the title, **"Excellency."** while their wives go by the title, **"First lady"** These titles convey a sense of respect, dignity and worth. Yet, it is not uncommon to find the holders of these titles embezzle public funds, live immoral sexual lives and engage in all kinds of atrocities and crimes. By so doing, such people bring disgrace to the title, **"excellency."** It is unfortunate that secular titles have also found their ways into the house of God. Today, in some Churches you find pastors having long lists of high sounding titles, while their wives go by the title, "First lady" as if the Church is competing with the world (Read 1 John 2:15-16). If Christ were to be physically present, would He go by these titles? If you are called by God, your ideal title is that of your calling (Read Ephesians 4:10-11).

Verse 1-2 of our text read, *"The wilderness and the wasteland shall be glad for them, and the desert shall rejoice and blossom as the rose; It shall blossom abundantly and rejoice, even with joy and singing. The glory of Lebanon shall be given to it, the excellence of Carmel and Sharon. They shall see the glory of the LORD, the excellency of our God."* The Lord in His might will restore your spiritual wasteland and make you enjoy the excellency of His glory.

Reflection: Do you enjoy the excellency of God in your life?

Word for today: *God's excellency makes us excellent in Christ.*

337

THE NEED FOR CONFESSION

"Ezra the priest stood up and said to them, 'You have transgressed...now therefore, make confession to the LORD God of your fathers, and do His will...'" (Ezra 10:10-11

READ: 1 JOHN 1:8-10

Our text reads, *"If we say that we have no sin, we deceive ourselves, and the truth is not in us. If we confess our sins, He is faithful and just to forgive us our sins and to cleanse us from all unrighteousness."* (v8-9). There is need for us to confess our sins to God, but such confession should not be hypocritical. To confess one's sin, while still living in it makes mockery of confession. Confession is a statement of admission of guilt. Therefore, whenever we confess our sins to God, we are admitting guilt for such sins and will not continue in them.

There are seven kinds of confession of sin people could make.
1. Personal confession—*the confession of sin you make asking God for the forgiveness of your personal sin* (Read Psalm 51:1-2).
2. Intercessory confession—*the confession of sin you make on behalf of others*. Daniel made this kind of confession during his prayer God's restoration, after seventy years of Babylonian captivity (Read Daniel 9:1-19).
3. Corporate confession—*the confession of sin made to God as a corporate body*. Ezra and Nehemiah initiated this kind of confession among the people, as they both championed the rebuilding of the temple and walls of Jerusalem (Read Ezra 10:10-12; Nehemiah 9:1-2). **4. Reciprocal confession**—*the confession of sin which people make to one another to receive the blessing of healing*. This kind of confession is between the sick and anyone with whom the sick one needs to be reconciled. **5. Hypocritical confession**—*the kind of confession of sin people make, while continuing to live in it* (Read Proverbs 28:13). **6. Faithless confession**—the *confession of your sin without believing that God has forgiven you*. Satan is behind this kind of confession (Read 1 John 1:9). **7. Genuine confession**—*the confession of sin you make wholeheartedly to God, with the resolve never to go back to it* (Prov. 28:13; 2 Corinthians 7:9-11).

Reflection: Do you confess your sins to God and forsake them?

Word for today: *Sins genuinely confessed are sins forgiven.*

338

THE UNVEILD GOSPEL

For the message of the cross is foolishness to those who are perishing, but to us who are being saved it is the power of God (1 Corinthians 1:18).

READ: 2 CORINTHIANS 4:1-6

The gospel of salvation in Christ is available and free to all. This means that it doesn't cost anyone money to be saved. All one needs is to believe in the finished work of Christ, who is the Author and Finisher of the salvation of the human soul (Hebrews 12:2). God is wise! Can you imagine what would have happened, if God had placed a price-tag on salvation? Certainly, the rich and the powerful of the world would have bought it up and resold it to people at such exorbitant price that the poor would have complained of lack of money to purchase it. As a result of this, salvation would have become a thing for the rich and privileged in the society. But, God who is wiser than men has made salvation to be free to all, so that no person would have any excuse for not being saved. Sometimes, when something is free, its value is under appreciated. This is what happens among people today! Some don't appreciate salvation, because it is free, while others try to make it look costly by working hard for it.

God's salvation to mankind is free and unveiled, yet not everyone has embraced it. Verses 3-4 of our text give us a clue as to the reason for this. We read, *"But even if our gospel is veiled, it is veiled to those who are perishing, whose minds the god of this age has blinded, who do not believe, lest the light of the gospel of the glory of Christ, who is the image of God, should shine on them."* The "god of this age" is none other than the devil (John 12:31). The devil is responsible for people not paying heed to the gospel and as a result, the light of the glorious gospel, which dispels darkness of sin is prevented from reaching their human soul. God does not force salvation on anyone. Rather, He offers it freely to as many as are willing to receive it. The gospel in an unveiled gift. But, when the gospel is rejected, it becomes veiled in the minds of those who have refused to accept it. When this happens, such people live through this life in spiritual darkness and continue in the same way in hell for eternity. When someone's mind is blinded, he cannot perceive the truth.

Reflection: Has the gospel been unveiled in your heart?

Word for today: *The unveiled gospel unveils the sinner's heart.*

HAVE AN ETERNAL PERSPECTIVE

Now faith is the substance of things hoped for, the evidence of things not seen.
For by it the elders obtained a good testimony (Hebrews 11:1-2)

READ: 2 CORINTHIANS 4:16-18

Physical vision is the ability to see physical objects which are temporal, while spiritual vision is the ability to see things from God's perspective. The Bible declares, *"God is Spirit and they who worship Him, must worship Him in spirit and in truth."* (John 4:24). Since God is Spirit, it behooves His children to be spiritual, and this includes having an eternal perspective to life. Those who are spiritual mind the things of the spirit, while those who are carnal mind the things of the flesh (Read Romans 8:5-8). This means that one's perspective of life is dependent upon one's spiritual values. For instance, if one's spiritual values are built on the truth—the Word of God, one's value in life will have eternal components to it. But, if on the other hand one's spiritual values are built on lies and myths, one's value in life will be worldly and ungodly. In verse 16 of our text, Apostle Paul wrote about the need for Christians to have an eternal perceptive to life. From Paul's statement, we are encouraged that though, our physical body perishes, yet our hope for the spirit body, which never dies, is renewed daily as we put our trust in Christ. So don't lose heart due to the sufferings you go through in life (Read 1 Corinthians 15:50-53). Verse 18 of our text reads, *"We do not look at the things which are seen, but at the things which are not seen. For the things which are seen are temporary, but the things which are not seen are eternal."* Indeed, as believers in Christ, we should not be spiritually myopic as to behold only the visible blessings of this world, which are temporal. Rather, we should focus on the blessedness of eternal life.

Having eternal perceptive of life enabled the Old Testament believers to die in faith, "not receiving the promises, but having seen them afar off and were assured of them…" (Hebrews 11:13). Stephen had an eternal perspective of life, as such, he was able to see the vision of an open heaven with Christ "standing on the right hand of God." (Acts 7:56). Having an eternal perspective of life will help you grow spiritually.

Reflection: What kind of perspective do you have of life?

Word for today: *Eternal perspective of life leads to eternal life.*

DIVINELY RESISTED

"Likewise you younger people, submit yourselves to your elders. Yes, all of you be submissive to one another, and be clothed with humility..." (1 Peter 5:5).

READ: PROVERBS 3:33-35

Our text reads, *"The curse of the LORD is on the house of the wicked, but He blesses the home of the just. Surely He scorns the scornful, but gives grace to the humble."* (v33-34). God blesses the humble and all he does, but makes curses the inheritance of the wicked, alias, the proud. In James 4:6 we read, *"But He gives more grace. Therefore He says: 'God resists the proud, but gives grace to the humble.'"* The word "resist" means to strive against, to pull down and to dethrone.

The Bible records three personalities whose pride led to incidents in which they were resisted by God. The **first** was Lucifer, who later became known as Satan. In Isaiah 14:12-15 we read, *"How you are fallen from heaven, O Lucifer, son of the morning! How you are cut down to the ground, you who weakened the nations! For you have said in your heart, 'I will ascend into heaven, I will exalt my throne above the stars of God; I will also sit on the mount of the congregation, on the farthest sides of the north; I will ascend above the heights of the clouds, I will be like the Most High.' Yet you shall be brought down to Sheol, to the lowest depths of the Pit."* Lucifer in his pride used the phrase, **"I will"** five times in our text: "I will ascend into heaven."; "I will exalt my throne"; "I will sit on the mount."; "I will ascend above the heights"; "I will be like the Most High." (v13-14). Lucifer was known as the 'son of the morning" due to his beauty. But, God resisted his pride and brought him down "into the lowest depths of Pit –called hell, and turned him into an ugly personality (v15). The **second** was king Nebuchadnezzar, whose pride the LORD resisted by making him to spend seven years in the wild. One day, as king Nebuchadnezzar walked on the balcony of his palace, he made this proud statement, *"Is not this great Babylon, that I have built for a royal dwelling by my mighty power and for the honor of my majesty?"* (Daniel 4:29-33). The **third** was king Herod, who was resisted by God for his pride (Read Acts 12:21-23).

Reflection: How do you handle the temptation of pride?

Word for today: *It is a fearful thing to fall into God's hand, due to pride.*

341

QUENCH YOUR SPIRITUAL THIRST

On the last day, that great day of the feast, Jesus stood and cried out, saying, "If anyone thirsts, let him come to me and drink." (John 7:37).

READ: EXODUS 17:1-7

The children of Israel were in dire need of water in the wilderness on their journey to the Promised Land. As they complained to Moses for lack of water, Moses cried out to God. In response, the LORD who knew what the people needed pointed Moses to the rock. We read, *"And the LORD said to Moses, 'Go on before the people, and take with you some of the elders of Israel. Also take in your hand your rod with which you struck the river, and go. Behold, I will stand before you there on the rock in Horeb; and you shall strike the rock, and water will come out of it, that the people may drink."And Moses did so in the sight of the elders of Israel."* The LORD instructed Moses to strike the rock and when he did, water gushed out from the rock for the people to drink. As they drank, little did the people know that they were drinking spiritual water as well, which was capable of quenching their spiritual thirst. Unknown to the children of Israel, they were physically and spiritually thirsty and needed both physical and spiritual water. Even though their physical thirst was quenched, after drinking the water from the rock, their spiritual thirst lingered due to unbelief. Apostle Paul was quick to point this out in his letter to the Corinthian Church. In 1 Corinthians 10:4 we read, *"And [they] all drank the same spiritual drink. For they drank of that spiritual Rock that followed them, and that Rock was Christ."*

One afternoon, our Lord Jesus, *"being wearied from His journey sat by a well known as Jacob's well."* Then came a Samaritan woman to the well to fetch water. Jesus said to the woman, "Give me a drink." (John 4:6-7). In a snobbish response, the woman said, *"How is it that you being a Jew, ask a drink from me, a Samaritan woman? For the Jews have no dealings with Samaritans."* (v9). As the conversation continued, Jesus made a remarkable statement about spiritual water (Read John 4:13-14). Jesus is the Water of life (John 4:14; 7:37) and the Bread of life (John 6:48). He satisfies all those that are spiritually hungry and thirsty.

Reflection: Are you spiritually thirsty? Drink from the Rock—Lord Jesus.

Word for today: *Only Christ can quench your spiritual thirst.*

A CAMOUFLAGE CHRISTIANITY?

"In the morning, as He returned to the city, He was hungry. And seeing a fig tree by the road, He came to it and found nothing on it but leaves..." (Matthew. 21:19).

READ: MARK 11:12-14

Genesis 3:7 gives an account of a typical spiritual camouflage. It reads, *"Then the eyes of both of them were opened, and they knew that they were naked; and they sewed fig leaves together and made themselves coverings."* Adam and Eve became aware of their nakedness after eating the fruit from the forbidden tree. So, in order to cover their nakedness, they made coverings of fig leaves for themselves. The fig leaves covered their physical nakedness, but could not cover their spiritual nakedness of sin. It took God's intervention to cover their spiritual nakedness of sin. God clothed them with animal skins, which involved the shedding of animal blood, for *"without the shedding of blood, there is no remission of sin."* (Hebrews 9:22b and Leviticus 17:11). Just as God provided Adam and Eve with better coverings, so does He provide sinners with better covering in Christ due to the shedding of His blood on the cross.

Just as the fig leaves failed Adam and Eve, so did the fig tree fail Christ. Our text gives us an insight into what took place between Christ and a fig tree. We read, *"Now the next day, when they had come out from Bethany, He was hungry. And seeing from afar a fig tree having leaves, He went to see if perhaps He would find something on it. When He came to it, He found nothing but leaves, for it was not the season for figs. In response Jesus said to it, 'Let no one eat fruit from you ever again.'"* From our text, we notice three problems with the fig tree. **First,** it had leaves without figs. Usually, the presence of leaves on a fig tree was an indication of fruitfulness. **Second**, it failed to satisfy its Maker, when it mattered most. Christ was hungry and needed to eat from the fig tree. **Third,** the fig tree had leaves at the wrong time—a time not meant for figs. Just like this fig tree, some Christians live camouflage lives; they have all the trappings of outward Christianity, but lack Spiritual fruits.

Reflection: How genuine is your Christianity?

Word for today: *A camouflage life has no place in heaven.*

'AND HIS CUP WAS FULL'

But Elymas the sorcerer (for so his name is translated) withstood them, seeking to turn the proconsul away from the faith (Acts 13:8).

READ: ACTS 13:4-12

One's cup becoming full is an idiomatic expression of when someone is caught up in his evil ways; a time to receive a recompense for one's evil deeds. When people practice wickedness without any regard to God, a time comes when their 'cup becomes full' and God's judgment takes place. God is longsuffering and He gives a sinner a long time to repent, due to His mercy. But, if God's mercy is rejected and rebuffed, then the cup of such an individual becomes full when God unleashes His wrath, at which time, there may be no opportunity for repentance. In our text we notice what happened to Elymas, the sorcerer, when his cup become full. During their missionary journey to Cyprus, Paul and Barnabas were invited by a man named Sergius Paulus—a proconsul "to hear the word of God." But, one Elymas *"withstood them, seeking to turn the proconsul away from the faith."* (v6-8). Elymas must have been profiting a lot from his sorcery and didn't want to lose his grip on the proconsul and his subjects. In response to Elymas' resistance against the gospel, Paul pronounced a curse of blindness upon him, and immediately Elymas became blind, with the result that the proconsul became a believer in Christ (v9-12).

Judas was a man whose cup was full, and as a result, he went and hanged himself. Judas was appointed among the twelve apostles. He traveled with Jesus, slept with Jesus and ate with Jesus, but had a hidden agenda—seeking an opportunity to betray his Master (Read Luke 22:3-6). During God's covenant with Abraham, He told Abraham that after fourteen generations, the cup of the Amorites would be full and He would unleash His wrath upon them and give their land to Abraham's descendants (Read Genesis 15:15-16,18). When one's cup is full, it may be too late for one to engage in any 'damage control' effort. Hence, it is very crucial to respond to God's gift of love by accepting Christ as Lord and Savior today, if you haven't done so yet.

Reflection: Don't wait for your cup to be full, make peace with God now.

Word for today: *God's cup of wrath begins when one's cup is full.*

THE TREES OF GOD FOR ADAM

I made it beautiful with a multitude of branches, so that all the trees of Eden envied it, that were in the garden of God (Ezekiel 31:9).

READ: GENESIS 2:8-9

God, the Creator of the universe, has a purpose for everything He has created. This means that nothing is created purposeless. For instance, out of the ground, God called into being "the grass, the herbs that yield seed, and the fruit tree that yields fruit according to its kind, whose seed is in itself." (Genesis 1:11-12). Then God created the Sun and Moon—the Sun to give light during the day and the Moon to give light at night (Genesis 1:14-18). Having created all animate and inanimate objects, God decided to create man to take care of all His creations. We read, *"And the LORD God formed man of the dust of the ground, and breathed into his nostrils the breath of life; and man became a living being."* (2:7). After creating man, "God planted a garden, eastward in Eden, and there He put the man whom He had formed." (v8).

In verse 9 of our text, we notice that in the garden of Eden where God placed Adam, there were four kinds of tree. **First** was the tree that was "pleasant to the sight.," **Second** was the tree that was 'good for food" **Third** was "the tree of life" and **fourth** was the "tree of the knowledge of good and evil." Each of these trees played some significant roles in the life of Adam. For instance, the tree that was "pleasant to the eyes", beautified the garden for Adam. By planting this kind of tree, the LORD added aesthetic beauty to Adam's environment. Any wonder, why human beings enjoy the beauty of nature? The tree that was "good for food", took care of Adam's hunger. Adam didn't need to work for food; all he needed to do was to eat from the fruits of the tree meant for food. The "tree of life" was meant to sustain Adam's life. Initially, God did not create Adam to die. It was sin that brought about suffering and death (Genesis 3:17-19,23). The "tree of knowledge of good and evil" was meant to test Adam's obedience to his Maker. God drove Adam from the garden to avoid him eating from the tree of life (v24). Today the tree of life is in heaven awaiting the saints (Revelation 2:7; 22:2,14).

Reflection: Do you depend on God for the sustenance of your life?

Word for today: *The tree of life is God's symbol of eternal life.*

"MESSAGE OF THE CROSS"

"I have proclaimed the good news of righteousness In the great assembly;
Indeed, I do not restrain my lips, O LORD, you Yourself know." Psalm 40:9).

READ: 1 CORINTHIANS 1:18-19

Verse 1 of our text reads, *"For the message of the cross is foolishness to those who are perishing, but to us who are being saved it is the power of God."* There are two important words in our text that merit close attention. One is the word, **message** and the other is the word, **cross.**

What is the message? The message is the gospel—the good news about Christ's death, burial and triumphant resurrection for the salvation of mankind.

What is the cross? The cross refers to the cross of Christ. There are many crosses. Christ's cross is not **a cross,** but **the cross**. Apart from the cross of Christ, there are many other crosses. They range from cultic cross to sun cross, Coptic cross, Canterbury cross, Occitan cross, thieves cross, papal cross, cross eminence and so on. Each of these crosses has something it represents. So, we notice that the message of the cross is nothing but the news of how Christ died on the cross for mankind, and the need for man to respond to His sacrificial death in order to be saved. The gospel is closely linked with the cross of Christ. The **cross** *symbolizes* Christ's suffering and death, while the **gospel** *speaks* of the victory His death ushers to mankind over sin and death.

There are four truths about the message of the cross.

1. It sounds foolish to those who are on their way to destruction (1 Corinthians 1:18a).

2. It is the power of God to those who are being saved (v18b).

3. Believers should not be ashamed of it (Romans 1:16a).

4. It is the power of God that brings salvation (v16b).

5. It reveals God's righteousness from faith to faith (v16c).
Message of the cross is that Christ died on the cross for our sins. Refusal to accept it sends one to hell.

Reflection: Have you embraced the message of the cross yet?

Word for today: *Christ's death on the cross is the power of the gospel.*

AN ABUNDANT LIFE INVITATION

"I have come that they may have life, and they may have life more abundant-ly." (John 10:10b)

READ: ISAIAH 55:1-5

When people invite guests to a party or luncheon, they do so within the limit of available resources like food, time, space and manpower. But, when God makes an invitation, He does so within His limitless available resources. Human invitation is selective; God's invitation is universal, human invitation is temporal; God's invitation is eternal, human invitation is subject to change and cancellation due to prevailing circumstances; God's invitation is permanent due to His sovereign power. God made two abundant life invitations in the Bible—one in the Old Testament and the other in the New Testament. The Old Testament abundant life invitation reads as follows, *"Ho! Everyone who thirsts, come to the waters; and you who have no money, come, buy and eat. Yes, come, buy wine and milk without money and without price."* (Isaiah 55:1-2). Only God can make such a universal invitation for people to feed and drink freely, due to His Omnipotent providence. God's invitation is aimed at satisfying people's spiritual hunger and thirst. Are you spiritually hungry and thirsty? Respond to God's invitation by accepting His Son, Jesus Christ as your Lord and Savior today and it will be well with you forever.

The second of God's invitation is found in the gospel of Matthew and it reads as follows: *"Come to Me, all you who labor and are heavy laden, and I will give you rest."* (Matthew 11:28). Incidentally, the Old and New Testaments' invitations of God point to the Person of Christ. He is the living water, that gives life (John 4:10, 13-14). He is also the food—the Bread that gives life (John 6:48,51). Verse 3 of our text reads, *"Incline your ear, and come to me. Hear, and your soul shall live; and I will make an everlasting covenant with you—the sure mercies of David."* The only way to benefit from God's abundant life invitation is by responding to Him. He says that if you do so, "your soul shall live." Respond to God's invitation and be blessed.

Reflection: Do you enjoy an abundant life in Christ Jesus?

Word for today: *Abundant life flows from God of abundance.*

347

BELOVED OF THE LORD

"[Neither] height nor depth, nor any other created thing, shall be able to separate us from the love of God which is in Christ Jesus our Lord" (Romans 8:39).

READ: JOHN 3:16-18

During His earthly ministry, our Lord Jesus openly revealed the love of God in the following statement, *"For God so loved the world that He gave His only begotten Son, that whoever believes in Him should not perish but have everlasting life. For God did not send His Son into the world to condemn the world, but that the world through Him might be saved."* (John 3:16-17). In deed, God loved the world so much that He sent His son, Jesus Christ to save her from eternal condemnation. Every sinner is beloved of God. The word, **world** means the entire human race. The entire human race came from Adam. When Adam sinned against God, the human race was in Adam's loins. As a result of this, the human race inherited the guilt of Adam's sin. Apostle Paul gives us some insight into the guilt and suffering of the human race based on Adam's sin and the righteousness of the believer based on Christ's righteousness. We read, *"For if by the one man's offense death reigned through the one, much more those who receive abundance of grace and of the gift of righteousness will reign in life through the One, Jesus Christ. Therefore, as through one man's offense judgment came to all men, resulting in condemnation, even so through one Man's righteous act the free gift came to all men, resulting in justification of life. For as by one man's disobedience many were made sinners, so also by one Man's obedience many will be made righteous."* (Romans 5:17-19). Even though the world (human race) was in enmity with God due to Adam's sin, nonetheless, God still loved her by sending Christ to save her.

So we see that no matter how sinful a person may be, the love of God is still available for such a person. God loves the sinner, but hates his sin. That is the truth! God did not send Jesus to condemn the world, but to save it. This means that in Christ, God has predestined salvation for the human race.

Reflection: Do you know that God still loves you?

Word for today: *Sin may destroy a sinner, but not the love God has for him.*

BE STEADFAST IN THE LORD

"For we have become partakers of Christ, if we hold the beginning of our confidence steadfast to the end." (Hebrews 3:14).

READ: 2 PETER 3:14-18

Another word for **steadfast** is "firmly loyal or constant." One can be steadfast in the Lord or in the world; in righteousness or sin; in love or in hatred. When a person is steadfast in the Lord, he or she stands to reap the benefits accruing from such steadfastness. In 1 Corinthians 15:58 we read, *"Therefore, my beloved brethren, be steadfast, immovable, always abounding in the work of the Lord, knowing that your labor is not in vain in the Lord."* As believers in Christ, we ought to be steadfast in our hope for the Lord's return, in our service to Him and in our giving to His work. When we do these, we will be "found by Him in peace without spot and blameless" when He returns, and will not be "led away with the error of the wicked" in our Christian journey (2 Peter 3:14, 17). A good number of people who had professed faith in Christ in the past have fallen by the way side in their Christian journey today, due to lack of steadfastness in their faith.

The children of Israel exhibited some acts of unsteadfastness in their walk with the LORD. For instance, they were not steadfast in their faith, when sent out to spy the land of Canaan. As instructed by God, Moses "sent from the Wilderness of Paran, twelve spies made up of the heads of the children of Israel" to go and spy out the land of Canaan (Numbers 13:1-3). Ten out of the twelve spies, brought back a discouraging and disheartening report as follows: *"We went to the land where you sent us. It truly flows with milk and honey, and this is its fruit. Nevertheless the people who dwell in the land are strong; the cities are fortified and very large; moreover we saw the descendants of Anak there. We are not able to go up against the people, for they are stronger than we...we were like grasshoppers in our own sight, and so we were in their sight."* (27,28,33). The above report lacked steadfast faith in the LORD. The people forgot God's victory over Pharaoh and his mighty army at the Red Sea (Exodus chapter 14).

Reflection: How steadfast are you in your walk with the Lord?

Word for today: *A steadfast walk ensures a steadfast growth in the Lord.*

AWAY WITH A 'ZIG-ZAG' LOYALTY

Moreover it is required in stewards that one be found faithful (1 Corinthians 4:2).

READ: PSALM 78:32-37

Loyalty is an act of being faithful to an ideal, course or person. God demands an absolute loyalty from us, if we claim to be His children. One cannot claim to be a child of God when one is not willing to be loyal to God. Another word for loyalty is faithfulness. The children of Israel had problem maintaining a consistent loyalty before God. The writer of Psalm recalled their zig-zag loyalty to God. Rather than maintain a straight course of loyalty, they chose a zig-zag type in which they were quick to sin against God and when chastised, they returned back to God, only to turn away from Him again, and then returned back to Him thereafter and the cycle continued. Our text reads, *"In spite of this they still sinned, and did not believe in His wondrous works. Therefore their days He consumed in futility, and their years in fear. When He slew them, then they sought Him; and they returned and sought earnestly for God. Then they remembered that God was their rock, and the Most High God their Redeemer. Nevertheless they flattered Him with their mouth, and they lied to Him with their tongue; for their heart was not steadfast with Him, nor were they faithful in His covenant."* (v32-37). God is not happy with a zig-zag kind of loyalty. Living for God today and for the world tomorrow amounts to a zig-zag loyalty before God. God does not want a divided loyalty from His children.

In His parable of the unjust steward, our Lord Jesus Christ condemned a divided loyalty, alias 'zig-zag' loyalty to God, when He said, *"No servant can serve two masters; for either he will hate the one and love the other, or else he will be loyal to the one and despise the other. You cannot serve God and mammon."* (Luke 16:13). Indeed, it takes unalloyed loyalty to faithfully serve a master. Therefore, no one can serve God and the world at the same time, without compromising one's loyalty for the other. Judas was a servant with a divided loyalty. As he tried to serve Christ and money, he got into a big mess which led him to take his own life (Read Matthew 26:14-16; 27:3-5).

Reflection: As a Christian, what is your loyalty to God like?

Word for today: *A zig-zag loyalty takes people to hell.*

DELIVERED AND PRESERVED

"The LORD shall preserve you from all evil; He shall preserve your soul...your going out and your coming in from this time forth, and even forevermore." (Psalm 121:7-8).

READ: PSALM 140:1-8

Psalm 140 was written by David as prayer to God for His deliverance from the evil men. David used two words in his prayer —**Deliver** and **Preserve.** We read, *"Deliver me, O LORD, from evil men; preserve me from violent men, who plan evil things in their hearts; they continually gather together for war. They sharpen their tongues like a serpent; the poison of asps is under their lips."* (Psalm 140:1-3). Like David, we all need to pray and ask God to deliver us from the "evil men" and preserve us from the "violent men." The world in which we live is full of evil and violence. No day passes without the news about acts of violence and evil across the globe. The acts of violence and evil being perpetrated by men are so mind bugling that people's hearts are beginning to fail them (Luke 21:26). Right now, there is no safe and peaceful place in the world. Yet, the Bible says that this is only the beginning of sorrows—an appetizer to human suffering (Read Matthew 24:7-8; Mark 13:8).

If you are a child of God, there is a good news for you. The LORD has promised to deliver you from the evil one—the devil, and to preserve you from the forces of darkness. Psalm 91:14-16 reads, *"Because he has set his love upon me, therefore I will deliver him; I will set him on high, because he has known my name. He shall call upon me, and I will answer him; I will be with him in trouble; I will deliver him and honor him. With long life I will satisfy him, and show him my salvation."* The LORD knows how to deliver and preserve those who trust in Him from the hands of evil and violent men. For instance, He delivered and preserved Joseph from Potiphar's wife who lied against Joseph—a fabricated lie that sent him to jail (Genesis 39:7-20). But the LORD was with Joseph (v21). The LORD delivered and preserved Daniel in the lion's den and caused his false accusers to reap the seed they had sown (Read Daniel 6:1-24).

Reflection: No matter what your problem may be, God's deliverance is available always.

Word for today: *God delivers and preserves all those who trust in Him.*

351

STRENGTH THROUGH WEAKNESS

"For though He was crucified in weakness, yet He lives by the power of God. For we also are weak in Him, but we shall live with Him by the power of God..." (1 Corinthians 13:4).

READ: 2 CORINTHIANS 12:7-10

Apostle Paul was the most used, most persecuted, and most gifted of all the apostles of Christ. He alluded to the vision given to him by God fourteen years earlier, in which he was *"caught up to the third heaven...into paradise and heard inexpressible words, which it is not lawful for man to utter."* (2 Corinthians 12:2,4). Paul did not want to boast about the revelations he was given, nor the spiritual gifts in his life. Rather, he chose to boast in his infirmities so that "the power of Christ might rest upon him." (v5, 9). In our text, Paul made mention of the "thorn in his flesh" from Satan to buffet him. Three times he asked the Lord to take away that physical ailment. But Christ's reply to him was simple, *"My grace is sufficient for you, for my strength is made perfect in weakness." (*v9). Paul tells us why the Lord allowed the thorn in his flesh to remain. In verse 7 we read, *"And lest I should be exalted above measure by the abundance of the revelations, a thorn in the flesh was given to me, a messenger of Satan to buffet me, lest I be exalted above measure."* Sometimes, the Lord allows certain things to come our way to make us depend on Him. In Paul's case, the thorn in his flesh was a physical ailment, possibly an eye problem resulting from his encounter on the Damascus road (Read Acts 9:3, 8-9,18). Paul, in his letter to the Church in Galatia alluded to his bad sight as his physical ailment. We read, *"You know that because of physical infirmity I preached the gospel to you at the first...for I bear you witness that, if possible, you would have plucked out your own eyes and given them to me."* (Galatians 4:13-15).

There is no doubt that God used Paul's infirmity to teach him humility. According to the Life Application Bible Commentary, "Those who are strong in their own abilities or resources are tempted to do God's work on their own, and that can lead to arrogance. Those who struggle with weakness tend to rely on Christ's power."

Reflection: Are you physically weak, rely on Christ's strength.

Word for today: *Our weakness becomes strength in Christ Jesus.*

MOUTH & HEART CONSECRATION

Every way of a man is right in his own eyes, but the LORD weighs the hearts (Proverbs 21:2).

READ: PSALM 19:12-14

Verse 14 of our text reads, *"Let the words of my mouth and the meditation of my heart be acceptable in your sight, O LORD, my strength and my Redeemer."* In this text, David referred to two important human organs in his prayer to God—the **mouth** and the **heart.** The heart conceives ideas, while the mouth expresses such ideas in words. Hence, the heart and the mouth are closely connected. Look at what our Lord Jesus said about the closeness of the human heart to the mouth in Matthew 15:18-19. It reads, *"But those things which proceed out of the mouth come from the heart, and they defile a man. For out of the heart proceed evil thoughts, murders, adulteries, fornications, thefts, false witness, blasphemies."* Our mouths and hearts need constant cleaning and consecration. In Isaiah 6:4-6, we notice how Isaiah's mouth was cleansed and consecrated in order to become God's mouthpiece. Isaiah saw his unworthiness and cried out, *"Woe is me, for I am undone, because I am a man of unclean lips.* In response to Isaiah's cry, *"One of the seraphim flew to me, having in his hand a live coal which he had taken with the tongs from the altar. And he touched my mouth with it, and said: 'Behold, this has touched your lips; your iniquity is taken away, and your sin purged."* (Isaiah 6:4-6). Since God cannot use a defiled vessel, He first of all cleansed Isaiah's lips before making use of it. In order for the words of your mouth and the meditation of your heart to be acceptable to God, both your mouth and your heart need to be cleansed and consecrated.

Why is it necessary for the human's mouth and heart to be cleansed and consecrated before God? **1.** It is because the human heart is "deceitful above all things and desperately wicked." (Jeremiah 17:9). **2.** It is because the heart expresses itself through the mouth (Matthew 15:18). **3.** It is because what comes out of the mouth can defile the whole body (James 3:6). A crooked heart and defiled lips cannot glorify God because God is holy.

Reflection: Do you keep your mouth and heart consecrated for the Lord? Do you live a holy life?

Word for today: *Consecrated heart and mouth come from a consecrated life.*

ALONE WITH THE LORD

"Thus says the Lord GOD, the Holy One of Israel, 'In returning and rest you shall be saved; in quietness and confidence shall be your strength.'" (Isaiah 30:15).

READ: MARK 1:35-39

We live in a busy and noisy world. Unfortunately, the world has succeeded in conditioning us to be comfortable with noise and crowd, thus robbing us the opportunity of being quiet and alone with the Lord. Due to busyness of life, we hardly make out time to be alone with the Lord and as a result, we are unable to "hear what God the LORD will speak." (Psalm 85:8). In spite of the busy schedule of our Lord Jesus Christ, He made out time to be alone with His Father. We, His followers cannot do otherwise, but to follow His example. Verse 35 of our text reads, *"Now in the morning, having risen a long while before daylight, He went out and departed to a solitary place; and there He prayed."* By the time Christ had finished being alone with His Father in prayer, Simon and others who were searching for Him said to Him, *"Everyone is looking for you."* (v37). Jesus knew that the crowd needed Him, but He did the first thing first, by spending some time alone with His Father. May God help us to follow in the footsteps of Christ.

Five reasons why we should learn to be alone with the Lord
1. It will enable us to hear God's voice better. God spoke to Elijah in a "still small voice" while he was alone (Read 1 Kings 19:11-13).
2. It enables us to express our worship to God better. The Bible enjoins us to be silent before the Lord (Read Habakkuk 2:20 and Zephaniah 1:7).
3. It enables us to express our faith in the Lord. Psalm 62:5 reads, *"My soul, wait silently for God alone, for my expectation is from Him."* Whenever you are alone with the Lord in quietness, you tend to focus on Him and reflect on His faithfulness better. 4. It enables us to be physically and spiritually refreshed (Read Mark 6:31-32).
5. It enables us to seek God's will (Read Luke 6:12-13).
God likes to communicate His will to us in a quiet environment.

Reflection: How much time do you spend being alone with the Lord daily?

Word for today: *Alone with the Lord opens the door to divine communication.*

THE 'UNBELIEVING BELIEVERS'

But the multitude of the city was divided: part sided with the Jews, and part with the apostles (Acts 14:4).

READ: ACTS 28:23-27

Whenever people say that they believe in God, but refuse to believe in Christ Jesus, they earn the name, 'Unbelieving believers.' Unbelieving believers claim to know God, yet they refuse to believe what God says about His Son. If you believe what God says about Christ—His son, you are likely to be a 'believing believer. But, if on the other hand, you refuse to believe what God says about His Son, then you are nothing, but an 'unbelieving believer' irrespective of your claim of knowing God. **What does God say about His Son?** The gospel of Matthew has the answer. God made two important statements regarding Christ's identity: One was during His baptism at River Jordan; the other was at His transfiguration. In spite of angelic announcements about Christ's identity prior to His birth (Matthew 1:21,23; Luke 1:31-32), God Himself spoke from heaven about Christ's identity prior to the beginning of His ministry. In Matthew 3:17 we read, *"And suddenly a voice came from heaven, saying, 'This is my beloved Son, in whom I am well pleased.'"* Matthew 17:5 also reads, *"While he was still speaking, behold, a bright cloud overshadowed them; and suddenly a voice came out of the cloud, saying, 'This is my beloved Son, in whom I am well pleased. Hear Him.'"* Why did God make these two-fold announcements? It is to fulfil the law about witnesses in a matter (Read Deuteronomy 19:15b). In Matthew 3:17, God's announcement was informational. But, in Matthew 17:5, His announcement was both informational and a warning. He added "Hear Him!"

Our text reveals four character traits of the unbelieving believers:
1. They hear the Word of God, but fail to understand it (Acts 28:26a).
2. They lack spiritual discernment of the truth (v26b). See also 1 Cor. 2:14.
3. They have hearts that "have grown dull" (v27a).
4. They have ears that are "hard of hearing" (v27b)
5. They have spiritual eyes that are closed (v27c)

Reflection: Who are you—a 'believing' or an 'unbelieving' believer?

Word for today: *Believing and obeying God make a genuine believer.*

GIVE AND GAIN

Then Peter answered and said to Him, "See, we have left all and followed You. Therefore what shall we have?" (Matthew 19:27).

READ: MATTHEW 19:27-30

The saying, "Nothing ventured, nothing gained" is true. You have to give up something in order to gain something of greater value. For instance, if you give up your time, talent and treasure to the Lord, you will gain hundredfold of what you have given, including eternal life. In reply to Peter's question about the reward in giving up something to gain God's Kingdom, Jesus said, *"Assuredly I say to you, that in the regeneration, when the Son of Man sits on the throne of His glory, you who have followed me will also sit on twelve thrones, judging the twelve tribes of Israel. And everyone who has left houses or brothers or sisters or father or mother or wife or children or lands, for my name's sake, shall receive a hundredfold, and inherit eternal life."* (Matthew 19:28-29). If you give up relatives for Christ's sake, you will gain hundredfold of relatives in Christ, here and hereafter. Also "if you give up a secure job for Christ's sake, you will find that God offers you a secure relationship with Himself now and forever. If you give up your family's approval to serve the Lord, you will gain the love of the family of God." Abraham gave up his relatives in obedience to God's call in his life. In return, he gained the fatherhood of the nation of Israel through whom 'all the families of the earth have been blessed." (Read Genesis 12:1-3; Acts 3:25-26). What are you willing to give up for Christ's sake?

The principle of giving and gaining was demonstrated by Christ Himself. He gave himself up to die in order to gain many souls into His father's Kingdom. John 12:24 reads, *"Most assuredly, I say to you, unless a grain of wheat falls into the ground and dies, it remains alone; but if it dies, it produces much grain. And I, if I am lifted up from the earth, will draw all peoples to Myself."* Indeed, by His sacrificial death, Christ has drawn and continues to draw many souls to Himself. Amen! Anyone who is not prepared to give up his or her old lifestyle of sin will not gain eternal life in Christ Jesus.

Reflection: Write down three things you have given up for Christ's sake.

Word for today: *Lose the world, gain Christ; gain the world, lose Christ.*

THE GOD OF BREAKTHROUGHS

Beloved, I pray that you may prosper in all things and be in health, just as your soul prospers (3 John:2).

READ: 2 KINGS 4:1-7

God is the God of breakthroughs. In fact, He is the Source of every breakthrough in people's lives. *A breakthrough is an act of major accomplishment or success in one's life.* Our text is a classic example of how God can orchestrate a financial breakthrough in a person's life. A widow had a huge financial problem. Her husband had just died, leaving her with an unpaid debt and the creditors were about to take her two sons as slaves. As she approached Elisha with her financial problem, Elisha asked her, *"What do you have in the house?"* She replied, *"Your servant has nothing in the house, but a jar of oil."* Then Elisha said to her, *"Go, borrow vessels from everywhere, from all your neighbors—empty vessels; do not gather just a few. And when you have come in, you shall shut the door behind you and your sons; then pour it into all those vessels, and set aside the full ones."* This widow obeyed the instruction of Elisha. As she poured the little oil she had into the empty jars of oil behind closed doors, the oil became inexhaustible. Instantly, her little 'oil jar of poverty' became several 'oil jars of plenty.' As soon as the empty vessels got finished, the oil stopped flowing. Then the widow came and told Elisha what had transpired. Elisha told her, *"Go, sell the oil and pay your debt; and you and your sons live on the rest."* (v7). It is amazing how this widow went from financial hardship to financial breakthrough in one day.

There are three important spiritual lessons in this story:
1. God wants you to make available the little you have, so that he can multiply it. It is not how much you have that matters; it is how willing you are to make it available to God that matters. **2.** The more empty space you have for the Lord, the more He fills you up. As long as the widow had more empty vessels, the oil kept flowing. But, when the jars finished, the oil flow stopped. Do you have a space for Christ? **3.** God deals with us behind closed doors. When you spend time with the Lord in prayer behind closed doors, your breakthrough begins.

Reflection: Do you want a breakthrough in life? Come to Christ in faith.

Word for today: *A breakthrough comes from the God of breakthroughs.*

REJECT GOD, REJECT LIFE

Thus says the LORD of hosts, the God of Israel: "Amend your ways and your doings, and I will cause you to dwell in this place" (Jeremiah 7:3).

READ: PROVERBS 1:24-33

When people hate their lives, they end up committing suicide for variety of reasons. Similarly, when people hate and reject God—the Giver of life, they commit spiritual suicide and end up in hell. God says, *"He who sins against me wrongs his own soul; all those who hate me love death."* (Proverbs 8:36). Solomon, the author of our text paints a pathetic picture of those who reject God and refuse the wisdom that comes from knowing Him. He mentions four things God will do to those who reject Him.

1. God "will laugh at their calamity" (v25-27). God is a merciful God, but when He laughs at one's calamity, one is done for good.

2. God 'will turn a deaf ear to their cry" (v28-30). When someone has a serious problem, he or she looks for solution to such a problem by crying to God. But, woe betide a person whom God gives a deaf ear to his or her cry.

3. God will "punish them in kind." (v31). In other words, "they shall eat the fruit of their behavior and be gorged on their own devices."

When Jeremiah was commanded by God to go and confront the children of Israel for their rebellion against God, they refused to listen to Jeremiah's message and by so doing rejected God. They said to Jeremiah, *"As for the word that you have spoken to us in the name of the LORD, we will not listen. But we will certainly do whatever has gone out of our own mouth, to burn incense to the queen of heaven and pour out drink offerings to her, as we have done, we and our fathers, our kings and our princes, in the cities of Judah and in the streets of Jerusalem. For then we had plenty of food, were well-off, and saw no trouble."* Today, some people still behave like the children of Israel. They stubbornly reject God by refusing to accept the salvation that He has made available in Christ Jesus Are you one of such people? God is the Source of life, therefore, anyone who rejects Him rejects life—eternal life. But he who receives Him, receives life.

Reflection: Are you sure that you have eternal life? Read John 3:36.

Word for today: *Don't reject God, if you love your life.*

DECEMBER

DEVOTIONALS

362

IN SEARCH OF WISDOM?

The fear of the LORD is the instruction of wisdom, and before honor is humility (Proverbs 15:33).

READ: JAMES 1:5-8

The Bible enjoins us to get wisdom and understanding. We read in Proverbs 4:5 *"Get wisdom! Get understanding! Do not forget, nor turn away from the words of my mouth."* Wisdom is the ability to understand the secret things of God and to apply such knowledge in problem solving. The Source of wisdom is God! If you are in search of wisdom, the best Person to approach is God and the best tool to use is His Word. In Psalm 111:10, we read, *"The fear of the LORD is the beginning of wisdom; a good understanding have all those who do His commandments."* The "fear of the LORD" means having a reverential fear for God as your Creator. There are three kinds of wisdom. First is the worldly wisdom—*wisdom that comes from the world* (Read James 3:13-16). Second is the heavenly wisdom—*wisdom that comes from God* (v17). Third is Satanic wisdom—*wisdom that comes from Satan* (Read Exodus 7:8-12; Acts 16:16-19).

Daniel possessed the heavenly wisdom and as a result he was able to interpret God's writing on the wall for Belshazzar. During a wild party in his palace, king Belshazzar saw an inscription on the wall of his palace. The immediate effect of what he saw, *"changed his countenance, and his thoughts troubled him, so that the joints of his hips were loosened and the knees knocked against each other."* (Daniel 5: 6). In order to find interpretation to the dream, Nebuchadnezzar put all his wise men to task, who worked so hard, but *"could not read the writing, or make known to the king his interpretation."* (v8). But, king Belshazzar sought Daniel's help because he heard that the Spirit of God *was in Daniel* and *that* light and understanding and excellent wisdom were found in him. Due to the wisdom God gave to Daniel, he was able to interpret the writing on the wall to king Belshazzar (v24-28). Verse 5 of our text tells us to ask God if we lack wisdom...who gives to all liberally and without reproach. Verse 6 tells us how to ask—by faith, with no doubting .

Reflection: Are you in search of heavenly wisdom? Begin with God.

Word for today: *God—the Source of wisdom gives wisdom to people.*

THE BIG AND LITTLE FOXES

O Israel, your prophets are like foxes in the deserts (Ezekiel 13:4).

READ: SONGS OF SOLOMON 2:15-16

Foxes are "slightly smaller than a medium-size dog, with a flattened skull, upright triangular ears, a pointed, slightly upturned snout, and a long bushy tail." As "nocturnal mammals, foxes go out at night to hunt for prey, which include mice, birds, other small mammals and insects. Foxes and dogs look and behave very much alike. It is fair to say that foxes are wild dogs—since they live in the forest, while dogs are domestic animals, since they live in homes. Most of the time, little foxes break the hedges and creep into vineyards to destroy the roots of the vine by "gnawing on them." In so doing, they spoil the vine.

Verse 15 of our text reads, *"Catch us the foxes, the little foxes that spoil the vines, for our vines have tender grapes."* Our text paints a spiritual picture of what goes on in the Church. **"The vines"** *represent* believers in the Church of Christ Jesus (Read Isaiah 5:1-7); **"the tender grapes"** *represent* young Christian believers who are not deeply rooted in Christ and His Word, while the **"little foxes"** *represent* the 'little' sinful habits that Church goers live in. In the Church today, we have the big and little foxes. The "little foxes" are the 'little' sinful habits people commit. Although no sin is smaller than the others, some people have chosen to consider some sins as little sins—such as little gossip, little prayerlessness, little telling of lies to get off the hook, little un-forgiveness and so on. These 'little' sins are ruining the spiritual growth of the Church— leaving it vulnerable to all kinds of demonic attacks. A fox, though small in size remains a dangerous animal. It is crafty and carnivorous in nature. No wonder our Lord Jesus Christ likened Herod to a fox, due to his craftiness and blood-letting behavior (Read Mathew 2:7-8,16 and Luke 13:32). The 'big' foxes in the Church are the greedy, sweet-tongued, so-called men of God, who have devised all sorts of means to enrich themselves at the expense of the flock. Since they consider the Church their personal property, they take over the front seat, call the shots and give Christ the back seat in His Church.

Reflection: Beware of the 'big and 'small' foxes.

Word for today: *Allowing foxes in Christ's vineyard is dangerous.*

364

BREAK NOT THE DIVINE HEDGE!

Whoever digs a pit will fall into it, and he who rolls a stone will have it roll back on him (Proverbs 26:27).

READ: ECCLESIASTES 10:8-10

Our text reveals five important truths about life. First truth is that, *"He who digs a pit will fall into it."* (v8a). "Digging a pit" is a phrase depicting an evil plan against an innocent person. Haman dug a pit in the form of gallows on which he planned for an innocent Mordecai to be hanged. Since the Scripture must be fulfilled, Haman ended up being the one hanged on the gallows he made for Mordecai (Read Esther 7:9-10). Second is that, *"whoever breaks through a wall will be bitten by a serpent."* (Ecclesiastes 10:8b). Do you know that as a believer in Christ, the Lord has hedged you around? God hedges His people with divine protection. When God spoke highly about Job's faithfulness and uprightness, listen to Satan's reply, *"Have you not made a hedge around him, around his household, and around all that he has on every side? You have blessed the work of his hands, and his possessions have increased in the land. But now, stretch out your hand and touch all that he has, and he will surely curse you to your face!"* (Job 1:10-11). Contrary to Satan's expectation, Job did not curse God (v22). God also hedges His people against financial lack and demonic attack (Read Philippians 4:19 and Luke 10:19). Third truth is that, *"He who quarries stones may be hurt by them."* (v9a). Just as stones do not respect anyone, so does an evil plot not respect the plotter—it could boomerang. Whoever plays with fire will be burnt by it. Fourth truth is that, "He *who splits wood may be endangered by it."* (v9b). There are consequences for embanking on any evil plan. Fifth truth is that more strength in needed when using a dull ax. In other words, the ungifted will have to work harder than the gifted in fulfilling some objectives or attaining certain goals in life.

Don't break the hedge of divine **protection, provision** and **power** which the Lord has made around you by indulging in sinful behaviors. As long as you continue to align yourself with the Lord, His divine hedge will always remain.

Reflection: Have you broken the divine hedge? Ask God for His forgiveness.

Word for today: *Whoever breaks the hedge is vulnerable to the devil's attack.*

365

RESPECT GOD'S HOUSE

Then He said, "Do not draw near this place. Take your sandals off your feet, for the place where you stand is holy ground." (Exodus 3:5).

READ: ECCLESIASTES 5:1-3

Who can step into a court room without abiding by the court protocols, such as removing your cap—if you are a male, or standing up to usher in the judge, keeping quiet while the court is in session and addressing the judge with respect and dignity? If this is the case with a human judge, whose life is short-lived, what makes us think that our God—the Maker of heaven and earth deserves anything less, whenever we walk into His house of worship. Verse 1 of our text reads, *"Walk prudently when you go to the house of God; and draw near to hear rather than to give the sacrifice of fools, for they do not know that they do evil. Do not be rash with your mouth, And let not your heart utter anything hastily before God. For God is in heaven, and you on earth; Therefore let your words be few."* We should learn to respect the house of God, and avoid doing things we know that we cannot do before our President or a Judge. I don't know of any one who will be chewing gum while talking to our President or a Judge. Chewing gum while talking to a Judge in the court room will be considered a disrespectful behavior, which amounts to contempt of court—punishable by fine or imprisonment. Yet, some people come to Church with chewing gums in their mouths—-they sing and pray to God while chewing gums. I know that some people do this unknowingly. If this has been your habit, you had better stop it—it is an act of disrespect to God. Some people also spend time gossiping during a Church service, while others engage in something unrelated to what goes on during the Church service. Worse still, there are those who make financial pledges in the house of God for show—pledges which are never kept or redeemed. Are you guilty of this kind of behavior?

Can you make a pledge before a Judge and fail to redeem such a pledge? Certainly, doing so will land you in jail. It's a pity that since people don't see God, they think He is unaware of their rude and bad behaviors towards Him.

Reflection: How respectful are you of God's house?

Word for today: *Respect God's house and it shall be well with you.*

THE FUTILITY OF IDOLATRY

Will a man make gods for himself, which are not gods? (Jeremiah 16:20).

READ: PSALM 135:15-18

An idol is an image that is made with human hands and worshipped as a deity; it is anything that is worshipped and adored in place of God. Lately, a television program entitled, "An American Idol" has become very popular. The reason for using the word **Idol** is to make the winners of this competition feel like heroes, deserving respect, praise and honor. No wonder why some people tend to worship celebrities in our society. It is safe to say that anything that takes the first place in a person's life has become his or her idol. Unfortunately, some people have made their wealth, high social status and impressive academic achievements their gods—symbols of worship. Those who make idols their gods are foolish and rebellious. Foolish because they worship and ascribe deity to something that is man-made; rebellious, because they refuse to accept and acknowledge God as their Maker.

Our text reveals seven awful characteristics of an idol:
1. They are made of "silver and gold" (v15a). In some cultures, idols are made of silver and gold, while in other cultures, they are made of wood and clay or sand.
2. They are the "work of men's hands" (v15b). How can a human being make a deity for himself?
3. They "have mouths, but cannot speak" (v16a).
4. They "have eyes, but cannot see" (v16b).
5. They "have ears, but they do not hear" (v17a).
6. They lack "breath in their mouths" (v17b).
7. They are like those who make them and "those who make them are like them" Indeed, idol worshippers are as haggard and unkempt as their idols.
In Isaiah 41:21-24, the LORD through prophet Isaiah, confronts idols of the nations—that if they are really gods, they should tell of the past and predict the future by revealing "things that are to come hereafter." Anyone who indulges in idol worship is not wise.

Reflection: Do you practice idolatry? Do you know of anyone who does so?

Word for today: *Idolatry is an attempt to make God an idol.*

LORD, DRAW ME NEARER

Let us hold fast the confession of our hope without wavering, for He who promised is faithful (Hebrews 10:23).

READ: HEBREWS 10:19-25

By the inspiration of the Holy Spirit, Fanny J. Crosby composed a hymn which has become very popular today. The lyric of the hymn is as follows:

I am Thine O Lord, I have heard Thy voice, And it told Thy love to me;
But I long to rise in the arms of faith, And be closer drawn to Thee.
Refrain: *Draw me nearer, nearer, blessed Lord,*
To the cross where Thou hast died;
Draw me nearer, nearer, blessed Lord, To Thy precious bleeding side.

Just like Crosby, our prayer daily ought to be that Christ should draw us nearer in three important aspects of our Christian journey. First, we should pray that Christ should draw us nearer to **Himself.** By drawing us nearer to Himself, we are able to hear Christ clearer, love Him deeper and serve Him better. When we are drawn closer to Christ, the world will be farther away from us. Second, we should pray that Christ should draw us nearer to **His Cross.** By drawing us nearer to His cross, we will be able to appreciate what Christ did for us on the cross and willing to "take up our cross and follow Him daily." (Luke 9:23). Thirdly, we should pray that Christ should draw us nearer to **His Word**. By drawing us nearer to His Word, we will be able to read, study and meditate on His Word daily.

Verse 23-24 of our text read, *"Let us hold fast the confession of our hope without wavering, for He who promised is faithful. And let us consider one another in order to stir up love and good works."* It is when we are drawn closer to Christ that we will be able to *"hold fast the confession of our hope without wavering"*, and *"stir up one another to love and good works."* The closer we are to Christ, the more fruitful we become. Christ says, *"I am the vine, you are the branches. He who abides in me, and I in him, bears much fruit"* (John 15:5).

Reflection: How closely do you walk with the Lord?

Word for today: *The closer to Christ; the farther from the world.*

SEVEN THINGS GOD HATES

Woe to those who call evil good, and good evil; who put darkness for light, and light for darkness; who put bitter for sweet, and sweet for bitter! (Isaiah 5:20).

READ: PROVERBS 6:16-19

Our God is an embodiment of love. 1John 4:16 reads, *"We have known and believed the love that God has for us. God is love, and he who abides in love abides in God, and God in him."* Although God is love, there are things He hates. Our text reads, *"These six things the LORD hates, yes, seven are an abomination to Him."* (v16). The writer of our text used a "numerical progression—six, even seven, as a rhetoric device to embellish his poetry, provide a memory aid, and build a climax." According to Nelson's Study Bible, this kind of writing "gives the impression that there is still more to be said about a topic." For instance, "the word **hate** progresses to **abomination**, which is the strongest expression of hatred."

Let's consider the seven things that God hates:
1. **"A proud look"** (17a). Psalm 101:5b reads, *"The one who has a haughty look and a proud heart, Him I will not endure."* God cannot tolerate a proud look, hence He *"resists the proud, but gives grace to the humble."* (James 4:6).
2. **"A lying tongue"** (17b). David prayed, "Deliver my soul, O LORD, from lying lips and from a deceitful tongue." (Psalm 120:2). *"Lying lips are an abomination to the LORD."* (Proverbs 12:22).
3. **"Hands that shed innocent blood"** (v17c). Proverbs 28:17 reads, *"A man burdened with bloodshed will flee into a pit; let no one help him."* Those who shed innocent blood will live in the pit of guilt until they die.
4. **"A heart that devices wicked plans."** (v18a). Read Proverbs 24:2; Jeremiah 18:18; Mark 14:1.
5. **"Feet that are swift in running to evil"** (v18b). Read Isaiah 59:7-8.
6. **"False witness who speaks lies."** (v19a). Read Proverbs 19:5,9; Matthew 26:59-60.
7. **"One who sows discord among brethren"** (v19b). Read Proverbs 6:12-15. Hate what God hates; love what God loves, and it shall be well with you.

Reflection: Do you love what God hates?

Word for today: *Loving what God hates sends people to early grave and hell.*

MULTITUDE-DRIVEN CHRISTIANITY

You shall not follow a crowd to do evil; nor shall you testify in a dispute so as to turn aside after many to pervert justice (Exodus 23:2).

READ: EXODUS 12:37-39

Verse 37-38 of our text read, *"Then the children of Israel journeyed from Rameses to Succoth, about six hundred thousand men on foot, besides children. A mixed multitude went up with them also, and flocks and herds—a great deal of livestock."* When the children of Israel left Egypt, a mixed-multitude went with them. The mixed multitude most likely included, the Egyptians who saw God's mighty hand during the ten plagues and other ethnic groups who wanted to get away from Pharaoh. The mixed multitude caused a lot of trouble "when things did not go smoothly or as anticipated." (Numbers 11:4). Wherever there is a multitude of people, a mixed multitude is never wanting. Just as the mixed multitude blended well with the children of Israel, so do mixed multitude consisting of unbelievers blend very well with believers in the Church today. A mixed multitude is often found in a multitudinous Church for the following reasons: **1.** To feel good about themselves. Multitudinous Church believers feel empowered by the crowd and a magnificent Church building (Read Matthew 24:1-2).
2. To have the sense of belonging to a 'winning team'. Such people feel that, "the bigger the crowd, the closer they are to God" **3.** To avoid commitment in serving. Sometimes people who go to crowded Churches are really not committed in such Churches. Rather, they perch from Church to Church. **4.** To blend with believers in Christ, while living in sin (Read Matthew 13:30).

Numbers 11:4-7 read, *"Now the mixed multitude who were among them yielded to intense craving; so the children of Israel also wept again and said: 'Who will give us meat to eat? We remember the fish which we ate freely in Egypt, the cucumbers, the melons, the leeks, the onions, and the garlic; but now our whole being is dried up; there is nothing at all except this manna before our eyes!'"* Multitude-driven believers crave for worldly things, complain unnecessarily, lack spiritual depth and doubt God's ability to provide.

Reflection: Are you a mixed multitude or multitude-driven believer?

Word for today: *God is the God of the faithful, not of the crowd.*

SEED, SOIL AND STONE

Some fell on rock; and as soon as it sprang up, it withered away because it lacked moisture (Luke 8:6).

READ: ISAIAH 5:1-7

Seed, Soil and Stone are closely associated with planting. These three elements play significant natural roles in the quantity and quality of harvest a farmer reaps. For instance, if a farmer sows good quality seeds, he will in turn reap good harvest. But, if on the other hand, he sows poor quality seed, he will consequently reap poor harvest. No matter how good the soil is, the quality of seed sown determines the quality and quantity of the harvest a farmer reaps. A farmer cannot sow a poor quality seed and expect the soil to change the dynamics of the of harvest he reaps. The soil enables the seed to germinate, but the ultimate harvest depends on the quality of seed sown. If a farmer sows his seeds without clearing the stones, no matter how good they are, the seeds will fail to germinate due to lack of mineral nutrients from the soil. Stones play a natural role of erosion prevention, not germination of seed. This means that for farmer to expect a good harvest, he must get rid of stones and sow good quality seed in a good soil.

In our text, the LORD through prophet Isaiah gave disappointing parable of a vineyard. We read, *"My Well-beloved has a vineyard on a very fruitful hill. He dug it up and cleared out its stones, and planted it with the choicest vine. He built a tower in its midst, and also made a winepress in it; so He expected it to bring forth good grapes, but it brought forth wild grapes. And now, O inhabitants of Jerusalem and men of Judah, Judge, please, between me and my vineyard."* (v1-3). The "choicest vine" *speaks* of the Word of God; the "stones" that were cleared *speaks* of the obstacles that were removed to enable the seeds germinate and grow. The soil *speaks* of the hearts of the men of Judah, while the "wild grapes" *represent* the oppression, injustice and unrighteousness perpetrated by the people. Things have not changed much. Today, we find people who claim to be hearing the Word of God, attending fellowship and praying regularly, but still indulge in acts unbecoming of children of God (James 1:22-25)

Reflection: As you sow, what kind of dividend do you harvest?

Word for today: Seed, Soil and Stone, if well handled, produce a good harvest.

SKEPTICS OF GOD'S POWER

He who is not with me is against me, and he who does not gather with me scatters (Luke 11:23).

READ: LUKE 11:14-23

Due to our human frailty, we tend to be skeptical about God's power, even though we claim to believe in Him. Sometimes, when people read the Biblical account of God's miracles in the Old and New testaments, they conclude that such things don't take place anymore today. This is not true! Our *"God is still the same yesterday, today and forever."* (Hebrews 13:8). 12 years ago, when under God's leading the ministry of The Agape Christian Church was birthed, a number of people expressed some skepticism. From a human perspective, there were much odds against its survival being a non-indigenous ministry, considering the poor survival rate of such non-indigenous Churches in Baltimore, in the past. Our ministry started with three families in a home basement, without any parent Church and with practically nothing, except our Bibles and faith in God. Three years later, the Church bought her first property and eight years later, it bought a gigantic facility with provisions to accommodate any kind of school. This kind of progress for a non-indigenous ministry in the United States without a parent Church, wouldn't have been possible, if God's hand wasn't in it. To Him be ascribed all the glory and honor!

In our text, we notice how skeptical Christ's Jewish audience was about His ministry. After witnessing the great miracles Christ performed, rather than believe in Him, the people accused Him of using the power of demons in casting out demons. Verse 15 of our text reads, *"But some of them said, 'He casts out demons by Beelzebub, the ruler of the demons.'"* One thing about skeptics is that they always look for a reason to be skeptical, even when one does not exist. Accusing Christ of casting out demons with the power of "Beelzebub, the ruler of demons" smacks of elevating Satan above Christ. In spite of the miracles Christ performed, some of the people "sought from Him a sign from heaven." (v16). Had Christ given them a sign from heaven, they still would not have believed Him. It is hard to convince a skeptic who doesn't like you.

Reflection: Are you a skeptic or a believer in God's power?

Word for today: *A skeptic suffers from the sepsis of unbelief.*

372

FREEDOM WITHOUT PROBATION

"A slave does not abide in the house forever, but a son abides forever. Therefore, if the Son makes you free, you shall be free indeed." (John 8:35-36).

READ: JOHN 8:31-36

Whenever someone serving a jail term is discharged from the prison on probation, he or she is free, but not totally free. If the provision of the probation is violated, he or she can be rearrested and sent back to jail. But, the freedom that Christ Jesus gives is different—it is total and has no probation clause attached to it. Verse 36 of our text reads, *"Therefore if the Son makes you free, you shall be free indeed."* In fact, only Christ has the ability to set a sinner totally free from the bondage of sin and Satan (Read Galatians 5:1).

Christ *"said to those Jews who believed in Him, 'If you abide in my word, you are my disciples indeed. And you shall know the truth, and the truth shall make you free."* (John 8:31-32). Christ's statement contains a four-fold truth. **First,** it takes believing in Christ to abide in His Word. No wonder Christ directed His statement to those Jews who believed in Him? **Second,** it takes abiding in Christ's Word to become His disciple. **Third,** it takes both believing in Christ and abiding in His Word to know the truth. **Fourthly,** it takes knowing the truth to be set free. In John 15:7 our Lord Jesus made a similar statement in relation to abiding. We read, *"If you abide in me, and my words abide in you, you will ask what you desire, and it shall be done for you."* What does it mean to abide in Christ and for His Word to abide in you? The word **Abide** means "to remain", "to continue" Therefore, "to abide in Christ" and His Word "to abide in you" means to remain and continue in Christ as His Word remains and continues in you. As a believer, you must continue to obey the Word of Christ to be His disciple—a learner. The reply of the Jews to Christ's statement underscores their ignorance about spiritual freedom to which Christ referred. They argued, *"We are Abraham's descendants, and have never been in bondage to anyone. How can you say, 'You will be made free?'"* Jesus pointed them to the freedom from sin (v33-34).

Reflection: Are you totally free from sin and Satanic bondage?

Word for today: *Freedom in Christ is a freedom indeed.*

GODLY& UNGODLY SUBMISSION

"The household of Stephanas...have devoted themselves to the ministry of the saints—submit to such, and to everyone who works and labors with us." (1 Corinthians 16:15-16).

READ: ACTS 4:18-20

As believers in Christ, the issue of submission is written in the Bible. Paul writes, *"Wives, submit to your own husbands, as to the Lord. For the husband is head of the wife, as also Christ is head of the church; and He is the Savior of the body. Therefore, just as the church is subject to Christ, so let the wives be to their own husbands in everything."* (Ephesians 5:22-25). This text is a very popular one with husbands who want their wives to be submissive to them, even though they themselves may not be submissive to Christ. There is no doubt that the Word of God enjoins a wife to be submissive to her husband, because the husband is her head . We notice that believers in Christ are also enjoined to be submissive to their leaders (Read Hebrews 13:17). With regards to secular government, we are enjoined as well to be submissive. In 1 Peter 2:13 we read, *"Therefore submit yourselves to every ordinance of man for the Lord's sake, whether to the king as supreme, or to governors, as to those who are sent by him for the punishment of evildoers and for the praise of those who do good."* There are two kinds of submission: one is godly—prompted by God; the other is ungodly—prompted by the devil. A godly submission occurs when what you are asked to submit to does not counteract the Word of God, but honors God. On the other hand, an ungodly submission seeks to disregard God and promote Satan. If faced with the issue of submission to an ungodly command, what do you do?

The Bible has an answer! In our text we notice how Peter and his colleagues handled the issue of ungodly submission. After the miraculous healing of a man born lame, they were commanded to stop preaching in the name of Jesus (v14-18). Since the command was ungodly, Peter and others refused to submit to it (v19-20). As a believer in Christ, any command that is against the Word of God is ungodly, and therefore, does not merit your submission (See Daniel 3:13-18).

Reflection: To whom do you submit—the world or Christ?

Word for today: *Submit to God and His Word and it shall be well with you.*

SPIRITUAL PEP-TALK

"Comfort each other and edify one another, just as you also are doing." (1 Thessalonians 5:11).

READ: 1 THESSALONIANS 5:12-22

Team managers or coaches often give pep-talk to their players to boost their confidence, instill enthusiasm and bolster morale. Just as players need pep-talk to enhance their performance during games, so do we as believers in Christ need spiritual pep-talk to do well in our Christian journey.

In our text we notice that Apostle Paul in his letter to the Church in Thessalonica, listed seventeen (17) ingredients of spiritual pep-talk for Christian living. **1. Respect the Church leadership** (v12). You may not agree with them always, but respect them. **2. In love, hold the Church leaders in high esteem** (v13a).Thank them for their efforts; don't be a critic-bug.
3. "Live in peace with all" (v13b). Learn to get along with others (Romans 12:18)
4. Warn the unruly among you (v14a). Encourage others to plug into God's work. **5. Encourage those who are fainthearted** (v14b). Try to instill confidence in others (Read 2 Timothy 1:7).
6. "Uphold the weak" (v14c). Pray for the weak in faith.
7. "Be patient with all" (v14d). Be calm in the face of provocation.
8. Don't be vengeful (v15a). Through love you can win over your enemy.
9. "Pursue what is good for yourself and others." (v15b). Be willing to accommodate others for the common good.
10. Be joyful (v16). Even when the going is tough, rejoice in the Lord.
11. Be prayerful (v17). Prayer is talking to God—learn to talk to Him.
12. Be thankful to God in everything (v18). Remember God's goodness and thank Him. **13. Don't quench the Holy Spirit** (v19). Read Ephesians 4:30.
14. Avoid treating prophecies with contempt (v20).
15. "Test all things" (v21a). Be discerning. (Read 1 John 4:1).
16. "Hold fast to what is good." (v21b). Ensure a moral uprightness.
17. "Abstain from every form of evil" (v22). Don't compromise on sin.

Reflection: Which of the above pep-talks do you observe?

Word for today: *No spiritual pep-talk, no spiritual walk with the Lord.*

QUINTESSENTIAL RELEVANCE

Not that we are sufficient of ourselves to think of anything as being from ourselves, but our sufficiency is from God (2 Corinthians 3:5).

READ: JOHN 15:1-5

Verse 5 of our text reads, *"I am the vine, you are the branches. He who abides in me, and I in him, bears much fruit; for without me you can do nothing."* The above text underscores the fact that Christ is quintessentially relevant to our spiritual, physical, emotional, academic, economic and financial success in life. Indeed, human beings can do nothing without Christ! Any success people seem to have made outside of Christ is temporal and of no eternal value.

There are four things worthy of note regarding the quintessential relevance of Christ.:

1. In **Creation,** Christ is quintessentially relevant. John 1:1-3 reads, *"In the beginning was the Word, and the Word was with God, and the Word was God. He was in the beginning with God. All things were made through Him, and without Him nothing was made that was made."* Without Christ, creation would not have taken place. Christ was the spoken Word of God that brought every created being into existence. (Read Colossians 1:16-17).

2. In **Salvation,** Christ is quintessentially relevant. Genesis 3:15 reads, *"And I will put enmity between you and the woman, and between your seed and her Seed; He shall bruise your head, and you shall bruise His heel."* While on the cross, Christ, the Seed of the woman, bruised the head of Satan, while Satan bruised His heel through his seed—the unbelieving Jews and Roman soldiers.

3. In **Provision,** Christ is quintessentially relevant. Philippians 4:19 reads, *"And my God shall supply all your need according to His riches in glory by Christ Jesus."* Christ fed five thousand with five loaves of bread and two fish.

4. In **Protection**, Christ is quintessentially relevant. The Bible declares, *"At the name of Jesus every name must bow, of things in heaven and those on earth, and those under the earth."* (Philippians 2:10). If you trust in the Lord, He will protect you against all evil. (Read Isaiah 54:17 and Psalm 34:7).

Reflection: Is Christ quintessentially relevant in your life?

Word for today: *Christ's divine nature makes Him quintessentially relevant.*

SPARE THE ROD, SPOIL THE CHILD

Chasten your son while there is hope, and do not set your heart on his destruction (Proverbs 19:18).

READ: PROVERBS 13:24-25

An undisciplined child is like a time bomb waiting to explode at his or her adolescent age. When a child grows up without proper training and discipline, the parents in particular and the society as a whole suffer. He or she leads a wayward life, gets into trouble with the law, and ends up in jail. On the other hand, a disciplined child usually grows up to lead a useful and successful life. Talking about discipline, it is important to distinguish between **child discipline** and **child abuse**. With child discipline, the intent is to correct the child's behavior, without inflicting a bodily injury or harm on him or her. But, in child abuse, the discipline is very intense, so much so, that bodily injury often occurs. **Discipline** is aimed at correcting the child's bad behavior, while **abuse** is aimed at harming the child bodily, mentally and emotionally. As a parent or guardian, the Word of God enjoins you to discipline your child.

Our text reads, *"He who spares his rod hates his son, but he who loves him disciplines him promptly* (v24). If you really love your child, learn to discipline him or her. Failure to do so will destroy the child. In western culture, it is not uncommon to find parents who for fear of their children being taken away from them by the Social Services, fail to discipline their children. Most of the children who are aware of this government imposed parental handicap brag about it. Some even have the boldness to say to the face of their parents, "If you touch me, I will call the police on you." Since no parent wants his or her child to betaken away, the child is left without discipline and rots in ignorance and bad behavior. Proverbs 22:6 has a very important warning for parents. *"Train up a child in the way he should go, and when he is old he will not depart from it."* The word **train** implies teaching by doing. Children learn faster and better when they watch the adults do what they are being taught. This means that as a parent, you should train up your child by doing what you teach.

Reflection: Do you spare the rod to spoil your child?

Word for today: *The genesis of a spoilt child in his or her upbringing.*

ORDER OUT OF CHAOS!

I beheld the earth, and indeed it was without form, and void; and the heavens,
they had no light (Jeremiah 4:23).

READ: GENESIS 1:1-5

The first two verses of the first chapter of Genesis seem contradictory. Verse 1 reads, *"In the beginning God created the heavens and the earth."* and verse 2 reads, *"The earth was without form, and void; and darkness was on the face of the deep. And the Spirit of God was hovering over the face of the waters."* A closer look at these two verses shows that they are not contradictory, but revealing. First, there was the first earth created in the beginning. Second, the same earth became "void, without form and filled with darkness" For the first earth created in the beginning to become void, formless and filled with darkness, means that something happened to it. Another word for void, formlessness and darkness is **chaos**. The chaotic condition of the first earth prompted God to create another earth. In other words, God created the present earth out of the chaos that existed in the former earth. There is a strong speculation amongst Bible scholars that the first earth was destroyed as a result of angelic fight that took place while Satan and his cohorts were being driven out of heaven. That incident left the former earth void and in complete darkness, prompting God to create another earth. The Bible does not tell us what led to the void and darkness of the former earth and how long it lasted. But, suffice it to say that it was in a chaotic condition.

God created order out of chaos. By a divine fiat, He created light first in order to eliminate darkness. He said, "Let there be light; and there was light." (Genesis 1:3). When God saw that the light He created was good, He separated the light from darkness (v4). In doing so, God called the light Day and the darkness He called Night. Hence, Day and Night have become divine tools for determining when morning and evening set in. Just as God brought order out of chaos during creation, so does He bring order in chaotic lives. For instance, Christ brought order and normalcy in the chaotic life of a lunatic possessed by legions of demons (Read Luke 8:26-39).

Reflection: Has God created order and calm in your life?

Word for today: *Only God can create order out of chaos.*

A POSITIVE INFLUENCE

"I have given you an example, that you should do as I have done to you. (John 13:15).

READ: 2 KINGS 5:1-7

How people influence others is not necessarily based on what they possess, but who possesses them. For instance, if someone is possessed of God, he or she will have a positive influence on those around him or her. But, if on the other hand, a person is possessed of the devil, he or she is bound to influence those around him or her in a negative way. This means that **positivity** produces positive result, while **negativity** produces negative result. Jezebel, the wife of king Ahab, was possessed of Baal—a Phoenician god. As a result, she influenced Ahab negatively to become a worshipper of Baal (Read 1 Kings 21:25-26).

In our text, we notice how a slave girl made a positive influence in the land of Syria. This little slave girl had every reason to be negative in life. **First,** she was a slave in captivity. **Second,** she was in a strange land, separated from her parents. **Third,** she found herself living under the same roof with a master who was a leper—a condition considered a taboo in the land of Israel from where she came (Read Leviticus 13:44-46). But, in spite of all the misfortunes against her, the slave girl chose to stay positive in order to make a positive influence in the place she found herself. She did not forget her God, nor did she stop testifying to the power of her God. Most people in her condition would have felt abandoned by God and stopped serving Him. But not so for this girls! She kept the faith. Verse 3 of our text reads, *"Then she said to her mistress, 'If only my master were with the prophet who is in Samaria! For he would heal him of his leprosy.'"* This slave girl did not keep quiet; she did three positive things: **1.** She influenced Naaman's wife positively by her **character**. Her godly character opened up the opportunity to introduce her God to Naaman's wife (v3). **2.** She influenced Naaman by her **testimony** (v4). Naaman's response to her testimony was fast. **3.** She influenced the king of Syria by her **faith** (v5).The Syrian king believed her before writing his letter.

Reflection: Has someone made a positive influence in your life?

Word for today: *Make a positive influence in someone's life today.*

379

A FUTILE RELIANCE

Thus says the LORD: "Cursed is the man who trusts in man And makes flesh his strength, Whose heart departs from the LORD." (Jeremiah 17:5).

READ: ISAIAH 31:1-3

As humans, we are dependent beings. Hence, you and I depend on God-the Creator who provides us all our daily needs for the sustenance of life. Since no one comes into this world with anything, we surely need something to survive in it. Unfortunately, some people have chosen to rely on God's creatures, rather than on God the Creator. There are those who rely on man-made gods for protection, provision, promotion and salvation, instead of relying on God Almighty—the Maker of heaven and earth. Some even rely on human effort to win spiritual battles, while others rely on good political and social connections with those in corridors of power to succeed in life. It is futile to rely on human beings, because they can fail you, when you least expect it. If you rely on God, He will use human beings to bless you. It is true that your job enables you to pay your bills and meet other financial obligations, but you should not rely on it in order to succeed in life. Rather, you should rely on God who through your job and career meets your financial obligations. God is the Source of your livelihood, while your job or career is the means through which He meets your need. Do you know that putting your job or career before God is like putting a cart before a horse? Doing so does not make for a successful spiritual ending.

The children of Israel struggled a lot with the issue of reliance on God in times of trouble. Rather than rely on God, they chose to rely on idols and heathen kings. Our text is a case in point. Each time the children of Israel were threatened by a neighboring kingdom, they were quick to seek help from Egypt, instead of God. Rather than repent and ask God for His help, they rebelled against Him by gravitating toward Egypt. God made it clear to them, *"The Egyptians are men, and not God, their horses flesh, not spirit."* When He *"stretches out His hand, both the helper and the helped will perish together."* (v3). As a user of this Devotional, in whom do you rely on? God or man?

Reflection: When last did you rely on God for a breakthrough?

Word for today: *Man will fail you, but God will not. Rely on Him!*

GOD'S INSEPARABLE LOVE!

"If the LORD delights in us, then He will bring us into this land and give it to us, 'a land which flows with milk and honey.'" (Numbers 14:8).

READ: ROMANS 8:31-39

I t is not uncommon to find a couple who claim to have love for each other end their relationship and part ways. When this happens, the love that once bound such a couple fizzles out. But this is not the case with God. The love that God has for those who put their trust in Him is inseparable and eternal. In verse 35 of our text, Apostle Paul asks an important question, *"Who shall separate us from the love of Christ? Shall tribulation, or distress, or persecution, or famine, or nakedness, or peril, or sword?* In verse 38-39, Paul answers his question in these words, *"For I am persuaded that neither death nor life, nor angels nor principalities nor powers, nor things present nor things to come, nor height nor depth, nor any other created thing, shall be able to separate us from the love of God which is in Christ Jesus our Lord."* The following are evidences and benefits of God's inseparable love towards us:
1. No one can be against us (v31). **2. God did not spare His Son from dying for us** (v32). **3. No one can bring a charge against us** (v33).
4. No one can condemn us (v34). **5. No one can separate us from the love of Christ** (v35). **6. We are more than conquerors in Christ** (v37).

People do separate themselves from God's love by running away from Him, but God does not separate His love from people. No matter how deep someone is in sin, God's love is till available. God loves a sinner, but hates his sin. God demonstrated the depth of His love by sending His only begotten Son to die for us. John 3:16-17 read, *"For God so loved the world that He gave His only begotten Son, that whoever believes in Him should not perish but have everlasting life. For God did not send His Son into the world to condemn the world, but that the world through Him might be saved."* When we realize the inseparable nature of God's love toward us, we cannot but, fall down before Him in humility and worship Him with gratitude in our hearts. In Ephesians, Paul summarizes the dimensions of God's inseparable love towards us (Read Ephesians 3:18).

Reflection: Have you responded to God's love in Christ?

Word for today: *Just as God is inseparable from Christ, so is His love for us.*

PATIENCE AND PERSEVERANCE

But you, O man of God, flee these things and pursue righteousness, godliness, faith, love, patience, gentleness (1 Timothy 6:11).

READ: JAMES 5:7-12

Patience and perseverance are among the virtues needed as Christians on our spiritual journey to heaven. We ought to be patient for the coming of the Lord and persevere as we go through trials and persecution for the Lord's sake. In waiting, you are patient; in suffering, you persevere. Verse 7 of our text reads, *"Therefore be patient, brethren, until the coming of the Lord. See how the farmer waits for the precious fruit of the earth, waiting patiently for it until it receives the early and latter rain."* James urges us to be patient until the coming of the Lord. He compares the patience we ought to exercise regarding the Lord's coming to that of a farmer who patiently waits for the "early and latter rain" on his crops. Patience goes hand in hand with expectation and anticipation, while perseverance goes hand in hand with hope and reward. Christians of the early Church waited with expectation and anticipation of the Lord's return. Unfortunately, some Christians of today, pay lip service to the Lord's return. They wait with little or no expectation or anticipation of the Lord's return. Sermons regarding the Lord's imminent return is no longer popular among Christians, because worldliness, riches and fame have taken a prominent position in their hearts. It is when our hearts wait patiently that we can be established *"for the coming of the Lord"* which is at hand (v8).

The farmer has no control over the weather—the weather is out of his control. Nonetheless, by faith he believes that the early and latter rain will take place to water his crops and give him fresh fruits. Similarly, "the timing of the Lord's return is beyond our control. Paul, Peter, James, John and other faithful believers in Christ believed that Christ could come back in their life time. According to the Life Application Bible Commentary, "We ought to live with the same conviction. Christ may come back today; at any time, His return may be near, for we do not know when it will occur. But, we do know that it will occur." (Matthew 24:27, 37, 39; 1 Thessalonians 5:2; 2 Peter 3:10).

Reflection: Are you patient and persevering—waiting for the Lord's return?

Word for today: *Patience and perseverance are pivotal to faith in Christ.*

A TIME TO PONDER!

And his brothers envied him, but his father kept the matter in mind (Genesis 37;11).

READ: GENESIS 37:9-11

Three things made Joseph's siblings to hate him. The **first** was the special love his father—Jacob had for him, because he was "the son of his old age." (Genesis 37:3). The **second** and **third** things were *the dreams Joseph had. In narrating his first dream, Joseph told his siblings, "There we were, binding sheaves in the field. Then behold, my sheaf arose and also stood upright; and indeed your sheaves stood all around and bowed down to my sheaf."*(v7). Joseph's brother understood the meaning of his dream and were quick to question him, *"Shall you indeed reign over us? Or shall you indeed have dominion over us."* In fact Joseph's dream fueled the hatred his siblings had for him (v8). As if that wasn't enough, Joseph had another dream, in which he saw the sun, moon and eleven stars bowing down before him (v9). Joseph's father who had a good interpretation of his dream, *"rebuked him and said to him, 'What is this dream that you have dreamed? Shall your mother and I and your brothers indeed come to bow down to the earth before you.'"* (v10). Joseph's dream had a two-fold outcome: his brothers envied him, but his father kept the matter in mind." (v11).

It is not a bad thing to ponder over things as Jacob did—things like your personal relationship and walk with the Lord. Another word for **ponder** is **reflection**. Whenever we reflect or ponder over things, we tend to get a better understanding of what is going on. Sometimes, the Spirit of God gives us more insight into what He wants us to know during a time of reflection. Daniel was a guy who pondered over things in his life. After pondering over King Nebuchadnezzar's delicacies, Daniel refused to eat of it (Read Daniel 1:8-9). Later, when Daniel received an interpretation regarding the vision from God, he reflected on what he saw. As he pondered over it, "his thoughts greatly troubled him and his countenance changed, but he kept the "matter in his heart." Mary also pondered over the things that were told her about Jesus (Luke 2:16-20).

Reflection: Do you ever ponder before you speak or act?

Word for today: *Pondering over God's goodness strengthens your faith.*

911 CALL TO HEAVEN

"Call to me, and I will answer you, and show you great and mighty things, which you do not know" (Jeremiah 33:3).

READ: PSALM 70:1-5

Davd, the author of Psalm 70, used the phrase, "Make haste" three times in our text. *"Make haste, O God, to deliver me!"* (v1a). *"Make haste to help me, O LORD!"* (v1b). *"Make haste to me, O God!"* (v5). It is not bad to ask the Lord to hasten the answer to your prayer; David did the same thing. He asked God to make haste to deliver and help him. David was in distress and made what could be considered a 911 call to God. In the United States, 911 telephone number is the number you can call in time of emergency. This makes a 911 call synonymous with emergency. With a 911 call, one usually receives a quick or immediate response. Those who respond to 911 call are always ready 24/7. Just as there is a mundane 911 number to call in times of emergency, so is there a heavenly 911 number to call in times of emergency. You access it through prayer and the access code is Jesus. *A 911 call to heaven is the prayer you offer to God in time of distress, danger and dismay.*

In our text we notice the content of David's 911call to God. He used the word, "Let" in introducing his request, due to his faith in the LORD and conviction that the LORD would answer his distress call. We read, "**Let** them be ashamed and confounded, who seek my life." "**Let** them be turned back and confused, who desire my hurt." (v2). "**Let** them be turned back because of their shame." (v3). "**Let** all those who seek you rejoice and be glad in you; and **let** those who love your salvation say continually, '**Let** God be magnified!'" (v4). God answered David's 911 call and delivered him from the hands of king Saul. Are you going through some difficulties and challenges, why not make a 911 call to God today! He will respond to you as He did to David. Hannah was a woman who made a 911 call to God (1 Samuel 1:8-18). There are three characteristics of her 911 call to heaven. **First,** it was made out of grief and anguish (1 Samuel 1:10). **Second,** it involved a heart-felt talk to the LORD (v13). **Third,** it received a surprise response from the LORD (v20).

Reflection: Have you ever made a 911 call to heaven? If not, why not?

Word for today: *Answer to a heavenly 911 call is guaranteed in Christ.*

THE GODLY

"The LORD has set apart for Himself him who is godly...." (Psalm 4:3).

READ: PSALM 15:1-5

The Webster's English Dictionary defines the word, **godly** as "having a great reverence for God." This means that the godly are those who have great reverence for God. Are you godly? In their fallen state, human being find it difficult to have a genuine reverence for God—their Maker. This kind of attitude is backed by Satan who manipulates the mind of people to doubt, disbelief and disregard God to the extent of denying His existence. God regards such people as fools, no matter how highly placed or educated they may be. Read Psalm 14:1; 53:1.

Our text spells out eleven characteristics of the godly.
1. He is upright in his dealings with others (v2a). Read Psalm 24:3-4; Isaiah 33:15-16).
2. He is righteous before God—meaning he is in right standing with God based on faith in Christ (v2b). Read 1 Corinthians 1:30-31; 2 Corinthians 5:21).
3. He is truthful—meaning he speaks the truth from his heart, not from his lips (v2c).
4. He does not backbite, nor slander—meaning he does not engage in unprofitable side talks (v3a).
5. He does not perpetrate evil to his neighbors (v3b). Read Exodus 23:1)
6. He does not "take up a reproach against his friend" (v3c)—meaning he does not stab his friend at the back.
7. He "despises a vile person" (v4a)—meaning he does not support an evil person's behavior.
8. He "honors those who fear the LORD" (v4b).
9. He fulfils his vows to the LORD, no matter what (v4c). Read Judges 11:35.
10. He does not lend money with interest to a brother (v5a)—meaning he does not make a profit out of a brother in need of financial support. Read Leviticus 25:36-37).
11. He does not take bribes (v5). Read Exodus 23:8; Deuteronomy 16:19).

Reflection: Are you living a godly life? If so, how?

Word for today: *The godly fears and honors God; the ungodly does not.*

HAVING CHRIST'S DNA

For you are all sons of God through faith in Christ Jesus (Galatians 3:26).

READ: JOH 1:12-13

In a layman's term, DNA (Deoxyribonucleic acid) is the hereditary material in a person which caries genetic information about the individual. Hence, due to DNA, individuals from the same parents or genealogy are likely to carry identical genetic code. From a Christian perspective, there are two kinds of DNA: One is Adamic and physical in nature; the other is Christ-like and spiritual. Just as our physical DNA reveals our natural make-up, so does our spiritual DNA reveal our spiritual make-up. In other words, physical DNA defines our natural identity, while spiritual DNA defines our spiritual identity. This means that for one to possess Christ's DNA, one has to be born of God.

Our text reads, *"But as many as received Him, to them He gave the right to become children of God, to those who believe in His name: who were born, not of blood, nor of the will of the flesh, nor of the will of man, but of God."* (v12-13). Just as a child who is born into a family carries the DNA of his nuclear family, so does a person born into God's family carry Christ's DNA. On the issue of having Christ's DNA through spiritual rebirth, the Life Application Bible Commentary couldn't have put it more succinctly, "All who welcome Jesus Christ as Lord of their lives are reborn spiritually, receiving new life from God. Through faith in Christ, the Holy Spirit changes such people from the inside out—rearranging attitudes, desires and motives. Being born of our parents makes us physically alive and places us in our parents' family, while being born of God makes us spiritually alive and joins us with God's family." As members of God's family, we possess Christ's DNA. Whenever a sinner is born again by accepting Christ in his life, he sheds off his Adamic DNA and picks up Christ's DNA. When this happens, four things become obvious:

1. He begins to hate sin and love righteousness (Romans 6:20-22).
2. He becomes heaven conscious (Colossians 3:1-3)
3. He begins to fellowship with God and the brethren (1 John 1:3).
4. He becomes dedicated in serving God (Deuteronomy 6:5:John 12:26).

Reflection: What kind of DNA do you have— Adam's or Christ's?

Word for today: *Without Christ's DNA, you can't claim to be a child of God.*

THE JOY OF CHRISTMAS

Then the shepherds returned, glorifying and praising God for all the things that they had heard and seen, as it was told them (Luke 2:20).

READ: LUKE 2:8-14

Christmas means a different thing to different people. For instance, to the worldly and party-going guys, Christmas is a time of shopping, organizing wild parties and getting drunk; a time of celebrating the holidays, instead of Christ, the purpose for the holidays. But, to believers in Christ, Christmas is the time of a joyous celebration of Christ's birth. The joy of Christmas flows from the message of God's peace to mankind for the forgiveness of sin, offer of salvation and gift of eternal life in Christ. Hence, the celebration of Christmas without Christ in the life of the celebrant is like attending a party without being invited. No wonder so many people steal, get drunk, fight, kill and do all sorts of atrocities in the name of Christmas? It is unfortunate that the world which does not know Christ has hijacked Christmas celebration and renamed it, "holiday celebration" If Christ has not be born into your life, celebration of His birthday is meaningless (Read John 1:12-13).

On that cold winter night, when an angel of the Lord stood before a group of a country-side shepherds to announce the birth of Christ, the Bible records that "the glory of the Lord which shone around them made them to be greatly afraid." (Luke 2:8-9). But, in the midst of their fear, the angel told the shepherds, *"Do not be afraid, for behold I bring you good tidings of great joy, which will be to all people. For there is born to you this day in the city of David a Savior, who is Christ the Lord."* (v10-11). Soon after the announcement of Christ's birth by the angel, "a multitude of angelic host joined him in lavishing praises to God." The lyric of their praise-song was wonderful:

"Glory to God in the highest,
And on earth peace, goodwill toward men!" (v14).

The angel referred to the deity of baby Jesus as, "Christ the Lord." As Lord, Christ is God who came down from heaven in human form. As you celebrate Christmas today, remember what Christ's birth has done.

Reflection: Has Christ been born in your life? If so, Merry Christmas!

Word for today: *The joy of Christmas—God came to earth in human form.*

SACRIFICIAL SERVANTHOOD

[Christ] made Himself of no reputation, taking the form of a bondservant, and coming in the likeness of men (Philippians 2:7).

READ: MARK 10:41-45

Christ whose birthday we celebrated yesterday, was born as a King to die, not to rule. In most dynasties, when a child is born, he or she falls in line in succession of the reigning monarch. In the history of mankind, Christ is the only person who was born as a King to die, instead of to rule. The Bible records that on hearing of the birth of King Jesus, Herod the king "was troubled, and all Jerusalem with him." (Matthew 2:1-3). King Herod was troubled because he thought that King Jesus was going to unseat him. But, little did Herod know that Christ was not born to rule, but to die, in order to save mankind from sin (1:21). Indeed, Christ was born as a sacrificial lamb to take away the sin of the world (John 1:29). Prior to His incarnation, our Lord Jesus Christ knew what His mission was going to be—to suffer in the place of mankind (Read Isaiah chapter 53). During His earthly ministry, Christ did not keep His audience in doubt regarding His mission. On a number of occasions, He told them about His sacrificial death. Matthew 16:21 reads, *"From that time Jesus began to show to His disciples that He must go to Jerusalem, and suffer many things from the elders and chief priests and scribes, and be killed, and be raised the third day."* While in Galilee, Christ also told His audience, *"The Son of Man is about to be betrayed into the hands of men, and they will kill Him, and the third day He will be raised up."* (17:22-23). See Luke 9:21-22.

In our text we read of how Christ reminded His disciples of His servant-hood mission. After narrating how He would be mocked, scourged, killed and be raised the third day, James and John the sons of Zebedee made a request to Christ. They wanted to be granted the right to sit on His right and left hands in heaven (v37). But when the other ten apostles heard about the lofty request of John and James, they were greatly displeased. Then Jesus gave them a lesson on sacrificial servant-hood: "Whoever desires to be first shall be a slave of all." Christ cited His mission as an example of sacrificial servant hood (vs44-45).

Reflection: How do you serve Christ and others?

Word for today: *The way to get served is by serving others.*

388

A BLURRED SPIRITUAL VISION!

And He spoke a parable to them: "Can the blind lead the blind? Will they not both fall into the ditch?" (Luke 6:39).

READ: MARK 8:22-26

When people have a blurred vision, they seek the help of an optometrist and may eventually wear eyeglasses to improve their vision. The same thing happens spiritually. Our Lord Jesus Christ came into a town called Bethsaida, and "they brought a blind man to Him, and begged Him to touch him." (Mark 8:22). Jesus took the man out of the town, spat on his eyes, placed His hands on him and asked him if he saw anything. The blind man *"looked up and said, 'I see men like trees, walking.'"* (23-24). The guy had a blurred vision experience having not seen before. Then Jesus put His hands on him the second time and asked him to look up. The Bible records that the blind man "was restored and saw everyone clearly." (v25). This particular healing paralleled the healing of a man who was deaf and dumb in Mark 7:32-35. These two miracles had four things in common: **1.** Christ was begged to touch them (Mark 7:32; 8:22). **2.** Christ took them away from the public view (7:33a; 8:23). **3.** Christ used saliva in the process of healing them (7:33b; 8:23b) **4.** Christ commanded them not to publicize their miracles (7:36; 8:26).

If we take a closer look at the healing of the blind man, we shall discover four spiritual truths. **First,** physical blindness is analogous to spiritual blindness. Just as the physically blind cannot see physical objects, so can the spiritually blind not see spiritual truth. **Second,** one needs the touch of Jesus to deal with one's spiritual blindness. Just as Jesus touched the eyes of the blind man in order for him to see physical objects, so do the spiritually blind need Christ's touch to see spiritually. **Third,** spiritual sight restoration can occur instantly (See John 9:1-10). **Fourth,** spiritual sight restoration can also come progressively. Like the two-part healing of the blind man, "insight into salvation or one's spiritual life may be progressive for some converts." We need the Lord's touch for a clear vision of what He is showing us and where He is leading us. Do you have a blurred spiritual vision? With it, you can't go far!

Reflection: When last did the Holy Spirit minister to you?

Word for today: *Walk into eternity with a clear, not a blurred vision!*

389

DIVINELY RELOCATED

"Arise, go to Zarephath, which belongs to Sidon, and dwell there. See, I have commanded a widow there to provide for you." (1 Kings 17:9).

READ: 1 KINGS 17:1-10

Our text is a classic example of how God can relocate someone. As a punishment for Ahab's disposition to idol worship, Elijah proclaimed a drought in the land of Israel. Verse 1 of our text reads, *"And Elijah the Tishbite, of the inhabitants of Gilead, said to Ahab, 'As the LORD God of Israel lives, before whom I stand, there shall not be dew nor rain these years, except at my word."* Interestingly, Elijah was not spared the effect of the drought he pronounced. Sometimes, the righteous do suffer the effects of God's wrath upon the wicked. As the drought intensified over time, Elijah needed water and food. Then God relocated him. Verse 2-4 of our text read, *"Then the word of the LORD came to him, saying, 'Get away from here and turn eastward, and hide by the Brook Cherith, which flows into the Jordan. And it will be that you shall drink from the brook, and I have commanded the ravens to feed you there."* Elijah relocated to his new venue and was fed by the ravens, while he drank from the brook. After a while, the brook dried up due to the intensity of the drought. Again, God relocated Elijah. This time to a widow in the land of Zarephath (v8-10). God knows how to divinely relocate His people. For instance, God divinely relocated Joseph from his father's house to the land of Egypt to save the lives of his family members (Genesis 45:3-7). God also divinely relocated a slave girl from Israel to Naaman's house to point Naaman to God in order to heal him of his leprosy (2 Kings 5:1-3). Sometimes the process of divine relocation is bitter as was the case of Joseph and the slave girl.

God owns the Church and may relocate you from one Church to another to enable you render a more effective service to His glory. When you are divinely relocated, three things will happen: **First,** you will not lack just as Elijah never lacked. **Second,** you will become a source of blessing to others. Elijah's relocation blessed the widow. **Third,** you will experience God's miracle like Elijah did. Being fed by the ravens and a widow are miracles of divine provision.

Reflection: Are you sure that you are where God wants you to be?

Word or today: *With a divine relocation comes a divine blessing.*

STAY TRUE TO THE END

"I know whom I have believed and am persuaded that He is able to keep what I have committed to Him until that Day." (2 Timothy 1:12).

READ: 2 TIMOTHY 4:6-8

A very popular Scripture Union chorus with following lyric reminds us of the need to stay true to the end as believers in Christ:

Keep me true, Lord, Jesus keep me true,
Keep me true, Lord, Jesus keep me true;
There is a race that I must run, there are victories to be won,
Give me power every hour to be true.

Towards the end of Paul's Christian journey, he made a statement that looked like a valedictory speech in our text: *"For I am already being poured out as a drink offering, and the time of my departure is at hand. I have fought the good fight, I have finished the race, I have kept the faith. Finally, there is laid up for me the crown of righteousness, which the Lord, the righteous Judge, will give to me on that Day, and not to me only but also to all who have loved His appearing."* (v6-8). Paul summarizes what our attitude to the Christian race should be: 1. We must "fight the good fight of faith"—*meaning to withstand every attempt of the devil to dislodge our faith in Christ Jesus.* 2. We must "finish the race"—*meaning to persevere in serving the Lord to the end.* 3. We must "keep the faith"—*meaning to abide by the sound teaching of God's Word.* 4. We must be expectant of the Lord's return. Unfortunately, many Christians do not follow the spiritual principles outlined above. Some fight the good fight of faith, but fail to finish the race; while others finish the race, but don't keep the faith.

Paul likens the Christian race to a physical race. A physical race involves four things: The athletes, the umpire, the rules to follow and the crown to be won. Similarly, in a Christian race, four things are involved: The believers in Christ, the Holy Spirit, who serves as the Umpire, the Word of God, which provides the rules to follow and the heavenly reward. In the Christian race, it is not how well you started, but how well you finished.

Reflection: Let our daily prayer be to stay true to the end for the Lord.

Word for today: *Remember, no victory, no crown!*

FALSE PROPHETS

For false christs and false prophets will rise and show signs and wonders to deceive, if possible, even the elect (Mark 13:22).

READ: 2 PETER 2:1-3

Verse 1-2 of our text read, *"But there were also false prophets among the people, even as there will be false teachers among you, who will secretly bring in destructive heresies, even denying the Lord who bought them, and bring on themselves swift destruction. And many will follow their destructive ways, because of whom the way of truth will be blasphemed."* In the Old Testament, there were false prophets and in the New Testament they are not lacking. As we consider false prophets, it is important to seek answers to four pertinent questions about false prophets:

1. Who are the false prophets? False prophets are those who use demonic means to foretell the future, perform miracles, teach doctrines that are contrary to the Word of God and make them appear to be from God.

2. Why are there false prophets? There are false prophets today in fulfilment of God's Word (Read Mark 13:22). Those who hate the truth like to hear lies.

3. Who is responsible for the false prophets? Satan is responsible. Since the angelic conflict in which Satan and his cohorts were cast down from heaven, Satan has raised many followers in the form of false prophets to deceive people and cause them to doubt God and His Word.

4. How do we respond to false prophets? The best way to respond to false prophets is by not listening to or patronizing them. Satan likes to mimic God. For instance, God has genuine priests and worshippers, while Satan has counterfeit priests and worshippers in the form of idol worshippers. God has genuine power, while Satan has pseudo power (Exodus 7:8-13; 1 Kings 18:25-40).

After reading the following Scriptural passages, try to discover and write down the character traits of a false prophet: 1 Kings 22:11-12, 24; Jeremiah 28:10-11. Compare your findings with the humility and effectiveness of a true prophet in 1 Kings 22:25-38; Jeremiah 28: 12-17). For the reward of false prophets and their followers, read Ezekiel 13:1-10.

Reflection: To whom do you listen? False prophets or God?

Word for today: *False prophets and their followers will end up in hell.*

BE SPIRITUALLY PREPARED

Prepare your outside work, make it fit for yourself in the field; and afterward build your house (Proverbs 24:27).

READ: AMOS 4:12-13

As you stand on the threshold of a new year, it will be good to do three things: **1. Reflect** on the journey of the current year. **2. Thank God** for the end of current year's journey—for His guidance, protection and provision. **3. Get prepared** for the journey of the next year, which starts tomorrow. In our text, God through prophet Amos, told the children of Israel to prepare themselves to meet Him, having refused to obey His Word. Verse 12 reads, *"Therefore thus will I do to you, O Israel; because I will do this to you, prepare to meet your God, O Israel!"* It is good to prepare one's self to receive God's blessings, rather than His anger and wrath. As you get ready to enter into a new year, it is good to prepare yourself spiritually for God's blessings. The saying, "He who fails to prepare, prepares to fail" holds true for everything we do in life, including our walk with God. The Bible makes it clear, *"God is Spirit and those who worship Him must worship Him in spirit and in truth."* (John 4: 24). This means that if by any reason you have served God in the flesh this year, come next year, you must be prepared to serve Him in spirit and truth. Our Lord Jesus declared, *"It is the Spirit who gives life; the flesh profits nothing. The words that I speak to you are spirit, and they are life."* (John 6:63).

Come tomorrow, the journey of next year will begin. The question before you is this: Are you prepared for the journey of 2016? If so, how spiritually prepared are you? Remember, no one ever embarks on a journey without some measure of preparation. Just as a physical journey requires some preparation, so does the spiritual journey. In fact, your spiritual journey should demand even a better preparation, due to the eternal value attached to it. There are four ways in which you can be spiritually prepared for next year. **First,** resolve not to allow your past define your future. **Second,** resolve to be prayerful in 2016. **Third,** resolve to make God's Word your standard in 2016. **Fourth,** resolve not to enter the new year with bitterness and anger in your heart towards anyone.

Reflection: Have you gotten your copy of 2016 Heavenly Banquet Devotional?

Word for today: *A journey well prepared is a journey well begun.*

393